NAVAL POWER IN ACTION

NAVAL POWER IN ACTION

Seizing the Initiative in the
New Cold War with China

BRENT DROSTE SADLER

Foreword by JOHN LEHMAN
U.S. Secretary of the Navy, 1981–87

NAVAL INSTITUTE PRESS
Annapolis, MD

Naval Institute Press
291 Wood Road
Annapolis, MD 21402

© 2025 by the U.S. Naval Institute

All rights reserved. No part of this book may be reproduced or utilized in any form or by any means, electronic or mechanical, including photocopying and recording, or by any information storage and retrieval system, without permission in writing from the publisher.

Library of Congress Cataloging-in-Publication Data

Names: Sadler, Brent Droste author
Title: Naval power in action : seizing the initiative in the new cold war with China / Brent Droste Sadler.
Other titles: Seizing the initiative in the new cold war with China
Description: Annapolis, MD : Naval Institute Press, [2025] | Includes bibliographical references and index.
Identifiers: LCCN 2025000572 (print) | LCCN 2025000573 (ebook) | ISBN 9781682475775 hardcover | ISBN 9781682475782 ebook
Subjects: LCSH: United States. Navy—Forecasting | Sea-power—United States | Sea-power—China | Shipbuilding—United States—Forecasting | Shipping—United States—Forecasting | United States—Military relations—China | China—Military relations—United States
Classification: LCC VA50 .S226 2025 (print) | LCC VA50 (ebook) | DDC 359.030973—dc23/eng/20250620
LC record available at https://lccn.loc.gov/2025000572
LC ebook record available at https://lccn.loc.gov/2025000573

♾ Print editions meet the requirements of ANSI/NISO z39.48-1992 (Permanence of Paper). Printed in the United States of America.

9 8 7 6 5 4 3 2 1

Why a maritime approach to the new cold war that is upon us? The pages that follow will lay out the rationale and an action plan, but there is another reason. I am a product of several generations of naval service, and my earliest days were quite literally held in the arms of a sailor. A childhood surrounded by all things maritime likely predisposed me to a strategic maritime approach. But given world events, it is the best way forward. For this reason, this book is dedicated to my parents.

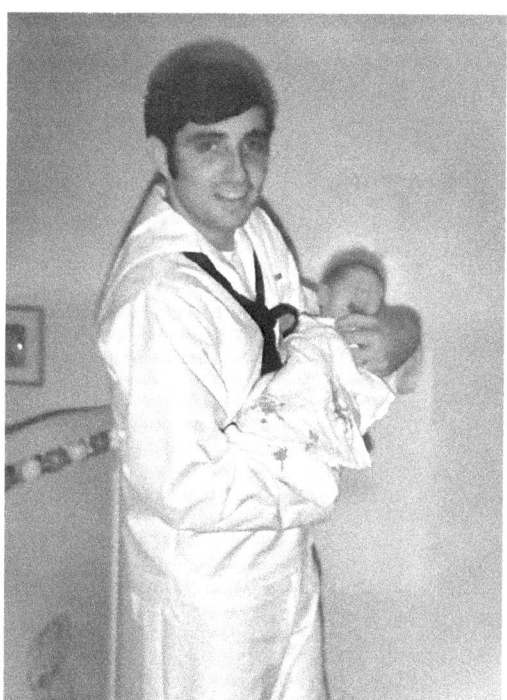

The author and his father, spring 1971 *Author photo*

CONTENTS

List of Illustrations ix

Foreword by John Lehman xiii

Preface xvii

Introduction: Naval Power in Action 1

PART ONE. THE COMPETITION FOR POSITION AND PREVENTING A CCP FAIT ACCOMPLI 21

CHAPTER 1. Fortify the Nation, Prepare to Strike: China's Evolving Global Military Basing Construct 23

CHAPTER 2. Naval Statecraft Operationalized 56

CHAPTER 3. A New Operational Approach in Decisive Maritime Theaters 83

PART TWO. STRENGTHENING THE HOMELAND TO WAGE PROTRACTED WAR AND RESILIENCY TO COERCION 99

CHAPTER 4. Enhancing Operational and Industrial Energy Resiliency 101

CHAPTER 5. How a Revolution in Shipping Can Regain American Maritime Strength 124

CHAPTER 6. A Twenty-First-Century Naval Act for Ships, Shipyards, and Sailors 171

PART THREE.	REORGANIZING FOR A NEW COLD WAR TO SEIZE AND RETAIN THE INITIATIVE 187
CHAPTER 7.	A Maritime Department 189
CHAPTER 8.	A National Security Council for a New Cold War 207
CHAPTER 9.	A Fleet Structure for Great Power Rivalry 236
	Conclusion 252
	Notes 257
	Selected Bibliography 311
	Index 315

ILLUSTRATIONS

FIGURES
1. *Great Power Multitasking*   xxi
2. Chinese aggression equation explanation   18
3. Chinese aggression equation, part 1   21
4. Heavy-lift and repair ship   76
5. Chinese aggression equation, part 2   99
6. The concept of multimodalism   152
7. Creating a Defense Department innovation market bridge incubator   158
8. Chinese aggression equation, part 3   187
9. Forming a U.S. maritime department   201
10. Proposed NSC structure for waging the new cold war   219
11. Current Navy structure versus recommended future structure   243

GRAPHS
1. Window of Opportunity: How China Sees Its Strategic Future   15
2. Strategic Petroleum Reserve at Dangerously Low Levels   108
3. Where the U.S. and China Compete for Crude Oil   113
4. U.S. Refinery Capacity Has Declined Since 2020   116
5. Operationally Important Fuels: Production, Consumption, and Reduced Refining Capacity   119
6. Fewer Ships Transiting Suez and Bab-el-Mandeb   143

MAPS

1. Navy Maritime Threats around the World 4
2. China Has Built or Funded Ports across Western Africa 45
3. The Importance of Ascension Island 46
4. Key Components of the Pacific Quad 59
5. Cancer to Capricorn Strategic Framing 67
6. Notional Deployment Sites for ESDs 72
7. Distance between Four South China Sea Flashpoints 86
8. China's Formidable yet Localized Missile Threat 91
9. Screen to Reposition First Island Chain Littoral Forces 94
10. Strike Group Surge under First Island Chain Covering Force 95
11. Major Sources of U.S. and Chinese Oil Imports 114
12. How U.S. Ports Can Currently Accommodate Large Container Ships 144
13. Opportunities for New Intermodalism 153
14. New Multimodalism Proof-of-Concept: Detroit-Toledo-Chicago 164
15. New Multimodalism Comprehensive Proof-of-Concept: U.S. East Coast and Puerto Rico 164
16. Regional Offices of New Cold War NSC 220
17. Current U.S. Navy Fleet Boundaries 239
18. Current Joint Geographic Combatant Commands 240
19. Modified U.S. Naval Fleet Boundaries 244

TABLES

1. Critical Chinese Distant Seas Naval Vessels 38
2. Ports with Potential Chinese Military Utility 50
3. Cost of Deepening U.S. Harbors to Accommodate Large Container Ships 129

4   Top Maritime Nations   130
5   A Modern Naval Act of 2023   182
6   A New U.S. Navy Fleet Structure: Mission Tasking   247

TEXTBOXES
1   Proposed Draft National Security Directive:
    Sealift and Formation of the Maritime Department   204
2   Proposed Draft 2025 National Security Strategy   225
3   Proposed Draft Executive Order Reorganizing
    the Executive Office of the President   230
4   Proposed Draft Presidential Strategic Decision Memo
    Establishing NSC Structure and Processes   233

FOREWORD

During my service as President Ronald Reagan's secretary of the Navy, I came to appreciate—and use frequently—the Navy's cadre of highly skilled and knowledgeable strategic planners and politico-military experts. These often included retirees who continued to perform valuable service to the operational Navy and the nation while serving in think tanks, graduate schools, war colleges, consultancies, private companies, and on Capitol Hill. Their unique perspectives, wisdom, and experience have had vital—if often unrecognized—influence on decisions made in the Pentagon and on Navy staffs worldwide.

Among the most talented and prolific of those active today is the Heritage Foundation's Brent Sadler, a thoughtful retired U.S. Navy submarine officer with impeccable operational, staff, and diplomatic experience. Brent's heartfelt and deep concern for the future of our country and our Navy has been expressed—and often acted upon—for years in conferences, blogs, memoranda, and studies. In May 2023 he published a highly influential magnum opus: *U.S. Naval Power in the 21st Century: A New Strategy for Facing the Chinese and Russian Threat*. The book, an appeal for America to adopt an approach to the world that Brent called "naval statecraft," was well received and well-reviewed by U.S. and allied defense cognoscenti.

Rather than resting on his laurels, however, he continued to think and write, fleshing out details of the naval statecraft concept and expanding his thinking to encompass what he is now calling "maritime statecraft." *Naval Power in Action* is very much a sequel to and an elaboration on the recommendations Brent made in his earlier book.

Not surprisingly, I'm a big fan of Brent and much of his thinking. I've been down many of the roads he's traveling, albeit a half century ago. It's become a cliché, of course, that twenty-first-century China, Russia,

Iran, and North Korea aren't the Soviet Union. And the United States of today isn't the United States of the Cold War. Nevertheless, there are approaches we took and things we did back then that—brought up to date as Brent does in this latest book—should prove useful today. And tomorrow.

As complements and elaborations to Brent's observations and recommendations, I would urge the following actions:

▶ Go to sea often and in demanding conditions to hone your war-fighting skills, including on the doorsteps of China, Russia, Iran, and North Korea. This was a central theme of our exercise program of the 1980s and of my 2018 book *Oceans Ventured*. Especially refine and build in state-of-the-art electronic warfare and cover and deception operations and tactics. Brent argues for using the lessons of Exercise Ocean Venture to create follow-on exercises he calls Exercises Pacific Venture and Southern Hook. As we did, Brent recommends folding in appropriate allied militaries.

▶ Know what and how the Chinese, Russians, Iranians, and North Koreans think and how they fight. Understand their unique strengths and weaknesses, and resist the urge to "mirror image" them.

▶ Build well on the tried-and-true foundation of existing naval and maritime institutions, especially the numbered fleets, the Naval War College, the Naval Postgraduate School, the Naval Institute, and the Center for Naval Analysis (or CNA, the Navy Department's federally funded research and development center).

▶ Create new institutions when necessary. We did this with the Strategic Studies Group, the Naval Strike Warfare Center, and "Super CAGs," among other initiatives. Brent's cogent and detailed calls for a new maritime department, task-organized National Security Council (my own old stomping grounds), and a new fleet structure should be examined, discussed, and acted upon.

▶ Develop and use a compelling modern-day equivalent of our highly successful Maritime Strategy. As Brent points out, we need

a National Maritime Strategy for the twenty-first-century that goes well beyond the Navy and includes all the major government maritime offices and agencies.
- Identify the most aggressive experts in strategy, operations, tactics, force planning, and cost-cutting; foster their development; and put them in positions of influence. I had my corps of well-educated and operationally experienced naval operator-strategists. Today's Navy and its supporters are fortunate to have an equivalent corps of clear-minded navalists with appropriate talents to exploit, of which sailor-diplomat Brent Sadler is a shining example.
- Analyze real-world operations while they are occurring and get their lessons learned out quickly to the fleet. We did this with our operations in the Middle East, off Grenada, and with the British and Argentine war over the Falkland Islands. Today's naval operations—especially in the South China Sea, Taiwan Strait, Black and Red Seas, Eastern Mediterranean, and NATO's northern flank—need to be just as assiduously mined.
- Adopt justifiable and achievable force goals, consistently sticking to them and ensuring they are resourced. We did this with our six-hundred-ship Navy goal, and our goals for fifteen carrier battle groups and one hundred submarines (helping to win the Cold War in the process).
- Cut procurement costs, especially through competitive, firm, fixed-price contracts. Mightily resist the urge to gold plate and constantly redesign our ships, aircraft, and systems. Upgrade existing systems when you can, and eschew chasing wasteful research and development "rainbows."
- Treat Congress and the incumbent administration with respect and as partners, identifying supporters of American naval and maritime power on both sides of the political aisle. My own efforts in dealing with Senators John Tower (R-TX) and Scoop Jackson (D-WA) and with Representative Charlie Bennett (D-FL) and others on the Hill were appreciated and rewarded.

- Finally, integrate and carry out these initiatives through strong, thoughtful, and aggressive civilian, Marine Corps, and Navy leadership at the very pinnacle of the sea services. Brent cites my choice of Adm. James A. "Ace" Lyons for a series of vital senior positions in need of both tactical and operational brilliance and strategic and political savvy. But there were many other such bold leaders as well, not the least of which was the president himself.

The times call for a major overhaul in how our nation thinks about and uses its vital naval power—a critical element of American strength and success throughout history that has unfortunately been neglected and under-resourced for more than a generation. Meanwhile, we have been fortunate to have continued to spawn knowledgeable and passionate thinkers like Brent Sadler to keep the flame of American navalism burning brightly. This book and the ideas it puts forth and recommends—if studied and used—will assist mightily in a rebirth of U.S. Navy power and American navalism that is sorely needed.

JOHN LEHMAN
Secretary of the Navy (1981–87)
October 19, 2024

PREFACE

Among duck hunters there is a saying that describes our nation's current predicament in the competition with China—shooting behind the duck. It means that the actions our leaders have been taking for many years have been reactive and ineffective; said another way, they are missing their mark. To correct this requires adjusting for the target's—China's—reaction and anticipating its course to aim for an interception point. This book aims to inform a near-term (within four years) approach to lead in this competition with China. And there is not much time to begin getting the aim right.

Since my book *U.S. Naval Power in the 21st Century* was published in May 2023, changing world events have made it clear that an explicit and urgent action plan is needed for the United States to take the lead over China. Doing this requires a revitalized maritime industry, a strengthened Navy, and a new approach to American statecraft. Naval statecraft as the central framework must inform explicit near-term actions for successful competition with China. At a remarkable event at Harvard University in September 2023, the secretary of the Navy made the case for a new statecraft. This speech is one high-water mark in the growing realization that a novel approach is required, one the secretary called "maritime statecraft." This is similar to the premise of *U.S. Naval Power in the 21st Century*, which fuses naval presence with developmental economics and proactive diplomacy. While the concept is gaining traction among policymakers in Washington, D.C., there is much work yet to do.

In recent years China and Russia have advanced their interests by sowing confusion and strategic distraction among our national leadership; while 2023 stands out as a particularly bad year for this, it must not become a harbinger of future years. In Asia, China has secured a security arrangement with the strategically placed Pacific nation of the

Solomon Islands and is suspected to have a similar deal with Vanuatu. All the while, China has been running a maritime insurgency in the South China Sea that is heating up. No longer limited to gray-zone tactics, Chinese navy and coast guard vessels have entered the fray to harass neighbors and undermine the rules-based order—notably in the violent June 2024 interference and collisions with Philippine vessels near Second Thomas Shoal. On the other side of the world, Russia continues its bloody assault on Ukraine into a third year. It has also been rattling its nuclear saber in numerous tests and developments of deadly new weapons, like the nuclear-powered cruise missile Burevestnik, and revoked the Comprehensive Nuclear Test Ban Treaty. Adding to the strategic chaos, both China and Russia have benefited from and supported the October 2023 assault on Israel by the Iranian proxy Hamas in Gaza. The effect has been strategic confusion in Washington, as the nation contends with various national challenges across the globe, placing Americans in direct threat. Strategic clarity is required and can be achieved by leveraging the mobility afforded by the oceans while pursuing a proactive maritime effort that regains the strategic initiative.

There is urgency to act; China's leaders realize they have a window of advantage that closes as this decade concludes. In March 2021 Navy admiral Philip Davidson, the former commander of the U.S. Indo-Pacific Command, cautioned Congress that China is preparing to move against Taiwan by 2027. That assessment has since been echoed by subsequent Indo-Pacific commanders; the CIA director, William J. Burns; and Mike Pompeo, a former secretary of state and ex-CIA director. Why 2027? Eyeing negative economic and demographic trends and the regional military balance, Chinese leaders worry that the odds they will be able to achieve their long-held goal of conquering Taiwan will fade with each passing year afterward. And the people of Taiwan, in polling over many years, are growing less and less inclined to willingly join the communist mainland. The fact of the matter is, for the United Sates to avoid a major war with China hinges on holding off such an attack this decade. After embracing a decades-long strategy of hoping China would democratize or moderate its behavior to become a responsible stakeholder, China has instead pursued a massive military modernization and expansion. To blunt this force and instill doubt in Communist Chinese leaders requires urgent action, including bolstering our military presence in the region. But the bigger bill will be investments that grow the capacity of the United States to wage and sustain what would be a prolonged years-long war, for which it is in 2024 unready.

The challenge before us is how to act with what is at hand to deter China while setting the conditions for a sustained competition well into the future. Bore-sighting on China, while necessary, can be dangerous if it blinds the United States to other dangers—our nation must be prepared and armed, must be able to "chew gum and walk" as often eloquently stated by our political leaders. Sadly, this has rarely been the case, as domestic politics have a way of fixating leaders on whatever issue is at hand, all the while distracting needed action at the detriment of enduring vigilance as China's military rose beginning in the late 1990s. A maritime approach can mitigate this but will require investment and action along several lines of effort.

Top of the "to-do" list is bolstering our economy's defense to coercion via a variety of vectors—cyber, sanctions, direct attacks. Most urgent is addressing the paucity of shipping on which the nation's economy floats. Without adequate, reliable shipping, keeping the lights on and factories humming during a confrontation with China is an open question. For our military to keep the fight "over there" also places demand on shipping that we just do not have today. The issue is more than simply finding and leasing ships and hiring crews; America must regain its competitive edge in the maritime industrial sector. It can do this by merging several emerging technologies and some existing ones into a potent new logistic framework that will revolutionize shipping and give the nation a comparative advantage.

Like shipping, the nation's industrial base has softened to a degree that is unhealthy and, as the war in Ukraine has exposed, unable to meet urgent military needs. Case in point is the inability to meet Ukraine's need for simple artillery rounds. The problem is similar in torpedo production, naval shipbuilding, and repair. Moreover, shocks to global supply chains—notably, the Covid-19 pandemic—has made clear that the danger is real, resulting in efforts to on-shore rare-earth element production critical in exquisite defense items and expanding production of microelectronics at home. The problem, however, is much larger, and targeted homeland industrial strengthening is required, including actions to prevent an enemy from holding hostage our economy and actions to build the capacity to meet our wartime needs. This book picks up on this from *U.S. Naval Power in the 21st Century* and focuses on improving national energy resiliency.

To some, the war with China is already underway. Part of this current fight is one China has been waging for years and has a wide lead: control over access to markets and strategic infrastructure such as ports. Winning this positional competition with China can deter conflict and set conditions that complicate Chinese military and strategic aims.

Through economic inducements and strong-arm coercion, China has gained de facto control of many strategic ports, near dominance of maritime chokepoints, and an ability to sustain military presence in decisive theaters—that is, the South China Sea. This is where naval statecraft will be helpful and most visible in the near term. Should the United States lose this positional competition, it will give China the confidence it seeks to affect a fait accompli subjugation of Taiwan before the United States and its allies could effectively act. This positional competition is merely the preliminary round of a longer competition that China has embarked to rewrite the world to its liking. Chinese success in this first round will hasten a showdown, but war is not a foregone conclusion, and there is much the United States can do today to compete more effectively. Doing so requires retooling the nation's institutions to exercise national power by better integrating economic, diplomatic, and naval activities into a new naval statecraft. This will require reorganizing the government for the tasks.

This book refines ideas presented in *U.S. Naval Power in the 21st Century* and focuses attention to the present, laying out a case for acting in three areas: strengthening the homeland to economic coercion, modernizing and reorganizing institutions to successfully compete, and winning the positional fight with China. Achieving success in these three areas requires urgent action with effects following in waves—increased maritime presence followed by improvements in national industrial resiliency and capacities. As the nation once again finds itself entering a new cold war, this time with China and Russia, there is a need to reorganize and retool our institutions and laws to optimize for the unfolding fight. The objective is to deter a confrontation with China this decade while waging an enduring but eventually successful new cold war. This book aims to spark creative thinking, invigorate leadership, and generate overdue action so our nation can stop shooting behind the duck.

FIGURE 1. *Great Power Multitasking* Grace DeSandro

INTRODUCTION
Naval Power in Action

No major proposal required for war can be worked out in ignorance of political factors.
—CARL VON CLAUSEWITZ, *On War*, 1832

The once comfortable lead enjoyed by the United States in comprehensive national power (military, economic, and diplomatic) over China has rapidly eroded. China, buoyed by favorable treatment after being allowed to join the World Trade Organization (WTO) in 2001, has leveraged its state-led economy for massive windfalls—moneys that have been invested in its military, fueling a massive modernization and expansion unrivaled since the end of the Cold War, adding 112 modern warships to its navy between 2005 and 2023 while the U.S. Navy shrank by three warships.[1] By 2020 the U.S. Department of Defense had acknowledged China's military lead in shipbuilding, conventional ballistic and cruise missiles, and integrated air and missile defenses.[2] Simply outspending China, as was done by the United States in its comprehensive competition with the Soviet Union, is not an option today. Instead, smarter application of U.S. influence, industry, and military presence is required.

Most importantly in the near term, as the comprehensive power between the United States and China has narrowed, success in world events will be determined by who retains the strategic initiative. It is a lesson the communist Chinese learned during their rival nationalists' fifth campaign of 1933, which nearly resulted in their annihilation in the Chinese Civil War (1927–49).[3] Far from the peasant forces of the 1930s, today's People's Liberation Army (PLA) of the Chinese Communist Party (CCP) is a modern Goliath backed by the world's second-largest economy. Its navy, the People's Liberation Army Navy (PLAN), has since 2015 overtaken the United States as the largest fleet, and it routinely deploys to distant seas. This is not a bolt from the blue; in fact, China has since 2008 routinely deployed the PLAN to the Indian Ocean, initially in support of counterpiracy operations. Today China has the global reach to create problems for the United States at its choosing, a military to back up its diplomacy in tangible ways, and an economy that fuels its global ambitions. Grudgingly, U.S. political leadership has only recently come to terms with this challenge in a so-called China consensus that sees the bilateral relationship defined by rivalry. Having ceded the initiative to China for more than a decade, it is well past time for the United States to get moving in what will be the defining relationship of the twenty-first-century.

REGAINING THE INITIATIVE AND SUSTAINING THE PEACE IN A DANGEROUS DECADE

Recent world events make clear that the United States—and, more broadly, the West—has lost the initiative in the great-power competition with China and Russia. Consider the inability to neither anticipate nor deter Russia from its second invasion of Ukraine in February 2022—preparations that were plainly visible for many months. In March 2022 a secret security pact signed between the embattled prime minister of the strategically located Solomon Islands and China became known. This left Washington reeling, playing catch-up to impress Prime Minister Manasseh Sogavare to reverse course but too late to have any tangible effect. Then there is the October 7, 2023, barbaric assault on Israel by Hamas that was missed by U.S. and Israeli intelligence. This led to the targeted killing of over 1,200 innocents in southern Israel. The confused response from America was emblematic of a nation that had lost its strategic north star. On one hand, the American president supported Israel's right to wage war against Hamas after this attack while, on the other hand, also calling for an immediate ceasefire as Hamas continued to hold several hundred hostages and lobed rockets into civilian areas of Israel. This is an inherently dangerous time, and the United States seems unsure of how to make sense of it and regain the initiative.

Complicating matters for the United States is that American leaders have been too accustomed to running the world's post–Cold War agenda. Today these leaders find themselves amid a new era where mere diktat, shuttle diplomacy, or military flexing alone will not carry the day. It is a new era that a growing group of experts are calling a new cold war.[4] Whatever you call it, the nation is witness to the beginning of a long contest with China as the principal adversary. But, unlike the last cold war, the nation must confront a dangerous coalescing cabal of adversaries—notably, Russia, North Korea, and Iran. As the nation struggles to find its footing, its rivals in Beijing, Moscow, and Tehran have been restive; increasingly willing to test America's resolve—perhaps soon even directly. Preventing a major confrontation is of upmost importance, and against the designs of China, a smarter use of national treasure and military resources is needed. But sustaining deterrence and ensuring peace also requires a military positioned and with the capacity to fight a major war and win. The most dangerous scenario America's military must be ready for is a prolonged war with China over the future of democratic Taiwan.

This will require achieving a dual goal—smarter statecraft and stronger military—in time to be effective against the principal threat, China. Given the yawning disparity of military power and weakening global position of the United States, urgent action is required along three lines of effort: reorganizing for today's new cold war, winning a positional competition with China, and bolstering the nation's economic resiliency. Advances in these three efforts will not be cheap, but the bill after thirty years of a so-called post–Cold War Pax Americana is finally coming due. With this, hard power's relevance has returned in a big way, exemplified with Russia's 2022 invasion of Ukraine.

Regaining the initiative requires better strategic discipline in Washington than has been the norm, and key in this process is preventing strategic distraction from the principal threat—China. This means building several adequate options for national leaders. Having multiple options allows leaders under domestic political pressure tools to respond to world events in ways that do not take away from longer-term enduring efforts. In one regard the United States is well positioned. After decades of the Cold War, the nation has an unrivaled network of allies and like-minded partner nations. However, this network of friends will only act in concert and bring to bear resources if given the confidence of U.S. leadership and readily available military presence. That said, sometimes a heavier U.S. hand will be required. This has been the case since the barbaric October 7th attacks, on that day Hamas killed thirty-five Americans and took ten hostages. Fortunately, there already was a sizable naval presence (a carrier strike group and special forces on a large amphibious warship) in the eastern Mediterranean since Russia's February 2022 invasion of Ukraine. This serves as a reminder that limited U.S. naval forces must be sustained where they can have the greatest strategic impact and respond to crises with high domestic political interest. Sadly, the failure of that naval presence to deter Hamas or its supporter, Iran, from those attacks reminds us that effective naval presence must be part of a broader strategic effort. This is a point detailed in the 2023 book *U.S. Naval Power in the 21st Century: A New Strategy for Facing the Chinese and Russian Threat*: "Navies exist to assure access to markets and influence events on land for political ends."[5]

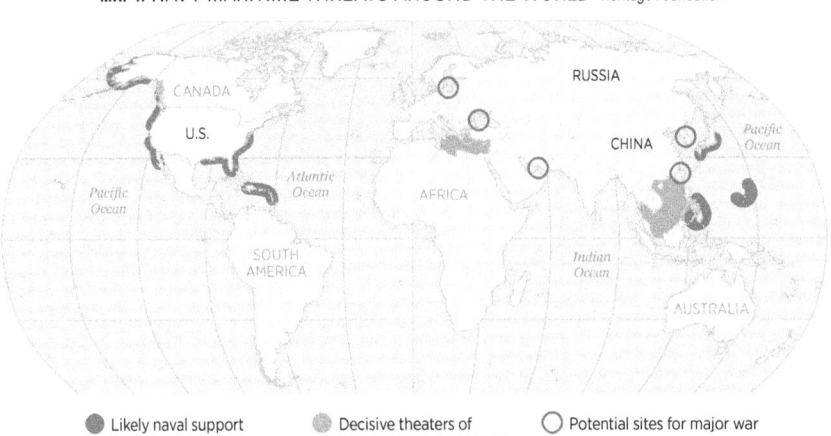

MAP 1. NAVY MARITIME THREATS AROUND THE WORLD *Heritage Foundation*

Russia's 2022 invasion of Ukraine and Hamas' 2023 assault on Israel illustrate the importance of correctly picking the decisive theaters. Today for the United States, the decisive theaters are the Eastern Mediterranean and the South China Sea. In this new cold war, naval power is again the tool of choice for seizing and retaining the initiative, but to be effective and sustainable, naval power must be paired with forceful diplomacy and economic statecraft. While diminished, naval power remains an American advantage in a new great game with China where maneuver and rapid response are the deciding factors. When forcefully employed, U.S. naval power's renowned ability to rapidly reposition and assert sustained strike power offshore attracts allies and partner nations while deterring adversaries. To be effective in the new cold war, naval power must be exercised in a new framework—naval statecraft.

In a nutshell, naval statecraft emphasizes naval and maritime power to present adversaries' strategic dilemmas while using that presence to enable economic engagements that demonstrate the supremacy of U.S. capitalism and governance in delivering prosperity for the most people. In time, this sets the stage for long-term alignment of common national interests able to withstand the worst influences of China, Russia, and other adversaries. Simply put, naval statecraft merges maritime with economic power enabled at strategic points by focused diplomacy. Our principal adversary—China—is not ten feet tall, but it represents a challenge unlike any our nation has ever confronted, necessitating an updated conceptualization of statecraft. The earlier book, *U.S. Naval Power in the 21st Century*, details the rationale and application of naval statecraft now and though the next fifty years. Building on that work, this book focuses on applying naval statecraft to regain the strategic initiative in the great game with China.

Informing this approach is a keen awareness of how the CCP at the helm of China have embarked on a long-term effort to supplant the United States and its rules-based order. Readers of *U.S. Naval Power in the 21st Century* will recall that the CCP is looking to win this new great game preferably by not firing a shot this decade. Author Michael Pillsbury, in *The Hundred-Year Marathon*, details a nine-point approach that captures China's peacetime competitive approach—one anchored in deception.[6] Failing that, the CCP's leaders have also been assiduously working to fight from a position of advantage diplomatically, economically, and of course militarily this decade. CCP military planners have studied the American way of war and know that victory will come, as Elbridge Colby asserts, as a fait accompli.[7] Averting what could highly likely be the most destructive war in human history requires winning the peace while being ready to win a prolonged war that could last years. Before moving on, it is worth reviewing in brief the CCP approach to great-power competition.

CHINA'S APPROACH TO GREAT-POWER COMPETITION: A BRIEF SUMMARY AND HISTORY

China has engaged in decades-long great-power competitions before; this current contest with the United States is nothing new to Beijing. Such a strategic rivalry, however, is unique in the American democratic experience. The closest to this is the military and ideological Cold War with the Soviet Union that lasted more than fifty years. The United States is engaged in a military, economic, and ideological contest with the CCP, but until recently the ideological aspect was largely ignored. This has gone on for thirty years, as former deputy national security adviser and China expert Matt Pottinger argued in an influential 2021 *Foreign Affairs* article.[8] Confounding many conventional thinkers for too long was a simple question: Why would the CCP chose competition when clearly the Open Door policies begun under Deng Xiaoping in 1979 had massively enriched the country? The answer defied Western understanding as too often policymakers mirrored their own values on their counterparts in Beijing—this has proven definitively wrongheaded. The first revelation that the CCP was engaged in a new cold war would come in 2001.

The Tiananmen Papers leaked to the public in 2001 detailed firsthand accounts of CCP deliberations before, during, and immediately after the massacre of Chinese democracy protestors in June 1989. That event was a shock to the CCP, which still reverberates today, and its memory is strictly censored. The months-long protests posed the greatest threat to the CCP's legitimacy to rule the nation since its victory in 1949. Those documents made clear the CCP began seeing the United States as its preeminent enemy in the early 1990s, especially a leaked State Security Ministry document on ideological and political infiltration from the West.[9] This fear of the West would be amplified by two other major world events completing what Rush Doshi has called a "traumatic trifecta."[10] The rapidly unfolding events of Tiananmen Square (1989), Gulf War (1990–91), and the fall of the Soviet Union (1991) then solidified in the CCP a sense of being under assault.

This should not surprise anyone who is familiar with Marxism, for at the core of the CCP's world view is an ideology that survives by fomenting strife, whether class warfare or racial unrest through critical race theory. This conflicted nature of Marxism is captured in Aleksandr Solzhenitsyn's *The Gulag Archipelago*: "If only there were evil people somewhere insidiously committing evil deeds, and it were necessary only to separate them from the rest of us and destroy them.... But the line dividing good and evil cuts through the heart of every human being. And who is willing to destroy a piece of his own heart?"[11] The lesson is that Marxist regimes are never at peace with themselves and always fearful given their war against human nature. The Marxist nature of the CCP's world view has inevitably led it to a new cold war, which began in the heady days of the early post–Cold War era when many in the West declared the "end of history" and the end of ideological warfare.

Despite this danger, many people on both sides of the Pacific made lots of money while remaining blind to China's growing comprehensive power. Until Xi Jinping's arrival at the helm of the CCP in 2012, the policy was "to hide one's capabilities and bide one's time" [Tao Guang Yang Hui (韬光养晦)] until the balance of power had shifted to China's favor. This was classic Chinese strategic deception, and it worked.[12] The United States would soon seek and win WTO membership for China on December 11, 2001. The CCP would use its newfound access to Western markets and finances to underwrite rapid economic growth and, with it, the fastest modernization and expansion of its military not seen since the coldest years of the Cold War.

Yet, the CCP remained too weak militarily, and its economy was too over-reliant on the West to risk uncovering its designs to rewrite the world to its communist wishes. Between WTO accession and the rapid militarization of the South China Sea in 2015, China continued to bide its time and hide its capabilities. It was what Deng's successor, Jiang Zemin, called "a period of strategic opportunity" [Zhànlüè Jīyù Qī (战略机遇期)].[13] Jiang saw this as a time for China to solidify its economic leadership while the United States was preoccupied with its war on terrorism following the September 11, 2001, al-Qaeda attacks. It was also a time for setting its rivalry with Russia aside to rebuild its military for the type of confrontation it would face against the United States.

Militarily, the moment that crystalized the need for modernization of the PLA was the third Taiwan crisis (1995–96). Jiang viewed Taiwan's then president, Lee Teng-hui, as moving the island toward independence from the mainland and sought to use military force to pressure him and influence coming elections. The plan backfired spectacularly with Lee being elected president in Taiwan's first democratic national elections, as two U.S. Navy carrier strike groups effectively blunted the CCP's military pressure.

While the CCP had already begun to address its need to modernize in 1993 with the initial purchase of four Russian *Kilo*-class submarines, it would accelerate its modernization after the third Taiwan crisis. In 1996, six months after that crisis, Russia sold two newly built *Sovremenny*-class destroyers to China.[14] This sale would help propel the PLA's rapid development of its own destroyers from 2001, the *Luyang* and *Renhai* classes. Of course, the biggest development was the 1998 purchase from Ukraine of the ex-Soviet aircraft carrier *Varyag*—now operational in the PLAN as the *Liaoning*.[15] In June 2002 China penned a contract for eight additional *Kilo*-class submarines, this time with the capability to launch long-range antiship cruise missiles—the Novator Alpha 3M-54E export variant of the Kalibr family of missiles.[16] In six years the PLA had acquired the most modern naval equipment money could buy from Russia and would begin to use this to modernize its fleet. While the PLA was serendipitously getting sensitive defense information from overseas commercial and academic contacts, the clearest statement of intent was these procurements of Russian platforms—the CCP intended to contest the oceans.

It would not take long for China's next leader to issue guidance that would make Alfred Thayer Mahan proud.[17] In 2004 Jiang's successor to lead the CCP, Hu Jintao, issued the so-called new historic missions, which were further clarified in a subsequent defense white paper at the 17th Congress of the CCP.[18] These new missions meant that the PLAN would be responsible for securing overseas markets and defend national interests far from the mainland. The first tangible product of this new direction was the December 2008 deployment of a three-ship PLAN flotilla to the Arabian Sea to support ongoing counterpiracy operations. At the time many China watchers saw it as an indication of China taking a supporting and constructive role, upholding the rule of law. They were wrong.

Prior to his ascension to party leadership in November 2012, Xi Jinping was thought to be a reformer who would accelerate China's alignment with the existing order. The *New York Times* in February 2012 speculated that Xi would make reforms to improve the common Chinese lot through an "economic overhaul"—meaning liberalization.[19] Not only did this not happen, but Xi would unify the party behind him by eliminating rivals through cascading anticorruption purges.[20] Xi has been so successful in solidifying his party hold that he broke Chinese Communist orthodoxy and secured a third term as general secretary and undisputed leader of China.[21] The last leader of China to do this was Mao Zedong, whose prolonged party leadership had enabled past excesses such as the Cultural Revolution. By the time Xi had secured his complete and uncontested leadership of the CCP, he had also benefited from and secured for China massive economic and military power.

As the third Taiwan crisis was ending in 1996, Chinese leaders knew that to contest the United States in the future, the PLA would need a sizable modern military, and achieving this would require two things: securing border disputes to allow resources to be shifted to the seas, and access to Western intellectual property and its finances to effect military modernization. WTO membership greatly eased the CCP's access to needed resources to modernize its military. However, if China were to focus those resources for the type of naval and air battle it would face against the United States, it would need to resolve border disputes. Top of the agenda was settling the long simmering rivalry with Russia, which had induced violent border clashes—the most remarkable of which took place March through August 1969. That clash was a year in the planning by the CCP aimed at undermining Soviet prestige at a time it was reeling from its 1968 Czechoslovakia intervention.[22] Eventually Soviet firepower and willingness to attack along its long, shared border saw the initiative shift by August. Fearing they would be unable to control the course of the conflict, CCP leaders sought to deescalate, opened diplomatic channels with Moscow, and established a code of conduct along their border.[23] A limited military incident with strategic objectives would be repeated in 1979 against Vietnam to punish it, principally for its strategic partnership with the Soviets.[24] Failing to execute its preferred rapid, punishing military strike, and after prolonged fighting, the CCP settled for making its point with the capture of the strategic northern city of Lang Son and then withdrew. As the CCP's strategic sights shifted in the early 1990s to countering the United States, it would need to put its Russian threat to rest. This was achieved with ratification of a 2001 treaty that cemented their strategic partnership and essentially settled their borders.[25] This treaty was quietly renewed for another five years on the eve of Russia's second invasion of Ukraine later that same month, in February 2022.[26] WTO accession and relative stability along China's land borders enabled China to turn to the seas and, after the financial crisis of 2008, to ramp up its economic statecraft and begin building a sprawling sphere of influence through its Belt and Road Initiative.

This brief history raises two points worth stressing: First, CCP leadership will take its time to set up and use limited military forces, including allowing casualties among its forces, for a "peacetime" strategic objective. Second, the CCP's actions can be blunted or constrained if it is uncertain over its ability to control the risk. In both incidents, the Russian border conflict and 1979 Vietnam invasion, fighting subsided rapidly once Beijing began to lose control of the political and diplomatic outcomes.

Another important feature of the CCP is its strategic opportunism. As China was entering the WTO and laying the foundations for its military modernization, two events opened a strategic opportunity for it to rapidly close the power balance with the United States. The first was the terrorist attacks on the United States in September 2001 and subsequent American invasion of Iraq in 2003, ushering in a twenty-year war that distracted the United States. The second event was the economic collapse of 2008, which saw for the first time Chinese leaders profess that the unipolar world had ended. China was not immune, of course, from economic or terrorist dangers. So in 2001 China founded and hosted the Shanghai Cooperation Organization (SCO), building on the 1996 Shanghai Five, which originally focused on lessening border military forces. The SCO would grow to facilitate greater coordination in defense, especially against insurrection and terrorists, and region-wide economic integration—while also working to exclude extra-regional powers. The SCO would aid in stabilizing China's eastern border but also provided it greater access to critical energy resources. Unconstrained by exposed shipping routes and markets, China could dominate this region far from Western influence.

The 2008 economic crisis was the trigger for a rapid expansion of Chinese economic presence with the creation in 2013 of the One Belt, One Road initiative (later renamed Belt and Road Initiative, or BRI). With the United States distracted by fighting insurgencies and battling economic crises, the CCP had what then–general secretary Jiang Zemin predicted in 2002 would be a twenty-year period of strategic opportunity.[27] During this time, and aided by the BRI, CCP influence rapidly spread across the world, providing the CCP diplomatic leverage, access to critical resources that the West could not easily switch off, and an independent financing mechanism—the Cross-Border Interbank Payment System (CIPS). On the heels of inconvenient sanctions on Russia following its annexation of Crimea in 2014, China formally established CIPS.[28] This has provided the CCP an effective means of executing deals beyond the prying eyes of Western financial entities, which is all the more potent as the dollar's dominance of international trade slackens.[29] The CCP's deliberate efforts after twenty years secured potent global economic influence connected by its alternative financing system and focused its military development for a contest with the United States. While long-term efforts like the BRI have strengthened the CCP's economic and diplomatic hand, it is not unassailable, and the leaders in Beijing know this.

At the 20th Party Congress in October 2022, a gathering of CCP officials every five years charged with laying out the strategic direction, the theme was: "Hold High the Great Banner of Socialism with Chinese Characteristics and Strive in Unity to Build a Modern Socialist Country in All Respects."

CCP confidence in delivering on this theme rests on three pillars: a favorable regional military balance, assured market access for critical imports like energy, and political assurances from a growing network of countries with entrenched interests. Weakening the CCP's confidence in any of these pillars would impact its strategic calculus—likely pushing the CCP to a defensive posture.

On the military front, Xi Jinping has not been shy regarding his displeasure with the PLA's readiness, claiming that "five incapables" bedevil the PLA.[30] Notable is concern for the military's political orthodoxy or trustworthiness, which in 2023 has seen unusually numerous purges of senior military leaders.[31] To enhance the PLA's modern war-fighting capabilities, major joint military reforms were launched in 2014—and ten years later the jury remains out on how effective these have been.[32] The conclusion is that the PLA may have new weapons but, without proven competency, there remains uncertainty in Beijing for how the PLA would fare in a modern war.

Even if there is some uncertainty within the CCP regarding the PLA's ability in a modern war, Chinese economic statecraft would make up for it in coercion. Or maybe not. There has been growing discontent with China's economic approach—missed obligations of the BRI, lopsided benefits of overseas investments going to Chinese entities, and failure to deliver financial assistance when most needed. Case in point: the 2022 protests in Sri Lanka as its economy tanked (GDP shrinking by 7.8 percent; inflation at 60 percent) while its China-supported leader, President

Gotabaya Rajapaksa, fled.³³ Amid this turmoil, China resisted responding to Sri Lankans' pleas for financial assistance and loan restructuring, which analysts assessed as accounting for 20 percent of total official debt; almost two years later, as of October 2023, a solution had yet to be found.³⁴ And to further make the point, in the middle of this turmoil, China's space surveillance vessel, the *Yuan Wang 5*, was initially in early August 2022 denied a port call by Sri Lanka's foreign ministry, which was later allowed on condition it would not conduct any surveillance while in port.³⁵ Despite China holding over 50 percent of its bilateral debt, the Sri Lankan government in December 2023 considered a moratorium on Chinese maritime research vessel visits.³⁶ Events in Columbo indicate that despite significant debt held and economic ties, Chinese influence can be blunted. Bottom line, a Chinese deal is never final and is always up for renegotiation.

A third factor informing CCP confidence is economic security or, as the CCP itself has judged in the past, sustained economic growth. Given a host of factors, China is facing sustained downward pressures on its economic growth to levels not seen since the Tiananmen Square sanctions regime of the early 1990s. Most notably since 2020 there has been the added downward pressure on the economy from the Covid-19 pandemic. Pandemic policies like zero-Covid shut down major ports and factories for prolonged periods when even a single positive test of Covid was found among the workforce.³⁷ Add to this Moody's December 2023 downgrade of China's credit rating to negative territory, signaling more than domestic unease with the state of China's economy under unsustainable debt.³⁸ Given these economic pressures—some of which were unavoidable, like demographic shrinkage—has led CCP leadership to rewrite the social contract to focus on so-called values-based legitimacy backed by a sustained propaganda and nativist campaign.³⁹ Whether this shift in party legitimacy convinces the people is still unknown, but clearly the CCP is concerned that it will not be able to deliver on its promise of prosperity.

Operationalizing this knowledge for strategic effect on China will be key. Events between the spring and fall of 2023 provide a test case for how these three factors (economic stability, military balance, and political control) influence CCP decision-making. After almost a year of heightened military presence around Taiwan following the August 2022 visit to Taiwan by Nancy Pelosi, the U.S. Speaker of the House, President Joe Biden's administration in the spring 2023 started sending overtures that it wanted to improve relations and was willing to make a deal.[40] Initial attempts at sending senior White House or State Department officials to Beijing ran into headwinds. That is, until a presidential policy meeting on April 6 led to two senior commerce officials traveling to Beijing to open economic discussions with Beijing.[41] Those overtures worked, and in succession secretaries of treasury and commerce made their way to Beijing.[42] Chinese hosts made clear their expectations at briefings before and after the visits: "China requires the U.S. to cease the suppression of Chinese enterprises, lift bans on Xinjiang-related products, and take concrete steps to respond to China's major concerns in economic relations between the two countries."[43] Washington, however, was hoping for a more broad cooling of tensions involving renewed military dialogues. Instead the PLA maintained a heighten level of military presence around Taiwan and continued to intimidate Philippine resupply missions to its South China Sea garrison at Second Thomas Shoal.[44]

Rather than play up incidents like a Chinese spy balloon that flew over the United States, the U.S. administration tried to suppress or diminish these news reports in pursuit of engagement.[45] To the CCP, this made their military hand stronger and gave them confidence as to what Washington's narrow intents were—dialogue. The only pressure applied to China during this time was the public information campaign the government of Philippines ran exposing Chinese coercion in its waters around Second Thomas Shoal and a limited and unchanged U.S. military presence in the region.[46] As a result, Beijing was compelled to neither moderate its military activities nor meaningfully engage in military exchanges until after extracting several economic engagements. To cap months of diplomacy, Xi Jinping secured a summit meeting with the U.S. president that bolstered his efforts to stabilize a faltering Chinese economy.[47] Alternately, the first tangible outcome for the United States would be a late-December phone call between the chairman of the Joint Chiefs

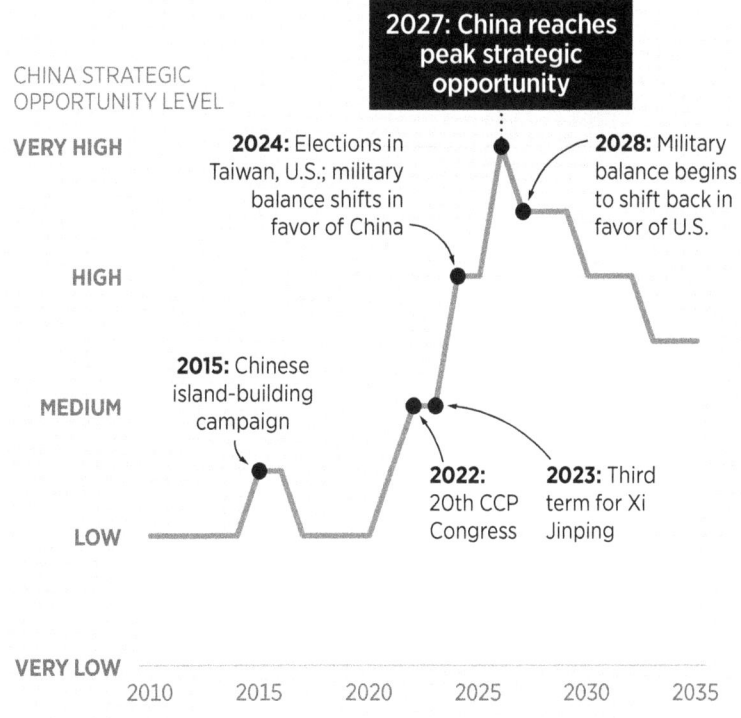

GRAPH 1. WINDOW OF OPPORTUNITY: HOW CHINA SEES ITS STRATEGIC FUTURE
Heritage Foundation / The Daily Signal

China currently holds a small military advantage over the U.S. and its allies in the Pacific, but that advantage will be temporary. Meanwhile, elections in the U.S., China, and Taiwan may contribute to a rise in strategic opportunity for China, which would peak in 2027 then quickly drop.

of Staff, Gen. Charles Q. Brown, and PLA general Liu Zhenli.[48] Liu would retire and be replaced by a new PLAN admiral within days, making the call of questionable value. Given the weakness of China's economy, the United States had a strong hand in seeking concessions but, by not pressing its advantages, had allowed Beijing to effectively cede nothing. A key tenant of this book is that more effective engagement with the CCP is possible by comprehensively coordinating actions that undermine confidence in Beijing's ability to sustain a favorable military balance and economic stability and to retain effective political or diplomatic control of events.

DECONSTRUCTING CHINESE STATECRAFT FOR PROACTIVE U.S. ACTION

The previous sections can be condensed into an equation that describes the interplay of three primary factors informing CCP strategic calculus. Since it is Chinese aggression that is sought to be deterred, the equation focuses on that and not alternatively on containing CCP activities. That said, the equation is:

Chinese Aggression = Military Balance + Secure Economy + Effective Political Control

The structure of this book uses the above equation as a guide for the actions recommended to sustain deterrence through this most dangerous decade—2025 through 2035. Each term of this equation correlates to a section of this book: Part 1 focuses on how increased western Pacific military presence in concert with allies and partner nations will shift the regional military balance away from China's favor. Part 2 focuses on how securing the U.S. economy will strengthen U.S. ability to resist Chinese economic coercion and, if needed, sustain a long war. Part 3 then addresses how reorganizing for the new cold war can enhance U.S. proactive, effective control of events or incidents instigated by the CCP. The additive effect of these actions would raise uncertainty in Beijing that enhance deterrence.

This deterrence is not only against military assaults, as Chinese aggression also operates on a spectrum and not a binary peace or war dialectic. This spectrum of rivalry, as CCP confidence grows, will be more willing to take risk and instigate confrontations with the United States. The impossibility of knowing precisely all the factors weighing on Beijing's calculus renders a macro view most useful for using trend analysis to ascertain future outcomes. As such, each term of the above equation judges CCP perception regarding relative strength and trends. To get a sense of how this works, what has been playing out since House Speaker

Pelosi's visit to Taipei in August 2022 is a good test case. Since that time, the daily thirty-day floating average of Chinese military presence around Taiwan has seen a fourfold increase at levels that have persisted until the publication of this book.[49] During this time China has also made increasingly provocative actions such as ramming Philippine coast guard cutters in the South China Sea and conducting drills focused on stopping and inspecting shipping headed to Taiwan.[50] Using this equation can help us understand and predict CCP behavior; let's apply some "trend analysis" to another recent event.

Test Case: China's Increased Provocations Following President Tsai Ing-wen's April 2023 Meeting with Speaker of the U.S. House of Representatives, Kevin McCarthy

1. In March, forty-two Chinese Maritime Militia and a PLAN warship were spotted in the Philippines' exclusive economic zone near Thitu Island.[51] This is far smaller than previous levels; over two hundred Maritime Militia had massed around Whitsun Reef in March 2021. From April 9, the PLA instigated military exercises focused on Taiwan. The net effect on military balance was muted given the largest-ever U.S.–Philippines major exercise, Balikatan, and nearby two U.S. carrier strike groups and two U.S. amphibious ready groups.[52]
2. China's economy, under pressure since the 2020 Covid-19 pandemic, started to see recessionary pressures begin to abate.[53] Not wanting to risk this recovery, the CCP announced several trade investigations but refrained from implementing new economic sanctions against Taiwan.[54]
3. Military activities begun April 8 focused on Taiwan, while paramilitary activity in the South China Sea was at a lower level than the same time in recent years. The effect of these activities seems to have enhanced CCP political control of events around Taiwan and prevented a crisis in the South China Sea.
4. On April 6 the Chinese Fujian maritime safety administration launched a provocative three-day drill to stop shipping headed

FIGURE 2. Chinese aggression equation explanation *Author illustration*

to Taiwan.[55] By the end of April, despite significant military presence and live-fire drills, no Taiwan commercial ships had been interdicted by Chinese forces. The implication is that a too-narrow military predominance and potential economic blowback restrained more aggressive activities that Beijing may have been planning.

This trend analysis (see Figure 2) is inexact, but it provides an accessible approach marrying the art and science of deterrence specific to China. Each of the following three parts of this book focus on one term of the model equation. The intent is to assess specific actions to enhance deterrence and shift the strategic initiative to Washington.

PART ONE: "THE COMPETITION FOR POSITION AND PREVENTING A CCP FAIT ACCOMPLI"

Part 1 lays out several efforts to stabilize and then shift the military balance in Washington's favor, starting with the Indo-Pacific. This will involve confounding the CCP's positional competition for overseas basing and strategic market dominance. Achieving this requires competing against the CCP elite-capture influence campaigns and the BRI.

PART TWO: "STRENGTHENING THE HOMELAND TO WAGE PROTRACTED WAR AND RESILIENCY TO COERCION"

The second part of the book focuses on undermining the CCP's ability to coerce or manipulate global supply chains to influence U.S. political decisions. Chapter 4 focuses on securing operational energy needs and associated transportation so that a wartime economy can function and military units kept fueled. Chapter 5 addresses the associated need to secure vital shipping and regaining American shipbuilding capacity, both important for an effective Navy and for sustaining a wartime economy.

This is followed by chapter 6, which details a modern naval act to grow the Navy drawing on the insights laid out in *U.S. Naval Power in the 21st Century* with a focus on setting the conditions for a rapid industrial rearmament, should the nation find itself in war.

PART THREE: "REORGANIZING FOR A NEW COLD WAR TO SEIZE AND RETAIN THE INITIATIVE"

The final part of this book focuses on reorganizing the government to better execute a sustainable competitive strategy against China. Chapters will deal in turn with creating a Maritime Department focused on securing critical shipping and regaining American maritime commercial competitiveness (chapter 7); proposing a new National Security Council structure tailored to executing specific strategic objectives and not to manage the various departments and agencies of government (chapter 8); and detailing an oceans-centered naval fleet versus being aligned to joint force regional combatant commands (chapter 9).

CONCLUSION

As 2023 ended, Xi Jinping made two important personnel appointments for the PLA that have implications going well into this century, into what will be years that decide the peace. The first was the Christmas day promotion of submarine officer Admiral Hu Zhongming to lead the PLAN. Days later, on December 29, 2023, the first naval officer—Admiral Dong Jun—was named to lead the PLA as minister of defense. Both officers have firsthand joint operational experience in theaters where they have commanded forces near the militaries they would fight in a war across the Straits of Taiwan. This focus on naval warfare currently fits into a long-term approach to preparing for a contest this decade over Taiwan.

At a March 2021 congressional hearing, the commander of the U.S. Indo-Pacific Command cautioned that China was preparing to move against Taiwan by 2027. That warning has since been affirmed by current and past directors of the Central Intelligence Agency, secretaries of state, and senior military leaders. Moreover, numerous factors are conspiring to present the CCP as having a closing window of time to act on Taiwan and to instill urgency for Xi Jinping to act this decade. This is not unlike Jiang Zemin's twenty-year "strategic opportunity" that informed CCP decision-making during the pivotal years of 2002–22, which witnessed the PLA's modernization and rapid growth.

Regaining the initiative against the CCP's decades of running an ambitious program to rewrite the world order is late in coming. This book hopes to lay out some actionable ways to do this in the near term while setting the conditions for successfully waging a new cold war against the CCP that is of their choosing. Success will require executing coherent efforts across multiple governmental agencies, civilian organizations, commercial interests, international organizations, allies, and not-so-friendly nations. Each of these efforts, like the parts of a warship's reduction gear, will spin at different speeds, involve different gearing patterns, appear offset from other gears but all will drive a common effort—competition with China. Adding more gears to this system adds horsepower but not speed, meaning that there is only so much time available for the United States to take effective action. The ideas that follow can inform that action and stop the nation's proclivity for "shooting behind the duck" in the great-power game we find ourselves.

PART ONE

THE COMPETITION FOR POSITION AND PREVENTING A CCP FAIT ACCOMPLI

Chinese Aggression = Military Balance + Secure Economy + Effective Political Control

FIGURE 3. Chinese aggression equation, part 1 *Author illustration*

Part 1 presents initiatives to posture naval forces to better contest Chinese economic statecraft and to complicate PLA efforts to secure overseas bases or access militarily useful infrastructure. The effect of these efforts will be to shift the military balance at key strategic locations in the south and central Pacific and Southeast Asia. To achieve this initiative, it is necessary to understand how the CCP guides its overseas investments and redirects them for its strategic purposes. This knowledge can then be used to shape naval operations in support of coordinated maritime economic statecraft to advance U.S. interests and to prevent the PLA from taking a threatening military posture. This is naval statecraft in action to regain the strategic initiative in the near term. The net effect of these efforts is to diminish CCP confidence that the PLA can effectively execute strategic objectives in peacetime or execute effective war plans.

CHAPTER 1

FORTIFY THE NATION, PREPARE TO STRIKE
China's Evolving Global Military Basing Construct

先為不可勝, 以待敵之可勝
[Fortify the nation, prepare to strike]

The Chinese idiom opening this chapter is from a classic Sun Tzu script about tactical disposition. Its direct translation in short is, "first put themselves beyond the possibility of defeat, and then wait for an opportunity of defeating the enemy." This idiom, especially the complete section of Sun Tzu's ancient text on tactical disposition, reflects a still-relevant discussion about the importance of military posture in waging protracted military campaigns.[1] Today China's acquisition of ports and naval bases overseas should likewise be seen as a competition for strategic position.

This effort was first recognized in 2004 when a Booz Allen Hamilton analyst coined the term "String of Pearls" for a study of potential Chinese naval bases in the Indian Ocean. Since then, concern has only grown over where and for what purpose the Chinese navy would seek overseas bases. In recent years the strategic implications of Chinese global dominance of ports, made more pronounced since the supply chain crises of the Covid-19 pandemic has come into clearer focus.[2] This concern has sharpened as Chinese leaders turn ostensibly economic interests into security presence—exemplified by China's protestations for years that it did not seek a military base in Djibouti only for it to happen.[3] This has become a too familiar pattern by Beijing; deny then acquire military access to overseas bases. Since 2022, this has been playing out in the Solomon Islands and Cambodia's port of Ream.

That said, the study of Chinese overseas basing is complicated by opacity regarding their plans, activities, and official strategy. What can be seen appears to be an inconsistent Chinese Communist Party's (CCP) military—the People's Liberation Army (PLA)—approach to achieving global strategic position. As such, there may in fact be no formal plan but a nonlinear amalgamation of central party direction, economic profit seeking, and policy pragmatism guiding China's overseas basing. However, the operational demands of being ready for a conflict over the future of Taiwan by 2027 are driving the CCP to take risks in securing a favorable strategic position. This chapter sheds light on this dynamic process in which the PLA is acquiring overseas naval bases and proposes ways to complicate it.

CCP CORE INTERESTS AND THE MILITARY TOOLS TO DELIVER THEM

The CCP's often-stated long-term objective is "national rejuvenation" by its centenary in 2049. In recent speeches, Chairman Xi Jinping has made clear this includes unification of the mainland and Taiwan as well as advancing economic prosperity.[4] This does not mean war is a foregone conclusion, but domestic political pressures and recent developments in the military and economic balance may be accelerating Beijing's desire to move sooner on the military front. If this is in fact true, there will be added pressures for the PLA to establish a favorable strategic position and secure critical energy and raw materials for the regime while presenting a daunting military obstacle to any intervention against it. If allowed to advance unabated, the CCP could soon assault Taiwan without facing an effective counterattack in what Elbridge Colby has called a fait accompli conquering of the island. This may explain recent moves to secure basing in the Pacific and Southeast Asia.

Moreover, tensions with the United States have grown amid economic pressures wrought by the Covid-19 pandemic and a deteriorating business environment in China. As China's comparative advantage in cheap labor has waned, manufacturing has increasingly moved out of mainland China. A contributing factor is a worsening business environment according to a 2021 survey of European companies doing business in China. Respondents indicated that in recent years, heightened politicization under Xi has caused a markedly deteriorating business environment—a trend that predated the pandemic and persists in late 2024.[5] If Western companies continue to move out of China, this will place greater importance on overseas replacement sources of raw materials and markets for the CCP. This search has been assisted since 2013 by the Belt and Road Initiative (BRI) but has in recent years been losing momentum. The strain of its debtors' shaky financials has imperiled the $1 trillion BRI investments made by China across Africa, Latin American, and Asia.[6] In turn, a financially overleveraged CCP could face added impetus to use its military presence to backstop compliance by strategically important CCP debtors—for example, the deep-water port Hambantota, Sri Lanka. The point is, economic and military interests are converging and incentivizing the PLA to secure more overseas bases.

To achieve sustained security to the CCP's overseas economic interests, the PLAN would need to develop new capabilities and experience operating in distant seas. Following CCP general secretary Hu Jintao's 2004 "new historic missions" pronouncement, analysts pointed out the PLAN would need to develop platforms that could project CCP power beyond its coastal waters, new tactics, and more naval support vessels and bases to support distant operations.[7] The first tangible execution of these new missions was the December 2008 deployment of two PLAN warships and a supply ship to participate in antipiracy operations in the Horn of Africa region.[8] After sustaining a naval presence in the region for years, in 2017 the PLA established its first and, as of August 2024, only formal overseas military base in Djibouti, where recent pier upgrades are assessed able to host the PLAN's largest warships.[9] The military value of nearby logistics demonstrated by the base in Djibouti to naval operations off the Horn of Africa likely contributed to the CCP's 2013 decision to rapidly and massively build an archipelago of man-made islands in the South China Sea.

By late 2015 the PLA had erected seven man-made islands in the South China Sea, which have since been thoroughly militarized. Subsequently, there have been frequent stops to these bases by PLAN warships, PLA Air Force (PLAAF) aircraft, China Coast Guard (CCG) cutters, and the paramilitary maritime militia.[10] The true value of these features is not for waging war with the United States but to sustain an economic-military campaign to exert greater control over these waters.[11] It is what naval historian and researcher Hunter Stires calls "an insurgency at-sea" waged by the CCP to rewrite the norms of economic and military behavior in the region.[12]

Prior to the PLA's construction of ports and airfields there, the CCG and PLAN were only able to maintain a limited naval presence out to one thousand miles from the nearest naval base on Hainan Island. For the PLAN, these man-made islands provide a place to refuel, provision, and repair its warships on extended deployment, thereby freeing its limited number of logistics ships for more distant operations. The importance of these bases is greatest for sustaining a fleet of smaller CCG and maritime militia vessels far from mainland bases. For smaller patrol vessels like the PLAN's Type-22 missile boat (also called *Houbei* class), coast guard cutters, and repurposed fishing vessels of the maritime militia, there is no viable at-sea replenishment option.[13] However, after these forward bases were established, sustained Chinese maritime presence has skyrocketed and remains high around several key disputed features. In 2022, total CCG vessel-day activity included[14]

> **Scarborough Shoal**—344 days, an increase of 57 days over 2020 data
> **Second Thomas Shoal**—279 days, an increase of 47 days over 2020 data
> **Luconia Shoals**—316 days, an increase of 37 days over 2020 data
> **Vanguard Bank**—310 days, an increase of 168 days over 2020 data
> **Thitu Island**—208 days (no data available for 2020)

Likewise, recent years have seen a marked increase in maritime militia presence throughout the South China Sea.[15] In the intervening years, life at these garrisons has settled into routine for PLA forces. State television reported there are even grocery stores for military personnel on several of these outposts, where only years ago was a partially submerged coral reef.[16] Unmentioned in these government media posts is the tremendous economic potential from fishing as well as seabed resources like petroleum that these persistent naval forces secure for China. This economic potential drives half of CCP interest in the region, with CCG and maritime militia carrying the effort. The other half of the equation is the influence of and deterrence by a strong regional military presence based there that complicates potential U.S. intervention in crisis. These man-made islands have enabled a larger and sustained PLA and paramilitary presence that is now a fixture of life in the region. The overall effect has been to incrementally "box out" the United States, leaving claimant states like Malaysia or the Philippines to confront China in a lopsided daily naval competition or else cede their claims.[17]

Given the 2004 new missions, experience off the Horn of Africa, and success in the South China Sea, Beijing clearly appreciates the strategic importance of logistic bases to sustain forward naval presence. This has informed future PLA's overseas basing requirements, shaped the types of warships built, and determined the port facilities required. In the South China Sea, the PLA was able to occupy and build its bases on top of submerged or partially submerged features, but this is not an option further afield—there, a different approach is needed to secure and sustain a forward naval presence. This would also require greater combined effort within China's government agencies as well as CCP political consensus for such efforts to succeed.

PRAGMATISM, OPPORTUNISM, AND ENTROPIC WARFARE

Regarding PLA port access, a unity of effort, or civil-military fusion, has become a fixture of the CCP approach. Xi Jinping understands the importance of seaborne trade to meeting long-term rejuvenation goals, publicly stating in 2017 that the country conducted 90 percent of its trade on the ocean with six hundred ports worldwide.[18] Beginning with 1999's "going out" policy and accelerating after 2013's BRI, the CCP has used incentives and material support rather than directing commercial or PLA investment to develop access to specific ports.[19] This loose approach has incentivized a collective effort that, by late 2022, gave China through its state-owned and private enterprises control of over one hundred foreign ports in more than fifty countries along critical shipping lanes.[20]

Not all these ports rise to national-level attention or focus, but sometimes an overseas port rises in strategic value to merit added political and military attention. If a port's value crosses this strategic threshold, it triggers greater diplomatic engagement and government directed investment. In this regard, Xi Jinping's November 2019 visit to the Greek port of Piraeus stands out. Xi's visit capped a years-long progression beginning from April 2016 when China's state-owned shipping company, COSCO, took control of Piraeus port operations, followed in July 2017, when three PLAN warships visited the port for four days.[21] Importantly, Xi's visit to Piraeus came ahead of a contentious decision to allow COSCO to acquire 67 percent ownership of the port despite not meeting prior development agreements.[22] The trajectory of ever-greater Chinese control of this port has since stalled due to unmet public expectations for greater Chinese investment and associated job growth, and there has not been a repeat PLAN visit since a series of court cases in 2020 protesting further development of the port.[23] During a visit to Athens in January 2023, I witnessed China's attempts to control Piraeus. Similar patterns can be seen as China sought access and development of other militarily useful ports.

For two decades China has been actively securing access to a sea lane stretching from China's southern coast through the Straits of Malacca, Persian Gulf, East African coast, through the Suez Canal and into southern Europe—the so-called Maritime Silk Road. When reviewing Chinese efforts along this route, a similar pattern emerges—commercial access begets political attention that leads to military utility. This is not always driven by China; in Egypt's case, the government there courted Chinese presence. On the heels of an August 5, 2019, deal with China's Hutchison Ports, a PLAN warship stopped in Alexandria naval base for a technical stop.[24] This technical stop likely allowed the PLAN to assess feasibility for conducting future repairs at the port as well as conduct minor maintenance given the short visit—four days. These developments came after sustained engagement by Egypt's president, Abdul Fattah al-Sisi, who visited China six times since taking office in 2014 prior to attending the signing of the August 2019 agreement with Hutchison Ports.[25] Setting the stage for these events, Xi visited Egypt in January 2016 to meet with al-Sisi focused on opening a comprehensive strategic dialogue; the meeting culminated in the signing of twenty-one investment deals.[26] A subsequent summit between them occurred in December 2022 in Riyadh, Saudi Arabia.[27] This summit was followed in March 2023 with the announcement of a $2 billion steel pipe production investment in the Suez Canal Economic Zone.[28] In the coming years, should the political relationship remain strong and anchored on mutual economic benefit, it is likely there will be more port calls by PLAN warships that increasingly conduct repairs and replenishment, further underscoring China's comprehensive investment in Egypt. Access to and potential leverage over the Suez Canal Authority would afford the CCP an ability to complicate adversarial naval action or delay commercial shipping, slowing other countries' economies in a form of sanctions with Chinese characteristics. Of course, the same thing is playing out in Panama, with Hutchison Ports operating ports on either end of the Panama Canal.

A final example of an evolving CCP approach to gaining access to militarily important ports has occurred in the Solomon Islands. What is unique in this case is a willingness by the CCP to take advantage of domestic political disputes to secure deals. Events began following violent protests and a narrowly won December 2021 no-confidence vote amid claims of corruption over vote buying by China. In turn, leading opposition leaders sought a referendum that divided the country with the embattled prime minister, Manasseh Sogavare, claiming external interference—a claim aimed at Australia.[29] In March 2022 a secret pact negotiated by Sogavare and the PRC came to light that allowed Chinese security forces access to the country amid speculation China was also looking to establish a naval base in Isabel Province.[30] Sogavare's rationale seems to be "regime survival," as the deal would afford him Chinese protections and assistance against future public dissent.[31] U.S. reaction was tardy, and a series of high-level engagements were unable to turn the tide—notably, the April 2022 and March 2023 visits of senior National Security Council coordinator for the Indo-Pacific, Kurt Campbell.[32] At the same time, several nefarious deals that would ostensibly grant the PLA access to the country had heightened local awareness of China's influence in the Solomon Islands' 2024 general elections.[33] This risky and divisive diplomatic approach is what regional expert Cleo Paskal has called "entropic warfare" and is causing consternation among Pacific island nations' typically harmonious relations.[34] While Sogavare withdrew from consideration as the prime minister again, the deal that opened the door to sustained Chinese security and military presence remains in place with a new government.

The cases of Greece, Egypt, and the Solomon Islands illuminate a diverse CCP approach—on the one hand, courted by a host; and, on the other hand, a riskier, coercive approach. Looking ahead, it is clear the CCP will tailor its actions to changing conditions on the ground as seen in Piraeus in response to rising popular dissatisfaction. At the same time, it will allow commercial interests to lead and prepare conditions for more robust military presence, as in Egypt, or to seize on local opportunities as in the Solomon Islands. Once a port gets national CCP attention, several organizations important to realizing the port as militarily useful will come into action.

BRIDGING COMMERCIAL VALUE TO POLITICAL STRATEGIC ACTION

CCP interests in a foreign port for military purposes seems to be triggered once it gains enough viability economically and politically as a reliable host. If the relevant port serves strategic interests, such as securing energy shipments, it likely gains added national government attention as well as resources. Today such decisions and actions are likely to work through three bodies: the Central Military Commission (CMC), the Central Commission for Integrated Military and Civilian Development (军民融合发展委员会), and the Central Organization Department.

To date, the only situation in which such decision-making has played out was the 2016 establishment of the base in Djibouti. This occurred prior to the founding of the Central Commission for Integrated Military and Civilian Development that came in January 2017. Prior to its establishment, the principal decision-making body for military affairs was the CMC, chaired by Xi Jinping. For several years beginning in 2014, speculation had mounted against PRC protestations that the PLA was seeking a base in Djibouti.[35] At the time the CMC had only one PLAN officer detailed to the commission—the influential admiral Wu Shengli, who played a key role as PLAN commander initiating the PLAN Horn of Africa antipiracy patrols.[36] Admiral Wu had a substantial operational career, unlike his successor to the CMC, Admiral Miao Hua, who was a career PLA political officer who only became a PLAN officer in 2014 and subsequently was promoted to admiral in 2015.[37] However, the PLA's drive for overseas naval bases could be reenergized as the first PLAN admiral, Dong Jun, took the helm on December 29, 2023, as minister of national defense.[38]

On January 22, 2017, a new body was established that could play a key role in decisions involving overseas basing and access to foreign ports—the Central Commission for Integrated Military and Civilian Development. The commission's importance was underscored by the frequency of meetings—June and September 2017 and March 2018—and the fact that it is chaired by Xi Jinping.[39] Another sign of the commission's importance was the seniority of its original members, including three Politburo Standing Committee members (Li Keqiang, Liu Yunshan, and Zhang Gaoli) and two CMC vice chairs: PLAAF general Xu Qiliang and PLA general Fan Changlong.[40] One early topic of this new commission was planning for the thirteenth five-year plan (2016–20) regarding implementing civil-military integration in military logistics, which seemingly covers access to overseas ports for repair, sustainment, and basing of PLAN vessels.[41] Personnel assigned to this commission, aside from Xi's continued chairmanship, since the Twentieth Party Congress remain unknown. However, it is likely to continue to include CMC uniformed leadership as well as senior members from agencies focusing on transportation and foreign affairs.

Finally, the third organization involved is the Central Organization Department, which is responsible for all personnel decisions within the party and even senior corporate leadership. The ability to direct senior executive personnel assignments has a compelling impact on Chinese state-owned enterprises like COSCO.[42] For private companies, oversight of corporate decisions is exercised through constitutionally compelled party committees established in any organization with three or more CCP members.[43] This influence over corporate leadership selection and decision-making compels a unity of effort across Chinese political-economic society in line with CCP orthodoxy and dictate. According to interviews with State Council officials, BRI projects, with few exceptions, are not directed from national leadership, giving bureaucratic, corporate, and provincial interests leeway in pursuit of projects.[44] Given the commonality of BRI infrastructure projects sought for overseas military bases, it would not be a stretch to assume that a similar approach is at play in BRI. In fact, the PLA's base in Djibouti began with economic development, as has other ports the PLAN has increasingly visited. Considering the focus of these three organizations, it is highly likely they will play a role in the establishment of overseas naval basing and military access agreements.

Just as the CCP has implemented several reforms to enable greater civil-military fusion to advance its interests, the PLA has likewise reformed to better leverage commercial activities. In 2016 the PLA established the Logistics Support Department and the National Mobilization Department. These organizational reforms enable the PLAN to directly engage with commercial entities operating overseas ports or requisition shipping for military purposes.[45] Such reforms are already having results. Reporting from 2022 has uncovered design modifications to and exercises practicing the use of commercial car ferries able to deploy PLA tanks and amphibious assault vehicles.[46] Rather than conducting time consuming and expensive military construction of facilities, these administrative changes give added credence to the notion the PLA would instead leverage dual-use overseas facilities and commercial shipping. Since 2012 the PLAN has been aggressively using Chinese overseas ports to "show the flag" or resupply and increasingly to conduct significant repairs—nine times since 2017.[47] However, naval operational needs may still necessitate the PLA to dredge ports, expand piers, and construct facilities overseas. The next section assesses where the CCP is prioritizing recent overseas port access efforts against military operational need and strategic intent.

IMPACTS ON NAVAL FORCE STRUCTURES AS OVERSEAS BASES BECOME MORE IMPORTANT

In the Indian Ocean, what were once infrequently visited ports by the PLAN are increasingly playing a role in sustaining a growing regional naval presence. As the CCP is becoming more confident and the rhetoric heats up, the character of its overseas military presence has likewise changed. For example, the PLAN presence dedicated to supporting a counterpiracy effort in the Indian Ocean can secure access to critical sources of energy and raw materials and can evacuate its nationals from conflicts. This persistent naval presence came into action in April 2023 as violence flared between rival military factions in Sudan, and two PLAN ships arrived at Port Sudan to evacuate more than 1,300 Chinese nationals.[48] At the same time, the potential for sustaining the PLAN at sea in conflict is driving a focus on new types of basing that can sustain naval operations in the western Pacific. The indefensibility of South China Sea man-made island garrisons will drive the PLAN to find more secure nearby bases. Additionally, the CCP's need to secure a nuclear second-strike capability will require the PLAN and PLAAF to operate its strategic nuclear forces—submarine and bombers—further into the Pacific.

The changing strategic environment is trending toward confrontation, and the type of basing is likewise changing to support a forward-based military able to sustain combat operations far from home. This partially explains the diplomatically risky move to secure military access to the Solomon Islands. These developments have required changes to the CCP and PLA bureaucracy, as discussed already, but also PLAN organizational and warship design changes. Notably, PLAN warships intended for far-seas operations will need to operate at sea for months with limited replenishment, necessitating larger warships able to carry needed fuel and support systems. This trend is already seen in new designs of PLAN surface combatants like the *Renhai*-class destroyers, which increased operational range by three thousand miles and increased displacement 40 percent over its predecessor, the *Luyang* class.[49] A similar range and displacement trend is notable in the PLAN's newer fleet oilers, which are critical for refueling warships at sea and vital for sustaining distant operations. However, it is the development of modern nuclear submarines that will have a profound impact on PLAN operations in both the Pacific and Indian Oceans and their associated basing requirements.

Since 2015 the People's Liberation Army has been undergoing structural reforms to enable joint war-fighting.[50] Given developments in communications, deployment of submarine-launched long-range cruise missiles, and advanced combat control systems, the PLAN's submarines' role in joint strike operations should be anticipated. Publicly disclosed information does indicate a change to PLAN submarine missions, to include strike missions against U.S. installations in the western Pacific. However, little publicly available reporting indicates that new PLAN distant-sea deployments or new deterrent patrol areas are being planned. Regardless, recent years reporting of Chinese deep-water surveys in the Philippine Sea and placement of undersea sensors near Guam could be preparation for a sustained future PLAN submarine presence in these waters.[51]

Dramatic changes in the Chinese nuclear arsenal are pointing to a greater likelihood of PLAN's presence in the central Pacific. Since 2015 the PLA has undertaken a broad and still ongoing nuclear modernization effort.[52] In July 2021, it was revealed that China had built more than three hundred new intercontinental ballistic missile (ICBM) silos in the Gobi Desert, tripling the number of such silos. Pentagon assessments point to Beijing fielding seven hundred nuclear warheads by 2027 and at least one thousand by 2030—on track to become a nuclear peer of both the United States and Russia.[53] Strategic parity, to include viable second-strike nuclear capabilities from submarines and bombers, will increase the confidence of the CCP to press its interests overseas and increase the need to secure its long-range air and undersea nuclear forces. Securing these strategic platforms on deterrent patrol will strongly influence PLA basing posture in the Pacific and Indian Oceans.

Range limitations of current and projected PLAN nuclear submarine-launched ballistic missiles will necessitate closing the distance to the United States to have the desired deterrent effect. The PLAN's submarine-launched ballistic missiles, the JL-2 and JL-3, cannot hold the entirety of the United States within range from launch areas within the first island chain. To do so, PLAN ballistic missile submarines (SSBN) would have to venture well into the Philippine Sea or the north or central Pacific to hold all the continental United States at risk of nuclear attack. If Chinese leadership view targeting all the United States as a strategic priority, their SSBNs would have to conduct deterrent patrols far from mainland support. The operational challenge for PLAAF nuclear-capable H-6 bombers is much greater and would require formal basing far from mainland China. For this reason, it is more likely the PLA would seek logistic support bases instead for episodic deployments of strategic bombers and nuclear submarines to within range of U.S. targets. In this scenario, likely patrol areas include the Philippine Sea and central Pacific; there is no indication of the PLAN developing a SSBN capability to conduct under-ice deterrent patrols in the Arctic, like the Russians do. Of course, the PLAN could also develop a longer-range submarine-launched ballistic missile for the successor of the *Jin*-class SSBN. Or it could develop the capability to launch a fractional orbital bombardment system from a submarine, which the PLA successfully tested in 2021 traveling 25,000 miles.[54] But until the PLAN can deploy a submarine-launched ballistic missile with a range in excess of 10,700 miles, PLAN SSBN deterrent patrols within the first island chain will have limited strike capability against U.S. mainland targets, thus greatly constraining its deterrent effect.

PLAN WARSHIPS FOR SUSTAINED DISTANT OPERATIONS AND THEIR OPERATIONAL REQUIREMENTS

Not unlike the denials over its base in Djibouti, so too did the CCP and its military, the PLA, deny for years any intent of procuring aircraft carriers. Such denials weakened in the years between 1998 and 2000 with the purchase of the ex-Soviet carriers *Minsk*, *Varyag*, and *Kiev*.[55] According to Naval War College interviews with civilian and military experts in China, the consensus is that the decision to pursue an operational aircraft carrier fleet came with the announcement by then–general secretary Hu Jintao of "new historic missions" for the PLA, notably, for the PLAN to protect China's economic interests overseas. Since that time, as of August 2024, the PLAN has acquired three aircraft carriers—two indigenously built, one of a Chinese design. A fourth aircraft carrier (Type 004) is under construction.

This commitment to a fleet of aircraft carriers represents a significant investment in material and manpower. Moreover, a navy that has aircraft carriers is one focused on power projection, often while conducting distant operations far from home ports. PLAN aircraft carrier deployments and exercises in recent years indicate a clear intent and progression to such distant operations—to include "blue-water ops," when aircraft carriers conduct flight ops too far from land bases to divert in case of an in-flight emergency.[56] To protect the PLAN's massive investment in aircraft carriers, recent deployments have included air defense–capable warships, like the modern Type 055 cruiser or *Renhai*-class.[57] From its 112 vertical launch tubes and robust sensors, these multimission warships can defend against submarines, surface warships, and air and missile attacks.[58] Less reported: if the PLAN follows U.S. precedent, it should be expected that Chinese submarines would be nearby to detect any threats to the carrier. To support prolonged distant operations, a nuclear submarine's endurance and ability to sustain high speeds for long periods of time make it an ideal candidate for this mission. The PLAN had eight Type-093 *Shang*-class nuclear submarines in January 2024; follow-on variants are expected.[59] Unlike the PLAN's conventionally powered fleet that demands fuel to stay at sea, nuclear submarine at-sea endurance is a function of food for the crew.

The PLAN has also come to appreciate the versatility of large amphibious warships. These ships can put troops ashore using small armored amphibious assault vehicles or helicopters. Most notable in this category are the PLAN's Type 071 and larger Type 075 warships. The Type 075 looks like a small aircraft carrier, much like its contemporaries the Japanese *Hyuga* class or U.S. *America* class. Should the PLA develop short take-off and vertical landing fighter aircraft, or jump jets, like the West's venerable AV-8B Harrier or today's F-35B, the PLAN could potentially employ such aircraft from the Type 075 and later variants. The versatility of large amphibious warships makes them ideal for a host of peacetime missions such as noncombatant evacuations (e.g., Sudan in 2023), disaster response, and amphibious assault in wartime. For this reason, as is the case for the U.S. Marine Corps, such ships are likely to become a fixture of Chinese distant operations.

These ships represent the core of naval platforms performing PLAN distant operations well into the future. Today, keeping this fleet at sea and armed requires the PLAN to deploy logistic ships—oilers, munitions ships, and tenders for repairs. Notably, the PLAN has deployed a purpose-built logistic ship to sustain its aircraft carrier fleet in distant operations, the Type 901 *Fuyu*-class fast combat support ship.[60] These ships are designed to keep up with the aircraft carrier to replenish fuels and munitions, which will typically be required every three to five days during intensive air operations. Of course, older PLAN vessels will continue to deploy on distant operations, like the July 2023 port call in Nigeria that included a *Jiangkai II*–class frigate, *Luyang IV*–class destroyer, and a *Fuchi*-class oiler.[61] However, the considerable combat capacity and endurance of a few classes of modern PLAN warship make them well suited for distant operations. From this small group of warships, their physical size and operational needs inform the feasibility of certain overseas ports. These requirements and constraints inform the planning of warship overseas port visits (see table 1).

ELEMENTS OF A NAVAL PORT VISIT: DIPLOMATIC CLEARANCE, ARRIVAL, AND DEPARTURE

> *The amateurs discuss strategies, dilettantes discuss tactics: the professionals discuss logistics.*
> —**NAPOLEON BONAPARTE**

In late 2007, amid significant U.S. military operations in Iraq and Afghanistan and with tensions rising over Iran's nuclear and missile program, the need for militarily useful fuels was critical.[62] The U.S. military's demand for jet fuel and marine diesel was immense during those tensions. To sustain military operations while preparing for a military confrontation over Iran's nuclear program and its regional proxies, the U.S. military was required to increase its orders for fuel and double the

TABLE 1. CRITICAL CHINESE DISTANT SEAS NAVAL VESSELS

Warship	Length (m)	Beam (m)	Draft (m)	Ship's Fuel Use	Range (nm)	Endurance (days)	Crew	Helo / Aircraft
Type 002 aircraft carrier	305	75	9.5	Diesel	8,000	18.5		Y
Type 055 destroyer	186	19	7.5	Jet	8,000	18.5	250	Y
Type 093A nuclear submarine	110	10.5	9	Diesel*			105	N
Type 071 large amphibious warship	212	28	7	Diesel	6,000		120	Y
Type 903A oiler	172	24.2	9	Diesel	10,000	27.8		Y
Type 075/076 large amphibious warship†	226	36	8.1	Diesel	8,000	18.5		Y
Type 901 logistics ship†	240	32	10.8	Jet				Y
Type 003 aircraft carrier†	316	76						Y

*A nuclear power warship's endurance is a function of food and less a function of fuel; the diesel fuel used is for backup power generation in case the nuclear power plant needs to be shut down.

†Type 075/076, 901, and 003 warships are still in development and there is limited publicly available data.

SOURCES: Werner Globke and Weyers Flottentashenbuch, *Warships of the World 2020–2022* (Bad Neuenahr-Ahrweiler: Bernard & Graefe, 2020), 48–51, 54–55, 58–59, and 66–67; Conor M. Kennedy and Daniel Caldwell, "China Maritime Report No. 23: The Type 075 LHD: Development, Missions, and Capabilities," China Maritime Studies Institute, October 2022, 11–12 and 28, https://digital-commons.usnwc.edu/cgi/viewcontent.cgi?article=1022&context=cmsi-maritime-reports; "Type 901 Class Fleet Replenishment Ship," *Naval Technology*, November 29, 2017, https://www.naval-technology.com/projects/type-901-class-fleet-replenishment-ship/ (accessed July 17, 2023); and Andrew Tate, "China's Carrier Replenishment Ship Begins Sea Trials," *HIS Jane's Defence Weekly*, December 30, 2016, https://web.archive.org/web/20170125202609/http://www.janes.com/article/66613/china-s-carrier-replenishment-ship-begins-sea-trials.

number of tankers moving these militarily useful fuels to the Persian Gulf region.[63] Likewise, the PLAN will have to contend with the realities of sustaining a fleet on distant-deployed operations, and this requires access to resources via overseas ports.

Typically, a series of decisions are made before a warship visits a foreign port is even proposed to a host nation. Usually this starts with a political and diplomatic choice—is this port visit to sustain military operations or is the visit focused on diplomacy with the host nation or region? Most of the recent U.S. port visits have been for sustaining military operations, although the June 2023 port call to Vietnam by a U.S. aircraft carrier clearly serves a diplomatic end—to provide visible support of nations in maritime dispute with China.[64] The PLAN also uses port calls for political ends, as it did with the earlier mentioned visit to Nigeria and routine distant deployments of the PLAN's hospital ship *Peace Ark*, which visited Kiribati, the Solomon Islands, Tonga, Vanuatu, and East Timor in the summer of 2023.[65] When considering the strategic and political commitment to visit a specific country's port, it cannot be assumed that a naval ship can navigate to the desired port.

Getting a warship to a host nation's port requires sound navigational planning, including supplies such as parts, food, and fuel. Sound navigational planning specifically requires determining whether a warship can navigate safely to the port given the depth of water, weather, tide, and currents. These factors place physical limitations on the warships that can make the port visit as well as the support that will be needed, such as tugs. Tugboats are especially important for larger ships attempting to moor in challenging currents, which could easily push an unaided warship aground or into a pier, causing embarrassing damage. With the operational or diplomatic decision made and navigational planning begun, the focus shifts to the logistics and permissions required to execute the port visit.

The next step in this process involves diplomatic clearance for a warship to visit a host nation's port. This process can become highly politicized, with significant enduring policy ramifications. For this reason, the embassy in the host nation will be very involved with the naval attaché who plays a leading role in the effort. A diplomatic showdown over nuclear declarative policy and an ill-timed naval port call with long-standing ally New Zealand in 1986 led to a thirty-year absence of U.S. Navy port visits, despite the need for common cause to secure the south Pacific.[66] The PLAN had its own brush with this dynamic from July to August 2022, when its surveillance ship *Yuan Wang 5* was first denied and then eventually allowed to dock in the Chinese-run port of Hambantota.[67] Navigating local political sensitivities is sometimes made more intense if the proposed port visit is located in a sensitive region—say, in the South China Sea, where overlapping maritime disputes can rapidly turn a goodwill visit into a major unanticipated diplomatic statement.

While informal dialogue will occur well before, diplomatic clearances are formally sought much closer to the actual arrival of the warship. One reason for this timing is to control publicity and ensure some degree of operational security by limiting time for any hostile party to plan acts against the warship. Sometimes this is not enough to ensure the safety of a naval vessel's visit. This was the case when U.S. destroyer *Cole* was attacked in October 2000 while taking on fuel at the port of Aden, Yemen.[68] This formal process is handled through a diplomatic note to appropriate defense or foreign affairs agencies in the host nation, usually thirty days prior to the arrival of the warship. Sometimes, however, unforeseen circumstances warrant an emergent port call by a warship due to medical emergencies, material breakdowns, or to avoid dangerous weather. This last case is a long-standing navigational custom and memorialized in article 225 of the United Nations Convention on the Law of the Sea.[69] Nonetheless, nations have violated this precedent, as was the case in 2007 when, during a typhoon, small naval minesweeper vessels *Patriot* and *Guardian* were denied access to shelter in Hong Kong harbor.[70] This potentiality makes it prudent that PLAN naval planners consider multiple ports in a region to support distant operations. Moreover, should the need arise for an emergent port call, there will be added pressure to develop reliable partners with close diplomatic and security relations with Beijing.

Once a port and the timing for a specific warship's visit is agreed, specific logistic needs for the port visit become the focus. For the U.S. Navy, these specific requirements are requested via what is called a Logistic Request message, also known as a LOGREQ. These messages are transmitted to regional naval logistic commands (e.g., Pacific Fleet) and the embassy in the host country by the warship between forty-five to thirty days in advance of a planned port visit. These messages go into minute detail regarding access to port security, fuel, food, sewage handling, and so on.[71] Typically these services are contracted to husbanding agents that ensure the needed materials and support services, like electrical power (i.e., shore power), are ready when the ship arrives at the pier. This contracting process also has risk, as the U.S. Navy learned in the years-long corruption scandal involving port services contractor Glenn Marine Group. That scandal involved the embezzlement of millions of dollars and the arrests of several senior U.S. naval officers for corruption.[72] The PLAN, too, would have to rely on contracted services and the operational security risks associated, placing a premium on familiarity with trusted agents in the ports their warships visit.

Aside from the diplomatic or strategic objectives of a naval port visit, there is a very real material rationale for making these port calls—resupply, repair, even crew rest. Along these lines, the PLAN has limited the amount of time its sailors spend in port, but with more frequent and longer, distant operations, crew rest will be increasingly important. Nominally the U.S. Navy conducts at least one rest and recuperation port call lasting only a few days planned midway in a six-month overseas deployment. Such dedicated port calls would only include limited and emergent repairs and maintenance. Regarding resupply, the above mentioned LOGREQ or its PLAN corollary would request food, water, and fuel—notably, marine diesel or jet fuel used for naval aviation as well as modern warship gas turbine engines. The endurance of modern warships and the need for higher quality fuels does influence port call decisions. This is mitigated by the PLAN routinely deploying an oiler with warships on distant operations, which can extend the nominal eighteen-day endurance of the conventional warships. There is no such hindrance for nuclear submarines.

Commercial ships move cargo; warships move munitions. When warships expend those munitions, they need to replace them to continue executing their mission and defending themselves. Munitions can be replenished in port or transferred from another ship at sea. Replenishment of munitions at sea would rely on ships like the *Fuyu*-class logistic ship already mentioned, but some modern munitions—notably, those launched from vertical launch cells common on U.S. and Chinese warships—would have to be reloaded in port with special cranes for U.S. warships. For this reason, and the fact that ships like the *Fuyu* would also need to be reloaded with munitions, ports where the PLAN can store critical munitions will be a growing requirement. As of December 2024, there is only one PLA overseas base in Djibouti, which ostensibly has bunkers suitable for storing and pier services able to reload munitions on PLAN warships.[73] The need to replenish munitions would be an acute operational requirement in wartime or limited combat missions such as counterterror-related operations. As such, where the PLAN pursues overseas port access with the capacity to store or handle munitions would indicate where it considers having to sustain combat operations.

Another factor weighing on the selection of a port visit is the ability to effect repairs, including planned maintenance. The U.S. Navy conducts planned mid-deployment maintenance to ensure peak performance of a warship throughout its deployment.[74] Likewise, the PLAN has taken a similar approach since 2006, which it calls "active maintenance"—best understood as preventive maintenance.[75] The PLAN's active maintenance relies on the availability of replacement parts and the ability to move highly skilled maintenance experts to the port where the repairs are planned—so-called Tiger Teams. The U.S. Navy frequently employs Tiger Teams, with parts and technical experts flown to the port where a deployed warship is docked; this adds another factor in port selection—proximity to commercial or accessible host nation military airfields. Typically, these planned repairs would not involve substantial work. For major damage, the warship would need to be placed in a drydock, especially for unplanned emergent repairs, for example, from a collision or groundings that jeopardize the watertight integrity of the ship. In wartime, ready access to drydocks for such repairs becomes critical when battle damage is expected and repairs are urgently needed to save the ship and return it to combat. In the lead-up to the Pacific War, the U.S. Navy had limited drydocks and operated under the expectation that the Imperial Japanese Navy would cut off the U.S. fleet from forward bases. Thus, the U.S. Navy devised a novel war-winning solution—floating drydocks.[76] Today the PLAN has some deployable drydock capability with the heavy-lift ship *Yinmahu*, the second of two such vessels in the PLAN entered service in 2015.[77] The PLAN could also rely on state-owned vessels like COSCO's

MV *Xin Guang Hua* heavy-lift ship with a lift area 208 m long and 68 m wide, big enough for PLAN *Renhai* cruisers and *Shang* nuclear submarines but not aircraft carriers or large amphibious warships.[78] While the PLAN may have access to deployable drydocking capability, this does not completely obviate the need for access to overseas drydocks for urgent repairs that cannot wait for the slow-moving heavy-lift ships to arrive.

Once the warship's in-port diplomatic, strategic, and operational missions are completed, it will depart. But there will be lingering issues to resolve to ensure that the invitation remains open for future port visits. Sailors, being sailors, sometimes run afoul of local law enforcement, which necessitates agreements like Status of Forces Agreements. These agreements are entered to ensure mutual understanding on how such issues are adjudicated. The warship's priority is to get the servicemember back to the ship so they can fulfill their critical military role on board. Without such understandings, the warship could have its mission impacted with the absence of some of its crew and could exacerbate a diplomatic kerfuffle. One such situation occurred in the Philippines in 2014 when a U.S. servicemember murdered a local citizen. The U.S. retained custody of the servicemember while Philippine law enforcement led the investigation.[79] Another aspect to conclude promptly after a warship's departure is settling all outstanding bills. Without local contracting support officials, embassy staff would be responsible for settling these accounts. The U.S. Navy typically assigns contracting officials regionally to support port visits and settle such accounts. The PLAN, too, would rely on such contracting officials, likely working out of the Chinese embassy, or Chinese civilian contractors given CCP access to the global commercial port services of state-owned enterprises.[80] Given institutional changes detailed earlier, the PLAN has since 2017 markedly increased its technical (i.e., repair, refuel, replenish) use of civilian Chinese-owned or -operated overseas ports, with PLAN warships visiting all but four nations (Jamaica, the Bahamas, Taiwan, and Iraq) in which the CCP controls port assets.[81] This suggests a strong likelihood that PLAN warships will rely on Chinese state-owned overseas port operators in the future to conduct technical port visits.

WOLF WARRIOR DIPLOMACY ACCELERATING OVERSEAS PORTS ACCESS AND BASING

A first case of an invigorated and riskier approach by the CCP began to come into public awareness in 2019 over activities at the Cambodian naval base at Ream. A suspected secret pact signed in the spring of 2019 between China and Cambodia granted China military access and basing in return for infrastructure improvements—new piers.[82] Suspicions grew after the government of Cambodia refused U.S. access to small-boat facilities it had built and refurbished for the Cambodian navy.[83] Despite repeated public denials by PRC and Cambodian officials, subsequent extensive Chinese dredging, construction, and development of air defenses had made it impossible to sustain the fiction that the activity was for anything other than military use with Chinese assistance.[84] A June 2022 groundbreaking ceremony, attended by the Chinese ambassador, began naval port expansion to allow vessels up to five thousand tons to stay at two new piers—large enough to host a *Constellation*-class U.S. frigate.[85] Foreign Minister Wang Yi made frequent visits to Cambodia or met in China with national leaders from Cambodia in April 2019, October 2020, and August 2022, during heightened tensions during Speaker Nancy Pelosi's trip to Taiwan.[86] While a permanent PLA presence like Djibouti may not occur, the staging of munitions and ample port facilities at Ream can provide the PLAN a useful forward staging base.

A world away in West Africa, another Chinese effort was progressing. In October 2021 news broke after a U.S. National Security Council staffer traveled to Equatorial Guinea to forestall an offer to China for a naval base. The region is an important source of China's fuel imports; however, in recent years Equatorial Guinea's production and exports have dwindled, making up only 2.52 percent of China's imports in 2022.[87] While a base in the Gulf of Guinea would have strategic value to the PLAN proximate to sensitive U.S. missile testing ranges at Ascension Island, the diminished economic importance for China of Equatorial Guinea and U.S. attention likely cooled the effort.[88] Wang Yi has not traveled to Equatorial Guinea, having only met the foreign minister in December

2021 during a China-Africa Cooperation conference in Senegal and then on the sidelines of the UN General Assembly in New York in September 2022.[89] To date, the attempt at a base in Equatorial Guinea seems to have

MAP 2. CHINA HAS BUILT OR FUNDED PORTS ACROSS WESTERN AFRICA   *Heritage Foundation*

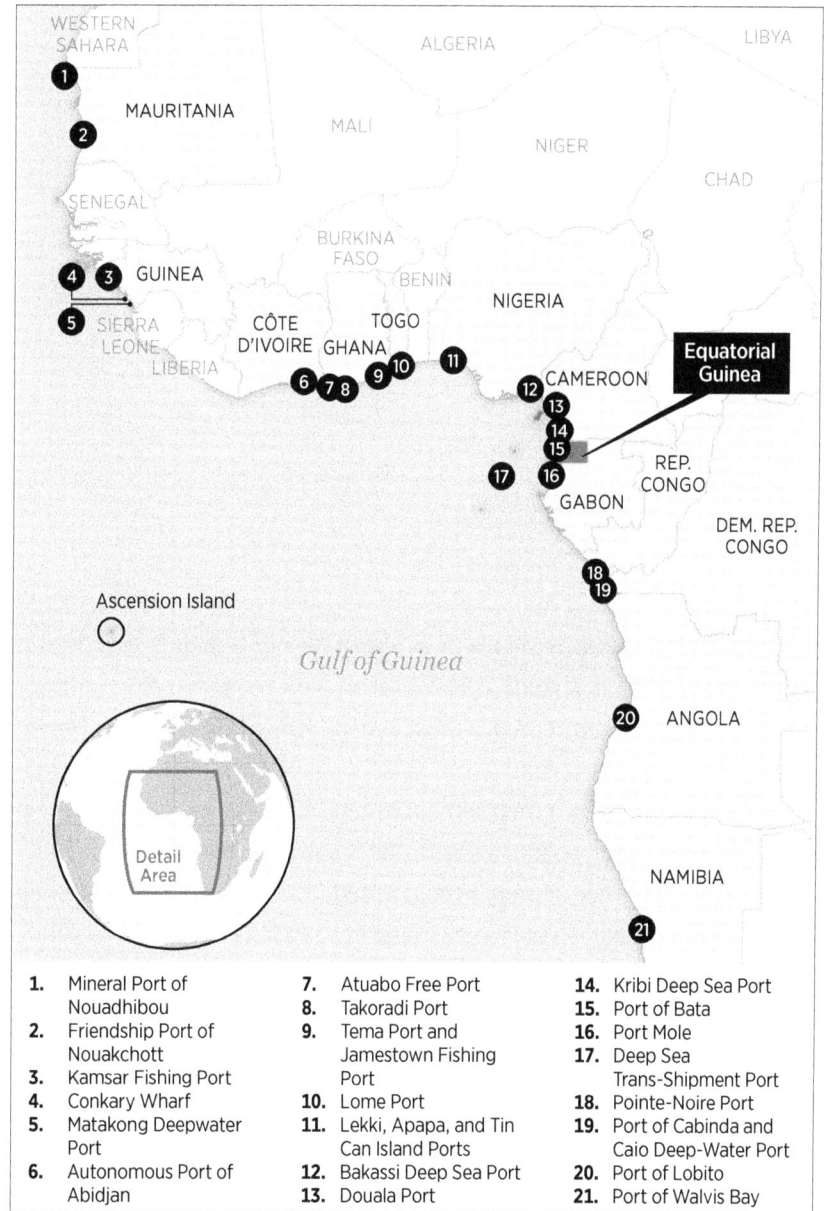

1. Mineral Port of Nouadhibou
2. Friendship Port of Nouakchott
3. Kamsar Fishing Port
4. Conkary Wharf
5. Matakong Deepwater Port
6. Autonomous Port of Abidjan
7. Atuabo Free Port
8. Takoradi Port
9. Tema Port and Jamestown Fishing Port
10. Lome Port
11. Lekki, Apapa, and Tin Can Island Ports
12. Bakassi Deep Sea Port
13. Douala Port
14. Kribi Deep Sea Port
15. Port of Bata
16. Port Mole
17. Deep Sea Trans-Shipment Port
18. Pointe-Noire Port
19. Port of Cabinda and Caio Deep-Water Port
20. Port of Lobito
21. Port of Walvis Bay

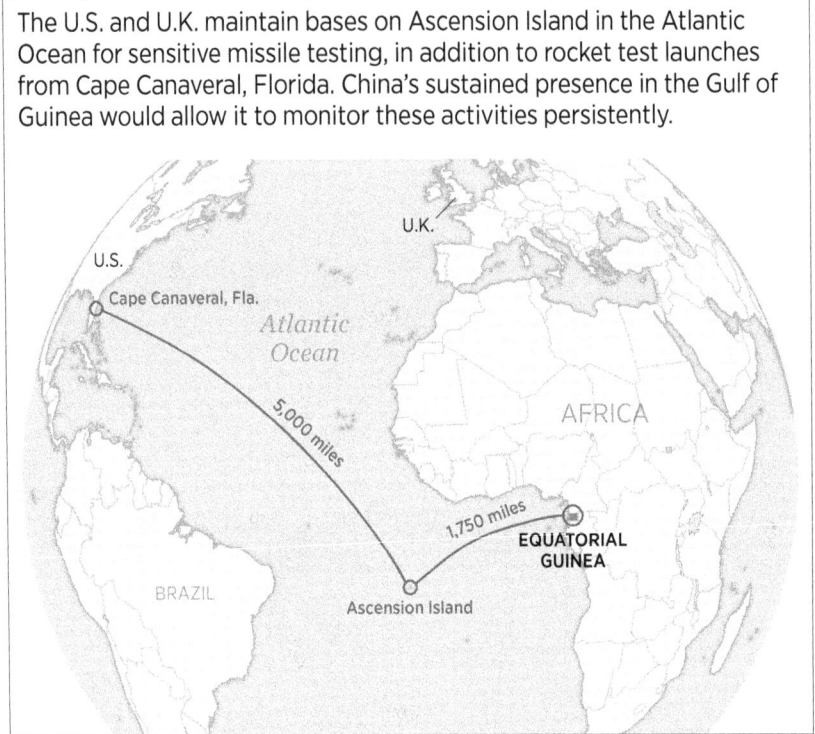

MAP 3. THE IMPORTANCE OF ASCENSION ISLAND *Heritage Foundation*

The U.S. and U.K. maintain bases on Ascension Island in the Atlantic Ocean for sensitive missile testing, in addition to rocket test launches from Cape Canaveral, Florida. China's sustained presence in the Gulf of Guinea would allow it to monitor these activities persistently.

stalled, but attempts may yet occur at one of twenty nearby West African ports where China is already invested. And with more pressing military needs in the Pacific and Asia, West Africa will likely remain a lower priority.

However, the most remarkable Chinese overseas basing effort was the secret agreement uncovered with the Solomon Islands in April 2022. Much of this story has already been covered, but it is worth emphasizing the military value of these islands along key sea lanes and near key U.S. bases in Kwajalein and Guam. Given the risks taken, China is prioritizing the Pacific islands. The most visible expression of that was Wang Yi's ten-day tour of Pacific island nations in May 2022, beginning with the Solomon Islands.[90] During this regional trip, Pacific island countries were presented a "Common Development Vision" and "Five-Year Action Plan on Common Development" that included proposals for cooperation in traditional and nontraditional security as well as network governance and cybersecurity.[91] This new regional engagement came after years of easy development money. Before the Solomon Islands entered the 2022 secret security pact, it received in 2019 about $730 million from China after switching diplomatic recognition from Taiwan to China.[92] Mutual interests, Prime Minister Sogavare's political survival, and the PLA's need for central Pacific military logistics support have sustained the pact. Since signing this pact, Chinese police delegations have conducted visits with provisions, like the nine-member team that visited in February 2023 and delivered Chinese riot control gear—twenty vehicles, two water cannon vehicles, and thirty motorcycles.[93] Amid a growing Chinese security presence, speculation persists as to whether the PLAN will gain a base in the islands.

WEIGHING PLAN OPERATIONAL CONSIDERATIONS FOR FUTURE NAVAL BASES

To recap, there are several key features of a port that make it viable for supporting naval operations. These factors include access to fuel, ease of navigation, port services (tugs, repairs, drydock, etc.), nearby airports, and proximity to sustained at-sea naval operations. In wartime, the need to store and load munitions and conduct battle damage repairs in capable drydocks becomes a significant concern for selection of forward naval bases. That said, the historical record of PLAN port visits and investments in commercial ports provides some important insight.

Since Hu Jintao announced "historic new missions," the PLAN has eagerly embraced them and has expanded its operations from regional to global. From 2002 to 2022 a pattern of PLAN port visits has emerged that indicates an operational focus as well as a geopolitical and economic strategy. The work of the National Defense University (NDU) and AidData stand out for helping discern the strategic direction of Chinese ports acquisition.[94]

The NDU, based in Washington, D.C., has tracked where PLAN warships have made port visits from 2002 to 2022. The pattern belies an operational focus in the Indian Ocean region, from where China relies on energy imports and since 2008 routinely participated in counterpiracy operations off the Horn of Africa.[95] Naval War College analysis of NDU's data has found a sharp uptick in PLAN port visits and bilateral naval exercises since 2008, with senior naval officer and diplomatic engagements rising through 2015 then tapering off to near zero, where it remained in 2023.[96] This would indicate an operational emphasis for PLAN port visits over military diplomacy. The only country that has since hosted a PLAN base is Djibouti, which also has limited repair capacity. The arrival in July 2023 of a large floating drydock in Djibouti does provide some local repair potential for PLAN warships like the Type 053 destroyer and Type 093 nuclear submarine but could accommodate ships no larger than the Type 071 amphibious warship.[97] This means the PLAN must continue looking for host nations where emergent or wartime repairs could be conducted while not obviating the potential of developing substantial repair capacities in Djibouti.

The AidData team took a comprehensive approach, drawing on their decade of financial forensics expertise to assess PLAN port visits. Their research in 2023 focused on predicting near-term potentials for future overseas naval bases. In a July 2023 report *Harboring Global Ambitions*, AidData weighed five factors potentially influencing a Chinese decision concerning where to place a future naval base: strategic value, strong bilateral relations, stability, United Nations voting alignment, and port characteristics.[98] As an aside, while China's investment in ports has persisted since the late 1990s, a notable increase of overseas maritime infrastructure investments was noted beginning in 2013 via China's Belt and Road Initiative.[99] Like NDU's analysis, AidData's analysis of Chinese financial activity from 2000 to 2021 confirms a focus of about one-third of total investment in Indian Ocean ports. Surprisingly, Atlantic Ocean ports in Latin America and Africa were a top focus (53.3 percent) for investment, which is likely representative of increased infrastructure improvements needed at more rudimentary sites. And Chinese investment in autonomous zones (i.e., Autonomous Port of Abidjan and Autonomous Port of Nouakchott) stood out where limited host central government oversight and control of port activities could afford Chinese entities more leeway to support military activities.

NDU and AidData did not assess all interesting ports, nor did they speculate on Chinese strategic intents. A few ports not covered by them are worth raising and are included in table 2: First, several Egyptian ports were added premised on the August 5, 2019, deal with Hutchison Ports and the subsequent PLAN technical stop in the Alexandria naval base.[100] Second, South Africa was added given its strategic position at the Cape of Good Hope and significantly developed ports as well as its recent multilateral naval exercises conducted with Russia over ten days in February 2023.[101] Third, the Russian port of Vilyuchinsk, which is collocated with a strategic missile submarine base, was added as a potential provisioning base for PLAN submarines on deterrent patrols able to range all of the United States. Last, the Solomon Islands was added to the table for review given news of a secret pact that would ostensibly allow the Chinese an enduring military presence there.

Analysis of the ports included in table 2 indicate several patterns and insights worth highlighting here. First, many ports are navigationally constrained or have limited pier infrastructure to host the most likely PLAN naval platforms conducting distant naval operations. That said, in some cases anchorages are available (e.g., Solomon Islands) that would allow for limited provisioning but are unlikely to allow for meaningful repair or significant movement of cargo or munitions. This raises another key factor: the resupply of munitions during conflict, which today only the PLA base in Djibouti could execute. However, should Chinese dredging and pier expansion proceed at Cambodia's naval base at Ream, it too could support munitions resupply of the PLAN's largest warships. Moreover, ports near or on a host nation's naval base also provide the PLAN with a means to store and load munitions and conduct sensitive logistic operations. That said, munitions support is possible at six ports studied: Vilyuchinsk, Doraleh, Galle Harbor, Jeddah, Al Jubayl, Ream, and potentially Honiara, should the Solomon Islands activate its security pact with China. Third, without significant dredging and port expansion, there are only eleven ports studied that could host the PLAN's aircraft carriers, to include its next-generation Type 003.

TABLE 2. PORTS WITH POTENTIAL CHINESE MILITARY UTILITY

Nation	Port Name	Type 002 Aircraft Carrier	Type 003 Aircraft Carrier	Type 055 Destroyer	Type 093A Nuclear Submarine	Type 071 Amphibious Warship	Type 075 or 076 Amphibious Warship	Type 903A oiler
Djibouti	Doraleh			X	X	X	X	X
Oman	Duqm			X	X	X	X	X
	Mina Raysut			X	X	X	X	X
	Mina Qabus	X	X	X	X	X	X	X
	Port of Sohar			X	X	X	X	X
Sri Lanka	Trincomalee			X	X	X	X	X
	Hambantota			X	X	X	X	X
	Galle Harbor*			X	X			X
	Colombo			X	X	X	X	X
Yemen	Al Mukalla							
	Aden	X	X	X	X	X	X	X
	Al Mukha			X		X		
	Al Ahmadi			X	X			X
	Salif			X	X	X	X	X
Singapore	Jurong Island	X	X	X	X	X	X	X
Pakistan	Karachi			X	X	X	X	X
	Gwadar	X	X	X	X	X	X	X
Bangladesh	Mongla			X		X		
	Chittagong			X		X		
Saudi Arabia	Jeddah*			X	X	X	X	X
	Dammam	X	X	X	X	X	X	X
	Al Jubayl*	X	X	X	X	X	X	X
Cameroon	Kribi			X	X	X	X	X
Vanuatu	Luganville		X	X	X	X	X	X
Cambodia	Ream*							
	Kampong Saom	X	X	X	X	X	X	X
Equatorial Guinea	Bata	X	X	X	X	X	X	X
	Malabo							
Mozambique	Nacala							
Mauritania	Nouakchott	X		X	X	X	X	X
	Nouadhibou							
Egypt	Alexandria	X	X	X	X	X	X	X
	N. Ain Sukhna			X	X	X	X	X
Solomon Islands	Honiara							
	Yandina							
	Port Noro							
South Africa	Durban			X	X	X	X	X
	Cape Town	X	X	X	X	X	X	X
	Richards Bay			X	X	X	X	X
	Simon's Town							
	Port Elizabeth			X	X	X	X	X
Russia	Vilyuchinsk							

*Port is near military facilities (airfield or port) that could support movement of munitions.

SOURCES: World Port Index, ver. 1.34.3.1, https://fgmod.nga.mil/apps/WPI-Viewer/; Google Earth, ver. 9.175.0.3; and Google Maps, https://www.google.com/maps/@37.5932461,-68.5613304,7.04z?entry=ttu; Navionics, ver. 19.1.

TABLE 2. PORTS WITH POTENTIAL CHINESE MILITARY UTILITY *(continued)*

Port Name	Type 901 Large Logistics Ship	Fuel (marine DSL)	Tugboat Available	Repair Services	Drydock	Explosive Handling	Medical Services	Airport within 50 Miles
Doraleh	x	x		Limited	x	x	x	x
Duqm	x		x	Major	x			x
Mina Raysut	x	x	x	Limited			x	x
Mina Qabus	x	x	x	Limited			x	x
Port of Sohar	x		x					x
Trincomalee	x	x	x				x	x
Hambantota	x							x
Galle Harbor*			x	Limited		x	x	x
Colombo	x	x	x	Moderate	x		x	x
Al Mukalla		x	x	Limited	x		x	x
Aden	x	x	x	Major	x		x	x
Al Mukha			x				x	x
Al Ahmadi		x		Moderate				x
Salif			x					
Jurong Island	x	x	x	Major	x		x	x
Karachi	x	x	x	Limited	x		x	x
Gwadar	x		x				x	x
Mongla		x	x	Limited			x	x
Chittagong		x	x	Limited	x		x	x
Jeddah*	x	x	x	Major	x	x	x	x
Dammam	x	x	x	Moderate	x		x	x
Al Jubayl*	x	x	x	Limited	x	x	x	x
Kribi	x	x	x					
Luganville		x	x	Limited			x	x
Ream*				Emergent		x		x
Kampong Saom	x	x	x	Limited			x	x
Bata	x			Emergent			x	x
Malabo		x	x	Limited				x
Nacala		x	x	Limited			x	x
Nouakchott	x		x				x	x
Nouadhibou		x	x	Limited			x	x
Alexandria	x	x	x	Major	x		x	x
N. Ain Sukhna	x	x	x				x	
Honiara		x	x	Limited			x	x
Yandina		x		Limited				
Port Noro							x	
Durban	x	x	x	Moderate	x		x	x
Cape Town	x	x	x	Major	x		x	x
Richards Bay	x	x	x	Limited			x	x
Simon's Town				Emergent	x			
Port Elizabeth	x	x	x	Moderate			x	x
Vilyuchinsk		x		Major	x	x	x	x

THE PAST AND FUTURE OF CHINESE BASING EFFORTS AND WHAT TO DO ABOUT IT

As 2027 draws nearer, the military operational imperatives of a showdown over Taiwan will drive the search for proximate naval basing in Southeast Asia and in the central and south Pacific. Bases in these regions more directly support wartime military operations in and around Taiwan; basing in the Pacific would support operations to threaten American logistics lines. Through this lens there is a clear rationale for the recent risks the CCP has taken in the Solomon Islands and Cambodia—both places where basing seems inevitable. The issue then becomes how to stymie or reverse the CCP and PLA's advances.

The CCP's approach and the PLA's organizational structure provide several avenues to stymie their efforts and seize the initiative in this positional competition. First, CCP efforts often rely on securing secret negotiated debt deals through elite-capture efforts without public scrutiny, for example, the Solomon Islands and Cambodia. Second, national leader engagement has been key to securing deals for basing, which also limits the number of such efforts that can be pursued at once, the port of Piraeus in Greece, the Solomon Islands, and the failure in Equatorial Guinea. Third, the PLAN will avoid local contractors and husbanding agents, preferring Chinese state–controlled enterprises overseas, thus limiting the economic benefit of their presence to the host nation populace. Fourth, the most important ports are those with strategic value both in military utility and access to strategically important markets and resources that garner significant CCP resources and attention. And fifth, as for all navies, the PLAN also must seek diplomatic clearance for port visits, which exposes their efforts to local political pressures; recall the Sri Lanka port visits the PLAN attempted amid domestic upheaval. Altogether, taking the initiative in this competition for tactical position and the urgency for the CCP to act this decade on Taiwan means that greater U.S. action in Southeast Asia and the south and central Pacific should be prioritized.

The objective of seizing the initiative in the positional competition underway with the CCP is to deter a violent confrontation over Taiwan.

This is done by blunting attempts at basing and access for the PLA that threaten U.S. military presence as well as holds at risk CCP war plans and assumptions for being able to sustain a major war. This will require an in-country presence in the form of embassies and consulates. But it must also include a persistent waterfront presence that enables U.S. naval and maritime economic activity while also monitoring Chinese activities. At the same time, the United States must provide a compelling economic-security proposition that partner nations would be willing to take over Chinese largess through the BRI's debt diplomacy and elite capture (i.e., bribery). Doing this will not break the bank and can be done rapidly, leveraging the U.S. Pacific legacy starting with the Compact of Free Association (CoFA) nations.

Following are five actions that can turn the tide in the positional competition of the Pacific and Southeast Asia and shift the initiative to the United States.

NEW EMBASSIES AND CONSULATES

Establishing new embassies in strategically important locations can enable better countermeasures to Chinese influence. Embassies are needed in the Solomon Islands, Vanuatu, Nauru, and the Federated States of Micronesia. Additionally, given the vast distances of the Pacific between embassies at capitols and key locations, consulates should be established at important maritime locations: Buka, Bougainville; Weno, Chuuk; Colonia, Yap; and Papeete, French Polynesia. Such a presence would ostensibly be able to blunt attempts such as the 2016 case of Chinese investors Cary Yan and Gina Zhou. The two were caught using bribery and money laundering in an attempt to create a new mini state at Rongelap, Marshall Islands, which locals felt was at the behest of Beijing.[102] Embassies and consulates enable business and people exchanges, focus national resources better in a host nation, and enable scrutiny of local Chinese efforts.

FLEET LIAISON OFFICERS

When a naval vessel visits a port, it requires tremendous diplomatic and contracting support, as detailed already. Having a persistent presence at key ports can ensure seamless and frequent visits by U.S. Navy and Coast Guard vessels at ports distant from U.S. embassies and consulates. The idea for these officers being posted at key ports was originally made in *U.S. Naval Power in the 21st Century*. Recapping that earlier proposal, such officials would be tasked with vetting local contracting and service support for visiting warships and military units. These officials would also assist the U.S. embassy in pushing back on Chinese narratives and efforts to confound such visits. An ideal first place to post such an officer is Malaysia's Kota Kinabalu on Borneo, with its large naval base and several strategically located ports. Other locations where a fleet liaison officer would make sense to enable more naval presence include Danang, Vietnam, where U.S. aircraft carriers have made several port calls; Phuket, Thailand, which is a frequent port stop of naval vessels; and Manus Island, Papua New Guinea, where the U.S. military has been improving port facilities for future use.

NEW COMPACT AGREEMENT FRAMEWORK

With the end of the UN trust territories managed by the United States with the Republic of Palau, Federated States of Micronesia, and Marshall Islands, a new arrangement was agreed with the island nations—the CoFA. These agreements have provided key services and eased immigration to the United States for the islanders while affording the United States unique security provisions important in this new cold war. A new framework for other island nations could replicate the successes of CoFA with island nations like Kiribati, Nauru, and Tuvalu. More on this in the next chapter.

DEVELOPMENT INFRASTRUCTURE AID AND MILITARY CONSTRUCTION

Military units like the Navy Seabees and Army Corps of Engineers excel at construction at austere and remote sites in support of military operations as well as for more prosaic efforts like building schools and local hospitals. The Development Finance Corporation, for example, was created by the BUILD Act in 2018 and is in effect a U.S. government development bank. It has not yet made any strategic impact, and this must change. The next chapter will detail how better focusing these efforts to maritime economic development with military utility can make U.S. military presence more beneficial and effective in the competition with China without BRI levels of spending.

AMERICAN SAMOA AS STRATEGIC HUB

Pago Pago served as a vital staging base early in World War II but was shuttered in 1951. At more than 2,600 miles from naval bases in Pearl Harbor and further from Guam, American Samoa provides a strategic hub to contest nearby Chinese encroachment and effective alliance work in the region with France, Australia, and New Zealand. How this will be done is the subject of the next chapter.

CONCLUSION

Given the deterioration in relations, prudent Chinese military preparation has focused on securing basing in the Solomon Islands, Cambodia, and potentially Vanuatu. With the first-ever PLAN officer, Admiral Dong Jun, as minister of defense since December 2023 on the CMC, it should not come as a surprise that naval distant operational logistics are increasingly informing Chinese strategic activities. The July 2023 return of Wang Yi as minister of foreign affairs after the purge of his predecessor, Qin Gang, is telling. He played a role in securing the base in Djibouti as well as the secret pact with the Solomon Islands and could likely repeat his past record.

For the United States, a new approach is required that can provide a compelling option to the economic security offered from the CCP. This will require the U.S. Navy sailors and Department of State diplomats work together to expand U.S. influence—an effort that will be enabled by port visits, focused economic development aid, military construction, naval exercises with partner nations, and the opening of new embassies and consulates. A great game is playing out in the south and central Pacific, and so far the United States has been late to arrive on the field.

CHAPTER 2
NAVAL STATECRAFT OPERATIONALIZED

Chapter 1 lays out China's comprehensive approach to a positional competition with the United States and China's next moves. That effort has centered in recent years on gaining military access, notably in Ream, Cambodia, and the Solomon Islands. It also aims to elbow out U.S. and wider Western economic and political influences. Arguably, China has used this approach since the "new historic missions" announced by General Secretary Hu Jintao in 2004. These missions have undergirded a gradual positioning of China's military to be ready to secure strategically important trade such as in energy, control maritime chokepoints, or complicate U.S. operations vital in a prolonged war.

In fact, China has been waging a competition for geostrategic position for decades primarily via economic inducements, but since 2019 it has shifted increasingly to security guarantees and coercion. As such, the risks are rapidly escalating. A response is long overdue, and the macro trends playing out to 2050 are raised in the earlier book *U.S. Naval Power in the 21st Century* to inform nearer-term positional initiatives—access to new bases, choice in strategic partnerships. That book also categorizes eight strategic maritime regions to prioritize to hold, build, or advance U.S. presence and interests.

To deter China this decade will require taking the initiative in the two build regions (south and central Pacific, Caribbean to Gulf of Guinea) and a decisively important advance region (South China Sea). For this book, the tropical maritime region stretching across the Caribbean to the Gulf of Guinea will be referred to as the Cancer to Capricorn Corridor. Finally, the previous chapter deals with the near-term positional efforts by China; this chapter lays out the response by operationalizing naval statecraft.

NAVAL STATECRAFT: A FRAMEWORK FOR WINNING THE NEW COLD WAR

American statecraft did not keep Russia's Vladimir Putin from invading Ukraine (twice, 2014 and 2022). Nor did it stop China's Xi Jinping from building an archipelago of man-made islands in disputed regions of the South China Sea, and it has not deterred him from firing missiles in the summer of 2022 over Taiwan. Reflexively our leaders fall back on reactive foreign policy based on repackaged "whole of government" pablum. A prime example is the U.S. government's vague notion of "integrated deterrence," described as planning, coordination, and operation of government agencies together, along with allies. Integrated deterrence talks up coordination among agencies but relies disproportionately on diplomatic maneuvers, which alone has ceased delivering for America. Naval statecraft offers a way forward.

A maritime presence can yield tremendous economic benefits while defending Americans and national interests. Case in point: Djibouti's economic rise in the early 2000s was sparked when U.S. naval forces arrived to carry the fight to al-Qaeda after the September 11th terrorist attacks. The increased maritime security presence enabled the deepwater port of Doraleh to become a regional commercial hub. Sadly, U.S. leaders failed to pair the naval presence with economic and diplomatic efforts. Years later Beijing filled that vacuum, and Djibouti has fallen deeper into China's orbit. Another example of naval statecraft came in 2020. Operating in international waters, a Malaysian-chartered oil survey ship, the *West Capella*, was subjected to Chinese harassment for months. The United States kept a measured but sustained naval presence near the ship while diplomats rallied international support in defense of Malaysia's economic rights. Eventually China ceased harassing the ship, and the region reacted with united antipathy toward China's behavior. Unfortunately, that success was more luck than planning. Naval statecraft embraces the reality that most nations must balance economic and security interests. But this causes problems for a U.S. government that typically approaches economics and security as distinct lines of effort championed by separate agencies. This has caused incoherence and inefficiencies that the nation's treasury cannot sustain; part 3 of this book takes up the challenge of overcoming this through reorganizing government.

With these historic examples in mind, there is an opportunity in three maritime regions to take the initiative from China in the positional competition. Driven by common cause to contain the scourge of narcotics trafficking, secure maritime resources, and grow trade, the Cancer to Capricorn Corridor is ready for a new approach. On the other side of the world, after years of failed delivery of shared economic development and codes of conduct to mitigate maritime harassment, Southeast Asia nations are increasingly resisting China over their economic rights and security in the South China Sea. Finally, a new great game is unfolding in what had been until recently an American lake—the south and central Pacific, where Pacific island nations are coalescing for common cause to secure economic rights from voracious Chinese distant fishing fleets, prevent seabed mineral poaching, and protect themselves from China's corrupting influence as it seeks military footholds in the region. Failing to act will cede to China the so-called Global South, with its growing populations, rich resources, and increasingly important strategic location.[1]

That said, the tools of conventional statecraft include diplomacy, information, military, and economic means—the so-called DIME. In naval statecraft, the military is focused on maritime presence, economic inducements proffered to increase maritime trade, and information and diplomatic initiatives that expose Chinese malfeasance, which in turn enables greater economic and naval presence. In this naval statecraft framework, the United States and its closest allies (e.g., Japan) have a distinct advantage over China and its strategic partners (e.g., Russia). The tools of naval statecraft include developmental economic programs like the United States' Development Finance Corporation (DFC) and the U.S. Agency for International Development. U.S. maritime presence is led by the Navy and includes littoral deployments of Marine Corps units like the new Marine Littoral Regiment, the Army's Multi Domain Task Force, and episodic shows of force by the Air Force. However, military construction units like the Navy's Seabees offer a unique blend of both maritime presence and an economic tool when employed in key maritime nations to enhance maritime infrastructure for military and economic use. Finally, the U.S. government has employed various informational tools in its decades-long war on terrorists, and the State Department has finally begun reestablishing consulates and embassies in these key regions. The most notable was the tardy February 2023 return of a U.S. embassy in the Solomon Islands only after it was discovered that China had sealed a secret security pact the year before with the island nation.

THE GREAT GAME IN THE SOUTH AND CENTRAL PACIFIC

In an arc stretching over 1,400 miles from Wake Island to Johnston Atoll and south 1,900 miles to American Samoa are six U.S. exclusive economic zones (EEZ), rich in fish and untapped natural resources on the seabed. Without improved U.S. maritime capacity and allied coordination, these U.S. maritime rights are at risk. However, it is far from just about fish: Should a conflict erupt in Asia, the United States will rely on secure

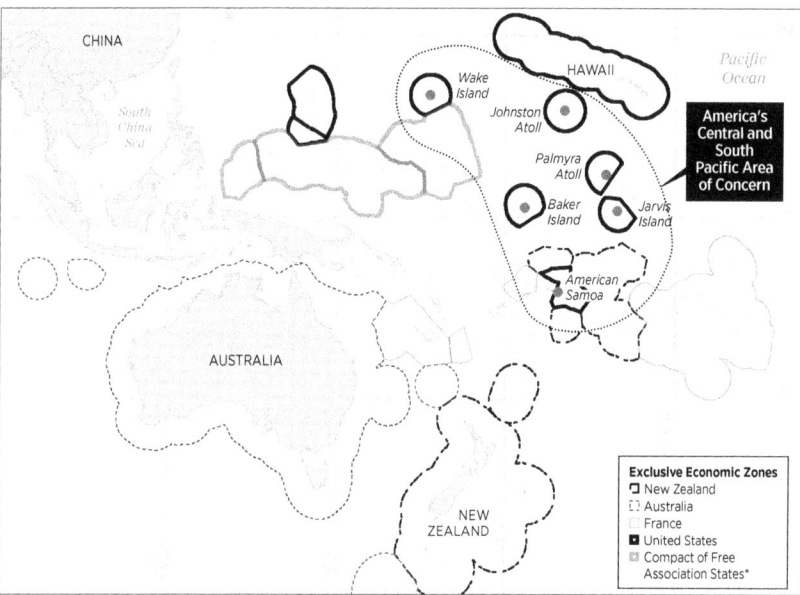

MAP 4. KEY COMPONENTS OF THE PACIFIC QUAD

* Consists of Micronesia, Palau, and Marshall Islands.
SOURCE: French Ministry for the Armed Forces, *France's Defence Strategy in the Indo-Pacific*, 2019, https://apcss.org/wp-content/uploads/2020/02/France-Defence_Strategy_in_the_Indo-Pacific_2019.pdf (accessed March 1, 2021), and Heritage Foundation research.

shipping and air freight across the region to support military operations. Without military access to these islands, the United States loses strategic positioning currently achieved at a low cost, hobbling its ability to sustain military operations in the western Pacific. The threat is very real.

When Kiribati (an island nation in the central Pacific) became unsatisfied that it would take years for America to finance the refurbishment of a World War II–era runway, it turned to China. If used for military purposes, that airstrip could support an enhanced Chinese military presence in the middle of American logistic lines and complicate military operations. China's leaders deny that this is a military project, but the world has heard that line before. Many in the region remember China's false promises regarding the militarization of reefs in the South China Sea or denials over the use of Ream to support the Chinese navy. Make no mistake: China has clearly prioritized the central and south Pacific. Over ten days from late May 2022, China's foreign minister visited eight Pacific island countries and presented them with the Common Development Vision and Five-Year Action Plan on Common Development. Regional experts at the time also whispered that security assurances also were discussed.

China makes it hard for Pacific islanders to resist its ploys. The Belt and Road Initiative is one way China is luring islanders with easy money. Such money enabled a controversial Chinese security pact with the Solomon Islands, which in 2019 received about $730 million from China after switching diplomatic recognition from Taiwan to China. Such investment is significant for the 724,000 Solomon Islands residents, assuming it reaches them. According to the World Bank at the time, this was equivalent to half of the Solomon Islands real gross domestic product. Regionally, from 2009 to 2019, China was the second-largest lender in the Pacific behind the Asian Development Bank. With a total population of less than thirteen million souls thinly dispersed across fifteen independent nations, Pacific islanders are greatly impacted even by small investments in resources and moneys. Yet many islanders have little affinity for China despite the potential payout. Case in point: although eventually going China's way, the Solomon Islands' April 2024 elections saw the pro-China Manasseh Sogavare barely win and his withdrawal for consideration to continue as prime minister. Pacific island nations are largely Christian and democracies, with islanders who care about religion and bread-and-butter issues, which complicates China's image in the region.

China's fishing fleets are globally significant both economically and ecologically. Since 2011 China's appetite for seafood has driven imports—tripling to $15 billion in 2019 and pushing its fishing fleets further afield. In 2021 China's fleets made up 38 percent of all global fishing activity.[2] In the Pacific, Chinese distant fishing fleets frequent waters near American Samoa, Guam, and Hawaii; the overall revenue loss to illegal fishing in the Pacific is estimated to be between $4.3 billion to $8.3 billion.[3] Complicating matters, these distant-water fishing fleets are largely unregulated. Nominal responsibility for this resides with the Chinese Ministry of Agriculture and Rural Affairs, operating under the guidance of China's Fisheries Law, now in its fifth version since its 1986 inception. However, these regulations lean more toward advocacy than regulation. Their provisions include providing financial support, fuel subsidies, and tax exemptions.[4] Additionally, while China's distant-water fishing fleet is largely off the books, it has been estimated to consist of up to 17,000 ships by using location data (e.g., AIS location data) and unique vessel identifier databases (e.g., Krakken's Fish Spektrum). Attempts to regulate this fleet are further hampered by opaque registration and ownership processes.[5] Additionally, Chinese maritime forces have shown a predilection to protect—not regulate—Chinese fishing fleets.

Chinese fishing fleet regulation enforcement is the responsibility of the Chinese Coast Guard (CCG), potentially supported by the paramilitary maritime militia that frequently operates in and among fishing fleets. This is worrisome given the reporting by the China Maritime Studies Institute regarding these forces "frequent use of intimidation" in the South China Sea.[6] One bright spot has been the CCG's enforcement of the United Nation's ban on drift-net fishing in the north Pacific since it joined in 2000 the North Pacific Coast Guard Forum.[7] Sadly, this bright spot has been dimming. Alarms were raised in September 2021 when a Chinese naval four-ship flotilla was unexpectedly encountered in Alaskan waters while a separately deployed CCG flotilla was nearby. This indicates China has the capacity to protect its fishing fleets as far afield as Alaska.[8] On top of this, in January 2022, the CCG escorted six Chinese Fisheries Company vessels that were threatened by pirates in the Gulf of Aden.[9]

The Coast Guard is the best tool for enforcing U.S. laws in its EEZs and for protecting marine and other resources. Thanks to the research of James Di Pane, it is clear that years of consistent underinvestment has left the Coast Guard poorly positioned to address growing challenges.[10] The Coast Guard's District 14 in 2022 patrolled the south, central, and western Pacific with ten cutters and maritime patrol aircraft.[11] That includes the July 2021 addition of three new Guam-based fast response cutters.[12] These smaller cutters are helpful but do not have the endurance to cover the vast spaces of U.S. Pacific EEZs. To mitigate their limited range (2,500 nm), the Coast Guard has used a buoy tender as a mother ship for deployments from Hawaii to American Samoa (2,000 nm) and Tahiti (3,000 nm).[13] Instead, these three new cutters will likely focus on the nearby EEZs of Guam and the Northern Mariana Islands. Keeping the distances involved in mind, Coast Guard procurement plans include eleven high-endurance national security cutters and twenty-five medium-endurance offshore patrol cutters.[14] This planned fleet is still likely inadequate and would arrive late to the task, given the scale of the maritime challenge from Chinese fishing fleets and its military. A 2011 Coast Guard study estimated that its planned acquisitions would only provide 61 percent of the cutters needed to fulfill the Coast Guard's missions, and a later analysis found it could take up to fifty-seven offshore patrol cutters to meet mission demands.[15] Complicating the Coast Guard's and the Navy's efforts to improve presence in this region is the lack of any permanently based ships in the south and central Pacific. The closest bases are in Guam and Hawaii, which include extensive EEZ patrol areas of their own. The problem is amplified as existing infrastructure (ports, airfields) are antiquated, most dating to World War II or to the early American space program, like the airfield at Canton

Island, Kiribati, which was shuttered in 1976. More naval forces are needed in the region with shore facilities for their sustainment in the south and central Pacific.

Building that presence will take time, which the nation and Pacific island partner nations do not have. As such, stronger collective action is needed now and can better safeguard U.S. maritime rights in the near term. This will also help resist Chinese military encroachment in the south and central Pacific. The United States thankfully has allies—Australia, France, and New Zealand—who are capable, resident, and for the most part share common interests in the region.

France has stationed significant forces (two surveillance frigates, three patrol vessels, and five maritime patrol aircraft) and has territory (New Caledonia and French Polynesia) in the Pacific. Furthermore, France is a member of the Pacific Quad (which includes Australia, New Zealand, and the United States) for coordinating security matters and, as party to the 1992 FRANZ Agreement, coordinates regional humanitarian assistance with Australia and New Zealand.[16] Because of other operational requirements, today's U.S. Navy is largely absent from the south and central Pacific. Fortunately, the Coast Guard has not had to deal with large illegal Chinese fishing fleets in U.S. waters—yet. Nevertheless, the day is fast approaching when it will, and today it has limited ability to interdict such illicit maritime activity in U.S. Pacific EEZs. Mobilizing the Pacific Quad for maritime security is an important step until more Coast Guard cutters arrive.

Australia is an important regional partner. Central to its efforts is the Pacific Maritime Security Program, a $2 billion (Australian dollars), thirty-year commitment of in-country staff sustaining a fleet of twenty-one patrol boats transferred to twelve Pacific island nations, providing regional aerial surveillance and underwriting efforts to enhance regional coordination.[17] However, overreliance on too few platforms can quickly open a gap of maritime security coverage. Case in point: the September 2021 grounding of Samoa's single Australian-donated patrol boat exposed the limits of the program, leaving the island with no way of patrolling its waters. New Zealand has limited resources. In 2020 it executed only 131 maritime patrol flying hours and 64 days at sea on fisheries patrols of its 1.6 million square mile EEZ.[18]

Given their extensive and dispersed EEZs, individually these Pacific Quad allies are hard-pressed to respond to large-scale poaching in their waters. However, better information-sharing and collective action can effectively focus limited naval resources to address the risk of large-scale illegal, unreported, unregulated (IUU) fishing and the theft of seabed resources (mineral, energy, etc.) and to protect important sea lanes.

Given the paucity of U.S. naval presence and the associated inadequate capacity to patrol its own EEZ, the United States will need to quickly grow its regional capacity. This will come with added investment in developing additional port, airfield, and repair facilities in the region to sustain the larger maritime presence. To focus resources and enable better regional coordination, a new Navy and Coast Guard detachment in American Samoa will be required. This headquarters would support operations, execute maritime training missions, and oversee infrastructure projects. Done well, this new detachment would synchronize operations like the U.S. Coast Guard's Operation Blue Pacific, with regional naval exercises and expanded dual-use (military and economic) infrastructure projects like pier expansion and ship repair facilities welcomed by regional partners.[19] Resourcing these activities would require a regionally focused maritime security capacity-building account, not unlike what Congress established with the Maritime Security Initiative of 2015. Additionally, this headquarters would coordinate naval deployments with allies like Japan and the United Kingdom. This is becoming increasingly important, with the United Kingdom deploying two patrol ships to the Pacific through 2026 and likely beyond.[20]

Annual Pacific Quad exercises should be pursued to practice wartime logistics, maritime patrol, convoy operations, and interdiction of large fishing fleets (e.g., the 2020 Galapagos Islands incident). Allowance should be made for future participation of Pacific island nation navies, notably from Fiji and Tonga. These exercises should serve to also standardize maritime policing practices with Pacific island nations. During the Covid-19 pandemic, there was good use of virtual policing to enable land-based third-party justices to authorize maritime policing in its waters. This should be expanded and standardized so that, at a minimum, Pacific Quad members can support policing in all the participating nations' EEZ.

At the same time, a new regional framework is needed that offers Pacific island nations an enduring political, economic, and security future better than what is offered by China. The work of Andrew Harding and Cleo Paskal has done much to bring Pacific island leaders together with the U.S. Congress and government, raise awareness of the stakes at play, and secure U.S. interests in the region. Their efforts directly contributed to the 2023 renewal for twenty years of the Compact of Free Association (CoFA). These agreements provide the Republic of Palau, Republic of the Marshall Islands, and Federated States of Micronesia access to U.S. federal social programs (e.g., Veteran Affairs), services (e.g., postal), and immigration to the United States as "habitual residents," with a high proportion serving in the U.S. military. In return, the United States is granted military access and the right to refuse any third party's military access to these islands. Unlike the U.S. territories of Guam and American Samoa or the Commonwealth of the Northern Mariana Islands, these three CoFA island nations vote at the United Nations and control their foreign affairs. Access to U.S. education, medical services, and jobs, to include military service, are strong attractors in many of these island nations—one I can attest to firsthand, having grown up in nearby Guam. That said, retaining national sovereignty is nonnegotiable, making an expanded CoFA an attractive alternative to China's debt diplomacy.

Sustaining the CoFA another twenty years was a strategic win for the United States, but it almost failed due to last-minute questions regarding its funding. The total bill was $7.1 billion over twenty years to secure one thousand islands spanning 2,500 miles across the central Pacific. At the same time, China's attempted regional economic and security pacts by Foreign Minister Wang Yi's 2023 regional tour remain a challenge to be addressed. Other Pacific islands like Nauru (population 9,892), Tuvalu (population 11,733), and Kiribati (population 116,545) need a new compact framework.[21] This new framework would include security access like that of the U.S.–Papua New Guinea Defense Cooperation Agreement signed in May 2023, paired with economic development. This new Pacific framework may even include limited access to U.S. services and immigration similar to, but not matching, existing CoFAs. The added cost would be small, given the populations in question and the proximity to U.S. territories on which services like Veterans Affairs and education already exists (e.g., Guam, American Samoa). Regarding economic development and military access, limited participation could be offered to Australia, Japan, and New Zealand. This diplomatic initiative would complement infrastructure projects tied to increasing naval presence and would improve local economic activity—e.g., port services, expanded piers, power stations. At the same time, efforts would proceed aimed at securing the maritime rights of the U.S. and Pacific nation partners through greater naval presence. Such an approach informs actions taken in the next region facing challenges that can be confronted from the sea.

THE TROPIC OF CANCER TO TROPIC OF CAPRICORN CORRIDOR

From the Tropic of Cancer to Tropic of Capricorn, U.S. influence and commerce with nations across Latin America and Africa is in peril. China continues to make deep incursions into these regions, employing a debt-trap model to advance its security footprint while simultaneously creating avenues for diplomatic, military, and political influence. This region spans an Atlantic corridor encompassing littoral West Africa, the Caribbean, and Latin America with 978 million people. *U.S. Naval Power in the 21st Century* made the case that this region will play an increasingly important role in global commerce and trade and will be a strategically important arena of the new cold war. According to the International Monetary Fund, by 2050 Latin American will have the lowest dependency ratio, 56 percent, a ratio of nonworking population versus working population.[22] The United Nations also projects that, through 2050, Africa will have the fastest growing population.[23] This Atlantic corridor is expected to account for 71 percent of the world's population growth through 2050, with Africa potentially adding $3 trillion in new consumer spending.[24] Therefore, it makes little sense not to devote more

MAP 5. CANCER TO CAPRICORN STRATEGIC FRAMING Chris Robinson

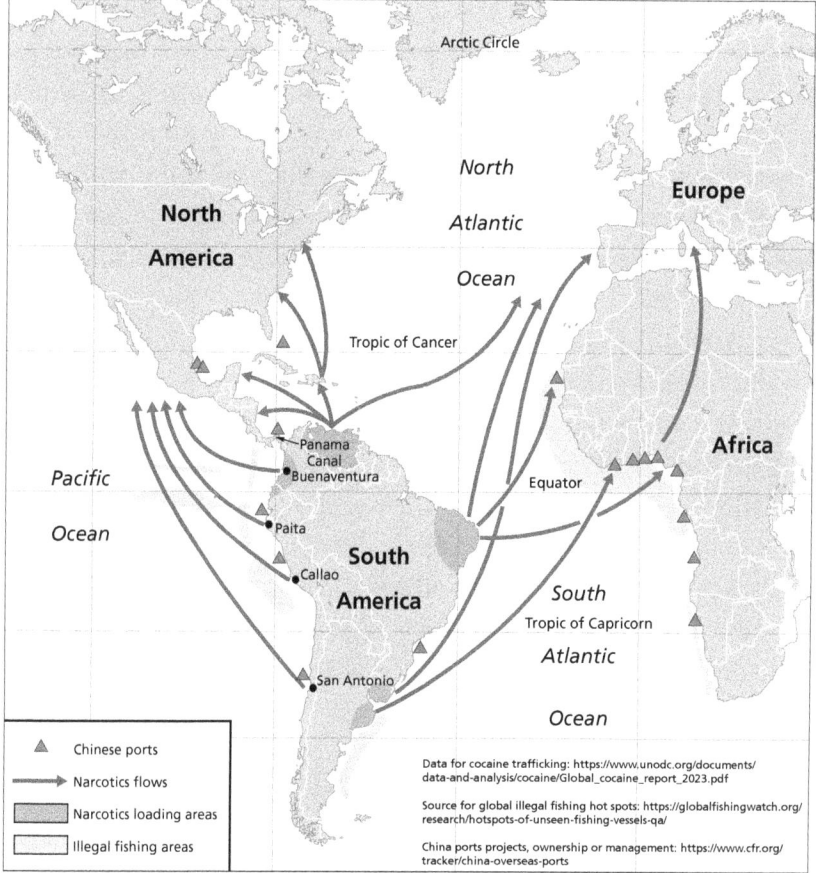

resources to the region and set the foundation for long-term trade growth and alignment of national interests. Despite this, U.S. investment in resources and presence has not kept pace with this opportunity or with the threat that China's encroachment presents.

Meanwhile, China has made common cause with the so-called Global South for economic development via the Belt and Road Initiative. However, in recent years, as mentioned in chapter 1, this effort is beginning to slow under the weight of significant debt. However, without a viable alternative, nations have no choice but to take on Chinese debt or forgo economic development. Making matters worse, Russia, Iran, and Cuba are also undermining regional security. Despite this, our nation shares a common threat with many across the region from narcotic cartels. Top of the list, the fentanyl epidemic in the United States represents a part of a broader shared threat from significant illicit commerce that courses through the region into the United States and Europe. Those same cartels facilitate and profit from illegal immigration via long illicit trafficking routes. Despite a multitude of differences among the individual states across this region, there is potential for common cause at sea—fighting the cartels' narcotic trafficking, protecting against illegal fishing, and developing trade.

It is time to offer an American response and reverse China's inroads into the Global South in concert with regional and European allies across the tropics. Despite this, the United States has prioritized other regions where the security risks are more prevalent and economic returns larger. As African and Latin American markets grow and the threat from China on our doorstep grows, this tendency toward neglect of this region will need to change. A first step would be to engage key regional partners sharing a common interest in combating the cartels, securing maritime rights, and seeking trade. Likely early partners include Argentina, Guyana, Morocco, Senegal, and Angola as well as the Netherlands, United Kingdom, and Italy.

European nations like the Netherlands, France, and the United Kingdom have possessions in the Caribbean that draw a sustained naval presence and coordination with the United States in counternarcotic efforts. Italy, too, has placed added emphasis on West Africa as a conduit for illegal migrants and access to energy resources. But it, too, as well as other European nations, is feeling the effects of narcotic trafficking, making the bridge to migrants' homelands via West Africa a growing concern. Guyana sought U.S. support in January 2024 as it came under increasing threat from neighbor Venezuela, which covets its resource-rich Essequibo region and its offshore energy reserves.[25] Other countries offer the potential for increased trade while growing their economies, and favorable governments look to expand their economic relations. Angola, with its large oil and gas sector, has recovered from a five-year recession in 2021 thanks to non–oil-sector growth.[26] The December 2023 election of Javier Gerardo Milei, an economist, to lead Argentina has ushered in a pro-growth government that offers new opportunities for greater monetary and trade relations.[27] A similar trend is playing out in Rome since Giorgia Meloni became prime minister in October 2022 with a proactive foreign relations agenda some have called a "new look" that aims to counter illegal migrant flows, open markets to access energy trade, and build a more muscular military presence (e.g., the 2024 deployment of Italy's F-35-capable aircraft carrier to the Pacific).[28] Other nations, too, may join in common cause on these issues, notably Brazil, but these countries more than most in the region share common interests with the United States that all would benefit from a new regional framework.

On the African end of the Cancer to Capricorn Corridor, the experience of a 2021 failed Chinese naval base deal with Equatorial Guinea indicates it is possible to stop China in the region. Key to that success were preexisting economic relations not beholden to Beijing.

In October 2021 a U.S. National Security Council staffer traveled to Equatorial Guinea amid troubling reports that China was being offered a naval base there. While China's attempt failed, it was typical of a multifaceted approach used to secure favorable policies by susceptible governments. According to the U.S. Department of Defense's annual report on China, influence campaigns include a wide array of resources focused narrowly on swaying select power brokers.[29] Since 1979 Equatorial Guinea has been led by Teodoro Obiang Nguema Mbasogo, with members of his family and close affiliates running the government, media, and the nation's oil business—which, since 2004, is the third-largest in sub-Saharan Africa.

China's interests in the region include a thirst for natural resources (e.g., cobalt and manganese) and fishing—sometimes illegally. Since 2013 the lion's share of China's pursuit of natural resources and markets has been via the Belt and Road Initiative, which comprised 21 percent of all inward investment to sub-Saharan Africa through 2021.[30] The capture of the Chinese fishing vessel *Hai Lu Feng* in 2020 by African pirates (and its recapture) exposed some uncomfortable truths. It was found that Chinese fishing fleets used registration and location data for multiple ships to skirt licensing fees, duties, and limits on fishing. This activity has caused overfishing—to the detriment of local fishers. Moreover, polling and research in Africa indicate that after a one-year honeymoon over Chinese investment, onerous loan-structuring terms and the exclusive use of Chinese firms has typically eroded local perceptions of China.[31] Today, after a generation of such behavior, Africans are open-eyed about China's largess and its strings-attached deals.

Conditions in Western Africa's Gulf of Guinea afford an opportunity to apply naval statecraft. On the U.S. side are significant oil-sector investments. Exxon Mobile's affiliate is the largest in-country oil producer in Equatorial Guinea since 2007. Oil revenue accounts for over 90 percent of Equatorial Guinea's exports, but it is sourced in the troubled waters of the Gulf of Guinea. Nearby oil-producing countries like Nigeria have also had to contend with piracy and maritime robbery. Additionally, the U.S. Navy has engaged nations of the region since 2007 through Africa Partnership Station, an initiative to enhance African military maritime security through port visits, short-duration training missions, and exercises. For example, Gulf of Guinea nations have, since 2011, come together for an annual maritime security exercise called Obangame Express. Led by the United States, in 2021 it had thirty-two participating nations, including Equatorial Guinea.[32] The exercise has helped improve regional maritime security against piracy, illegal fishing, and maritime crime. At the same time, the CCP is heavily invested in the region: In 2019 the region produced 11.4 percent of China's total fuel imports.

However, missing from the Chinese development model are the main income generators—small and medium enterprises (SME).[33] World Bank offers an important statistic: SMEs in developing economies create seven out of ten jobs.[34] The U.S. Agency for International Development and the DFC are well placed to connect Cancer to Capricorn Corridor SMEs with U.S. markets. Since being established in 2019, the DFC has shown little evidence of an increased focus on advancing U.S. national security and foreign policy with respect to countering Chinese influence.[35] Prosper Africa was established by President Donald Trump in late 2018; through 2021 it has effected eight hundred deals with forty-five African countries valued at $50 billion total. Of these deals, thirty-six were in the aerospace and defense sectors. As such, there has been inadequate focus of Prosper Africa and DFC on strategic ends let alone enabling military capacity building. Unaddressed, these programs will continue to miss an opportunity to focus future investments that can address pressing regional maritime security needs holding back local markets.

Providing an alternative to the Chinese model will be challenging, but the case of Equatorial Guinea illustrates it is workable. Long-standing U.S. business presence in Equatorial Guinea, (e.g., Mobil Corporation and Exxon) undoubtedly contributed to the success of U.S. pressure to back out of the Chinese base deal, something that was absent in the Solomon Islands before China secured its secret security pact there. Sadly, strategic economic presence in Africa is ending as Exxon-Mobil Corporation ended its African operations in mid-2024, ending its presence in Equatorial Guinea that stretches back to the mid-1990s.[36] Naval statecraft would focus on and incorporate economic statecraft to better encourage U.S. economic presence in strategically located markets. In concert with leveraging allied economic presence, a naval statecraft presence would further the opening of new markets that achieves trade diversification that mitigates regional reliance on China. Initially, visiting naval forces focus on addressing common concerns like piracy and illegal fishing, only gradually improving the maritime capacity of the partner nation through training and transferring naval equipment.

Illegal fishing and the need to secure maritime seabed rights in Latin America is not unlike the illegal fishing seen in the Gulf of Guinea. Added to this is the scourge of narcotics trafficking that has its tentacles spread through Central America and the Caribbean to the Americas and through South America via Western Africa to Europe. It is a shared threat that is spreading addictions and criminality and weakening governments. It is a particularly important threat in the United States.

The United States is suffering from a pandemic of illicit narcotics—notably, fentanyl, which killed more than 74,000 Americans in 2023[37]—facilitated by Chinese criminal maleficence across Latin America. Putting an end to this deadly trade will require strangling the drug cartels by

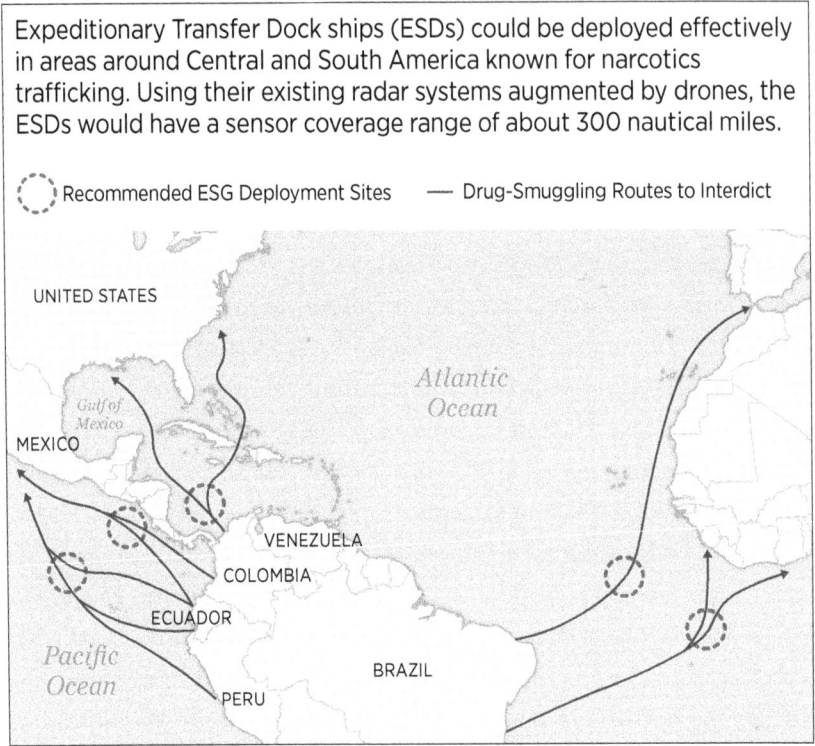

MAP 6. NOTIONAL DEPLOYMENT SITES FOR ESDs *Heritage Foundation*

cutting their illicit smuggling networks connecting Latin America, China, and the United States. In the fight to secure our nation from dangerous illicit drugs, the Joint Interagency Task Force South (JIATF-S), based in Key West, Florida, has been leading a successful regional coalition for decades. Despite this effort, victory has been elusive, given few resources and a constrained U.S. focus, allowing the cartels to adapt and survive.

Defeating the cartels behind the drug trade requires more than just cutting off the trade in fentanyl to the United States. The cartels deal in more than one drug and more than one market. Their trafficking services North American and European customers who have not lost their appetite for cocaine, a drug now experiencing a post-Covid surge valued at over $650 billion.[38] Hitting the cartels' bottom line will require intercepting both shipments of cocaine and the precursor chemicals needed for fentanyl production. Based on discussions at the JIATF-S in 2022, the cartels rely on several critical sea routes to move 90 percent of their drugs. The most important shipment routes cross the Pacific with precursor chemicals from China and cocaine from South America to intermediary stops before moving into the United States or via Europe's most porous border in French Guiana. Smugglers are attracted to French Guiana since, once inside, they can use local drug mules to access direct flights to Europe with fewer customs and immigration restraints.

Established in 1989, the JIATF-S has had measured success interdicting this illicit trade. In 2022 the JIATF-S enabled the capture of over $7 billion worth of narcotics, which is good but not good enough. Despite such seizures, it has not been able to deliver a knockout blow to the cartels' trade, with interdictions in 2017 accounting for only 1 percent in value of total cocaine trade.[39] Progress has been meaningful by leveraging twenty-one partner nations who directly contributed to 80 percent of all interdictions, but because of limited resources, this accounts for only about 10 percent of estimated cocaine traffic.[40] Enabling effective counternarcotic maritime operations, however, relies on sustaining forces at sea and providing wide area maritime domain awareness. The JIATF-S has been able to achieve modest improvement in this regard by contracting the ocean survey vessel *Kellie Chouest*.[41] From this ship, limited replenishment and surveillance has helped sustain multinational counternarcotics operations. It is estimated that almost two thousand tons of undiluted cocaine was produced in 2020, and a well-placed Coast Guard cutter can take fifty tons of narcotics out of supply. Ending the scourge of narcotics will require getting more players on the field in the maritime counternarcotics effort.

In the past, cartel transit routes have adapted as interdiction grew more effective in the Caribbean, with cocaine smugglers shifting to transit routes via West Africa to Europe. The cartels have expanded their European operations in recent years, making it a significant part of their bottom line. Unfortunately, the establishing legislation for the JIATF-S focuses only on routes from Latin America to the United States. This has prevented broader interdiction on a scale that would seriously threaten the cartels' bottom line. Fixing this will require reframing the current mandate of the JIATF-S to focus on cutting all the sea routes on which the cartels rely. An unholy alliance between the cartels and Chinese chemical suppliers is delivering massive profits to crime syndicates on both sides of the Pacific. As in Europe and Africa, increased criminality is weakening Latin American governments that are being exploited by the cartels and the Chinese criminal gangs—notably, the Bang group. This is already apparent as Venezuela slides deeper into criminality and active support of the drug trade while China courts a weakened Nicolás Maduro government. The bottom line is that China benefits by operating on both sides of the narcotics trade: Chinese criminal gangs generate income and influence while weakening local governments. Those weakened governments then turn to China for policing assistance to fight the very crime their criminal syndicates are spreading—see, for example, the experience of the Republic of Palau.[42]

Critically, focusing on only cocaine and fentanyl headed to the United States will not be enough to destroy the cartels behind the illicit narcotics trade. To up the pain on the cartels, the JIATF-S needs more cutters and aircraft to halt this illegal trade. Doing this better and more comprehensively targets the cartels' business model. Cutting off their access to sea routes would squeeze their bottom line where they are most exposed. A comprehensive approach building on the success of the JIATF-S with additional platforms and authorities could finally and mortally smash the cartels and take away from China an avenue to weaken and influence nations across the Global South. Moreover, focus should also be on the transit routes leading to Africa and onward to Europe. At the same time, a greater maritime presence enables better IUU prevention and law enforcement that further strengthens the common cause of nations across the Cancer to Capricorn Corridor.

A PLAN FOR COMPETITION IN THE CANCER TO CAPRICORN CORRIDOR

Resources should be directed to improving maritime security capacity, broadening maritime economic development, and increasing information exchanges. In August 2021 expeditionary sea-based ship *Hershel Williams* provided needed naval presence. The *Williams* operated in the region during a months-long deployment that included counterpiracy drills with the Brazilian navy. Embarked air and shipboard sensors enabled a wide area of surveillance to detect and record illicit maritime activities, which could be shared with regional governments. Additionally, this naval presence provided training that assisted partner navies to patrol their own waters. Such capacity-building efforts improve counternarcotics as well as IUU. Likewise, a new Cancer to Capricorn maritime security initiative will be needed modeled on the successful 2015 Maritime Security Initiative to improve South China Sea claimant states' maritime domain awareness capacity.

The U.S. Navy currently operates three ships, with two more planned, of the same class as the *Williams*—the *Lewis B. Puller* class. The lead ship, the *Puller*, is based in Norfolk, Virginia; the *Hershel "Woody" Williams* in Souda Bay, Greece; and the *Miguel Keith* in San Diego, California. These vessels provide a significant offshore presence best fitted to sustaining interdiction operations. As such, the U.S. Coast Guard has deployed helicopters and small-boat teams to these ships to support execution of maritime security training and capacity-building in the Gulf of Guinea. Such ships expand surveillance coverage over narcotics trafficking routes in the central Atlantic as well as the approaches from Latin America to Central America out to the waters surrounding the Galapagos Islands. However, operational demands are drawing the few of these ships on hand to other theaters, so an alternative to waiting for more ships to be built is needed.

A potential solution lies in the Navy's inactive fleet that can also address another operational dilemma—forward-area battle damage repairs. The Navy confronts a potential Pacific war with China that it is unprepared to sustain, with too few options for conducting forward-battle damage repairs. At the 2023 naval conference WEST, the Indo-Pacific Fleet commander, Admiral Samuel Paparo Jr., called for the capability to repair battle-damaged warships nearer the battle lines using deployable teams to meet and repair a damaged warship.[43] However, fly-away teams will be hard-pressed to effect major battle damage without gear like cranes, steel plate, cofferdams, and floating drydocks that

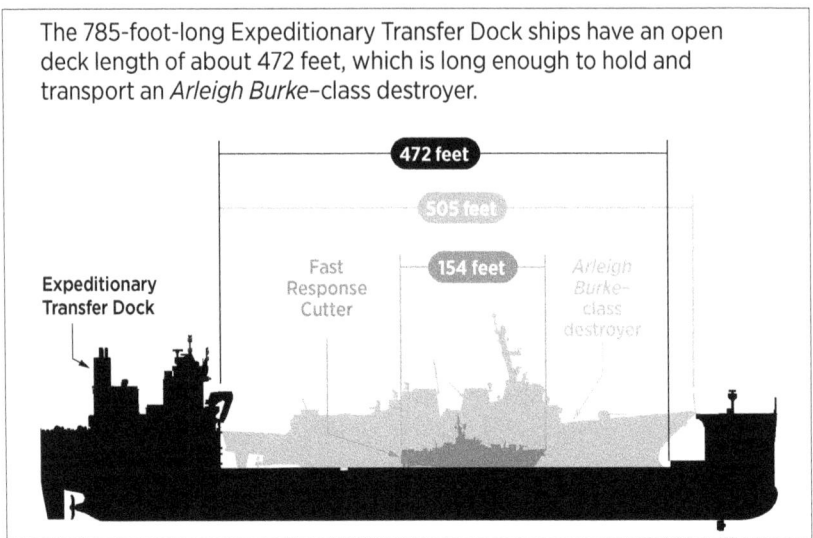

FIGURE 4. Heavy-lift and repair ship *Heritage Foundation*

proved instrumental in the Pacific during World War II.[44] To meet these needs today, new floating drydocks or modern heavy-lift ships will be needed.

A short-term remedy is returning to service and repurposing the two expeditionary transfer dock (ESD) ships, both in 2024 with a decade of life left. *Montford Point* (ESD-1) could be used as a mother ship in support of maritime counternarcotic operations in the Cancer to Capricorn Corridor. The second, *John Glenn* (ESD-2), could advance development of a heavy-lift repair ship and perfect expeditionary warship battle-repair techniques critical in a major war in the Pacific.

Both ESD-1 and ESD-2 are currently in an inactive reduced operating status, which means the Navy ensures these ships can be brought back to service—in these ships' case, within five days.[45] That said, a more reasonable timeline would be forty-five days to return these ships to an active status. Both ships are currently being maintained by the Military Sealift Command and remain on the Navy's registry of warships as of May 2024: *Montford Point* moored in Naval Station Norfolk, Virginia, and *John Glenn* moored in Oakland, California. The design of both ships is based on the *Alaska*-class crude-oil carrier built in 2011 by General Dynamics

National Steel and Shipbuilding Company and was the design basis for the *Williams*.[46] Importantly, these large ships have the deck space and support needed to sustain a range of drones that can greatly expand the sensor coverage detecting and then interdicting illicit maritime activities.

In recent years the Navy and the Coast Guard have developed unmanned platforms to provide persistent wide-area maritime domain awareness. Most notable has been the success of the Fifth Fleet, based in Bahrain, with the 2021 establishment of unmanned platform Task Force 59. The secretary of the Navy has since called for replicating this effort in the Fourth Fleet, responsible for the waters of JIATF-S patrols.[47] Unmanned platforms that both the Navy and Coast Guard operate like Saildrone, ScanEagle, or the Navy's unmanned surface vessels (large and medium), if operated from an ESD, would greatly enhance persistent at-sea sensor coverage.[48] Moreover, using the capacity of an ESD for repairing, reprovisioning, and refueling patrol vessels, many from regional partner nations, also facilitates greater capacity to effect interdictions and to destroy contraband (e.g., cocaine) at sea, preventing its potential diversion ashore. Altogether, an ESD acting as an unmanned and patrol fleet mother ship can enhance the effectiveness of maritime policing against activities like illegal fishing and narcotics trafficking.

An effective counternarcotic and IUU campaign in the Cancer to Capricorn Corridor has economic and security benefits but will not alone address the threat from China. Providing a compelling alternative to CCP largess—not merely "more and faster" than China can provide in infrastructure investment—is needed most. After all, the Obiang family regime has not shown any reticence or yet born any harm in dealing with China. If done well, naval statecraft provides a sustainable value proposition beginning with maritime security that enables economic development. This can bolster African and Latin American resiliency to potential Chinese coercion and align interests with the United States for a free and open community between the Tropics—Cancer to Capricorn. Sustaining such an approach requires U.S. public support earned from measurable benefits in homeland security and prosperity through expanded trade by applying Prosper Africa to this corridor and encouraging more domestic investments in maritime security. Americans will also rightfully expect results in battling the cartels. To achieve this, a broader mandate is required for JIATF-S, and platforms like the ESD should be returned to service to sustain maritime security operations from the Pacific coast of Latin America to the Gulf of Guinea. Finally, organizational realignment will be needed to execute this competitive strategy in the Cancer to Capricorn Corridor. Chapter 8 takes up how to realign for this task.

RUNNING A MARITIME COUNTERINSURGENCY IN THE SOUTH CHINA SEA

Today's tensions in the South China Sea can be traced to a series of events beginning with the 1986 Filipino "people power revolution" that peacefully toppled the dictatorship of Ferdinand Marcos. This set in motion events that culminated after the 1991 eruption of Mount Pinatubo and with the end of a century of U.S. military presence in the Philippines. The United States departed its major bases in Subic Bay and Clark Air Base, which created a power vacuum in the South China Sea filled by China. Likewise, action is long overdue centered on those regional nations in maritime dispute with China (Vietnam, the Philippines, Malaysia, Brunei, Indonesia). But given the Philippines' long-standing alliance with the United States and China's increasingly aggressive maritime tactics against it, a new regional approach that explicitly supports the Philippines is overdue.

To deter China overall, Washington needs a stronger military alliance with the Philippines, and leaders in Manila understand this. However, colonial memories and the multifaceted challenge from China requires a more comprehensive approach to bolster the bilateral relationship. To achieve this goal, the economic and military interests of both countries must complement each other while broadening and deepening the bonds between the two countries. After ten years, a bilateral security arrangement may finally be bearing fruit in this regard.

Signed on April 28, 2014, the U.S.–Philippines Enhanced Defense Cooperation Agreement (EDCA) has sought to bolster military cooperation. The intent was that rotational U.S. military forces would deploy to newly selected sites, thereby strengthening both nations' military presence. However, on the heels of successful arbitration against China's claims in the South China Sea, a change in direction toward China stalled the effort with the June 2016 election of President Rodrigo Duterte. Legal challenges against the EDCA fostered by Duterte's administration and the setting aside of the arbitration win have once again reversed with the June 2022 inauguration of a new president, Bongbong Marcos. Since the early months of 2023, the EDCA has accelerated with additional sites named and associated $128 million of defense investments unveiled at the April 2024 11th U.S.–Philippines Bilateral Strategic Dialogue.[49] Importantly, public statements regarding the EDCA by both governments have stressed its coincident economic benefits.

Sustaining this momentum requires making a compelling case to the Filipino people for how closer security relations with the United States addresses their needs. This requires a comprehensive approach that marries economic development with visible benefits of mutual security obligations ensconced in the bilateral Mutual Defense Treaty. Recent reporting from Philippine villages near EDCA sites indicate this may be working as residents of Santa Ana in northern Luzon welcomed the U.S. military and associated business.[50] At the same time, China is the Philippines' leading trade partner, at approximately $60 billion in 2019, but Manila's trade with certain free market allies (United States, Japan, Singapore, and South Korea) is comparable, at $65 billion.[51] When the virtues of economic development associated with the EDCA do not suffice, collaboration among allies clearly offers a much more compelling case representing more trade and investment than with China alone.

An example of such an allied economic statecraft occurred over the strategically important Subic Bay shipyard. When the South Korean company Hanjin went bankrupt in 2016, the shipyard was at risk of being taken over by China. Thankfully, the government-affiliated Overseas Private Investment Corporation—now the DFC—brokered a deal that forestalled a Chinese takeover of this port. Sadly, the DFC has not repeated such successes by developing infrastructure guided by U.S. economic interests and military operational needs, which is a departure from one of its original intents—to prevent the United States from being pushed out of friendly markets and security partnerships by the CCP. It was partly for this purpose that the DFC garnered bipartisan support when it was created in 2018, but it has since strayed from this intent considerably. Through a refocused DFC and invigorated collective economic action, a compelling economic case can be made to the wider South China Sea region. But success will remain elusive without addressing the maritime disputes with China.

In an influential 2019 essay, Hunter Stires lays out a compelling case for treating the CCP's efforts in the South China Sea for what they were—an insurgency against the rules-based order. Stires states it this way: "In the ongoing battle of legal regimes in the South China Sea, it is not: Which side would prevail in battle? but rather, Whose laws do the civilians follow?"[52] An effective response then requires taking a counterinsurgency approach in the region, where, according to the *U.S. Government Counterinsurgency Guide*, population-centric as well as adversary-centric actions are required.[53] Unfortunately, the United States has historically chosen to focus on the adversary by seeing the competition only as a maritime security dispute. This was evidenced in such statements like, "The United States will sail, fly, and operate wherever international law allows," which became an axiom that has been repeated verbatim by every secretary of defense since 2015. It completely misses the wider economic interests at play by our regional allies and partners. Stires' research has helped break long-standing strategic blinders and opened the way for a naval statecraft approach that incorporates both population- and adversary-centric approaches to the region.

Executing a population-centric campaign in this case will involve actions and policies intended to impact the fishermen, shippers, ferry operators, oil companies operating offshore rigs, and local governments directly benefiting from the South China Sea. As such, the focus will be the primary claimant states with the largest stakes at sea against China that include Vietnam, Malaysia, the Philippines, and Indonesia. In Malaysia, oil revenue contributes significantly to the government's bottom line and domestic politics. Taxes and dividends on Malaysia's state energy firm, Petronas, accounted for 35 percent of total government revenue in 2019.[54]

In Vietnam, the seafood industry employs 1.6 million people, and the country is emerging as a regional offshore oil and natural gas producer, contingent on its exploitation of oil reserves in its EEZ.[55] In the Philippines, fishing plays a significant part in the local economy, employing more than 1 million Filipinos and accounting for a sizable portion of gross domestic product.[56] During presidential campaign debates in January 2024, all Indonesian candidates affirmed the challenge of the dispute in the South China Sea as the most pressing flashpoint of conflict. The victor by a wide margin with 59 percent of the vote was the former special forces general and defense minister under the outgoing president, who vowed to continue past maritime policies.[57] Those policies referred to as Indonesia's "Global Maritime Axis doctrine" include building a stronger naval presence centered on Natuna islands in the South China Sea and reorganizing and strengthening its coast guard (Bakamla) to conduct enhanced maritime rights enforcement—often seizing and destroying violating Chinese fishing vessels.[58] Among the claimant states, the trend lines are clear—safeguarding their maritime rights requires a stronger maritime posture.

CONCLUSION

Naval statecraft will need to be first operationalized in three maritime theaters: the Cancer to Capricorn Corridor, south and central Pacific, and the South China Sea. All three theaters share common interests in improving maritime security: in varying degrees, against illegal fishing and narcotics trafficking. Moreover, all three regions' nations have interests in securing their maritime rights and economic development. This requires a persistent, tailored maritime presence that can foster maritime economic development enabled by that presence.

The approach in each of these three regions will differ in composition of forces and partner nation participation. In the south and central Pacific, the Pacific Quad will be a key partner in developing effective regional maritime domain awareness and security across the expanse of the Pacific Ocean. A new conception of the Compact of Free Association agreement will also be useful in securing for more Pacific island nations a secure, free, and open Pacific. In the Cancer to Capricorn Corridor, this will involve a collection of like-minded and geographically important partner nations working together to enhance maritime counternarcotics operations while growing trade via a Prosper Africa initiative expanded geographically to cover the entirety of this region in a Cancer to Capricorn trade corridor. Finally in the South China Sea, new naval fleet structures (chapter 9) and a maritime counterinsurgency (chapter 3) will be needed.

While waging an effective maritime counterinsurgency is overdue in the South China Sea, it also serves to deter China from a wider war. As discussed in *U.S. Naval Power in the 21st Century*, this sea will be a critical theater of operations in any potential war over Taiwan. Increasing uncertainty in the minds of CCP leadership about the success of its war plans over Taiwan also increases deterrence. As such, actions taken in this counterinsurgency will be guided by how it achieves this strategic effect. Getting the balance right between maritime counterinsurgency and deterrence is the focus of the next chapter.

CHAPTER 3

A NEW OPERATIONAL APPROACH IN DECISIVE MARITIME THEATERS

Aside from inherent military utility, naval operations in the immediate future must consider two audiences—the American public and that of our allies. This will necessitate a new naval operational approach that must achieve strategic impact on the perceptions of those operating on and making a living from the seas as well as influencing the calculus of our adversaries' leadership. Regarding the audience, the primary goal is to demonstrate to the American public that an endeavor of naval statecraft is working to deter our adversaries while rallying allies to common cause. As for our adversaries, the objective is achieved by demonstrating the futility of a military confrontation while winning the new cold war. This will require operating in three new ways: executing a maritime counterinsurgency, refining naval capabilities through modern Fleet Problems, and demonstrating resolve and confidence through flexible naval deployments. The strategic rationale for such an approach and where these must be focused is covered in depth in the previous book, *U.S. Naval Power in the 21st Century*.

In crafting new naval operations to achieve these aims, several key factors must be considered. First, within a wartime theater, consider where operations will be focused and with what kind of disposition (i.e., rules of engagement, proximity to hostile forces). Second, consider which forces are most appropriate to the mission. Third, consider how to most effectively conduct the planning and coordination required among U.S. agencies as well as key allies. By addressing each of these factors, this chapter provides a way to realize the type of new naval operations needed.

NAVAL OPERATIONS IN A MARITIME COUNTERINSURGENCY

Since its victory over South Vietnam in early 1974 for control of the Paracel Islands, China has waged a decades-long maritime insurgency. Things shifted into higher gear in 1992, after the United States vacated its bases in the Philippines, leaving a power vacuum that enabled China to employ a gradualist approach to impose its diktat across the South China Sea. Sadly, China's efforts were not fully appreciated until recently. China's goal has been to first delegitimize any claim other than its own and then to exercise effective control of the entirety of the South China Sea. This focus on political control of the South China Sea fits the conventional definition of an insurgency of U.S. joint doctrine.[1] Failing to recognize this fact, the United States spent years fumbling to counter China's South China Sea incursions. This changed thanks to the clever work of Hunter Stires, who in a groundbreaking 2019 article recognized it for what it was—a maritime insurgency.[2] As such, only by embracing a counterinsurgency framework would U.S. efforts hope to be successful in the region. Moving beyond this recognition, the focus must shift to how to implement an effective South China Sea counterinsurgency.

Two recent incidents are worth recounting briefly as they provide key insights on how to effectively counter China in the region. The first is the 2012 Scarborough Shoal standoff, and the second is the 2020 *West Capella* incident. Both incidents are extensively discussed in *U.S. Naval Power in the 21st Century*, but in short, these incidents illustrate the importance of persistent naval presence to stymie Chinese attempts of effective control over either a contested feature (e.g., Scarborough Shoal) or tied to specific economic interests (e.g., offshore oil exploitation of *West Capella*).[3] Readers of the earlier book will recall that the response at Scarborough Shoal failed because it ceded effective control to China when Philippine forces departed; in the *West Capella* incident, success was achieved by the sustained U.S. naval presence focused on supporting the economic activity of a partner nation—Malaysia.

The Chinese Communist Party has in recent years quickened the pace of its efforts to undermine U.S. security alliances and replace existing international maritime norms with Sino-centric ones. To do this, the Chinese have implemented unilateral fishing bans, harassed local non-Chinese fishermen, and strong-armed anyone who dares to conduct oil exploration in areas China considers theirs. To establish control of this sea, the Chinese in 2015 completed a massive building campaign that produced an archipelago of fortified man-made island fortresses—breaking a promise to then-president Barack Obama.

The CCP's gradual undermining of accepted maritime norms in the South China Sea is often equated to "boiling a frog." The metaphor suggests a pot where the heat is turned up so gradually that the frog does not notice until it is too late to escape. In this case, the Chinese government is heating up the South China Sea pot, and the frog is the United States. But all is not lost.

Three recent developments provide the pretext and legal basis for a new maritime counterinsurgency against China. First was the Philippines' 2016 win at the Permanent Court of Arbitration in The Hague declaring that China had no legal basis to claim the totality of the South China Sea. Originally, Philippine president Rodrigo Duterte had set aside this win to lure Chinese investment in his country. When the investment soured, he reversed course in 2020 and began pressing this arbitral win. Second, statements by then-commander of the U.S. 7th Fleet, Vice Adm. William Merz, and then-secretary of state Mike Pompeo during the *West Capella* crisis of 2020 signaled support for the legal right of nations in the region. Third, the January 2022 State Department *Limits in the Seas* report on China's South China Sea maritime claims made clear and specific the U.S. legal position regarding the extent of each nation's EEZs and territorial waters in the region.

A visible U.S. naval presence at four key locations can enhance the diplomatic message while bolstering the maritime rules-based order that is key to U.S. interests in the region. The United States should maintain its first naval presence at Vietnam's southern EEZ, where Chinese harassment of Vietnamese oil surveying and extraction has occurred. Importantly, this area is also not contested by Vietnam with its other regional neighbors—only China. The UN Convention on the Law of the Sea and customary international law, which all regional states—including

MAP 7. DISTANCE BETWEEN FOUR SOUTH CHINA SEA FLASHPOINTS Chris Robinson

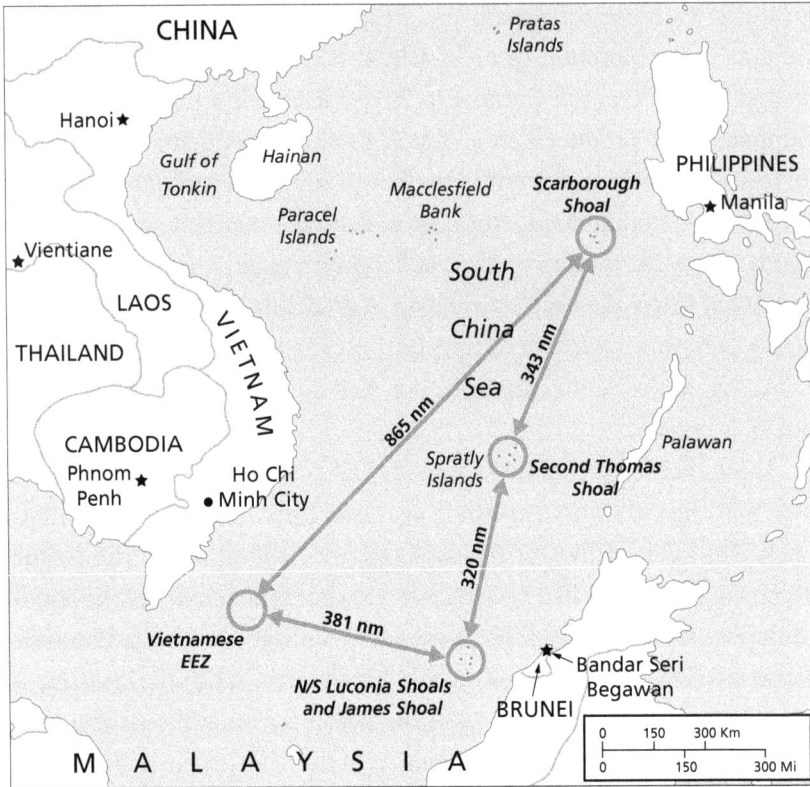

China—have agreed to, grants nations "sovereign rights for the purpose of exploring and exploiting, conserving and managing the natural resources." This presence would bolster the U.S. message to the region it upholds economic rights within a rightful EEZ.

The second naval presence should be near Scarborough Shoal, site of a 2012 dispute between the Philippines and China that drew in the United States diplomatically. Naval presence would serve to monitor and ideally deter further Chinese militarization of the shoal while highlighting China's duplicity in not honoring past promises to vacate the shoal. The message to the region would be that the United States will not accept coercive or unilateral changes at disputed features.

A third naval presence is needed at Second Thomas Shoal, home to a Philippine outpost and site of repeated Chinese harassment. Provocations have persisted since early 2023, frequently involving multiple Chinese Coast Guard vessels using water cannons to forcibly turn back Philippine resupply vessels headed to the garrison. This resulted in a rare rebuke from the United States that attacks on Philippine government vessels would trigger our Mutual Defense Treaty to defend Philippine forces.[4] Over several weeks in the summer of 2024, clashes at this feature between Chinese maritime forces and Philippine forces attempting to resupply their garrison turned violent in a dramatic escalation. Chinese sailors brandishing boat hooks and axes resulting in one Filipino sailor losing a finger.[5] A presence here demonstrates the viability of U.S. security treaties and the unacceptability of China's interference with another nation's maritime forces in its own waters.

The United States should maintain a fourth naval presence in the vicinity of James Shoal and the North and South Luconia Shoals within Malaysia's and Indonesia's EEZs. Importantly, both these nations have settled their maritime borders, leaving only China to contest their claims. As such, China has maintained a near-continuous naval presence near these shoals since completing its island building in 2015.[6] This area has been the target of repeated Chinese encroachment, and a U.S. presence would help deter Chinese intimidation of oil survey operations, local fishers, and local nations' maritime forces. The message to those at sea and regional states is that the U.S.-led, rules-based maritime order is the best guarantor of their rightful access to an area rich in oil and fish.

Unfortunately, the lack of U.S. strategic attention and sustained naval presence has been exacerbated by the years-long Fat Leonard corruption and bribery scandal involving dozens of U.S. naval officers and sailors in Southeast Asia. This sad saga and ensuing investigations have chilled port visits and engagements in the region for far too long. This situation has provided the Chinese a decades-long opportunity that they used to reset the region to their benefit. A course correction is needed, beginning with a renewed U.S. naval presence.

Posturing a persistent naval presence at these four locations will require a naval force fit for the mission. The principal Chinese forces are Chinese Coast Guard cutters, Chinese navy frigates, and maritime militia in repurposed fishing trawlers. Additionally, the winter months, November through March, see higher seas that tend to dampen smaller fishing trawler activity. Already the United States maintains a presence here consisting most often of littoral combat ships on rotational deployments and periodically deploys destroyers assigned to Destroyer Squadron 7 based in Singapore.[7] These ships can operate at speeds more than thirty knots and can embark helicopters and drones (e.g., ScanEagle)—easily within a day trip between the above four locations. A routine pattern of operations could see two of these warships at sea while deployed maritime patrol aircraft (i.e., P-8) provide overhead maritime domain awareness and rapid response capabilities. During typical periods of provocative Chinese activity during fishing bans in the winter months or major Chinese drills (July through September), the U.S. presence would be augmented by a deployed large amphibious warship with F-35 aircraft or by a carrier strike group and its air wing. Army forces deployed to the region as part of the Pacific Pathways program would bolster this maritime presence with its long-range antiship and air defense weapons.[8] In April 2024 the U.S. Army deployed to the Philippines with the Typhon weapon system, which is capable of launching Tomahawk and SM-6 missiles able to attack ships and aircraft, strike land targets, and defend from air threats.[9] The Air Force has deployed both fighter squadrons (theater strike package) and bombers (continuous bomber presence) to the region in episodic shows of force and training missions.[10] The effect is a visible and persistent presence that complicates Chinese operational planning and bolsters regional partner nations confidence in the United States.

These forces would be employed in a manner to raise doubt in Chinese military and political leaders and would not intend to instigate a direct confrontation. This effect is achieved by U.S. naval presence and the sharing of maritime domain information regarding the disposition of Chinese forces in the region with partner nations. This builds upon similar efforts exposing China's worst behaviors, which the Philippines has done with a so-called aggressive transparency campaign—a campaign that has seen the press corps integrated on resupply vessels and coast guard cutters operating in proximity to harassing Chinese forces and producing videos that end up online within minutes of the events. The public shaming of bad Chinese maritime behavior is not new, but the Philippine government made it a public policy in early 2023, garnering support in its stand against China's encroachment and interference of resupply missions to its garrison at Second Thomas Shoal.[11] Where the Chinese are present in force, an overwatch posture should be taken. On the other hand, where the Chinese are absent, a more present and forceful presence to monitor activities should be made—such as at open waters in Vietnam's southern EEZ or South Luconia Shoals. To counter well-known Chinese gray-zone tactics—shouldering, water-cannoning, and using maritime militia swarming tactics—nonlethal crowd-control capabilities could find great utility. The Department of Defense calls these intermediate force capabilities options, which include low-energy microwaves that instill burning sensations to exposed skin, sound weapons that cause pain, laser dazzlers that disorient, and even "goo" that can foul a ship's propeller, stopping it in the water.[12] The intent is to control escalation by providing naval warship commanding officers options across a wider range of force.

Getting the ships, aircraft, and ground forces into the region in a mutually supportive manner requires planning. For maximum effectiveness, Army and Air Force units deployed to the region would need to coordinate their operations with the naval forces led by Destroyer Squadron 7. These coordinated, joint operations would act within strategic guidance issued by Indo-Pacific Command in Hawaii and coordinated with key agencies in Washington, D.C., such as the State Department. Given the strategic implications of these maritime counterinsurgency operations, the complexity of joint operations, and the need to engage host nations supporting the joint forces in the region as well gain access to port facilities critical to sustaining a persistent naval presence, a regionally focused fleet is needed. How to establish such a new numbered fleet with joint force embedded staff officers is taken up in chapter 9.

However, the contest over the South China Sea involves more than besting the CCP's military and paramilitary forces. It is a competition over whose maritime order will prevail—a contest that has major economic and security implications for all nations of the region as well as the United States. In other words, the maritime order that benefits the most players and that can be firmly secured will prevail. This requires making a compelling value proposition to the people and governments of the maritime states that are in dispute with China. Doing so necessitates more than just naval presence, as detailed in chapter 2, but that presence is required to restore confidence in the existing maritime rules-based order—an order that best serves U.S. interests in trade and security. While waging a maritime counterinsurgency in the South China Sea, the Navy will also need to refine tactics, realistically evaluate new technologies, and challenge operational assumptions under challenging, real-world exercises. A dedicated regional fleet will also enhance greater engagement with regional partner nations' maritime police forces and the U.S. Coast Guard and Navy to adapt together as China evolves its own tactics.

MODERN FLEET PROBLEMS

Years in the planning, the Navy conducted its first large-scale exercise (LSE) in August 2021. The most recent and second iteration was conducted over August 9–18, 2023, and involved 25,000 sailors and marines across twenty-two time zones.[13] The exercise was intended to refine the coordination of global naval operations, with the 2023 iteration including ships at sea and thirty virtual units in every numbered fleet of the Navy. While a significant exercise, an LSE does not compare to the Fleet Problems that prepared the Navy for the Pacific war during World War II. Those large exercises sometimes included Army ground and air forces in twenty-one problems, or exercises. The Fleet Problems were held between 1923 and 1940 and typically involved a third of the Navy's warships, with the longest problem running fifty-two days; the average length of the exercises from 1934 was thirty-six days.[14] The Fleet Problems are credited with refining the war planning and techniques that would be successfully implemented against Japan in World War II. Today LSE does not fully assess the Navy's preparation for a war against China at scale under real-world problems of logistics, weather, and human error. A new modern Fleet Problem is needed.

MAP 8. CHINA'S FORMIDABLE YET LOCALIZED MISSILE THREAT *Heritage Foundation*

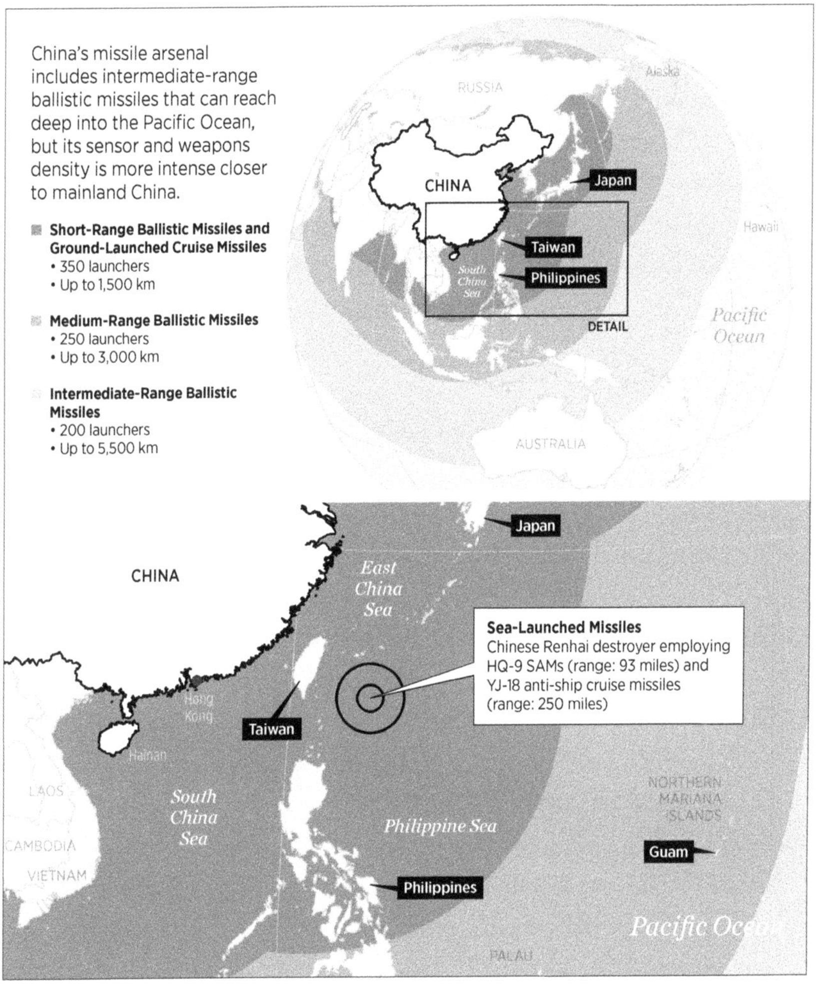
China's missile arsenal includes intermediate-range ballistic missiles that can reach deep into the Pacific Ocean, but its sensor and weapons density is more intense closer to mainland China.
Short-Range Ballistic Missiles and Ground-Launched Cruise Missiles
• 350 launchers
• Up to 1,500 km
Medium-Range Ballistic Missiles
• 250 launchers
• Up to 3,000 km
Intermediate-Range Ballistic Missiles
• 200 launchers
• Up to 5,500 km
RUSSIA
Alaska
CHINA
Japan
Taiwan
Philippines
South China Sea
DETAIL
Hawaii
Pacific Ocean
AUSTRALIA
CHINA
Japan
East China Sea
Sea-Launched Missiles
Chinese Renhai destroyer employing HQ-9 SAMs (range: 93 miles) and YJ-18 anti-ship cruise missiles (range: 250 miles)
Hong Kong
Hainan
Taiwan
LAOS
South China Sea
CAMBODIA
VIETNAM
Philippine Sea
NORTHERN MARIANA ISLANDS
Guam
Philippines
PALAU

In a war with China, there are three critical challenges to an effective war effort that have been openly discussed: surging into China's anti-access area denial (A2/AD) perimeter, conducting littoral operations in the first island chain, and contested logistics across the Pacific. A modern Fleet Problem would assess the military's planning, systems, and people under real-world conditions closely approximating those expected in a war with China. In the 1920s and 1930s, Fleet Problems were conducted in defense of the Panama Canal and often used geography that would likewise be expected in a Pacific campaign. The effect was that, by World War II, the U.S. Navy had experimented and prepared for every potentiality of the Pacific war, while strategically every campaign Japan operationally planned during the war failed—the successful Pearl Harbor attack and operations through May 1942 had been planned prewar.[15] Today's Navy has little reason to assume that its planning and unit-level training would hold up under the rigors of real-world fleet-level wartime operations. Modern Fleet Problems to improve this would include the actions described in the following paragraphs:

A NEW NIFTY NUGGET

Gen. Norman Schwarzkopf Jr., of Gulf War fame, is known for saying, "The more you sweat in peace, the less you bleed in war." This applies equally to preparation for a war with China likely over the fate of Taiwan. A 1978 logistics and mobilization exercise proved the value of testing the assumptions of war plans with real-world at-scale tests. That exercise, Nifty Nugget, exposed the inadequacy of readiness to execute a rapid mobilization to resupply Europe under a surprise Soviet attack.[16] Those lessons led to the creation in 1987 of Transportation Command, which proved pivotal in the success of operations Desert Shield and Desert Storm in the first Gulf War (1990 to 1991).[17] The challenge today is resupplying and sustaining a war effort in East Asia across the expanse of a contested Pacific Ocean. In recent years China and Russia have demonstrated the capacity to sustain naval and air operations deep into the central Pacific; Russia sent bombers to Indonesia in 2017 and a naval flotilla within twenty-four miles of Hawaii in 2021, and China dispatched a naval flotilla near Alaska in 2015, 2021, 2023, and 2024. Such demonstrations, along with both navies' nuclear submarines able to operate far from home ports, make assumptions of secure movement across the Pacific questionable. A modern Nifty Nugget could test assumptions, equipment, and training for such a massive endeavor.

THE THIRD VERSUS SEVENTH FLEET IN FLEET PROBLEM IX REDUX

The second key operational problem ripe for testing in a modern Fleet Problem is operating within China's A2/AD defenses while conducting offensive wartime operations. An arsenal of antiship ballistic missiles, long-range bombers, and submarines with antiship and land-attack cruise missiles extend China's A2/AD barrier to the second island chain—Guam and the Northern Marianas.[18] This does not mean actually conducting a Fleet Problem within China's A2/AD networks, which would be an operational security nightmare. Rather, like the 1929 Fleet Problem IX that advanced understanding of aircraft carrier operations, conducting such a Fleet Problem should be done in a region that geographically approximates the challenge. In this case, Guam and the Northern Marianas could double for the China coast, with U.S. forces on Guam simulated at Kwajalein. In such a scenario, the Third Fleet, deploying from the U.S. West Coast, would be tasked with conducting attacks on Guam, and the Seventh Fleet naval forces would act as an opposition force amid the islands of the Northern Marianas. Positioning and then rearming such a force would also be tested under simulated enemy fire as well as effectiveness of carrier strike operations under coordinated Chinese attacks played by forces in the Northern Marianas and Guam.

FIRST ISLAND CHAIN CONTESTED LITTORAL OPERATIONS

The Marine Corps and the Army have plans for a campaign of maneuver within the first island chain, which is intended to contest China's naval and air operations. For the Army, the concept of operations is multidomain operations.[19] The Marine Corps' concept is expeditionary advanced base operations and littoral operations in a contested environment.[20] These concepts inform the Marine Corps' Force Design 2030, which envisions a light, mobile amphibious force. The Army's concept is similar but less mobile and emphasizes long-range missile systems to include air and missile defenses. To succeed in the first island chain, both the Marines and the Army will need logistics ships and mobility to complicate Chinese targeting of their forces. This raises operational questions: How do we defend or secure the supply chain and the movement of forces?

To assess the adequacy of the current platforms, training, and operational planning, a corollary to the first island chain would be the Hawaiian Islands, which stretch just over 1,300 nautical miles, approximating the distance from Palawan island in the Philippines to Okinawa, Japan. To simulate Chinese ballistic and cruise missile strikes from the mainland, any Marine or Army forces that do not relocate in twenty-four hours would be attacked. Marine and Army forces along with invited allied nations (i.e., Japan and Philippines) in the Hawaiian Islands would be tasked with preventing the Third Fleet from crossing the island chain. Live-fire drills simulating attacks to suppress Chinese island garrisons such as Fiery Cross Reef could be conducted from Tinian to one of several uninhabited islands in the Northern Marianas. The distances are roughly equivalent and would include overflight of uninhabited islands similar to the challenges of avoiding friendly or neutral island garrisons in the South China Sea. Such a plan would resurrect a long-standing plan to establish a bombing range in the Northern Marianas.[21]

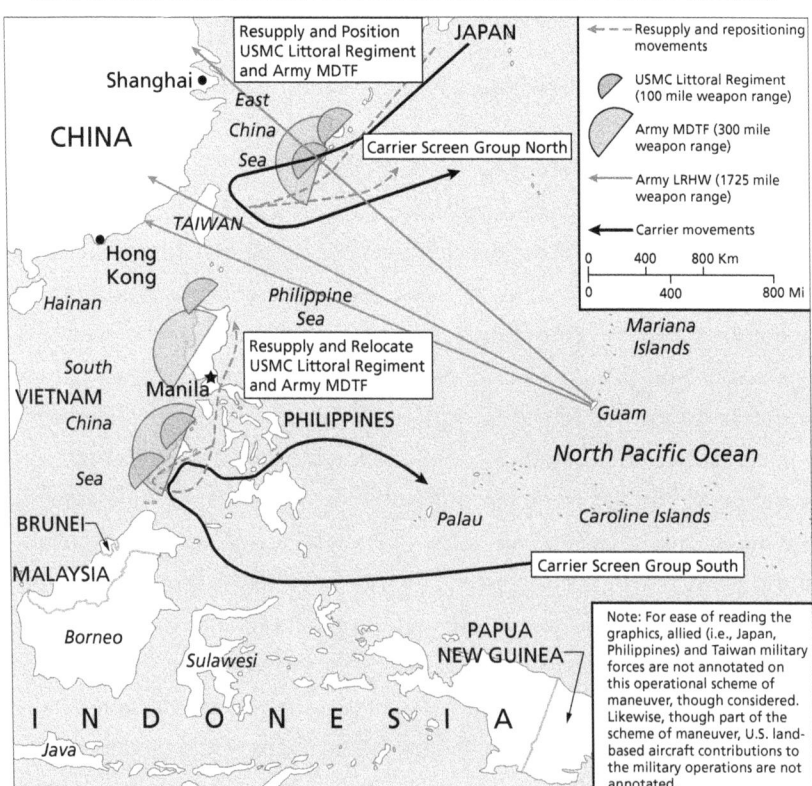

MAP 9. SCREEN TO REPOSITION FIRST ISLAND CHAIN LITTORAL FORCES *Chris Robinson*

MDTF: Multi-Domain Task Force
LRHW: Long-Range Hypersonic Weapon

Exercising at the fleet level with joint force participation (i.e., Army, Air Force), as appropriate, can test assumptions in current planning and rapidly refine the training and systems needed in a war with China. An example of the type of wartime maneuvers these problems would contribute to better understanding are summarized in schematics (see maps 9 and 10).

Too often the difference between planning assumptions and real-world realities in execution are huge. In 2019 a no-notice, large-scale logistics shipping readiness drill, Turbo Activation 19-Plus, made it clear that ships vital for sustaining military operations were only 40.7 percent ready—well below the target of 85 percent.[22] Had the logistic fleet performed like that in a real war, the potential of defeat would be unacceptably high.

That said, the proposed three Fleet Problems are not comprehensive, and similar Fleet Problems could be run that test the ability to contest

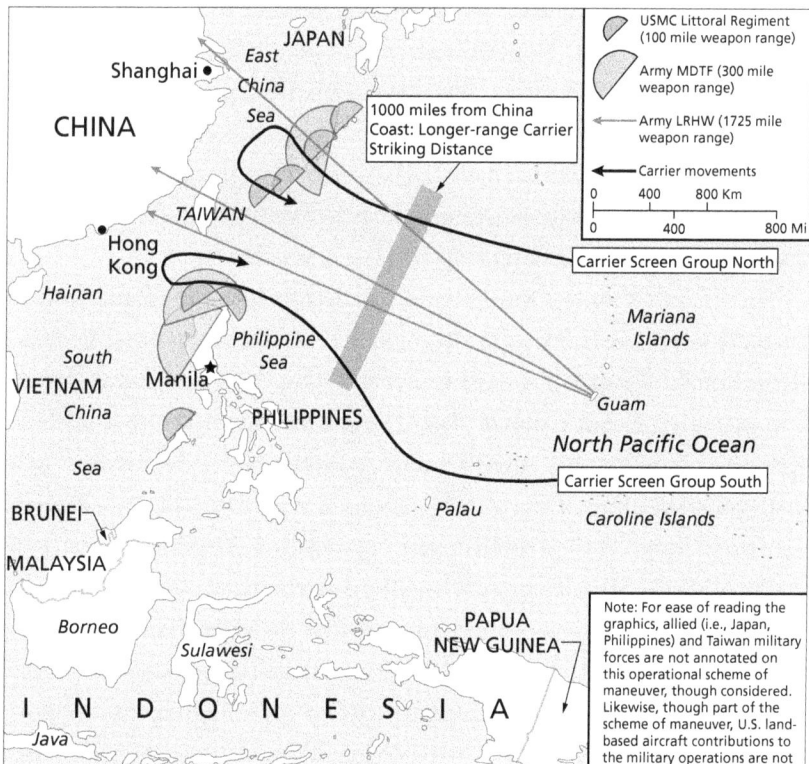

MAP 10. STRIKE GROUP SURGE UNDER FIRST ISLAND CHAIN COVERING FORCE *Chris Robinson*

a Chinese blockade of Taiwan as well as to intervene in an outer-island invasion by China, for example, the Senkaku Islands or Pratas. The experience of the Fleet Problems of the prewar era as well as Nifty Nugget make clear that real-world exercises are irreplaceable and relevant more than ever. Fleet Problems are not meant to influence adversarial thinking; that calls for a different type of operation.

SOUTHERN HOOK AND PACIFIC VENTURE

Fleet Problems are focused on the Navy and refining its planning for a future war; a naval demonstration, on the other hand, is intended to shape the minds of the adversary—and allies. Operation Ocean Venture 81 was just such an operation, which demonstrated in no uncertain terms the capability and willingness of the Navy to operate confidently in proximity to Russian forces. Ocean Venture 81 occurred seven months into the new Ronald Reagan administration at a time of austere budgets and high uncertainty of the Navy's ability to operate in the high latitudes under Russian threat. Nonetheless, these operations got the Russians' attention, and by 1983 it was clear from sensitive reporting shared with Congress that the investments made in the Navy were paying off. A similar effort is needed today to shape the Chinese strategic calculus and rally congressional support for sustaining a naval revitalization that will stand down the Chinese threat and help win the new cold war.

Success of Ocean Venture 81 was as a testament of the leadership of the secretary of the Navy, John Lehman; the personal support of the president, Ronald Reagan; but most importantly on the senior naval leadership executing it. Adm. James "Ace" Lyons was handpicked to lead these operations based on his aggressiveness, operational innovativeness, and clear understanding of the strategic dynamics at play.[23] Classified briefings with Congress directly from the man leading the effort, Lyons, and the intelligence agencies monitoring the Soviets made clear the strategy was working. The lesson of those times is that the right naval leadership, backed by the White House, with attuned intelligence can shape the adversary and make a compelling case to the American people to support the effort.

A modern Ocean Venture would build on the above lessons of 1981, with the focus today primarily on China. As such a Pacific Venture series of operations would intend to reduce Chinese confidence in their military's capabilities and increase uncertainty in their Navy's competencies to sustain itself in a long war. This would be achieved by effective fleet-level deception operations, combined operations with key allies, and sustained at-sea operations from a growing network of forward bases and facilities. Additionally, Pacific Venture would include an adjunct operation—Southern Hook—consisting of U.S. Atlantic forces and North Atlantic Treaty Organization (NATO) militaries deploying into Asian waters.

SOUTHERN HOOK

Drawing on naval forces from Europe and U.S. forces based in the Atlantic (Second and Fourth fleets), the operation would improve interoperability with key allies while repositioning from the Atlantic theater to the Indo-Pacific. This could include elements of nuclear submarines transiting under the polar ice cap and surface action groups transiting around the Cape of Good Hope and Australia into the central Pacific while implementing strict radio silence. Sailing in such a way requires atypical port stops and sustainment operations adding resiliency to logistic networks. It also adds complexity to operations that Chinese military planners will have to consider and work against.

PACIFIC VENTURE

Typically, warships deploying to the western Pacific race across the Pacific to their theater of operations, but in a Pacific Venture operation this will not be the goal. As in Southern Hook, one objective is to develop new port access and sustainment options along expected wartime transit routes. This means operating longer in the south and central Pacific and sustaining those operations from island logistic hubs nearby—American Samoa, French Polynesia, and so on. That said, the principal objective is to weaken Chinese confidence and make clear that any Russian involvement or support to China would come at a steep price. This would be achieved by demonstrating the ability to operate in force near Russian

Far Eastern centers of trade and military forces (i.e., Petropavlovsk and Vladivostok). As such, deception operations and radio silence would be practiced, creating an element of surprise and conditioning Chinese and Russian reaction over time to naval forces in the western Pacific. Taking a page from history, conditioning Chinese reactions to these naval maneuvers would be like Alexander the Great's victory over Indian King Porus across the Hydaspes River, splitting China's forces and ensuring the initiative remained with the United States.

These two operations, conducted with large naval formations, would over time favorably condition Chinese strategic calculus and operational disposition. The insights gained from their reaction to these operations would also further inform future operational planning and investments in future capabilities. Both Southern Hook and Pacific Venture would include, as appropriate, allied militaries leveraging current exercises like Pacific Vanguard with Australian, Japanese, and South Korean forces.[24]

CONCLUSION

Given the challenge of deterring a modern and larger Chinese naval force while keeping Russian adventures in check requires some fast operational learning and shaping of the adversary. This is best done by conducting naval operations like Pacific Venture to weaken Chinese military confidence and favorably condition their potential responses. Likewise, the Navy, in concert with the other armed services and those of key allies, must quickly refine their tactics and inform investments in new capabilities through a robust return to Fleet Problems. These problems would focus on improving contested logistic operations, capacity to execute strikes within China's A2/AD envelope, and maritime maneuver warfare along the first island chain. Finally, a first step to win the new cold war is to contest and roll back China's maritime insurgency in the South China Sea. These operations and activities are both necessary and costly, making sustained public support vital. Moreover, these activities cannot be sustained by a weak and vulnerable industrial backbone that will require hardening the homeland, which is covered in part 2 of this book.

PART TWO
STRENGTHENING THE HOMELAND TO WAGE PROTRACTED WAR AND RESILIENCY TO COERCION

Chinese Aggression = Military Balance + Secure Economy + Effective Political Control

FIGURE 5. Chinese aggression equation, part 2 *Author illustration*

In this part, the focus is on undermining the CCP's ability to coerce or manipulate global supply chains in order to influence U.S. political decisions. Chapter 4 exposes the dangers of a fragmented and under-resourced domestic energy sector that imperils military operations, a problem made even more stark when sustaining a wartime industry. This leads to, in chapter 5, a deeper analysis of the strategic vulnerabilities of a too-weak national maritime industrial sector. Solutions are offered that aim to secure vital shipping and regaining American shipbuilding capacity able to sustain a wartime economy. Chapter 6 lays out a naval building program introduced in *U.S. Naval Power in the 21st Century*, which is further developed with added focus on setting conditions for rapid industrial rearmament in war. The intent of these endeavors is to bolster the ability of the nation to sustain a long war with China that will weaken CCP confidence in prevailing in war, with peacetime confrontation incurring greater risk and cost to China.

CHAPTER 4

ENHANCING OPERATIONAL AND INDUSTRIAL ENERGY RESILIENCY

Energy security, the uninterrupted availability of energy sources especially to military units and the defense industry, directly impacts U.S. national security. China knows this and has bolstered its domestic energy production with the massive expansion of coal-powered electric plants, massive investment in renewable energy (i.e., solar, wind), and the addition of thirty-seven new civilian nuclear power plants between 2013 and 2023. Meanwhile, the United States has aggressively pursued a rapid transition to alternative "green" energy in recent years, in both commercial sectors and the military. Then, on March 7, 2022, the secretary of defense ordered the closure of a strategically important fuel depot on Hawaii—the massive underground Red Hill depot—due to leakage into the local aquifer. That decision, sadly, was made without first securing adequate tankers to move military fuels or to find locations to securely store it, leaving the military's operational energy needs at risk in the Pacific. Moreover, for the foreseeable future, military forces will employ ships, planes, and combat vehicles as well as significant components of defense infrastructure all dependent on an affordable, abundant, and dependable supply of petroleum.

While often good intentioned, such decisions have clear military implications of a too rapid and incomplete transition to alternative forms of energy. Given these risks, the U.S. government needs a more resilient framework of international partnerships and agreements and needs to facilitate and reduce barriers to domestic production, refining, and transport. This is all aimed at ensuring access to critical fuels for defense needs in the event of a prolonged military conflict. Remedies include rethinking the Strategic Petroleum Reserve (SPR) such that it is maintained to ensure adequate domestic energy supplies to support the military and industry in a war.[1] The size of this reserve will be a function of the nation's capacity to meet and sustain national energy needs in the transition from crisis to major war. The reserve would only be required if domestic crude production and refining cannot meet national wartime needs. Getting there will require unshackling American refiners, tapping into vast domestic energy reserves, and removing barriers to better connect the nation's energy to where it is needed. This will take time, and the nation will need stronger energy trade relationships with allies to ensure access to markets. Such access is needed to meet unfulfilled energy needs from domestic sources and refineries, sustain military units in the field, and ensure continuity of power for our allies' war efforts.

THE NATION AND ITS MILITARY CONVENTIONAL FUEL RELIANCE

America's transportation sector (trucking, rail, shipping, etc.) depends (90 percent) on gasoline, diesel, jet, and other conventional fuels; this is unlikely to change anytime soon.[2] In the transportation sector, for example, over 11 million commercial vehicles registered in the United States are diesel powered, including 97 percent of large "highway tractor-trailer size trucks."[3] Attempts by the Defense Department to shift its 170,000 nontactical vehicle fleet to electric remains a long-term endeavor and, amid congressional concerns, does not address the military's reliance on commercial logistics.[4] In the post–Cold War era, the military has become accustomed to moving critical repair parts on commercial carriers that can be subject to coercion and political interference from hostile nations. Before Congress in 2018, U.S. Transportation Command's commander stated that this situation includes potentially threatening access to energy as well as commercial carriers moving 90 percent of military personnel, and 40 percent of material shipments.[5] Without sufficient fuels, the American economy will markedly slow, which would have dire consequences for military operations reliant on a functioning domestic industry and logistic network.⁶ This problem would be especially dire during a prolonged war with China.

Deliberate policy, planning, and investments are needed to ensure that the nation can sustain prolonged military operations. This is especially true in a major war that disrupts overseas energy markets and normal shipping methods. Under such conditions, the United States will need more diverse and reliable overseas suppliers of energy for military operations. Given the global impact that a war with China would have, the United States urgently needs to ensure that it has enough fuel stocks and crude to allow the nation time to adjust to a wartime footing. In conjunction with this effort, we must also consider the time it takes to reconfigure existing refineries (years) or to build new refineries (a decade) to meet a wartime demand that cannot be securely sourced overseas, and we need to ascertain the U.S. domestic refining capacity to sustain many months of intense combat operations and wartime industrial activity with limited overseas access to refined petroleum products. In the recent past, part of the solution rested on using the global marketplace to meet domestic demand, but overseas access to markets would be constrained in a war with China.

PEACETIME MILITARY NEEDS ARE ONLY A FRACTION OF WARTIME ENERGY REQUIREMENTS

Between the years 2015 and 2020, the U.S. military consumed on average 93 million total barrels of fuel annually to sustain its operations.⁷ Almost half of this fuel was purchased from foreign sources to sustain deployed units.⁸ Military units based or operating in overseas locations typically purchase fuel from local distributors on the open market and under agreements with host nations.⁹ While these purchases are small relative to total national consumption (military consumption has averaged 0.16 percent of national consumption since fiscal year 2020), they can be impactful given that production rates have historically approximated consumption domestically.¹⁰ Because of this, the additional domestic demand to meet overseas consumption for military operations has been obscured. Transitioning to a wartime energy posture will take time, but the immediate burden of sustaining wartime operations will have to be carried by domestic transportation and energy suppliers. Those needs would specifically include refined crude oil in the forms of diesel, motor gasoline, and jet fuel.

According to the Defense Logistics Agency, which is responsible for the military's operational energy needs, it purchased 17.9 million barrels of diesel fuel in fiscal year 2022 to power logistic ships, trucks, and heavy equipment. Jet fuel, consisting of varying grades (i.e., JP4/JAB/JAA/JA1, JP5, JP8/JPTS), is used to power aircraft as well as modern naval warships using gas turbines. This represents the largest military operational energy need, requiring an average of 59.2 million barrels a year in 2020. Military requirements for motor gasoline averaged 1.2 million barrels a year since 2020.[11] Due to a heavy reliance on foreign sources, poor policy choices, and constrained transport of fuels, the U.S. military could be vulnerable to potential localized fuel shortages driven by Chinese economic coercion.

WARTIME FUEL NEEDS AND DOMESTIC SUPPLY

To sustain military wartime operations, as of March 31, 2024, the Maritime Administration (MARAD) maintained or contracted for eighty-nine vessels of varying classes as a National Defense Reserve Fleet.[12] This is augmented, as of January 17, 2024, by an additional sixty commercially active but militarily useful vessels that can be called on under terms of the Maritime Security Program.[13] This domestic fleet is woefully inadequate to sustain a nation at war. Moreover, the average age of these merchant ships is forty-five years, well over the industry end-of-life average of twenty years, and the Department of Defense faces a gap of approximately seventy-six fuel tankers to meet wartime sealift requirements.[14]

In practice, the MARAD fleet is intended to move fuel and matériel like ammunition to support combat operations. In a major prolonged war with China, this small fleet would be unable to meet combined military operational needs or to sustain a wartime economy. At the same time, this fleet would have to compete for tightening diesel fuel supplies—U.S.-flagged vessels are overwhelmingly propelled by diesel fuel.[15] Because of the scale of shipping required to sustain wartime operations and a wartime economy, the demand for shipping and energy at home would be larger than anything seen in the recent past and difficult to predict.

Moreover, if a conflict were to erupt with China, maritime trade would be massively disrupted, forcing the military to rely on fuel stockpiles—for a time. Most pressing in the early months of a conflict would be the potential loss under Chinese threat of overseas suppliers that the peacetime military has grown accustomed to using. To mitigate such shocks, the military stockpiles fuel at strategically important locations such as the Red Hill Bulk Fuel Storage facility in Hawaii. However, due to years of neglect, that facility is decommissioned and replacements remain to be found.[16] Without adequate fuel reserves or the ability to move fuel to the ships and aircraft using it, the military is in a potentially precarious position. In a war with China, the interplay between civilian and industry needs for fuel and that for wartime combat operations remains an unknown. Ostensibly, weathering this transition to a war footing would be eased by the SPR.

THE ROLE OF THE STRATEGIC PETROLEUM RESERVE NEEDS AN UPDATE

Legislation in 1975 established the SPR to mitigate energy shocks, such as the oil crises of the 1970s; the SPR is only mandated to hold a ninety-day reserve of crude oil, which is not based on wartime usage.[17] Since 2015 Congress has enacted seven bills mandating sales of up to 271 million barrels of crude oil from the strategic reserves. This was based on imports of crude narrowing as domestic production rose, making larger reserves seemingly unneeded. Importantly, due to historical market trends decades old, American refineries are predominantly tuned to process heavy crude oil, not domestic light sweet, which is one reason why the nation imports significant amounts of crude oil (heavy/sour).[18] Of course, many of today's American refineries, while tuned for heavy crude, can still process light crude but at a lower production rate.[19] Another factor weighing on U.S. energy imports is the use of the most economically accessible refined products. New England, for example, relies on nearby and cheaper Canadian-refined petroleum.[20] This situation is repeated in other parts of the country, which could provide an opportunity for an adversary to coerce the United States. According to Susan Grissom of American Fuel & Petrochemical Manufacturers, "U.S. refining capacity is already sufficient to produce enough product to meet US demand—it's just not produced in the region where it's needed and there isn't transportation infrastructure to move it economically."[21] For these reasons, the SPR and the crude-refining capacity alone are inadequate to minimize risk to access and transport of U.S. fuel. Actions are needed to ensure that the United States has adequate crude on hand and can refine it at rates needed for a wartime economy and that the military has the associated ability to move those fuels where needed.

Making matters worse is a political proclivity to tap the SPR, which is a reserve of crude oil, not refined petroleum products. Case in point: President Joe Biden's March 2022 decision and final sale in October 2022, ahead of the midterm elections, were a plainly visible attempt to suppress gas prices by releasing 180 million barrels for political benefit; the move ended up dropping inventories by almost a third.[22] By October 2022 only a twenty-five-day supply of distillate fuel (diesel varieties) was on hand in the nation—which would have been inadequate for managing the initial shock of a conflict.[23] The problem has not improved much since then, with inventories remaining at near-record lows as of November 2023.[24] While reserves remained at historic lows, President Biden once again sold historically large amounts of the SPR's crude, rationalizing these sales as in accordance with two 2015 laws; section 403 of the Bipartisan Budget Act of 2015 and section 32204 of the Fixing America's Surface Transportation Act.[25] In the meantime, the February 2023 sale of 26 million barrels drove the reserves down to 345 million barrels of crude—this, at a time when private inventories were precipitously dropping, leaving little surge capacity for a crisis.[26] On November 8, 2022, the Energy Information Administration (EIA) estimated that distillate fuel (i.e., fuel used in trucks, heavy equipment, heating) inventories in the United States were at "the lowest end-of-October level since 1951" and forecasted that these inventories in 2023 will maintain low numbers, at "17% below the five-year average."[27] The inventory has not moved much since, and as of

January 5, 2024, the SPR contained 355 million barrels of crude oil—a level not seen since 1983.[28] The SPR should be set aside so that when the nation finds itself in the middle of a crisis, it has the needed crude to refine into operationally useful fuels. Better yet, policies are needed in peacetime that allow drillers and refiners to drill and refine toward the capacity necessary—ideally meeting or exceeding capacities required in a major war, thus eliminating the need for the SPR.

In 2008 the Heritage Foundation conducted a computer simulation and war game assessing the impacts of a global energy crisis. The trigger for that crisis was terrorist attacks that effectively closed the Straits of Hormuz and Straits of Malacca, cutting off 24 percent of global crude shipments. The conclusion was not reassuring. Market forces, if pursued, would have seen a rapid recovery and adjustment of supplies, but this was found to be unlikely to occur.[29] The cause for this is that governments driven by narrow self-interest would be less inclined to trust markets beyond their control, especially in a crisis. It is worth noting that, at the time of this simulation, the United States had yet to realize the shale oil production boom and was more reliant on Middle East supplies. Also worth noting: In a modern war with China, the United States would likely be joined by allies Japan, South Korea, the Philippines, and Australia. These allies are reliant on petroleum from the Persian Gulf. As such, there would be even more demand for American petroleum to make up for supplies interdicted by China. Bottom line, the deficit in energy production among allies is dangerously low and vulnerable. Some of this was witnessed as NATO countries tried weaning themselves off Russian petroleum following its February 2022 invasion of Ukraine.

In 2015—given the inability of the Organization of Petroleum Exporting Countries (OPEC) to control markets, and amid abundant private inventories, untapped reserves, and open markets—the SPR seemed of little utility.[30] Recommendations at the time to sell off and terminate the SPR made sense because it was never intended to—nor arguably functioned effectively to—manipulate markets. Since then, however, China's military and economy have grown to be a major global influencer able and having demonstrated a willingness to apply economic statecraft and increase military coercion to impose its will. In this new reality, the role of the SPR will need to be reimagined as it relates to ensuring national energy security. This is critical against a foe with the wherewithal to interdict or delay fuel supplies, particularly in the combat theater but increasingly globally, given China's cyber, economic, and military reach. Specifically, the challenge is to ensure that the U.S. military and a wartime economy has adequate fuel supplies to conduct a prolonged war. This should guide an updated charter for the SPR and inform policies that would enhance the nation's energy security, which in time would diminish the need for the SPR.

To revise the SPR's charter would require changing political attitudes and legislation. So far, thinking about the SPR does not consider

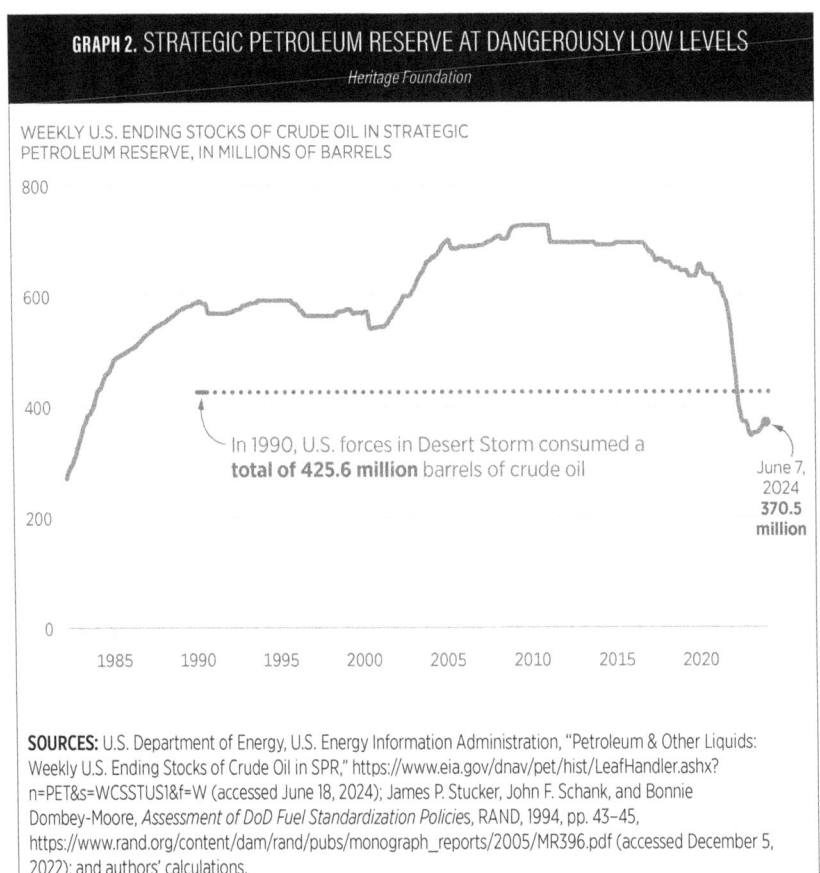

GRAPH 2. STRATEGIC PETROLEUM RESERVE AT DANGEROUSLY LOW LEVELS
Heritage Foundation

WEEKLY U.S. ENDING STOCKS OF CRUDE OIL IN STRATEGIC PETROLEUM RESERVE, IN MILLIONS OF BARRELS

In 1990, U.S. forces in Desert Storm consumed a **total of 425.6 million** barrels of crude oil

June 7, 2024
370.5 million

SOURCES: U.S. Department of Energy, U.S. Energy Information Administration, "Petroleum & Other Liquids: Weekly U.S. Ending Stocks of Crude Oil in SPR," https://www.eia.gov/dnav/pet/hist/LeafHandler.ashx?n=PET&s=WCSSTUS1&f=W (accessed June 18, 2024); James P. Stucker, John F. Schank, and Bonnie Dombey-Moore, *Assessment of DoD Fuel Standardization Policies*, RAND, 1994, pp. 43–45, https://www.rand.org/content/dam/rand/pubs/monograph_reports/2005/MR396.pdf (accessed December 5, 2022); and authors' calculations.

the implications for transitioning the nation to a war footing against China. To make matters worse, the Red Hill fuel storage facility closure compounds the shortfall of robust national fuel stocks near where the military needs them. And in a war where China is likely to use all means, including cyber, to slow or cut our domestic fuel transport, the federal SPR's four proximate locations in Texas and Louisiana are vulnerable. Having the SPR in one region eases an adversary's task to cut it off from where it is needed, so one key step to securing the fuel stocks would be moving crude and refined fuels to the West Coast, from where military operations in Asia would be sustained. Given a challenging geography (i.e., the Continental Divide and Rocky Mountains) and state regulatory environments, crude oil pipelines do not adequately connect the rest of the nation to the West Coast; only two refined petroleum pipelines make the connection.[31]

INADEQUATE TRANSPORT RENDERS STRATEGIC AND PRIVATE RESERVES OF LIMITED UTILITY

The concentration of the SPR and refinery capacity in the Gulf Coast region presents numerous challenges for getting needed fuels to the U.S. military. Limited energy transportation to the West Coast and New England complicates things; eastern states are heavily reliant on one pipeline. This fractured domestic energy logistic network makes getting fuel to where it is needed tenuous. For instance, New England has almost no pipeline connectivity to domestic sources, and the existing pipelines are maxed out. These are also prone to cyberattack, as demonstrated by a successful May 2021 attack on the Colonial Pipeline. That incident stopped for six days critical energy flows from Gulf Coast refineries to New York City.[32] Moreover, as former White House official Diana Furchtgott-Roth points out, recurring train derailments and ecological disasters, such as that in East Palestine, Ohio, in February 2023, should have been a clarion call for more and safer pipelines. While the Ohio train wreck involved petrochemicals, pipelines do safely transport crude, natural gas, and nonblended (not yet mixed with ethanol) gasoline.[33] Sadly, the Securities and Exchange Commission, the Board of Governors, and the Comptroller of the Currency have been standing in the way of new pipelines for what now is a misplaced ecological concern over common sense.[34]

The New England states made headlines in the fall of 2022 when fuel suppliers began rationing large consumers as fuel inventories shrank well below five-year averages. Then, in October 2022, Georgia-based Mansfield Energy issued a "code red" alert for a number of southeastern U.S. states, signaling widening diesel supply shortages.[35] At the same time, some wholesalers in northeastern states began rationing heating oil, preparing for winter with increased demand driving down reserves.[36] As previously mentioned, without sufficient pipeline capacity, New England is highly dependent on fuel inventories and imports via ships. Because Jones Act limitations make it cheaper and faster to import from foreign providers rather than domestic sources, compliant domestic shipping is rarely used and is too scarce to meet demand.[37] In a war, despite New England's industrial and military importance, the availability of wartime shipping is both critical and uncertain given the paucity of U.S.-flagged tankers.

California's situation is different because it has marginally adequate refining capacity.[38] But, as in New England, California's self-imposed constraints are undermining its energy security. California has passed a number of "net-zero" climate policies to eliminate the use of petroleum and other conventional fuels in a preference for electrification. This is representative of the state's decades-long effort, sending strong market signals to not invest in new oil production, pipelines, or refining capacity. This political isolation is made worse by a paucity of pipelines and transportation that, when it comes to energy supplies, are effectively isolated from the rest of the nation. This requires California to rely heavily on its own refineries to meet demand. Unfortunately, due to a combination of regulations driving consumers to renewables and environmental mandates, it has become more economical there for remaining refineries to transition to alternative fuels such as renewable diesel, or biofuels.[39] This trend will have a deleterious impact on California's existing refining capacity. The International Energy Forum notes that "output of a converted refinery is typically much lower."[40] In one example, California's Rodeo refinery produces 50,000 barrels a day of renewable fuel but had refined 72,000 barrels a day of fuel before retooling.[41] However, the actual total of refining loss is upward of 120,000 barrels a day considering that the associated Santa Maria refinery closed in the first quarter of 2023 to support the Rodeo refinery's conversion to renewables.[42] The effect is that, today, California refining capacity will be unable to meet future energy needs let alone needs during a crisis. Unsurprisingly, the EIA observes that California's fuel prices are extremely sensitive "and react strongly to relatively small changes in supply."[43] California is host to major military facilities critical to sustaining combat operations, making such systemic energy brittleness a strategic vulnerability in a prolonged war with China.

REMOVE SELF-DEFEATING RULES AND LEGISLATION— RETIRING ESG WARRIORS AND THE JONES ACT

When it comes to shifting political thinking and rules preventing adequate provision of energy needs for a war, two issues need to be addressed: first, to free American industry from the distraction of environmental, social, and governance (ESG) special interests; and, second, to begin the process of removing the shackles on American shipping imposed by the Jones Act. On the first, U.S. financial institutions have increasingly been pressured by progressive interest groups to adopt ESG policies, such as net-zero.[44] The effect of this pressure is to disincentivize investment in relatively clean, reliable, and affordable energy production in favor of renewables, markets for which—in battery production, solar cell fabrication, and wind turbine construction—China largely controls.[45] ESG is also affecting firms residing in treaty allies overseas, combining into a potential disaster that undermines U.S. foreign and national security policies.[46] ESG policies are increasing the United States' dependence on China for renewables, undermining attempts at energy independence, and weakening the nation's economic resiliency, thereby further opening the country to Chinese economic coercion.

The Jones Act, on the other hand, has not delivered on its mandate (see chapter 5) to ensure that the nation has a minimum of domestic shipping and merchant mariners to sustain the nation in war. The act's mandate that only U.S.-crewed and -produced ships may conduct shipments between U.S. ports has been unworkable for years. Too often Jones Act–conforming ships able to move fuels like liquefied natural gas are not available, requiring other ships to obtain waivers.[47] This exacerbates an underlying mismatch between the amount of fuel that the nation will need to fight and win a war with China and what would likely be available where it is needed.[48] Meeting wartime demands for fuel requires increasing access to foreign sources of crude, maintaining adequate domestic refining, and providing enough reliable transport to meet a wartime economy's needs.

WARTIME ENERGY NEEDS AND OVERSEAS SUPPLY

The recent diesel supply issues in New England reflect wider inadequacies of U.S. energy policies to ensure adequate supplies for all citizens in peacetime. In wartime, the situation could result in a dangerously inadequate supply to meet U.S. wartime needs. Following Russia's invasion of Ukraine, the United States accelerated its move off Russian petroleum imports—at the time, the nation's fifth-largest source of imported crude oil and petroleum products. In 2021 Russia accounted for 7.9 percent of all U.S. petroleum imports.[49] Without the normal influx of those Russian products, the United States has had to find alternative sources in the global market. This added to already increasing price of gasoline and diesel due to a raft of policies the then-new Biden administration implemented; from Inauguration Day January 2021 to the eve of Russia's invasion in February 2022, gasoline had increased in price 48 percent, and diesel rose 49 percent during the same time.[50] Moreover, beginning in early December 2022 through February 2023, European Union sanctions on Russian oil and petroleum products had ramped up into full effect.[51] The result has been further tightened fuel markets, driving buyers to find new suppliers to meet global demand while not falling afoul of sanctions (e.g., Iran, Venezuela, and Russia).[52] Confronted by the prospect of a shortfall in natural gas supplies, the European Union responded with mandatory reductions in energy use.[53] And things have only gotten worse with the

Houthis of Yemen attacking shipping passing through the strategically important Bab-el-Mandeb strait—a quarter of the world's shipping carrying 10 percent of global commerce passes this strait.[54]

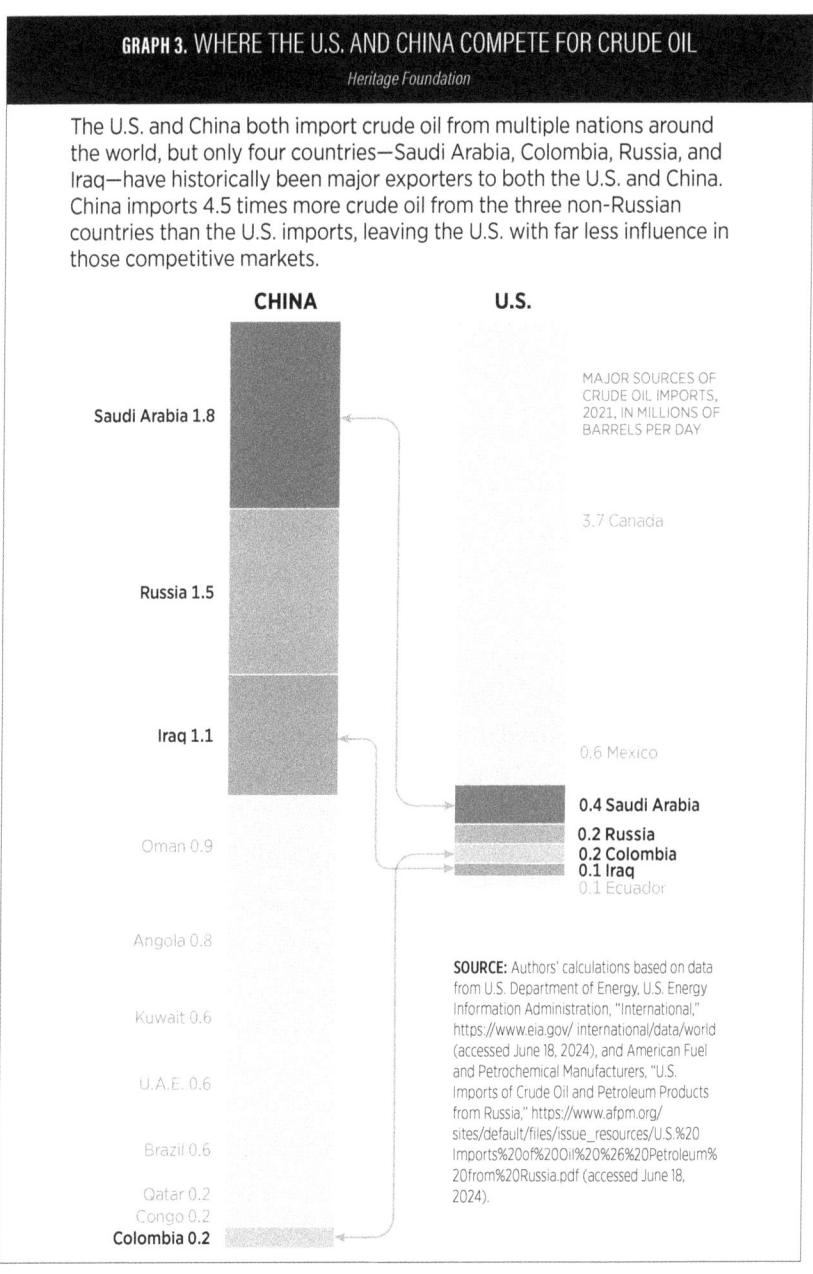

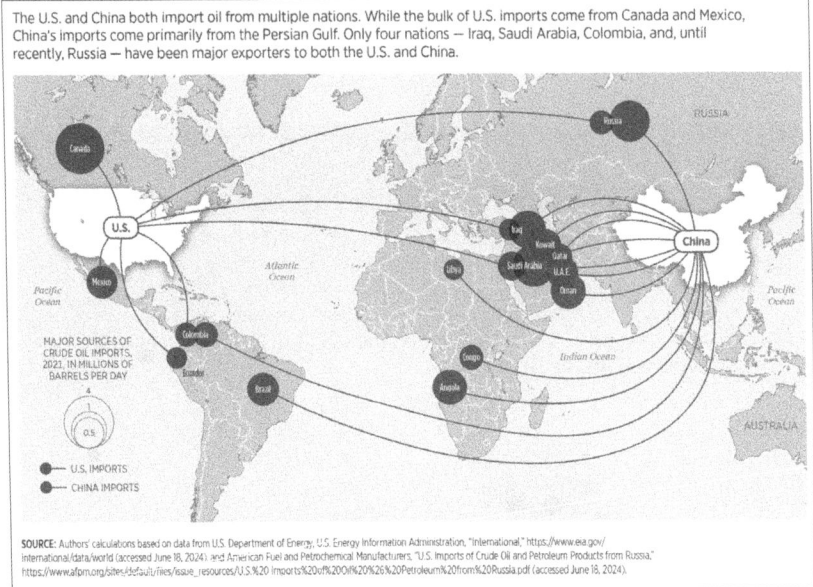

MAP 11. MAJOR SOURCES OF U.S. AND CHINESE OIL IMPORTS *Heritage Foundation*

The U.S. and China both import oil from multiple nations. While the bulk of U.S. imports come from Canada and Mexico, China's imports come primarily from the Persian Gulf. Only four nations — Iraq, Saudi Arabia, Colombia, and, until recently, Russia — have been major exporters to both the U.S. and China.

Additionally, during the Covid-19 pandemic, low fuel demand and consumption contributed to refineries facing major financial setbacks. Making matters worse was the Environmental Protection Agency's Renewable Fuel Standard that mandated "biofuels be blended into gasoline and diesel fuels."[55] This requirement burdened refineries with compliance costs that added downward pressures on the nation's refining capacity. Eventually, five U.S. refineries were permanently closed, shrinking overall capacity.

The U.S. military typically procures about half of its fuel from foreign sources to sustain deployed units.[56] In peacetime, sourcing fuel overseas near where it is needed makes good business sense. However, in war this may not be viable, especially as ports in East Asia become inaccessible due to Chinese long-range strikes or nations refusing U.S. deliveries for fear of Chinese reprisals. Nonetheless, the military needs several grades of fuel to operate.

Importantly, jet fuel is not only for aircraft but also for the gas turbines that power many of the nation's warships—as well as those of many allied navies.[57] Likewise, diesel fuel in several varieties propels large logistics ships and commercial shipping that an allied war effort will rely on to move material to any front. According to the United Nations and the International Maritime Organization, the world's commercial fleet of almost 54,000 large (greater than 1,000 gwt) vessels carried 10.6 billion tons of cargo in 2020 and is overwhelmingly propelled by several grades of diesel.[58] Moving this cargo required over 27 million tons of fuel (diesel/gas) consumed by ships worldwide. However, carbon zero (so-called net-zero) initiatives are today suppressing investments to grow global refining capacity. That said, the EIA reported that global refining capacity grew by 1 million barrels a day in 2022 and was expected to continue this growth by 1.6 million barrels a day in 2023 as new refineries in Southeast Asia and the Middle East came online.[59] However, without further growth, as the EIA predicts this decade, global refining capacity will top out at 105.2 million barrels a day by 2030.[60] This growth, however, is not pacing demand for refined fuels, which the EIA also reported grew by 2.2 million barrels a day in 2022 and projected demand would grow by 1.9 million barrels a day in 2023.[61] This situation, if it persists, will conceivably make it harder and more expensive for existing ships to source needed fuel until new, greener merchant ships come to market—which is not expected to begin until well into the 2030s.[62] In the meantime, there is no consensus on what this new fuel will be and how to economically transition to its use by merchant ships—in total, it is estimated the transition will cost $3 trillion and take decades to accomplish.[63]

The prolonged shocks of the Russian invasion of Ukraine and resurgent demands following the Covid-19 pandemic pressured the global supply of crude and refined petroleum products. At the same time, net-zero policies are having an immediate impact, driving down refining capacity and making global energy shortages more and not less likely, despite an abundance of crude oil.[64]

THE DILEMMA OF REFINING CAPACITY AND TRANSPORT

Petroleum refineries, whether at home or abroad, make products such as transportation fuels or heating oil processed from crude oil. In 2023 there were 124 U.S. operating petroleum refineries (5 were idle) with an

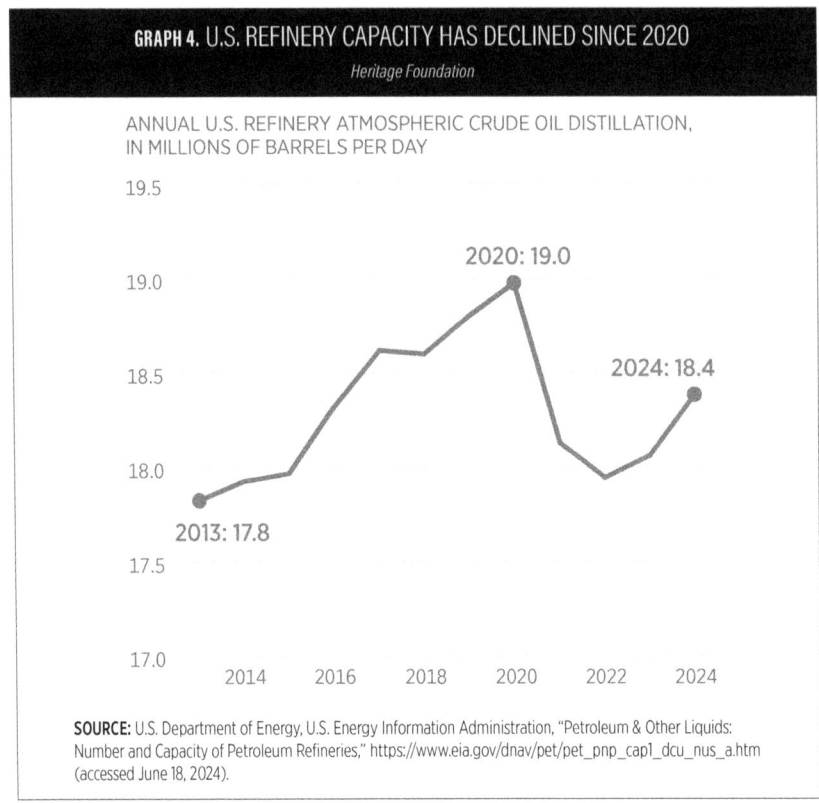

operable crude distillation capacity to process 17.9 million barrels of crude oil per day.[65] That is almost 1 million barrels less than the 19 million barrels per day in 2020 and is the lowest capacity since 2015.

American fuel security is a function of oil production, trade relationships, transportation, pipeline infrastructure, refineries, and inventories. Moreover, according to the EIA's International Energy Outlook, there is no scenario in which global demand for oil does not increase through at least 2050.[66] This new demand strains overseas stocks as most American refineries process heavy crude oil.[67] The current political environment in the United States is unfortunately working in ways that hampers the market response to surges in demand.

In 1949 there were 336 functioning oil refineries in the United States operating at a use rate of 89 percent and capable of refining 6.2 million barrels per day. While not a consistent decline, the number of American refineries has fallen every decade since then, and remaining refineries grew in capacity.[68] This has resulted in greater reliance on fewer refineries to produce more refined petroleum. The benefit of economies of scale with fewer but larger refineries is geographically concentrating the nation's refining capacity. A lesson of the strategic bombing campaigns of World War II and the bombing campaigns during the Vietnam War was that the energy industry's disposition to concentrated refining sites makes it easier for an adversary to target (with cyber, sabotage, etc.) energy supply with greater probability of significant operational impact.[69] Such risks should be considered, but consolidation is not, per se, a bad thing if it is driven by organic market pressures. However, in recent years harmful energy policies are driving this energy production geographic consolidation. Additionally, as seen in California and the northeastern United States, policy choices are affecting refining capacities.

Crude oil refinery capacity fell in the start of 2021 to the lowest level in the United States since 2015, with refineries closing, downsizing, or converting to renewable fuels.[70] That said, national refining capacity is not evenly distributed; in the East Coast region (PADD-1), there is little refining capacity. Today there are only seven refineries on the whole East Coast and zero operating U.S. refineries northeast of Pennsylvania.[71] Moreover, there is inadequate pipeline capacity north of Pennsylvania. The result: by the fall of 2022, inventories reached lows not seen for that time of year since 1974, when the EIA began collecting inventory data.[72] This has resulted in the region being reliant on overseas suppliers—even when the nation became a net energy exporter from 2019.[73] Altogether in wartime or a crisis, global trends in refinery capacity and inventories will constrain access to, or markedly increase cost for, supplying the military.

Added to this are non–market forces—sanctions, untold amounts of red tape, and decarbonization regulations—curtailing needed investment to sustain today's refining capacity and meet future energy needs. As a result, 2021 was the first year that net global refining capacity fell in three decades.[74] Roughly two-thirds of these losses occurred outside the United States.[75] The International Energy Forum states that "since March

2020, global refining capacity has fallen by 3.8 mb/d [million barrels per day], while global demand has grown by 5.6 mb/d."[76] However, very little investment is occurring in the United States or Europe where "net-zero" climate policies to forcefully phase out oil production and use are in place or being pursued. Refinery capacity in the United States fell again in 2023 with the closure of the 268,000 barrels-per-day refinery LyondellBasell in Houston to achieve "decarbonization goals" rather than upgrade the century-old plant.[77] This drop will be partially offset as the nearby new Beaumont refinery reaches its notional refining capacity of 250,000 barrels a day by the end of March 2023.[78] Despite an abundance of domestic oil—a competitive advantage for refineries in reducing costs and maintaining high use rates—there are no plans for any new, large refineries in the United States.[79] And should any plan come forward for new refineries, they would nominally take a decade to build and begin operations. Additionally, bans on Russian petroleum products have increased, and will continue to increase, competition for non-Russian fuel, limited available shipping to transport it, and forced regions like Europe into bidding competitions with higher-demand regions like Asia. The effect is higher costs but potentially limited availability of militarily useful fuels on the global open market, upon which deployed forces rely.

Moreover, a decrease in U.S. refining capacity directly impacts how much and how quickly America can meet surging diesel, gasoline, and jet fuel demands in a long war. In the United States, the gasoline used at the pump typically consists of 10 percent ethanol—produced as a renewable fuel additive.[80] According to EIA data, 95 percent of 2021 national ethanol production came from corn to be used as blendstock for oxygenate blending. For this reason, ethanol production is centered in the Midwest, given the region's corn farming.[81] Due to ethanol's oxygen-scavenging properties, blending typically occurs near to the customer or is shipped on trains, barges, or trucks using containers to avoid potential contamination with air or water. The nation exceeds its ethanol needs and meets its gasoline needs. But California, seeking carbon reductions, imports not-counted ethanol from Brazil over counted domestic sources to meet the state's low-carbon fuel standards.[82]

A less complex process is involved with jet fuel and diesel production, making an assessment more straightforward. Jet fuel consumption led production prior to 2020, but this reversed because of depressed demand during the Covid-19 pandemic. By 2022 demand met production but could widen again if production does not pace demand to pre-pandemic levels.[83] And, although diesel consumption levels have been lower than production in recent years, this margin is narrowing.[84] Overall, consumption and production are nearly matched in these three militarily useful fuels. Achieving this balance in 2022 involved importing crude oil at a rate of 6.3 million barrels a day—predominately heavy crude oil, to efficiently match domestic refining needs.[85] However, should overseas sources of heavy crude oil be disrupted, and should American refineries be forced to refine more domestic light sweet crude, production rates will slacken, upsetting the current balance between production and consumption. Moreover, in a war, regions like New England and California that are not well connected to domestic sources of fuels and that have limited refining capacity could face severe disruptions.

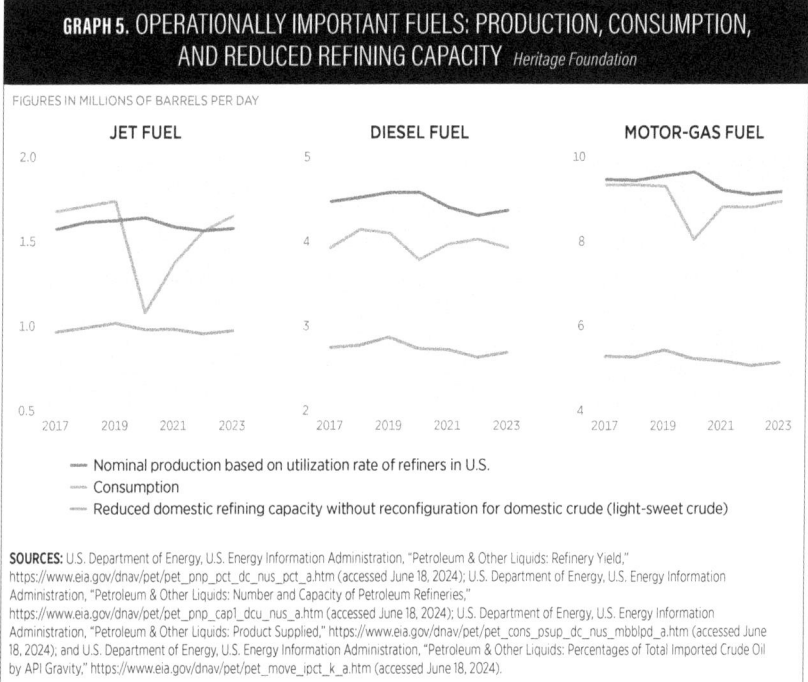

CONCLUSION

Ensuring the nation's wartime need for energy requires adequate domestic production and transportation to where the energy is needed. It also means addressing present shortfalls by securing access to overseas producers and appropriate shipping to move those fuels. To do this will require assessing the nation's comprehensive energy needs and vulnerabilities and entering more formal arrangements with allies to better ensure that deployed military forces in combat have access to needed fuels.

The first step is to assess the situation. This is no small task and will require defense, commerce, and energy-related agencies of the government to work with industry to determine what is needed. Initially, given the precariousness of the military's energy needs, the secretary of defense will need to identify the minimum level of reserves in diesel, gasoline, and jet fuel required to meet military wartime needs. This in turn sets a baseline for wartime energy needs to be met by the most secure sources of energy—domestic production or assured access from allies. This, however, is not enough, and as the nation transitions to a war footing, sustaining wartime industry will be critical. A fuller assessment of national wartime energy needs must therefore include the industrial energy needs to support military operations as well as industrial production. This forms what could be called a national wartime energy baseline. This baseline in turn should inform what reserves are needed in which fuels, minimum safe domestic refining capacity, and energy transportation needs in the case of a war with China.

To ensure readiness for a worst-case scenario, a war with China, it will be important to periodically assess the nation's energy resiliency—call these energy health reports. The secretary of defense and the secretary of energy would most likely be responsible for these reports, which should be provided to Congress on a quarterly basis. The reports would note domestic refining capacity in militarily useful fuels and the national inventories of these fuels—commercially and militarily. Included would be an assessment of inventories, adequacy of transport, and the time needed to transition existing refineries to produce militarily useful fuels from domestic crude oil sources, should overseas sources be disrupted. Such a report would require the Department of Defense to assure Congress that replacements for sites like Red Hill are in fact adequate. Altogether, these reports would inform recommendations for adjusting the size of the SPR. As domestic crude production increases and compatible domestic refinery capacity increases, the SPR could be reduced as the margin for meeting a national wartime energy need narrows or is erased.

Next, as the nation transitions from a peacetime market economy to a wartime one, there would be disruptions and unexpected developments impacting the sustainment of the war effort. Supporting allies' energy needs, too, would add to this dilemma, further stressing domestic energy production and transport. To mitigate these eventualities, it will be important to prepare for this transition. Building on the assessments just described, actions taken to ensure energy resiliency would be needed—and at the top of the list, reimagining the SPR.

Today's reserve, the SPR, does not function to meet national or military need for various types of fuels in a prolonged war. Given the global influence of China on markets and the ability to interfere with U.S. access to overseas energy, new legislation is needed that addresses this reality. Future strategic reserve legislation should ensure that the nation has robust access to energy markets in wartime and, in the worst case, adequate fuel reserves and refinery capacity so the United States and its allies cannot be coerced by China. Removing regulations meant to suppress investment in cleaner, efficient domestic petroleum refining will need to be rethought and greater capacity for refining at home will need to be sought. In peacetime this would make the nation a supplier of energy while, in war, the nation would have the latent capacity to meet wartime needs. This makes even more sense when considering that there are vast American reserves of petroleum. Waiting until a war to tap into these reserves and build the refining capacity needed would be too late.

Additionally, the examples of New England and California point to the need for more pipelines to move energy across the country safely and with confidence. The need for pipelines is made more necessary given a persistent paucity of U.S.-flagged tankers to move fuels during a crisis. This will require rethinking regulations and approaches to moving domestic crude from extraction to refining to customer. This will likely lead to a modern version of an energy highway akin to the Eisenhower interstate highway system that originally was meant to address military needs to move troops and equipment across the country quickly. Additionally, given the current reliance on foreign shipping and even rail in some cases, the secretaries of state and commerce will need to combine efforts and secure from key friendly crude- and refined petroleum–producing nations an agreement to ensure energy supplies during conflict. The Defense Logistics Agency currently has memoranda of understanding with several nations regarding provision of petroleum products to the military, and these should be reviewed with an eye to moving them to treaty obligations. In concert with this effort, agreements are needed with key shipping firms and their parent governments to ensure delivery during conflict. A vehicle for this is a maritime group of nations, discussed in chapter 5.

While informal multinational maritime organizations like a maritime group of nations would be needed, there is more the nation needs to do with partner nations. Top of the list is routinizing the exceptions often sought for foreign shippers to conduct business in the United States, especially during crises like natural disasters. A good example of this was the 2022 Jones Act waiver given to move supplies into Puerto Rico after Hurricane Fiona. However, modifications to the Jones Act in recent years have gone in the other direction. In a budget deal sealed in December 2022, Congress tightened Jones Act waiver processes, which has encouraged the import of foreign petroleum to northeast states since there are not enough compliant tankers available to meet demand.[86] The next chapter lays out a path ahead for regaining American shipping, which will take years to achieve. In the meantime, until adequate U.S. shipping is available to meet domestic demand, exceptions should be made lasting for ships registered, flagged, and crewed by select NATO countries, Japan, Philippines, and South Korea, to provide services between U.S. ports.

Shipping is one facet of the movement of energy to consider; pipelines are another. That said, Canada and Mexico are the United States' two largest energy trading partners, but they face unnecessary constraints.[87] The best example of this has been a decade-long resistance to the Keystone XL pipeline, which would have brought Canadian crude to American refineries in the south. On his first day in office as president, on January 20, 2021, Joe Biden revoked licenses needed and effectively killed the Keystone XL project. Without cross-border pipelines like Keystone XL, the nation is less able to mitigate shocks to its energy market with a trusted ally like Canada and neighbor Mexico. At the same time, countries in Latin America, Africa, Eastern Europe, and Southeast Asia are home to burgeoning energy resources but susceptible to investment from China and Russia known to weaponize energy markets for political control.[88] Aside from cross-border pipelines, improving the nation's access to energy markets will require a change in American diplomacy. Too often ESG and not national interests have shaped American energy diplomacy. Given the brittleness of the nation's current energy supply chain, a new theme for American energy and climate diplomacy should be energy resiliency. Given the higher standards of American energy production, this new focus would be complimentary to environmental improvement efforts as well as developing more resilient access to energy.

The nation's energy supply chain is too brittle; in some regions it is unable to easily adjust to surges in demand. In wartime, the consequences could be an inability to sustain military combat operations and a wartime industry unable to keep the nation armed. Readiness for this potentiality serves to deter China by presenting it a foe able to wage a prolonged war backed by a resilient wartime economy and industry. At the same time, an America self-reliant for its operational energy needs strengthens its overall strategic position over a China reliant on foreign fuels. Key in achieving this resiliency will be a strengthened American maritime industrial sector, taken up in the next chapter.

CHAPTER 5

HOW A REVOLUTION IN SHIPPING CAN REGAIN AMERICAN MARITIME STRENGTH

For too long the United States has neglected a core element of its security and prosperity—its commercial maritime strength. Of the more than 80,000 port visits by ships engaged in trade arriving at American ports in 2019, less than two hundred such ships were U.S. flagged, owned, and crewed.[1] The result is that American shipping and shipbuilding has dangerously atrophied. Yet our nation's overall domestic industrial sector and capacity for innovation remains strong. As such, this maritime problem can be solved. Doing so requires the United States to unleash latent American potential to address our critical maritime shortcomings. This will better ensure that the nation's security and prosperity are not hostage to the whims of unfriendly nations.

During the post–Cold War period the nation slowly ceded its economic security by increasingly relying on other nations' shipping and shipbuilding. Most concerning of these nations is China, which has relentlessly constructed a world-class merchant fleet, invested in over one hundred ports in sixty-three countries, and now has a commanding market share of the world's shipbuilding.[2] While the United States is fast losing its naval leadership, for many years it has not had the shipping fleet or the mariners to stay in a fight with China.

Critically, America has not sustained a viable merchant marine fleet worthy of its global economic reach or able to sustain the U.S. military in securing national interests abroad. Consequently, the nation today is vulnerable to economic interference—or potentially blackmail—by nations like China, a sample of which was evident during the Covid-19 pandemic, when China's zero-Covid policies shut down ports in China, holding up supplies for U.S. industry as well as, crucially, the containers in which to ship U.S. products, thus preventing U.S. container shipping from leaving U.S. ports.[3] A stronger and globally competitive U.S. maritime sector serves as a deterrent to Chinese economic coercion and military adventures because, with it, American trade can proceed with confidence even during a crisis with China, and the U.S. military could sustain combat operations with U.S.-flagged vessels. The nation needs a viable merchant fleet to ensure resiliency to crises and sustain a wartime economy, especially should the nation find itself in a major war with a country like China.

NEW THINKING REQUIRED

Getting the needed merchant marine fleet will require new thinking. Despite the best intentions of the century-old Jones Act, the few ships that are domestically produced, flagged, and crewed are not competitive in the world marketplace.[4] One estimate from the Department of Defense U.S. Transportation Command estimates that regulatory costs, mandates, and labor costs render U.S.-produced ships twenty-six times more expensive than sourcing overseas, costs that must be recouped via higher shipping rates.[5] This cripples the entire industry while saddling the nation with costs estimated at $9.8 billion per year.[6] In tandem with this decline, America's ability to sustain a Navy and merchant marine commensurate with its strategic interests in the competition with China and others has eroded to a dangerous level. The solution is not to pursue government remedies but rather to unleash American ingenuity in a bold new conceptualization of global logistics that, if properly executed, could reinvigorate the nation's maritime sector.

For the nation to modernize its domestic maritime sector, it must partner with dependable, longtime maritime allies such as Japan, South Korea, and the Philippines. This group of like-minded maritime nations can erase our cost disadvantage in both shipbuilding and crewing, which is necessary if we are to leverage cutting-edge technologies to revive the nation's leadership in the maritime sector. Just as America would not be able to dominate the tech sector without cheap microchips from Taiwan, America cannot compete in the maritime sector if it is locked into inputs costing twenty-six times the going rate. By creating these partnerships, the nation can leverage its human resources and technological and financing advantages to regain a competitive edge that would prove decisive in a prolonged conflict with China.

America today is far too dependent on hostile nations like China to convey its trade, leaving it vulnerable to economic coercion. Change is overdue. A revolution in shipping is needed for America to regain its economic resiliency and invigorate a maritime industry able to compete with an increasingly aggressive and confident China.[7] Several key technologies are maturing that, if combined, could form the basis of a new multimodalism, movement of cargo over multiple types of transport like truck and ship, which would revolutionize shipping and shipbuilding.[8] However, attracting the investments and political will to ensure America leads this new movement requires a proof-of-concept demonstration. This was how today's container shipping came about, which still dominates shipping.

A revolution in shipping would leverage innovation in distributed production, new cargo containers, seamless multimode transport, diversified port operations, and new massive cargo ships that hardly ever make port calls. These key innovations, tethered to a larger vision of a new multimodalism, constitute the revolution in shipping that could put the nation back on a trajectory of global maritime competitiveness. Delivering on this goal requires first reinvigorating a moribund industry, which can first be tasked with helping to deliver key capabilities the military needs today. The approach offered uses novel start-up business constructs like technology incubators and market bridges to kickstart America's maritime rejuvenation.

THE CURRENT STATE OF AMERICAN SHIPPING AND THE CALL FOR A BLUE OCEAN STRATEGY

American naval theorist Alfred Thayer Mahan's *The Influence of Sea Power upon History* (1890) remains a seminal work 130 years after its publication and continues to influence the world's navies. One of Mahan's key insights was the interdependence of maritime commerce fleets and navies, a point that remains valid today.[9] Seeing China's progress as a naval and shipping power, one might say that they have managed to "out-Mahan" the United States through an aggressive and focused prioritization of a powerful civil-military national maritime sector. A U.S. approach to remedy this state of affairs must be clear eyed—leveraging the United States' tremendous latent human capital and intrepid entrepreneurship.

Sadly, American maritime weakness has too often been on display. As the world recovered from the Covid-19 pandemic, demand for trade soared, exposing the brittleness of American global trade networks stubbornly reliant on seaborne shipping as ships queued at ports and store shelves went bare. Worsening world events served as a reminder that the nation is well served by a strong navy as well as adequate shipping. Americans were reminded of this as world energy and grain supplies were jeopardized as the war in Ukraine spread into the Black Sea. Direct attacks on shipping in the Red Sea by Iran's proxy in Yemen—the Houthis—served as one more reminder. Meanwhile, the Communist Party of China has grown to become a dominant maritime force. Indeed, China's management arrangements of many major foreign ports threaten to achieve global logistical overmatch as American shipping continues to fade toward extinction.

It is instructive to compare where the nation was on the eve of the end of the Cold War, when the United States had 530 U.S.-flagged merchant vessels but needed 650 to sustain a major war.[10] Today there are fewer than 200 ships for an economy that has since quadrupled in size and massively globalized its supply chains.[11] Worse still, the nation's shipbuilders have built typically no more than 20 large commercial vessels for years, and almost all those ships were for government agencies.[12] China, on the other hand, produced over 40 percent of the world's new commercial ships by tonnage and is delivering new modern warships to a fleet that will number more than 400 by 2025.[13] Conversely, the United States has struggled to grow a rapidly aging fleet and since 2002 has been unable to sustain more than 300 warships.[14] Commercial shipping and shipbuilding sectors share similar skilled workforces, drawing on common skills and engineering competencies, and—aside from nuclear-powered warships—share infrastructure needs—for example, graving docks, drydocks, cranes. In sum, the health of the U.S. maritime sector is poor, and with it the naval shipbuilding sector; this has potentially severe consequences for the nation.

By all accounts, America should be a maritime behemoth. American shipping and shipbuilding missed a rare opportunity for rejuvenation to regain and keep global competitiveness with the invention of container shipping. That novel approach to shipping was the brainchild of American businessman Malcom McLean. To improve his long-haul trucking business, he looked to maximize profits by taking advantage of cheaper and faster transit by sea. In April 1956, using a repurposed wartime cargo ship and strengthened truck trailers, he executed a proof-of-concept that sparked a revolution in shipping—containerization.[15]

Unfortunately for American shippers, the need for large port staging areas and the limited carrying capacity of early container ships conspired to slow what should have been a dominant American position in intermodal shipping. Failing to secure enough market share to be profitable, McLean lost the advantage to Japanese shippers and shipbuilders who had already embraced another American invention—modular ship construction. The lesson is that while a proof-of-concept like McLean's can galvanize investment and development of novel new modes of shipping, without first setting conditions for and developing a pathway to economic sustainability, any future multimodalism concept will remain vulnerable no matter how soundly engineered, economical, or environmentally beneficial.

A return to American maritime strength will not be easy or without its competitors—including the apex predator, China. In 2024 China has the largest commercial fleet (including Hong Kong), which is backed by the world's largest shipbuilding sector, enjoying both significant direct and indirect subsidies from the Chinese Communist Party (CCP). This situation poses an immediate threat to the ability of the United States

TABLE 3. COST OF DEEPENING U.S. HARBORS TO ACCOMMODATE LARGE CONTAINER SHIPS

Port	Cost (in millions of dollars)
Port of New York / New Jersey	$2,100.00
Charleston, South Carolina	$565.00
Jacksonville, Florida	$484.00
Port of Mobile, Alabama	$365.30
Port of Virginia, Norfolk, Virginia	$350.00
Boston Harbor, Massachusetts	$306.20
Mississippi River Ship Channel	$238.00
Savannah Harbor, Georgia	$507.20
Seattle Harbor, Washington	$61.20
Baltimore Harbor, Maryland	$33.00

SOURCE: Hannah Towey, "The U.S. Is Spending Billions of Dollars Deepening Port Harbors to Make Room for 'Mega' Container Ships That Are Only Getting Bigger," *Business Insider*, January 10, 2022.

to sustain a wartime economy that in peacetime has become reliant on foreign shipping and shipbuilding.[16]

China's "civ-mil" fusion blends civilian activities like shipping with military needs and has focused on achieving a dominant position in global shipping, shipbuilding, and port operations.[17] To this end, Chinese companies enjoy large amounts of government backing in addition to a regulatory environment that avoids the enormous costs of U.S. environmental, labor, and special-interest regulations. Between 2010 and 2018 Chinese shipbuilders received $132 billion in direct subsidies, which does not include vast indirect subsidies and a relaxed regulatory environment, giving them an artificial advantage over global competitors.[18] The risk is not just their military use of commercial ships and ports in war, but their ability to edge out market competitors and stifle any innovation contrary to CCP interests. China does not play by free market rules, which poses a threat to any disruptive new entrants to the shipping and shipbuilding sector. Contending with this challenge requires a multifaceted approach that challenges China's state-owned shipping sector, sets a favorable regulatory environment, and leverages the resources of several major players in this sector.

After decades of neglect, the U.S. maritime sector alone cannot take on China's Goliath state-controlled shipping and shipbuilding sectors, but a consortium of like-minded maritime nations could set the conditions for a successful revolution in shipping and renaissance of the American maritime industry. This group, similar to the Group of Seven (G7), would be an informal group composed of nations sharing common security and free-trade interests with significant presence in shipping, shipbuilding, or maritime workers.[19] Common interests regarding freedom of navigation, free trade, and a shared threat perception of China would serve to bind the group together. Given its informal nature, Taiwan could be included along with other major maritime players like Philippines, Japan, Greece, and South Korea. This new maritime sector–focused grouping—call it the Maritime Group—could together represent a formidable block critical to setting the conditions needed for an American-led revolutionary transformation in shipping to take hold.

TABLE 4. TOP MARITIME NATIONS *Heritage Foundation*

RANK	SHIPBUILDING BY TONNAGE, AS PERCENTAGE OF GLOBAL TOTAL		NUMBER OF MERCHANT MARINERS		NUMBER OF COMMERCIAL SHIPS OWNED*	
1	China	44.2%	Philippines	252,393	China (plus Hong Kong)	9,829
2	South Korea	32.4%	Russia	198,123	Greece	4,870
3	Japan	17.6%	Indonesia	143,702	Japan	4,007
4	Philippines	1.06%	China	134,294	Singapore	2,799
5	Italy	0.82%	India	113,474	Indonesia	2,411
6	Germany	0.63%	Ukraine	76,442	Germany	2,221
7	Vietnam	0.61%	United States	59,586	Norway	1,987
8	Finland	0.36%	Malaysia	35,000	Russia	1,833
9	Taiwan	0.30%	Vietnam	34,590	United States	1,783
10	France	0.29%	United Kingdom	33,743	South Korea	1,680
11	Norway	0.29%	Myanmar	33,290	Turkey	1,583
12	Russia	0.22%	Poland	31,222	United Kingdom	1,380
13	Turkey	0.22%	Greece	30,507	Netherlands	1,189
14	Netherlands	0.19%	Turkey	28,587	Vietnam	1,133
15	India	0.12%	South Korea	27,919	United Arab Emirates	1,087

▓ Ranked in top 15 in all three categories   ▒ Ranked in top 15 in two categories

Recommended Members of Maritime Group of Nations			
United States	Greece	Singapore	Indonesia
South Korea	Italy	United Kingdom	Netherlands
Japan	Turkey	Vietnam	Switzerland**
Philippines	Norway	Germany	

* Greater than 1,000 gross weight tonnage.
** Switzerland is a significant financier and owner of oceangoing vessels.
SOURCE: United Nations Conference on Trade and Development, "Review of Maritime Transport 2022,"
https://unctad.org/system/files/official-document/rmt2022_en.pdf (accessed August 3, 2023).

Regaining America's maritime footing will require policy and industry leaders to break long-standing, often politically entrenched norms and to implement a coherent, modern, competitive national maritime strategy. The primary task is to create a domestic landscape that can foster a sustainable competitive advantage in American shipbuilding, shipping, and logistics. In the near term, fostering stronger cooperation with allies can satisfy clearly defined national shipping needs in wartime.

To set these conditions for a successful revolution in shipping does not mean "outperforming" the principal threat: China's heavily subsidized and government-directed shipbuilding and shipping industries. Rather, it means changing the paradigm of modern logistics. In short, the nation should pursue a well-known management approach called a "blue ocean strategy"—an approach that creates new market space rather than continuing to compete in a conventional way.[20] Achieving this goal will require American leadership in devising novel, cutting-edge means of moving cargo, rethinking shore-to-sea connectors, and dispersing production by leveraging emerging technologies like additive manufacturing—in short, sidestepping the current Chinese dominated model of shipping.

Innovative U.S. leaders have done this before. Two innovations perfected in the United States shortly after World War II still shape global shipping—modular ship construction and the containerization of cargo. Modularization proved critical in World War II by rapidly connecting dispersed U.S. factories to rapidly outproduce all adversaries' shipbuilding combined. This is a technique used now at all competitive shipyards and taken to colossal scale in China. One factor in this loss of global competitiveness was organized labor's early resistance to modularization, which led to the erosion of U.S. commercial shipyards' market share. While China's cheap labor is becoming less cheap, it is still about half as expensive as skilled machine operators in the United States.[21] However, this is only part of the equation, as will be shown later; regulations and red tape at home are also having a deleterious effect on American competitiveness.

UNLEASH MARKET FORCES, NOT GOVERNMENT PROTECTIONS

Good ideas are insufficient if regulators stand in their way. The global and domestic maritime marketplace is already difficult for new entrants, and any innovator facing hostile regulators in the United States may look elsewhere. Thanks to the work by economist Peter St. Onge, we can see how various self-imposed forces are distorting and stymying efforts to regain our maritime edge. To illustrate the scale of our regulatory crisis in ship manufacturing, 2019 congressional testimony by the Department of Defense suggested there is a twenty-six-fold difference in costs to produce modern ships domestically rather than sourcing overseas.[22] Let's break this down. China's manufacturing wages are roughly 40 percent of U.S. levels, and labor costs make up roughly half of shipbuilding expense,[23] so it should be expected that only a 30 percent discount should be realized from cheaper labor, not the full twenty-six-fold difference. This leaves the lion's share of the cost difference being due to regulations and restrictions that render American shipping roughly eighteen times more expensive than it should be, labor costs aside. Conversely, while U.S. regulation handicaps shippers and shipbuilders, foreign government intervention and subsidies often present considerable advantages to competitors. Regarding purely commercial ships not built to military standards, U.S.-built cargo ships cost three to five times more than those of a similar design built overseas. This is due to foreign government direct and indirect subsidies as well as the shipbuilding discipline seen in South Korea using economies of scale by minimizing design differences across orders. Differentiation of products is another way to avoid this cost disadvantage, which would rely on American innovation in ship design.

Domestically, maritime innovation is stifled by a political landscape that rewards rigid adherence to an entrenched status quo. As an example, the Jones Act has, contrary to its intended purpose, paralyzed innovation and shackled the U.S. maritime sector. The Jones Act traces its legacy to a crisis that occurred in the lead-up to and involvement in World War I. On the eve of that war in 1914, America's U.S.-flagged merchant fleet carried about 10 percent of trade, with European nations conveying the remainder.[24] However, as European ships were redirected or sunk, the

American merchant fleet could not sustain the nation's trade, let alone bear the demands of combat three years later when it joined the war. Wartime necessity led to a massive government shipbuilding program, delivering a large merchant fleet that predictably diminished after the war, along with the Navy. However, Congress, seeking to ensure the nation's economy and security would never again be vulnerable, passed the Merchant Marine Act of 1920—the Jones Act. This act's preamble remains the best articulation of the importance of commercial shipping: "It is necessary for the national defense and for the proper growth of its foreign and domestic commerce that the United States shall have a merchant marine of the best equipped and most suitable types of vessels sufficient to carry the greater portion of its commerce and serve as a naval or military auxiliary in time of war or national emergency."[25]

Today the nation is in a dilemma similar to that in 1914, where the need for naval capacity necessitates a focus on regaining global maritime competitiveness. Overseas, the principal maritime competitor is China, which also poses a significant military threat. CCP government control, subsidies, and a willingness to use all national resources to gain a market advantage represents a strategic danger to the United States. In 1998 China prioritized a dynamic whole-of-government approach to building a globally dominant maritime sector.[26] Eight years later it would lead the world in shipbuilding.[27] Efforts by the United States to compete have amounted to little more than navel-gazing and policy paralysis. Overcoming these challenges requires leadership but is just the first step; attracting new talent into the maritime sector and creating market space for even a rudimentary novel concept of multimodalism will be critical. Getting underway on this new task will require addressing the China challenge and an unhelpful domestic maritime business landscape.

ADDRESS THE CHINA MARITIME THREAT

Competing for shipping and shipbuilding market share with Chinese corporations such as COSCO will require taking on the CCP. The risk to the United States is not just the military use of commercial ships and overseas ports by China in war but the ability to edge out market competitors and stifle any innovation contrary to CCP interests. Taking on a Chinese state–controlled commercial entity with massive financial backing will be no small feat for a U.S. start-up company and will require national leadership and supportive regulators to succeed.

As an example of this state sponsorship, on January 1, 2017, a new Chinese law, the National Defense Transportation Law, came into effect making clear that transport and associated infrastructure was a national asset as part of civ-mil fusion policies.[28] This built on a 2015 regulation, the Outline for Training and Evaluation of National Defense Transportation Specialized Support Teams, that mandated military training of personnel in so-called transport support teams for shipping, rail, air, and highway.[29] Naval analyst Thomas Shugart has tracked the development of Chinese civilian car ferries that could be used for a potential invasion of Taiwan, noting that training has been conducted on retrofitted ferries able to embark tanks and practiced the deployment of amphibious assault vehicles from them while at sea.[30] The reality is that Chinese commercial ships are also military assets, and so are the crews.

If there is doubt Chinese commercial shipping serves the CCP, consider recent research and reporting. A rare glimpse into the political life of COSCO crews was unveiled through the publication of several leaked corporate documents. These documents detail crews attending political study sessions, corporate political training given to ship captains, and even an oath-swearing ceremony for loyalty to the CCP.[31] According to these leaked documents, there are at least 10,000 party members and 150 senior special party cadre members in COSCO spread throughout its fleet and port operations. In fact, given troubling news of illegal overseas Chinese police stations, these documents also indicated that COSCO had 23 party members based in New York and 24 in Piraeus, Greece. The implication is that far more than commercial interests are driving COSCO, and its presence overseas often serves political purposes.

COSCO has embarked on a decades-long effort to become a global leader in shipping and port operations. Today it has stakes in approximately one hundred ports outside China, and one-third of these have hosted Chinese naval vessels. In September 2021 Germany's Tollerort terminal at the port of Hamburg became the ninety-sixth port outside mainland China with a major People's Republic of China stake.[32] The deal was finally struck, giving COSCO a 24.9 percent stake in the terminal over the objections of Germany's foreign office and five other ministries who were ultimately overruled by Chancellor Olaf Scholz. His argument was that Chinese money would go to another port in Poland if not Hamburg. The lesson is that Chinese investments in ports are guided by not only economics but strategic-political calculations with inherent risks to host nations.

So far the U.S. response to China's global maritime market ascendency has been muted. Instead, despite ardent support for Jones Act limitations, some U.S. shipping companies like Matson spend tens of millions on maintenance to their U.S.-flagged vessels in Chinese shipyards every year. The cost advantage of employing state-owned Chinese shipyards outweighs the 50 percent ad valorem tariff on foreign yard maintenance. This is particularly egregious given the possible counterintelligence value and the obvious deleterious impact to domestic shipyards. China's maritime industrial dominance poses another issue—cyber intrusion into shipboard systems, which has been a concern for some time.

On March 26, 2024, container ship *Dali* struck the Francis Scott Key bridge in Baltimore Harbor after losing power. The nature of the power loss remains as of August 2024 under investigation with lingering suspicions of a cyberattack, made worse when just days later, on April 6, the container ship *Qingdao* lost power near the Verrazzano Bridge in New York Harbor. The December 2020 National Maritime Cybersecurity Plan was intended to address vulnerabilities in the maritime sector such as these and would have required forensic cyberattack investigations.[33] While terrorism was ruled out quickly in the *Dali* incident, due diligence investigating cyberattacks is time consuming and requires exquisite skills; until recently, this level of investigation has been resisted. A month before the *Dali* collision, the White House issued an executive order to bolster cybersecurity of U.S. ports that granted additional authorities to the U.S. Coast Guard.[34] The day after this order was issued, the U.S. Coast Guard posted proposed cybersecurity regulation changes for public comment, which concluded on April 22, 2024.[35] Yet a May 14, 2024, marine investigation preliminary report by the National Transportation Safety Board failed to mention investigating cyber intrusions as a potential contribution to the incident.[36] Given that six people lost their lives in the *Dali* collision and given that the nation's then-tenth busiest port remained closed for two months, regaining full operations seventy-seven days later, the fullest investigation is warranted.

The safe and timely operation of harbors is supported by duties collected for the Harbor Maintenance Trust Fund (HMTF). These duties help finance periodic dredging of built-up silt, which is required to keep ports open. But the HMTF has not resulted in significant improvement of shipping access or modernized harbor infrastructure. In fact, U.S. ports perform below average in key metrics of wait times, unloading and offloading for container cargo, bulk cargo, and fuels.[37] As a result, no U.S. port has ranked in the world's top twenty-five of performance for many years, which impacts trade and adds costs.

To better enforce U.S. regulations, Congress directed a relatively small $6 million infusion as part of the Ocean Shipping Reform Act of 2022 intended for the Federal Maritime Commission to grow its staff with up to 170 new hires. These new regulators are to work through two hundred complaints that spiked during the post-Covid recovery and associated shipping backups at numerous American ports.[38] And increased cargo preference (e.g., government-impelled cargo to U.S.-flag carriers) has been proffered as a means of sustaining a minimum of American shipping with U.S. government cargo to keep these carriers afloat finically.[39] However, subsidizing increased government contracts further distorts the U.S.-flagged shipping market rather than allowing the United States to gain a competitive advantage against foreign competitors by increasing quality, productivity, and value. Moreover, MARAD remains skeptical that, even if all government cargo was mandated to be carried on U.S.-flagged ships (today it is 50 percent for nonmilitary cargo), there would be any appreciable impact on growing the American merchant fleet.[40] Cargo preference has a role, but it is not THE solution given the limited amount of cargo in question to make it lucrative for a competitive shipper.

When it comes to shipbuilding, Chinese companies enjoy healthy government backing on top of a regulatory environment that avoids the enormous costs of environmental, labor, and special-interest regulations found in the United States. Between 2010 and 2018 Chinese shipbuilders enjoyed $132 billion in direct subsidies, not including enormous indirect subsidies and regulations that give their shipbuilders a leg up on global competitors.[41] Favorable financing and supporting government direction enabled the massive merger of COSCO Group and China Shipping Group in 2016, and then the absorption of Hong Kong–listed Orient Overseas Container Line, to become today's COSCO. Such government support has created an irresistible shipbuilding market that benefits from foreign orders. Surprisingly, Taiwan's (the CCP's archenemy) Evergreen Marine Group purchased forty-four vessels from mainland Chinese shipyards in 2019. And between 2019 and 2021 China's four main shipyards (also producing warships) had 211 new orders, of which 64 percent were from overseas buyers.

Trying to "out-Chinese" the CCP's government-led and -backed shipping and shipbuilding model will not be effective. Rather, unleashing innovation and unshackling American industry should be the focus. One way of doing this is to remove legal and regulatory impediments that handicap our own industries to substantially narrow the competitive gap with China. Regulations constrain the market, like the Foreign Dredge Act, which regulates the dredging needed to keep the nation's ports open and makes new ports available for trade.[42] Another example is the redundant and politicized National Environmental Act (NEPA), which creates untold amounts of red tape that slows or discourages maritime infrastructure projects.[43] Other constraints include the Jones Act and an ad valorem tax on ship maintenance conducted on American-flagged vessels overseas. If pursued, policy reform needs to flow through all levels of the manufacturing supply chain, from inputs to labor and services, to the final product. Without such reform it is exceedingly difficult to imagine a return to competitiveness against China's shippers and shipyards.

As such, it is imperative that the nation moves away from handicapping domestic shipping toward the promotion of innovation and industry. The United States needs a national maritime strategy that includes enhancing transportation competitiveness and attractiveness of American ports connected to global markets. Doing this will also require reassessing the role existing incentives provided by MARAD while adhering to the Hippocratic oath: "do no harm" to a domestic industry overly dependent on the Jones Act.

MOVE AWAY FROM FLAWED TOOLS OF GOVERNMENT

Tools that have been used to sustain a minimum of civilian shipping to meet military operational needs include cargo preference laws and stipends to support U.S.-flag carriers and funding for the National Defense Reserve Fleet (NRDF), which has eighty-nine ships of varying classes as of March 31, 2024. This is augmented by an additional sixty commercially active but militarily useful vessels on retainer through the Maritime Security Program.[44] At the same time, a subset of the NRDF is the military-focused Ready Reserve Fleet that consisted of, as last reported in December 2022, forty-one roll-on/roll-off, two break bulk, and four crane ships.[45] Falling under the Department of Transportation umbrella, the Maritime Administration administers these support and readiness programs and was authorized in the National Defense Authorization Act of Fiscal Year 2021 to establish the Tanker Security Program (TSP) to expand access to commercial U.S.-flagged tankers for war sustainment through stipends that incentivize flagging of foreign tankers.

As the law is written, the new TSP program is not "scalable," and while ten ships are authorized, the reality is that in its first few years too few new tankers have been secured in TSP. Those ships that have signed up for TSP, according to industry experts, are doing so while concurrently benefiting from government cargo preference deals. The implication is that the stipend is too small—$6 million per ship maximum—when considering costs to modify commercial tankers to supply military vessels (e.g., CONSOL installation), the cost premium of an American crew, and relative market competition, making the TSP not lucrative enough as a business proposition. Bottom line, the stipend would have to be above $10 million per ship, and, realistically, there is not enough military cargo alone to make TSP participation lucrative.

As already detailed, the ability to clear ports and increase cargo is important, and rail transport serves a critical role. Unfortunately, U.S. rail carriers, after a decade of cost cutting, have too few engines driving fewer but longer trains, which the rails were not designed to handle, thus accelerating wear on existing lines. Hauling these longer trains is encouraged by regulations that discourage capital investments while layering additional requirements that may not ensure adequate safety; consequently, disasters such as the train derailment in East Palestine, Ohio, become more—not less—likely.[46] Pressures that nearly percolated to a national rail strike in 2022 could have cost the nation $2 billion daily.[47] The interconnectedness and need for competitiveness of American logistics—ports, airports, rail, highways—underscores the importance for a national maritime strategy or plan that past piecemeal approaches have repeatedly failed at improving.

The government protection and subsidy approach encapsulated in the Jones Act and various Maritime Administration programs, like the TSP and cargo preferences, has not worked. Statistics speak for themselves: 2019's Turbo Activation 19-Plus exercise demonstrated that only 64 percent of the Ready Reserve Fleet was able to deploy on time in support of national defense needs. Moreover, the average age of these merchant ships is forty-five years, well over the industry end-of-life average of twenty years, and "DoD faces a gap of approximately 76 fuel tankers to meet surge sealift requirements."[48] Administrator Mark Buzby of the U.S. Maritime Administration, while responsible for ensuring sealift for our military, warned in March 2020 that the merchant fleet is likely unable to deliver in a conflict and that, with only one shipyard able to build the needed logistic ships, the capacity to shift to needed production when necessary is questionable.[49] That said, simply discarding the Jones Act is not workable, and doing so would not ensure the nation access to critical shipping.

Despite over a hundred years of government intervention incentives intended by section 27 of the Merchant Marine Act of 1920 (the Jones Act), the government has failed to ensure that a fiducial merchant fleet is available for war. Moreover, past attempts at reforming or repealing the Jones Act have stalled due to a powerful combination of a captive industry and its well-funded legislative support—even though smart reform would allow access to cheaper, newer, safer, and more plentiful American-built shipping. The issue is a complex one, necessitating a national maritime strategy that sets American shipping and shipbuilding on a course to global commercial competitiveness, which inevitably would make Jones Act protections unnecessary. Whatever shape a future shipping model takes, it must be able to transport cargo securely on a competitive commercial basis.

DO NOT BOTHER WITH THE JONES ACT, MAKE IT UNNECESSARY
Congress has created several mechanisms for ensuring the nation can meet its military sealift needs. Despite the repeated testimonies by successive commanders of the Department of Defense Transportation Command citing the criticality of shipping, the issue has been a political football and has remained unresolved. Plans to help the U.S. shipbuilding industrial base and to bolster U.S. sealift capacity and reliability by replacing decrepit vessels has also fallen flat.[50] Limited American shipyard capacity has been squeezed to the brink of starvation and places emphasis on winning higher-value naval combatant contracts, further constraining the lower-end sealift construction base. The result is that, despite Jones Act protections, American shipbuilding is unable to sustain itself on government purchases as Beijing continues to build out its maritime logistical prowess. The American approach must change.

The reality today is, the Jones Act has failed to meet its stated intent. Due to a captive market, the domestic blue-water fleet the Jones Act sought to bolster has instead relegated itself to carriage of only the most inelastic cargo where no other alternatives exist. As already mentioned, market distortions the Jones Act has caused means U.S. commercial shipyards have become upward of 60 percent less efficient compared to overseas shipbuilders and are producing ships of limited value to the Navy's logistic needs at a 700 percent price premium.[51] The most modern, productivity-enhancing capital improvements, such as automated welding systems prevalent in leading shipyards globally remain elusive to domestic shipyards. Moreover, American carriers are punished with an ad valorem tax when conducting maintenance overseas at more modern and cost-effective shipyards—a vestige of the Tariff Act of 1930, (although this does not stop American carriers from doing this, given the considerable savings over domestic yard work).

Another failing aspect is ensuring an adequate number of available and certified U.S. mariners needed in a sustained crisis. While testifying before Congress in March 2020, former Maritime Administration head Rear Adm. (ret.) Mark Buzby drew attention to the inability to train and attract U.S. merchant mariners with viable jobs.[52] Another study from 2016 found a shortage of well over 15 percent of needed crew members (a gap of approximately two thousand trained and physically ready people). U.S. mariners today have an average age of forty-seven years.[53] While some experts have voiced serious concerns that this study underestimates the problem, there is consensus the nation has a problem ensuring it has enough merchant mariners.

Moreover, a lack of competition has driven the Jones Act fleet into a deadweight tonnage composition reflective of supply chains that have no alternatives. Now most of the fleet capacity is dedicated to domestic petroleum movements that do not have pipeline alternatives—and, as mentioned in chapter 4, that capacity is inadequate. This lack of fleet diversity presents a considerable challenge to the broader strategic mobility systems needed today and that Mahan envisioned for powerful navies bolstered by robust merchant fleets. Because the Jones Act fleet has retreated into these most inelastic domestic supply chains, repurposing tonnage for wartime use would deplete domestic energy security. For this reason, it is unlikely the Jones Act fleet would play a meaningful Department of Defense role in support of wartime strategic mobility.

An undersized American maritime sector severely constrains the nation's ability to mobilize for war, to sustain a wartime economy, or to sustain a war-fighting fleet. The result is a weaker deterrence to China, opening our nation to economic coercion. Consider that during the 1991 Gulf War, thirteen foreign-chartered vessels refused to enter the war zone, delaying delivery of military materials. In a 2020 study, military sealift in a major war that year would have needed to include a combination of domestic shipping, shipping with America's allies, and contractual obligations with third parties to meet a need for 19.2 million square feet of cargo capacity and eighty-six tankers.[54] Given the shuttering of Red Hill fuel depot on Oahu, Hawaii, and other factors, the real number of tankers needed is likely well above one hundred, not counting those connecting the various regions of the nation whose energy needs are not serviced by rail or road.

An interim solution would be to relieve treaty allies from the restrictions of the Jones Act by allowing Japan and South Korea to conduct shipping between U.S. ports. Waiving the Jones Act limits on ships built and registered in allied countries would avoid subsidizing Chinese shipyards and instead contribute to the allied shipbuilding industrial bases. Stipulations could be included in the deal that allied commercial ships must employ some number of U.S. merchant mariners and conduct some repairs and improvements in American shipyards. Waiving allies from Jones Act restrictions would be temporary as market forces and improvements at domestic shipyards and ports would lessen the need for protections like the Jones Act. In time, a larger, more competitive fleet would facilitate a modal shift of domestic freight to the water and expanding transportation-intensive American manufacturing industries.

FUNDAMENTALS OF THE NEXT INTERMODALISM

Being the first mover offers advantages that the nation can turn into a lucrative business attracting Americans to become merchant mariners and shipbuilders once again. A logical next step in this new multimodalism will be connecting new centers of industry and customers distant from existing connectors (e.g., airports, highways, ports) in a more disperse global trade that benefits far more Americans. Achieving this is no simple task, and as Malcom McLean did in 1956 with containerization, it will require first a demonstration of the approach's viability.

But first, to be successful, any new multimodal solution must address three fundamental outputs:

1. *Less time in port.* Reduce the time ships spend in port while maximizing overall capacity for revenue generating freight, at minimal overhead costs (e.g., port fees, longshore labor). Port-related fees are significant, increase as ships remain in port longer, and can rise as ships age and require more frequent maintenance. The goal would be to optimize a ship's deadweight tonnage utilization, a ratio of cargo tonnage versus miles traveled, as a measure for cargo ship productivity.[55]
2. *More trade pathways.* Increase the number of ports and alternative transit paths to improve resiliency against costly port or overland disruptions (e.g., natural disasters or conflicts).[56] The importance of this was made explicit when the Suez Canal was blocked by the ultra large container vessel *Evergiven* in March 2021 for almost a week, holding up 10 percent of global maritime trade at a loss estimated at $10 billion per closure day and causing prolonged shipping delays.[57] The point was reinforced beginning in October 2023 when Iran's proxy in Yemen, the Houthis, began attacking shipping in the Red Sea to dissuade support for Israel in its war against Hamas in Gaza. These attacks have had a severe impact on shipping that transits via the Suez Canal.

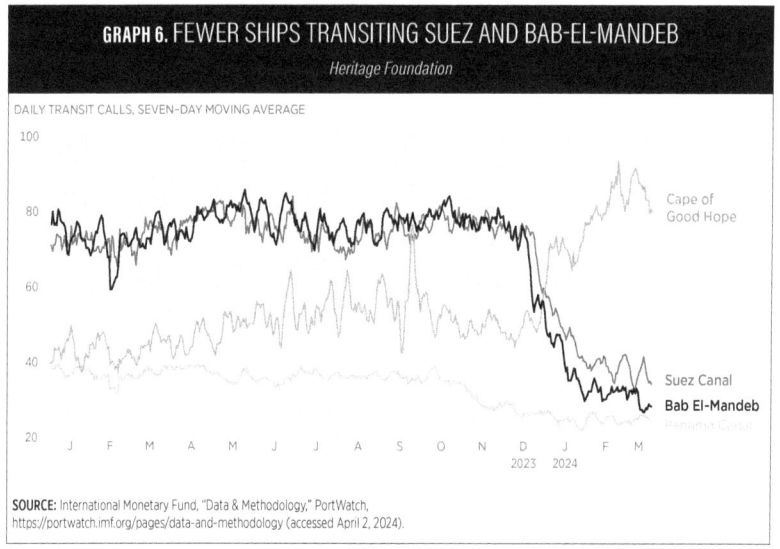

3. *More cargo throughput.* Increase the system throughput for cargo-carrying vessels to truly take advantage of economies of scale and reduce the per-unit cost for voyages. Any marginal increases in the economies of scale gained by larger ship capacity requires matched improvements to intermodal throughput rates—for example, more cranes, trucks, and rail chassis. Merely increasing ship capacity has the negative impact of ships so large that the number of ports in which they can call is dramatically reduced, and the benefits of larger cargo volume can be neutralized by the increased time to load and unload cargo. This is already being witnessed as container ships grow to massive proportions, in a so-called post-Panamax syndrome, named after ships too large to fit through the original Panama Canal.[58]

MAP 12. HOW U.S. PORTS CAN CURRENTLY ACCOMMODATE LARGE CONTAINER SHIPS *Heritage Foundation*

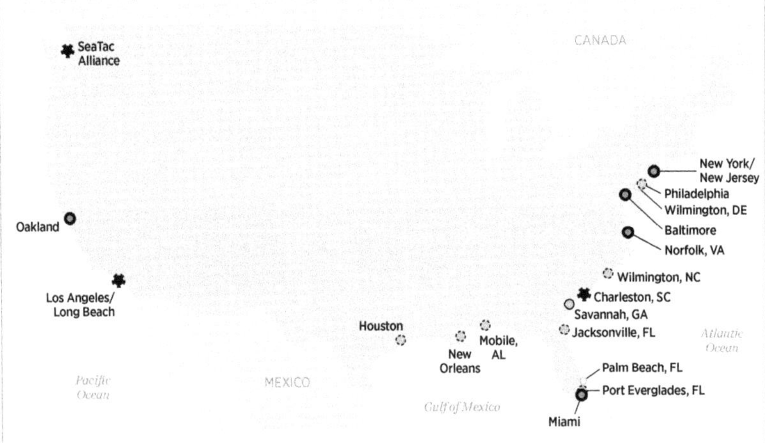

Category	Capacity in TEU*	Mean Low Water Channel Depth, in Feet
Panamax or less	4,200	Less than 38 feet
Panamax	4,500	39–40 feet
Post-Panamax I	6,000	41–45 feet
Post-Panamax II	8,000	46–48 feet
New Panamax	12,000	49–50 feet
Post Panamax	16,000	51 feet and above

* TEU refers to twenty-foot equivalent unit, which is a measure of volume in units of twenty-foot-long containers.
SOURCE: Jean-Paul Rodrigue, "Channel Depth at Major North American Container Ports," Hofstra University, Department of Global Studies and Geography, https://transportgeography.org/wp-content/uploads/Map-North-America-Container-Ports-Depth-1.pdf (accessed April 28, 2023).

Container shipping has been successful because it eased logistics and port operations while also increasing the security of cargo. Prior to container shipping, cargo was handled in bulk and repacked for movement off the pier, leading to high pilferage and breakage. This was overcome by packing cargo in containers that a truck would quickly move from the pier to its next destination. By conceptualizing shipping with the movement off the pier, container shipping represented an early step into intermodalism—the transfer of cargo across various means of transport. The next era in intermodalism will be multimodalism—made possible as several key technologies emerging now merge into a new global logistic network. Five elements of this potential brave new multimodal world include distributed production, new cargo containers, multimode transport, diversified port operations, and massive cargo ships that hardly ever make port calls. An overview of these five elements follows.

DISTRIBUTED PRODUCTION

At the end of the day, logistics—no matter how modern—is about moving cargo. Because of this, there are several elements that will persist: cargo-carrying platforms, cargo containers, sources of production, and customers. Two developments are quickly altering the landscape of today's logistics networks: intelligent networks and additive manufacturing. Additive manufacturing uses seven techniques to "print" using digital blueprints to build layer-by-layer complex components across a variety of materials, including metals. It does this with less waste and has enabled producing intricate and lightweight parts not possible by traditional milling or casting. This technology has the potential to massively distribute points of production. Realizing its potential, the Navy first installed an additive manufactured metallic critical flight part in one of its aircraft in July 2016 in a successful proof-of-concept and since May 2017 has focused on certifying additive manufacturing in operational (that is, at sea) settings.[59]

In January 2021 the Defense Department doubled down and committed all services to adopting additive manufacturing, identifying eight U.S. firms as additive manufacturing innovation institutes to help bring this technology to the military.⁶⁰ The implications to global supply chains are immense, opening new markets and centers of production. However, connecting these new centers of production requires a secure method of communication, tracking, and decision assistance. The recent technology of blockchain offers a solution.

While famous for its application to cryptocurrencies, blockchains offer dramatic improvements in logistics and manufacturing. They do this by effectively automating the verification and communication of data while cheaply offering increased security, transparency, and accountability. In simple terms, blockchains are decentralized registers of transaction data that function like a traditional database but can cheaply encompass a massive network to track the movement of cargo. Because blockchains natively operate across borders and languages and can use customizable permissions and rules paired with verifiable, immutable data inside smart cargo containers, they can ease customs processing and security of sensitive or perishable cargo. These features offer important safeguards against human error, fraud, illicit use, or corruption. Blockchains are already being widely researched and implemented in at least sixty-five industries including shipping, logistics, manufacturing, insurance, and national security applications.[61] Beyond these in-house efforts, blockchains attracted $25 billion in venture capital investment in 2021, up 713 percent from the previous year.[62] Paired with a powerful artificial intelligence (AI) decision-assistance program, the potential for adaptive-predictive logistics chains becomes more possible. Given the CCP's demonstrated history of usurping critical first-mover status in emerging technologies, the United States must guard its advances. Meanwhile, the United States and its allies must prioritize innovating and building market dominance in maritime blockchain technology. Furthermore, truly opening new logistic chains will also require a relook at the simple cargo container.

NEW CARGO CONTAINER

Container shipping is widely recognized as one of the most transformative technologies in the history of shipping. A new multimodalism will likewise be reliant on new thinking about the simple container. Although the shipping container transformed the way the world trades more than sixty years ago, the container has not been meaningfully updated to optimize modern trade. In fact, with U.S. container volume utilization hovering around 70 percent, shippers often pay to move nothing but air in mostly empty containers. Given the U.S. trade imbalance, volume utilization on the backhaul is often far lower. Optimizing container design for contemporary trade flows presents a considerable business opportunity. Moreover, limited container supply can hold up trade, as demonstrated during the Covid-19 pandemic recovery period, when containers stacked up in China. The situation is made worse by the near-complete Chinese monopoly on container production, making a superior, scalable alternative developed and fielded by America and its allies a priority.[63]

Today container shipping and air freight rely on common containers like the twenty-foot equivalent (TEU) or the forty-foot equivalent (FEU).[64] U.S. federal regulations stipulate upper truck (80,000 lb.) and rail car cargo (286,000 lb.) limits, which do not consider local bridge, state road, or environmental constraints. With these in mind, industry recommends that the TEU not exceed 44,000 pounds (22 short tons), including varieties with self-contained refrigeration units for moving perishables.[65] Air freight containers come in a wide array of sizes and shapes and are most often made using lightweight aluminum. Conventional steel TEU containers do not lend themselves to multiple shipping modes like airlift, limiting their use in a future with increased air transport that potentially alleviates road and rail congestion.

The recent development of so-called smart rail cars has allowed the movement of rail cargo to be tracked and reports sent when freight is accessed along the way; smart rail cars also provide monitoring of the environmental conditions in the container holding the freight.[66] Married with the technology of blockchains, shippers can get real-time data to inform delivery schedules, prompt customs clearances, optimize transit routes, and ensure that perishable cargo arrives without damage. Returning to the humble shipping container (i.e., the TEU), three Chinese companies in 2021 manufactured 96 percent of the dry cargo containers and 100 percent of refrigerated cargo containers.[67] During the Covid-19 pandemic recovery in 2021 and 2022, China's zero-Covid policies saw frequent port disruptions that delayed the movement of containers; without U.S. container manufacturing capacity, this meant cargo had to wait at U.S. docks for containers to arrive from China, the cargo emptied, and then delivered to the shippers. The results were significant delays and a doubling of shipping rates between U.S. ports and China between April 2020 and April 2021.[68] The scarcity of containers and Chinese policy impacts provides a lesson for the need for more distributed manufacturing of containers as well as for new designs that enable new intermodal shipping.

New containers will need some level of reverse compatibility so they can be carried on container ships side-by-side traditional TEUs. To do this, new air freight–capable containers could conceivably be connected into a TEU or FEU footprint for shipping but later broken down for air freight or smaller trucks. Another line of effort is to use new materials, like advanced composites, in the fabrication of shipping containers that would offer greater cargo capacity with less tare weight.[69] And methods of handling these new containers on container ships will need to enable transshipment at sea via support ships and vertical heavy-lift air platforms.

MULTIMODE TRANSPORT

The Department of Transportation monitors congestion on the nation's roads using a measure of travel time reliability to assess the adequacy of the nation's roads. These reports, dating back to 2010, show that the average time drivers are stuck in congestion is four hours and twenty-seven minutes.[70] So far, new roads seem to be keeping up with demand, but this congestion is costing trucking companies and commuters alike ($869 per commuter in 2022, or $81 billion total).[71] Despite potential bottlenecks on the nation's roads, trucks will remain indispensable in moving cargo, but new unmanned drone and vertical-lift technologies could be leveraged to alleviate some of the burden on roads and greatly expand access to new locations. Additionally, shifting a greater share of domestic cargo to sea and river networks will help alleviate driver shortages, minimize wear and tear on roads and trucks, and increase demand for American maritime jobs. However, emerging technology such as advanced lighter-than-air dirigibles and eVTOL (electric vertical take-off and landing aircraft) systems present an opportunity to lower legacy operational expenditure barriers to such transport of cargo.

The Navy has already demonstrated the ability to deliver fifty-pound cargo two hundred miles to a ship at sea using a Blue Water prototype drone in 2019.[72] For the Navy, this capability is just what is needed for the majority (90 percent) of its ship-to-ship cargo weighing less than fifty pounds. Commercially, however, these drones would have to be substantially scaled up to be useful.

A potential solution is a prototype dirigible designed for cargo transport between ship and shore. Dirigibles are attractive because they are cheaper than helicopters to operate and have the potential for greater carrying capacity and less environmental impact.[73] In June 2022 Air Nostrum purchased ten helium-lofted and electrically propelled dirigibles reportedly capable of moving one hundred passengers up to 249 miles at 80 mph.[74] When it comes to cargo, Lockheed Martin's LMH-1 dirigible can carry twenty-one metric tons of cargo at sixty knots for 1,400 nautical miles.[75] The airship company Aeros claims its working prototype rigid dirigible can be scaled up to carry sixty-six metric tons of cargo up to 3,100 miles at a speed of 120 mph.[76] Cost-effective vertical lift offers the potential to connect cargo flows to and from ships with more locations closer to rail and logistic hubs, with less time in or avoiding port holding areas altogether, avoiding the very factors that held back McLean's early container shipping.

According to the American Trucking Association, in 2022 there was a deficit of 80,000 drivers due in part to accelerated retirements during the Covid-19 pandemic, in a sector where the majority of drivers are over fifty-five years of age and there are too few new hires, given the difficult lifestyle and low pay.[77] In 2021 trucks carried 72.2 percent of domestic freight tonnage in 2021 on the nation's roads and transported 66.1 percent in value of trade to Canada and 82.7 percent to Mexico.[78] Beyond the existing deficit in drivers, meeting future demand will require an additional 90,900 new drivers to be hired by 2031, all for jobs that in 2021 paid an average of $23.23 an hour.[79] That said, the new multimodal approach has the potential of reducing the need for long-haul trucking with more short-haul trucking, keeping truckers closer to their families. But even if the trucks and drivers could be found, today's roads would require expansion and continual maintenance costing tens of billions of dollars annually. In 2022 the federal government spent $52 billion on national highways alone.[80]

The military has long had to contend with moving cargo over rough and contested terrain without roads, ports, or airfields. The helicopter proved critical in meeting this need and opened an entirely new element of naval and amphibious warfare. Helicopters were able to move between warships at sea without large flight decks. Fitted with submarine-detecting sensors and weapons, it became a formidable threat to hostile submarines. During the Korean War, helicopters acted as combat ambulances, moving the wounded rapidly from the front line to medical centers. The value of these missions validated the operating costs, ranging from the legacy CH-47 Chinook heavy-lift helicopter's approximate $4,000 per flight hour cost at the low end to the CV-22 Osprey tilt-rotor craft's almost $80,000 per flight hour cost.[81] Although the range, speed, and access to otherwise inaccessible locations are useful to the military and a great advantage, if the cost cannot be reduced, it is problematic in commercial applications.

Air freight, conducted on fixed-wing aircraft, is the most expensive commercial means of cargo transport, relegating it to the highest value and time-sensitive cargoes. According to several case studies carried out by the World Bank, air freight is four to five times more expensive than trucking and twelve to sixteen times more expensive than sea transport.[82] Comparing truck to rail transport, an analysis of the American market points to a cost advantage for rail by a factor of three (or one-third the cost per ton via trucking).[83] And detention and demurrage fees for cargo waiting for movement out of the port holding area can average $100 per day per TEU.[84] If the cost per ton per mile of air freight could be reduced by half, it would become competitive with trucking, especially over congested roadways or destinations not currently connected by rail. Short-haul air freight could then unlock potential savings by shortening the time cargo waits in port for movement and circumventing overland road and rail bottlenecks near ports of entry—and doing so without expensive new infrastructure projects.

$$\text{Relative Shipping Unit Cost} = 16 \text{ (miles via air freight)} + 9 \text{ (miles via truck)} + 3 \text{ (miles via rail)} + 1 \text{ (miles via ship)} + 100 \text{ (days in port)}$$

The cheaper-to-operate, high-productivity unmanned helicopter drones (e.g., K-MAX) and modern dirigibles present potential solutions to otherwise untenable air freight costs. There have been interesting developments in piloted and autonomously piloted so-called air taxis in recent years.[85] For example, widely available heavy-lift drones carrying up to five hundred pounds are now competitively priced compared to low-end helicopters, with ongoing improvements making them even more so.[86] The Navy has already demonstrated the viability of cargo-carrying drones with its Blue Water prototype; scaling up is the next challenge for commercial use.

DIVERSIFIED PORT OPERATIONS

The time cargo sits on a dock can be reduced by increasing the port cargo handling infrastructure or by diversifying the number of locations where a smaller volume of cargo can be handled. Bottom line, throughput can be maximized by tackling the principal bottleneck, which is often ship-to-shore transport. The heavy vertical-lift technologies mentioned previously can contribute to this, but avoiding ports altogether is not viable. Transshipment at sea offers a way to get around the navigation limits of massive new container ships that are unable to enter most ports.

Solving the challenge of keeping two ships stable enough to transfer TEU containers at sea also has military utility. Moving TEUs this way from massive container ships without coming to port requires smaller feeder vessels. Designing such a feeder vessel would benefit from the development of the Navy's light amphibious warship and its large

As maritime container ships grow larger, fewer ports will be able to accommodate their requirements for water depth, crane sizes, and offloading areas without incurring massive construction costs. One solution is to offload ship cargo without going to port.

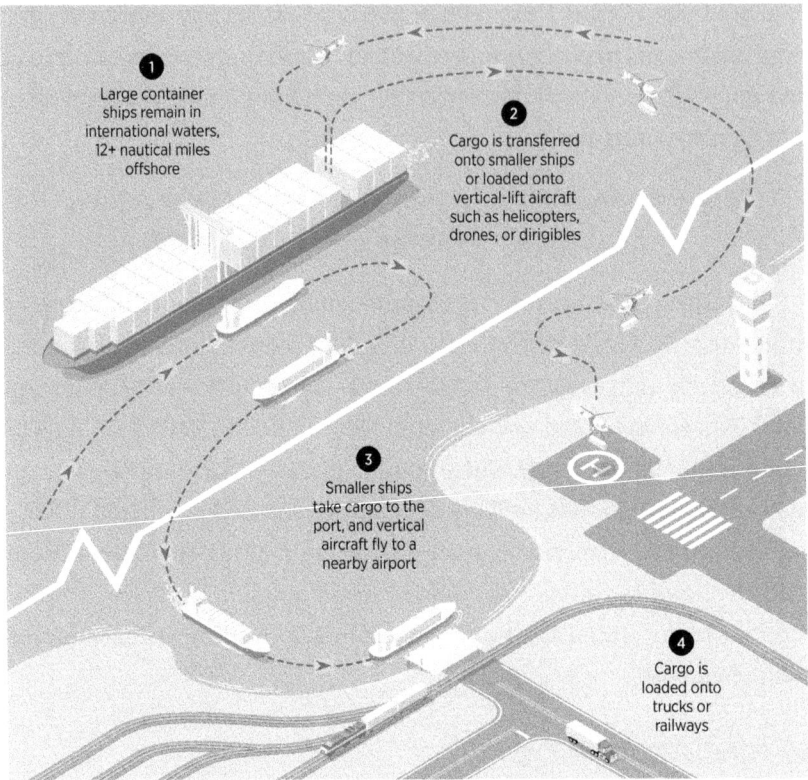

FIGURE 6. The concept of multimodalism   *Heritage Foundation*

unmanned surface vessel (LUSV), which is basically an automated offshore support vessel. Such stability between ships at sea is not a far-off development; it is a capability already used by support vessels that service offshore wind farms and oil rigs. The Navy's *Spearhead*-class expeditionary fast transports and experimental autonomous LUSVs have shallow drafts that would be ideal for feeder ships with the cargo capacity to open trade to previously inaccessible ports. This capability would provide greater logistical resilience with more secondary ports where cargo can be moved with minimal new infrastructure needed.

To manage today's shipping, companies like Flexport are streamlining the existing supply chain and transport networks. It is a lucrative business line but not revolutionary. When a container ship carrying thousands of TEU arrives in port, it is usually days before the cargo is on its way, and then longer still to reach its destination.[87] The actual time it takes is a function of crane and ground transport availability for onward delivery. If the cargo within a TEU container must be further

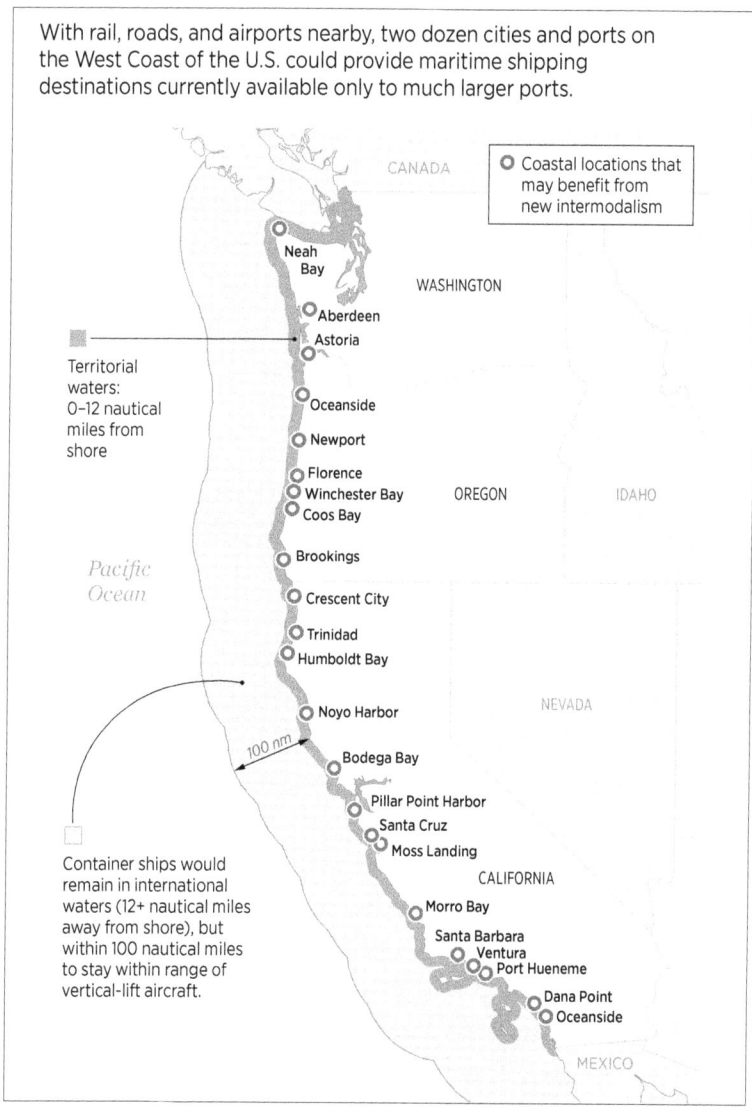

MAP 13. OPPORTUNITIES FOR NEW INTERMODALISM
SOURCE: Authors' research   Heritage Foundation

broken down for onward delivery, that adds still more time and requires warehousing, which can be in short supply. All this handling takes time and money. Reducing the need for these movements is where the next revolution in shipping resides. The key feature of Flexport's approach is getting cargo on and off the dock quickly. A new multimodalism must do this but much more.

Conducting cargo transfers to smaller feeder vessels opens shallow-water ports, often without the pier space or cranes to service modern and future container ships. A review of nautical charts, rail lines, and road maps between Los Angeles and the Strait of Juan de Fuca to Port Angeles, Washington, suggests there are at least sixteen ports that could achieve greater global trade connectivity using these types of feeder vessels. Today only three geographic locales service the vast majority of the American West Coast container traffic: San Francisco Bay (Oakland, San Francisco), Puget Sound (Seattle, Tacoma), and Los Angeles–Long Beach. Diversifying ports of entry would ease existing bottlenecks while increasing trade connectivity that would benefit Americans.

MASSIVE STAY-AT-SEA CONTAINER SHIPS

The current champion of container ships can carry 24,004 TEU. Built in China, it is the beast Ever Alot, measuring 1,312 feet long, 201 feet wide, and with a 55-foot draft. This immense size limits where it can dock.[88] Carriers are ordering these gargantuan ships from Asian shipyards because the shippers are able to reduce the delivered cost per TEU with economies of scale, but clean energy goals like IMO 2030 continue to mandate reduced emissions, which have significant design implications for future vessels and their energy sources.[89] Today marine diesel remains the primary fuel for large commercial maritime vessels, but environmental and energy efficiency concerns could ultimately see increased demand for maritime nuclear power.[90] Developments in other alternative fuels such as clean hydrogen and liquefied natural gas remain an aspiration but are not as "green" as nuclear power. Developments in small modular reactors offer a solution, powering massive merchant ships with the greenest of energies. Today, building such vessels in the

United States would be constrained based on a shortage of infrastructure such as graving docks, but vessels purchased on the open market could be modified in the United States until domestic production matures—that is, is forward nuclear compatible.

To achieve cost advantages from cargo-carrying economies of scale, massive ships will be needed. Using nuclear power for propulsion both serves to meet multinationally mandated green energy goals and frees the ships from frequent refueling, making them able to stay at sea for very long durations. Most importantly perhaps, nuclear propulsion enables sustained higher-speed ocean transits, effectively increasing overall cargo throughput with fewer ships. While competitors are forced to constrain their steaming speeds to meet emissions requirements, higher-value cargo could find its way aboard nuclear-powered high-speed cargo ships to help drive down inventory carrying costs. Regulatory uncertainty for this bold new future is, however, a real factor. Employing nuclear power on commercial ships will require new port-state permissibility and emergency preparedness readiness zones that set standoff distances from population centers in the event of a nuclear incident. While entry to some ports would be desired, moving cargo from these ships miles offshore using dirigibles and cargo-carrying feeder vessels minimizes the number of ports where these arrangements would be required.

As the world looks to green energy solutions, the International Energy Agency has emphasized nuclear power as a viable, cost-effective green energy production method.[91] Likewise, recent developments in small commercial reactors could usher in a renaissance of nuclear power at sea. This has been tried before, most notably in President Dwight Eisenhower's 1955 Atoms for Peace program and the related launching of a nuclear-powered commercial ship, the NS *Savannah*. The ship has been anchored since 1970 in Baltimore Harbor. The cost of operating and maintaining the earlier nuclear power plant and the lack of cargo-carrying capacity proved cost prohibitive, and the idea failed to become profitable. That could be changing with new advanced small modular reactors.

On July 29, 2022, the U.S. Nuclear Regulatory Commission approved NuScale Power's small modular reactor design.[92] NuScale's reactor uses passive means to cool its pressurized power plant by submerging it in water. It would produce six hundred megawatts of electricity in a twelve-reactor module grouping. At fifty megawatts each, one or two of these cores could potentially power large container ships using already proven electric-drive methods of propulsion. Other small nuclear reactor designs suitable for shipping are in the works, like TerraPower's molten salt reactor and a fifteen-megawatt heat pipe reactor being developed at the Los Alamos National Laboratory.[93] All these designs will drive electric power-generating turbines. For ship propulsion, electric drives are used instead of steam turbines attached through reduction gears to a propeller. The electricity generated powers an electric motor that turns the propeller with far less penalty to cargo capacity and simpler installation to replace conventional ship power plants. Electric drives are a proven design, having been used on various warships starting in the 1930s like the aircraft carriers *Langley*, *Lexington*, *Saratoga*, and others, and on five battleships like the *New Mexico* and others.[94] Based on this track record and technological advances, the latest U.S. Navy warships, like the destroyer *Truxtun* in 2018, have employed these systems with favorable results, including reduced fuel costs and ease of operations by the crew.[95] The more advanced *Zumwalt*-class destroyers have an integrated power system that also uses electric motors rather than large and very heavy reduction gears to reduce the high speed of turbines used for generating electricity into motive force directly. *Zumwalt*'s integrated power system can generate seventy-eight megawatts of power, using only seventeen of that to propel the ship at a speed of twenty knots.[96] Electric-drive propulsion has likewise matured in the commercial setting, with recent new-build cruise ships providing up to 20 percent fuel savings.[97]

KICKSTARTING A REVOLUTION IN SHIPPING—MARKET BRIDGES AND INNOVATION INCUBATORS

The development of new methods of shipping and shipbuilding will be a key element of the new multimodalism. In tandem with these engineering advances, the industry will need to attract workers to build, maintain, and run these new machines and get the concept to sea. Such a novel approach will need to bring together experts in finance, nuclear engineering, unmanned systems, education, and manufacturing. In the business world, start-up companies have benefited from so-called incubators that specialize in bringing diverse expertise and capacities together in one place to accelerate innovation and foster young companies. Inspired by business incubators, a similar approach can foster the early development of multimodalism while also attracting new entrants to the maritime sector and as merchant mariners.

An important advantage of the business incubator is its proximity to customers and associated business services. In the developmental phase, geographic proximity is important for small start-up enterprises to access business support services like financing, training of skilled workers, and workshops for producing working prototypes. Moreover, this collocation enables cross-communication for engineering and technical developments, such as between groups working to address power distribution systems in future nuclear-powered massive container ships with another group developing feeder vessel stability systems. Seemingly unrelated projects working in collocated workshops and labs are more likely to engender the needed commonality of support systems and interoperability. The approach would also accelerate the development and application of more mature technologies and processes like additive manufacturing in the fabrication process.

Given the imperative for the military to be postured for a war with China, this incubator would first focus on developing several key militarily useful capabilities—one example is vertical-launch system rearming at sea. Initially the incubator, while focused on developing solutions to vertical-launch rearming at sea, would also look for ways to apply such developed technologies to shipping and shipbuilding. Then, as prototypes are developed and operated, the lessons learned will inform the training of the workforce that builds, operates, and maintains them. Having training centers collocated with the developers would create a rapid feedback loop informing the training of future workforces.

An additional task of such an incubator is to encourage personnel to enter the maritime sector. This will require attracting a younger population with offers of meaningful work advancing exciting new fields with

The business world has long used an "incubator" to provide services to benefit start-ups. The Department of Defense could embrace this concept to produce prototypes, assist DOD procurement processes, and enter the commercial sector for appropriate innovations.

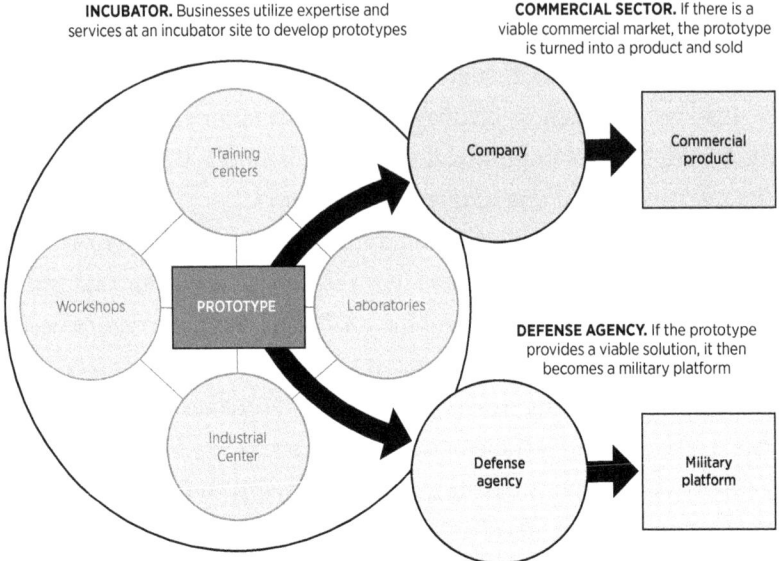

FIGURE 7. Creating a Defense Department innovation market bridge incubator
SOURCE: Authors' research Heritage Foundation

lucrative careers. This cannot be a ground-up approach, and leveraging the workforce of today will be needed to benefit from the decades of collective experience in shipyards and operating ships at sea. To do this will require a collocated training center focused on advanced naval architecture education, modern shipyard industrial techniques, and operational mariner proficiencies. However, getting shipyard workers and naval architects to leave their jobs for the prospect of improved skills will also require arrangements that benefit them as well as their employers. One way to do this is to create a program modeled on the Fulbright and Mansfield scholarship programs, which focus on exposing U.S. participants to international institutions and new ways of doing business.[98] A new maritime fellowship for aspiring maritime professionals and skilled industrial workers could be offered. This would bring together experts and skilled shipyard workers from around the nation and from some allied nations to share best practices, study, and advance relevant new processes and technologies like unmanned ships. The third element of this training institution would be the operators.

The United States currently has a deficit in able merchant mariners, and growing their numbers means providing options to pursue lucrative careers at sea. If a sustained crisis were to occur, the number of U.S. mariners (many of whom are approaching retirement age) needed would fall short. Addressing this shortfall is the duty of the Maritime Administration, which has tried to use student incentive payments to pay for college with associated obligations to serve in the merchant marine. However, without a viable industry to work in, many potential takers have forgone the $12,000 per year stipend. While more is needed to entice people to become merchant marine officers, more is also required to attract and retain more shipyard workers and the crews of modern merchant ships. Doing this will be important to sustain American shipping and shipbuilding. In addition to increased scholarships for college, longer associated service obligations (currently only three years) and new stipends targeting skilled laborers are needed to entice the next generation of shipyard workers with the cutting-edge technical skills needed. Additionally, until American shipping returns with a new multimodalism, career options need to ensure that enough American merchant mariners retain the skills required for operating at sea. One way of doing this is to offer salary offsets to those working for allied nations' shipping companies so they may retain mariner certifications. Eventually, these mariners would return to be trained to, and eventually would, take over the ships of a future American shipping fleet.

The Department of Defense is attempting something like this. In 2015 the Defense Innovation Unit (DIU) was established to accelerate the adoption of commercial and dual-use technology to solve military operational challenges.[99] The DIU does this by soliciting commercial venders to provide solutions on contract by leveraging authorities for rapid prototyping using other transaction authorities (10 USC sec. 2371b.f). Unlike the narrowly focused innovation incubator, the DIU has been broadly focused on a range of technologies and does not consider the commercial application of developed prototypes. The result has been predictable criticism of the DIU for failing to adopt at-scale new technologies that offer a return on investment to commercial participants. This is a sentiment echoed by Mike Brown in a 2022 interview at the end of four years as director of the DIU.[100] And the DIU's failure to scale innovations was a topic of discussion at the 2020 Aspen Security Forum that included the secretary of defense. At this forum, Shield AI chief executive officer Ryan Tseng captured the sentiment: "The DoD and the national security sector need to find a way to allow companies to generate returns for their investments in innovation.... Without the right incentive structure, little will get past research and development and prototype grants."[101] A multimodal innovation incubator can avoid the shortcomings of DIU by being narrowly focused on maritime operational problems and supporting the transition to commercial applications of developed technologies. Importantly, a maritime innovation incubator must accelerate innovation associated with scaled-up production informed by collocated research, production, and training facilities.[102]

Then, as the innovation incubator begins to deliver results, there will be a need for greater access to places with the associated infrastructure and platforms—albeit with comparatively less investment than port expansion and new intermodal connectors like roads, railways, and airports. The sites for new investment should take a page from the Trump administration's "opportunity zones" program. These were created in 2017 and intended to attract investment to economically distressed neighborhoods by providing investors a way to invest profits while avoiding capital gains taxes.[103] A similar approach could be applied to communities that would host nodes of the new multimodalism—ports, distribution centers, and so on. Infrastructure investments would in turn be incorporated and stocks offered as added incentives to investors. If they existed today, a beneficiary of such multimodal opportunity zones would be the investors in the port of Ponce, Puerto Rico. Scale AI has invested $2 million to turn the port into a smart port lab to mature technologies that could be used at other ports.[104] Technologies to be matured there include AI-enabled document processing, route optimization, object recognition, computer vision, and remote operations.

In October 2021 the Heritage Foundation hosted Dr. William Roper to discuss the concept of market bridges and how this could speed delivery of new technologies to the military. As director of the Defense Department's Strategic Capabilities Office and then assistant secretary of the Air Force for acquisition, technology, and logistics, Dr. Roper had seen firsthand the challenges of market entry for new innovative companies. His concept of a market bridge is straightforward—provide the demand and regulatory environment conducive for these small companies to produce innovative solutions to military needs.[105] A market bridge provides a regulatory bubble to proof key innovations that the Navy needs to actualize its war-fighting concepts, which can likewise advance multimodalism.

Kickstarting a revolution in shipping requires overcoming prohibitive developmental costs, regulatory constraints, and capital investments for manufacturing. One path forward is solving contemporary military problems like missile rearming of warships at sea and the need to sustain expeditionary forces far from logistic hubs. These are just some of the key operational problems the military is confronting as it thinks through what a war with China would entail using concepts like multidomain operations, distributed maritime operations, or expeditionary advance base operations.[106] All of these concepts rely on independent maneuver with coordinated effects across dispersed groups of marines, soldiers, aircraft, and ships. Actualizing such a construct is a focus of the Navy's 2022 Navigation Plan, which lays out six force design imperatives.[107] Of these several cross over into capabilities key in realizing multimodalism.

EXPEDITIONARY LOGISTICS

Expeditionary logistics is the ability to resupply forward-deployed units exposed to enemy attack, with rudimentary infrastructure, and dispersed over significant distances. Most notable in this regard has been the ongoing negotiations between the Marine Corps and the Navy in the design of a small logistics ship—the light amphibious warship (in 2024 called the medium landing ship).[108] Additionally, to minimize exposure to enemy attack (e.g., Chinese ballistic and cruise missiles), time in port or a fixed location during resupply operations would be held to a minimum. An example of this occurred during the war in Afghanistan. To avoid the threat from improvised explosive devices, the Navy and Marine Corps deployed autonomous K-MAX medium-lift cargo helicopters for a successful three-year resupply mission.[109] Developments in this area would benefit multimodal commercial use of feeder vessels and cost-effective vertical-lift cargo transport (helicopters, dirigibles, etc.).

RESILIENT LOGISTICS

Resilient logistics is the capacity to rearm, repair, and resupply ships far from major shipyards and industrial bases, at times under threat from an enemy. To this end, since a major speech at Columbia University in January 2023, the secretary of the Navy has prioritized the at-sea reload of vertical-launch systems. This would enable the Navy to rearm warships with an array of missiles that today must be done at a limited number of ports.[110] The Defense Department has also invested in additive manufacturing to alleviate reliance on long, easily interrupted supply chains by having onboard production of replacement parts.[111] Moreover, additive manufacturing plants have the potential to disperse manufacturing at an industrial scale, including, perhaps, on massive factory ships underway at sea. As the military develops vertical-launch system reloads at sea, this can also prompt the development of capabilities that enable cargo transfer at sea between massive container ships and feeder vessels. Likewise, the advancement of additive manufacturing will accelerate the dispersal of production, making a new multimodalism of greater utility.

EXPANDED DISTANCES

The Navy has focused substantial resources on extending the range of its weapons and its existing aircraft. Notably, the Navy has worked to develop the MQ-25 unmanned aircraft for in-flight refueling and surveillance missions.[112] The intent is to match and then exceed Chinese weapon ranges, but this work also indicates an awareness of the need for longer-range aircraft with higher fuel efficiencies, including increased use of unmanned aircraft for a range of missions. Improvements in engine efficiency and range, especially for vertical-lift craft, will make moving cargo from massive container ships at sea to inland locations more economically viable—a key feature of the proposed multimodalism.

INCREASED DISTRIBUTION

Increased distribution will require deploying a widely dispersed fleet of platforms connected via secure communications for a unity of effect. To achieve this, two related efforts of the Navy are important—communications network JADC2 and LUSVs. In the Navy's concept of distributed maritime operations, the aim is to enable rapid response to an enemy from numerous vectors of attack, thereby complicating an enemy's defenses. Doing so requires a resilient and reliable communications network connecting widely dispersed platforms—manned, unmanned, and autonomous. Joint All-Domain Command and Control (JADC2) is an effort to develop a common communications network linking all the U.S. military services to share sensitive data—a common analogy used is to compare it to the popular ride-sharing application Uber, which connects a rider with the most suitable driver.[113] LUSVs are experimental repurposed offshore service vessels with greatly automated and remotely monitored shipboard systems able to carry a variety of containerized cargoes.[114] In July 2022 the Navy successfully tested methods of autonomous ship control of an even larger expeditionary fast-transport ship that has a ramp that can accommodate roll-on/roll-off of an M1A2 tank and six hundred tons of cargo.[115] The goal is a fleet connected by a resilient network that enables manned and unmanned platforms to act in concert for a desired result. These military developments have utility in managing a global network of multimodal transportation across manned and autonomous platforms. Moreover, when paired with blockchain technology and new cargo containers, it can offer a secure method of monitoring cargo during shipment and ease customs at more varied points of entry.[116]

NO ONE CARES UNTIL A NOVEL MULTIMODALISM PROOF-OF-CONCEPT MAKES THEM CARE

Nothing galvanizes action like a visible demonstration of a new capability, whether it is the Wright brothers' first manned flight at Kitty

Hawk, Billy Mitchell's shocking first aerial bombing and sinking of the battleship *Ostfriesland*, and of course McLean's 1956 container shipping.[117] Similarly, a proof-of-concept is critical to demonstrate the viability of various technologies coming together in a novel multimodalism that is both profitable and not ecologically damaging. An effective proof-of-concept must also address the innovator's dilemma—"markets that don't exist can't be analyzed."[118] A successful demonstration of the

MAP 14. NEW MULTIMODALISM PROOF-OF-CONCEPT: DETROIT–TOLEDO–CHICAGO

SOURCE: *Authors' analysis.* Heritage Foundation

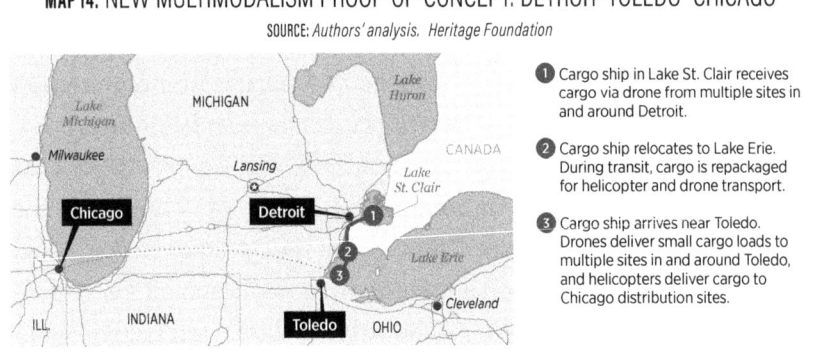

❶ Cargo ship in Lake St. Clair receives cargo via drone from multiple sites in and around Detroit.

❷ Cargo ship relocates to Lake Erie. During transit, cargo is repackaged for helicopter and drone transport.

❸ Cargo ship arrives near Toledo. Drones deliver small cargo loads to multiple sites in and around Toledo, and helicopters deliver cargo to Chicago distribution sites.

MAP 15. NEW MULTIMODALISM COMPREHENSIVE PROOF-OF-CONCEPT: U.S. EAST COAST AND PUERTO RICO SOURCE: *Authors' analysis.* Heritage Foundation

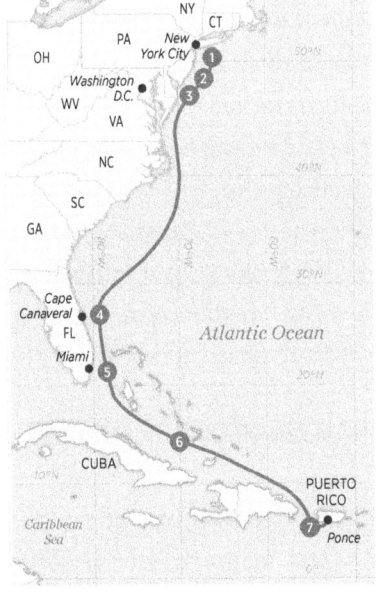

❶ Cargo ship is offshore of New York City. Cargo is delivered to cargo ship from various sites in and around the city. Feeder vessels deliver standard shipping containers from piers to cargo ship.

❷ Cargo ship relocates to offshore Delaware. During transit, it repackages cargo for distribution.

❸ Cargo ship arrives offshore Delaware and offloads cargo via helicopter for delivery to D.C. and Baltimore distribution sites.

❹ Cargo ship relocates to offshore Cape Canaveral, Fla., and delivers cargo via drones and helicopters to various sites to include potentially Patrick Space Force Base.

❺ Cargo ship relocates to Miami for conventional cargo operations.

❻ Cargo ship gets underway for Ponce, Puerto Rico. During transit, cargo is repacked for drone, helicopter, and feeder vessel transfers.

❼ Prior to mooring at Ponce, cargo transfers via drone, helicopter, and feeder vessels conducted to points on Puerto Rico. While moored at Ponce, "smart port" concepts and operations to be tested.

new multimodalism envisioned would provide key insights into the engineering challenges as well inform the operational costs of such a novel approach to shipping. Today there are several ports, technology companies, and local governments toying with key elements of this new multimodalism; a well-planned demonstration would show the way to link their efforts. This is why location for an initial demonstration will likely be centered on the Great Lakes, near current efforts to use drones for cargo movement; along the East Coast of the United States, where efforts are underway to reduce road and rail traffic, or in Puerto Rico, where there is work on smart ports.

CONCLUSION

If the United States cannot compete in global shipping and shipbuilding, the cost of building the necessary navy needed will increase, industrial capacity will be limited, and technology constraints may arise. Meanwhile, transportation-intensive industries across the economy will continue to flee to countries with more favorable maritime logistics and hinterland trade connectivity. Consequently, the nation's economy will increasingly rely on hostile nations for shipping, and the decline of the American maritime sector will continue. This conceivably entices increasingly provocative CCP adventurism as the Navy's downward trajectory progresses unabated. This can be reversed by bringing together know-how from disparate technical fields and expertise to create a domestic landscape that can host a sustainable competitive advantage in American shipbuilding, shipping, and logistics. American manufacturing produces near-record amounts, and this strength needs to be carried over to the shipbuilding and logistics fields.[119] Getting to this end state will require action from national leadership.

To plot a course for this recovery, the president will need to lead an effort to publish a national maritime strategy that is specific and enforceable, unlike past attempts, and lays out specific tasks and the agencies responsible for action. The goal is to regain American global competitiveness in shipping and shipbuilding while meeting current military needs. Such an endeavor is long term, which requires an associated execution plan to ensure progress can be monitored. Congress must sustain resourcing and oversight through a special committee on regaining American commercial maritime competitiveness. Congress has attempted this, calling for a Commission on the Future of the Navy in 2023, but it has yet to stand up that body. The nation deserves better going forward.[120] Like the select committee on the CCP, which has been stood up, the new committee would call hearings to assess and inform further actions to ensure the national maritime strategy is being adequately pursued.[121] Given the cross-cutting nature of the maritime sector, which covers commerce, transportation, and national defense, the committee's leadership needs to frequently hold routine hearings with leaders from the Maritime Administration, U.S. Coast Guard, and the U.S. Navy.

To ensure a favorable environment for an American revolution in shipping, several actions are needed. First is the establishment of an informal maritime group of nations to establish and sustain fair overseas conditions. The maritime group would aim to coordinate regulatory and commerce policies to facilitate a new multimodalism that leverages at-sea container traffic connected to shore via feeder vessels and further inland via vertical-lift craft (e.g., drones, dirigibles, helicopters). The initial meeting of the maritime group should be held in the United States with invitations for representatives from like-minded maritime nations; a list of recommended participants is provided in table 4. The agenda for the initial meeting would include setting new shipping environmental fuel standards, establishing assurances of access to shipping in crisis, and creating regulatory coherency regarding small nuclear reactors in commercial shipping. Administratively, this effort would be led by the secretary of transportation supported by interagency subject matter experts, for example, in the Department of the Navy, Coast Guard, Department of Energy, U.S. Trade Representative, Department of Commerce. Given the proposed agenda, initial membership should include South Korea and Japan as natural members given their treaty alliances with the United States; in practice, they are the only competitive countries to China in shipbuilding. Likewise, the Philippines, Indonesia, Vietnam, Poland, and Türkiye, with tens of thousands of experienced mariners, should be included. Greece, Singapore, Germany, Norway, and the Netherlands are countries with thousands of large commercial ships of their own, and they are currently developing novel methods of shipping today. And consideration should be given to include Switzerland, given its significant financial and chartered presence in the global maritime sector.[122] However, the maritime group is only part of the way ahead; the United States must better combat unfair Chinese maritime business practices and must incentivize U.S. shipping. To this end, the president will need to direct policy changes and seek increased resourcing for agencies like the Federal Maritime Commission to better combat harmful Chinese maritime business practices at home and abroad. Consideration should be given to updating laws for preferential sequencing of port access and services for U.S.-flagged vessels in U.S. ports and to eliminating port fees (i.e., the HMTF) for these U.S. vessels.

Setting conditions at home is critical and requires local, state, and national attention as well as working with industry. Getting the collective attention of this group and investors will require a proof-of-concept demonstration, such as McLean in 1956 with container shipping. Finding the next McLean in shipping will be critical to execute a new multimodalism proof-of-concept. While Congress and the executive branch should be engaged, it is industry and commercial investors who must bear the burden of executing a proof-of-concept. To get the greatest value and attract future investment, a more comprehensive demonstration should be executed involving the movement of cargo at Manhattan, Washington state, Miami, and Ponce, Puerto Rico. This comprehensive demonstration does carry more risk, so a scaled initial demonstration based on the Great Lakes should focus on vertical-lift and drone operations in high traffic and populated areas to an offshore cargo ship. This two-step demonstration (a scaled test and then a larger public demonstration) should exercise all facets of the new multimodalism envisioned, informing business models, informing needed regulatory relief or action, and galvanizing local and national attention.

We also need to create places where we can mature, test, and build various technologies. A promising way to do this is to establish a maritime innovation incubator. Venture capital–funded start-up companies already benefit from incubators, and the Department of Defense has experience with its DIU.[123] Using the lessons of these start-ups and the DIU, we need to create a maritime incubator with business and engineering support services, training centers, and waterfront access for demonstrating marketable prototypes that can attract new commercial entrants to the maritime sector. A maritime incubator provides an environment conducive to creating the technologies, workforce, and synergies across various technologies needed to realize multimodalism. Delivering at-scale solutions for shipping is likely not feasible initially, so providing solutions for the military's key operational problems is a good first customer. Done well, these militarily useful logistic capabilities can be made commercially viable and built and sold at a scale that makes it lucrative. At the same time, locations for expanded maritime trade connected even far inland will be needed to ensure that multimodalism matures in an economically viable manner. To do this, new multimodal opportunity zones should be created with favorable tax and other incentives to attract maritime industry investment. Such maritime opportunity zones would be the seed corn that would grow into the backbone of the new multimodalism—ports, inland distribution centers able to be connected directly to massive container ships at sea via heavy-lift aircraft, smaller cargo feeder vessels, and so on.

All this technology and new ship designs are worthless without the people to operate and maintain them. Today the maritime sector in the United States does not attract or train the needed workforce, so we will need to incentivize the competitiveness of American merchant mariners and shipyard workers. One way to get at this is to establish advanced mariner training centers and naval architecture advanced degree programs. If this training can be done at the maritime innovation incubators, there is added synergy in providing education and technical skill training where it is needed most. Innovation incubators should also have training centers that provide cutting-edge education in industrial skills, advanced degrees and certifications for naval architects, and advanced operational training relevant to the new multimodalism (e.g., unmanned ship operations, nuclear power). And there is a benefit for the existing maritime industry too. Stipends could be offered by state and federal agencies using existing educational grants refocused on skills important to the maritime sector. In fact, promising candidates in today's maritime sector could be assured that, upon completion of such training, they can return to their old jobs, bringing added expertise at little cost to the parent company—low investment / big return. New maritime fellowships that focus on graduate-level education (e.g., naval architecture) should also be pursued, both at U.S. institutions and in allied nations with a vibrant maritime industry (e.g., Japan, South Korea). Until there is a large and viable American shipping industry, stipends will be needed to offset the loss in salary to American merchant mariners serving aboard friendly foreign-flag ships, with the stipulation that, to receive this money, they must maintain relevant maritime certifications, stay in good health, and remain obligated for a predefined timeframe for recall to serve on U.S. merchant vessels in time of war.

The United States has neglected a core element of its security and prosperity—its historic maritime strength. As a result, American shipping and shipbuilding has atrophied, yet domestic industry and capacity for innovation remain strong. This advantage needs to be pressed by focusing on restoring American maritime competitiveness in pursuit of a new multimodalism. Returning to our roots as a maritime nation and manufacturing powerhouse and asserting the necessary innovations to do so in the modern era will be pivotal. If done well, fostering an American revolution in shipping can energize a lethargic industrial sector critical to the nation's defense and able to sustain a wartime economy.

A stronger and globally competitive maritime sector serves as a deterrent against Chinese economic coercion and military adventurism. With it, American trade can proceed unimpeded by dependency on others and with confidence that the U.S. military can sustain combat operations on U.S.-flagged vessels. In addition to serving American security needs, this revolution in shipping has the potential to mitigate environmental degradation, to promote domestic production, and to expand American exports to global markets, which can spur wider job growth and advance technological innovation in the United States. Getting underway on this project toward a renaissance of America's maritime sector begins with a proof-of-concept demonstration. One of the beneficiaries of and the rationale for undertaking this revolution in shipping is naval shipbuilding, which is the subject of the next chapter.

CHAPTER 6

A TWENTY-FIRST-CENTURY NAVAL ACT FOR SHIPS, SHIPYARDS, AND SAILORS

For years as China massively grew and modernized its fleet, the U.S. Navy has diminished to a point that tips the military balance in Asia dangerously against it—and its allies. Still, there is limited time to reverse this, and history points the way forward. The Naval Act of 1938, in response to the Washington Naval Treaty, naval shipbuilding violations by Imperial Japan, and Germany's annexation of Austria, galvanized naval shipbuilding just in time to deliver *Iowa*-class battleships, *Atlanta*-class light cruisers, the carrier *Hornet*, and other warships early in World War II. If the nation had delayed its response to these violations, it is unclear how much longer the war in the Pacific would have taken to conclude. Furthermore, if the nation had acted earlier, it is conceivable it could have prevented the war in the Pacific.

Today the nation confronts a rapidly deteriorating security environment, much as it did in 1938, but if we heed the lessons of history and apply them now, there is time to bolster our defenses—most importantly, the Navy. Doing this will require a modern naval act that begins an aggressive shipbuilding program, spurs recruitment for people, and develops needed shipyards. This effort should occur in tandem with the previous chapters' focuses on improving the nation's energy resiliency and strengthening of the maritime industrial sector, which are so critical to fielding an effective naval force.

A MODERN NAVAL ACT: SHIPS, SHIPYARDS, AND SAILORS

The 1930s domestic shipbuilding and defense industrial situation as well as the military balance have some similarity to the nation's predicament today: a lackluster defense industrial base, war in Europe, and rising threats from Asia. Reflecting on the success of the nation's defense industrial mobilization after 1938, one of the architects, Bill Knudsen, attributed the success simply to placing orders and financing plant expansion.[1] In short, if today's Congress and Navy can provide the demand for production with the predictability of payment, then perhaps the nation's naval shipbuilding capacity can be expanded. Sadly, this is something our nation's post–Cold War defense budgeting has generally lacked, especially when it comes to shipbuilding. Failing to pass budgets on time is the norm; in fact, according to the Government Accountability Office (GAO), the government has operated on stopgap continuing resolutions for all but three of the forty-six years between 1976 and 2022.

There is precious little time to act, as it takes two to three years to identify and qualify venders to produce the needed military-grade materials for ship construction. To grow the military industrial base before a looming showdown with China, we need to take action before the end of 2025. Otherwise, it will require substantially more investment and action to overcome our lack of readiness before China's confidence and capacity peaks. Unfortunately, without shipyard workers, none of this is possible, and the biggest competitor for human capital could be McDonald's with its twenty-dollar-an-hour wage. To compete, shipyard work must be lucrative for the individual, and meaningful in deterring China by delivering a greater capacity for building and crewing warships this decade. In short, a modern naval act must set in motion an expansion of naval shipbuilding that in turn spurs growth in shipyard capacity and workforce.

SHIPS

How many ships are needed? A consensus among policymakers has been building that China is planning to move against Taiwan this decade, with some asserting it will happen by 2027—see statements by current and past Indo-Pacific commanders and directors of the Central Intelligence Agency.[2] Yet, calls to grow the Navy to deter China—an endeavor that takes years to realize—have stalled consistently the last twenty years. The

Chief of Naval Operations (CNO) has voiced his concerns for a shipbuilding industry without the capacity today to build or support a larger fleet.[3] CNO Adm. Michael Gilday summed up what was needed to correct this, stating: "We need to give a signal to industry that we need to get to three destroyers a year, instead of 1.5, that we need to maintain two submarines a year. And so, part of this is on us to give them a clear set of—a clear aim point so they can plan a workforce and infrastructure that is going to be able to meet the demand. But again, no industry is going to make those kinds of investments unless we give them a higher degree of confidence."[4]

Moreover, the mission of the Navy is twofold, and has been since the nation's birth: to protect national interests in peacetime while being ready to wage war at sea. It is not an either/or proposition, making it odd that the secretary of defense in 2022 rejected an amendment to codify the Navy's peacetime missions.[5] Forward naval presence and its use in diplomacy is well known, and being nearer the threat means warships are ready and positioned should conflict become unavoidable. Sustaining a forward presence also has animated the Navy's long-range shipbuilding plans and the target number of ships needed. Therefore, this recent act by the administration belies a lack of appreciation of the role navies play in deterrence and securing peacetime interests. Further, it belies an effort to defer the cost of the Navy needed in pursuit of immediate budget cuts amid the promise of future wonder weapons. Already there are serious doubts that today's Navy has adequate resources to meet the threats facing the nation.[6]

In a break with convention, in 2022 the Navy began submitting long-range shipbuilding plans with three alternatives based on how Congress would resource it. When pressed, the CNO has said only the larger request would come close to meeting defense requirements—but still the fleet has grown smaller.[7] To reverse these downward trends as China rapidly expands its fleet, the CNO has on multiple occasions asserted that his budget will need sustained, year-on-year growth of 3–5 percent above inflation.[8] This would be a marked increase given post–Cold War norms, for sure, a time when defense spending averaged just over 3 percent of gross domestic product, with the Navy accounting for less than 30 percent of the defense budget. On the other hand, a return to such a level would approach the 1980s' naval buildup when defense budgets averaged between 5 to 6 percent of gross domestic product and the Navy averaged 37.6 percent of that annual budget.

In *U.S. Naval Power in the 21st Century*, the optimum naval force was calculated based on peacetime competition with China and Russia and what would be needed to win a long war with China. That fleet would be operated in eight maritime theaters with specific force requirements based on the seasonal maritime activity, threats, and the potential to shape the strategic environment. It was a threat-informed, math-based exercise that recommended a manned fleet of 390 warships by 2030. At the same time, the Navy's own Force Structure Assessment called for a fleet of 331 warships. Moreover, according to that Fleet Structure Assessment, as of the writing of this book, the Navy should have 314 warships but in fact has only 292—a reminder that the current approaches are not working. After nine years of at best treading water, the Navy will need an infusion of leadership and resources if it hopes to approach a fleet able to deter China this dangerous decade.

The task of deterring China is daunting, but there are options to bolster what little deterrence remains while setting the conditions at home for a national mobilization if war becomes inevitable. First, we need to give naval shipbuilding an unmistakable mandate and provide the necessary resources to build the warships that the Navy has long known it needs, such as destroyers, aircraft carriers, and nuclear submarines. But the Navy must rapidly ramp up production of unmanned vessels that can add both sensor coverage and firepower sailing in formation with traditional manned warships. Designs and concepts of operations are already being refined, but there is still work to be done before the most promising unmanned platforms like the extra-large unmanned undersea vessels (XLUUV) and the large (LUSV) and medium (MUSV) unmanned surface vessels can enter serial production. The Navy and Congress should continue to emphasize and apply due scrutiny of these programs through the normal National Defense Authorization Act (NDAA) budgeting and oversight processes while unshackling the Department of Defense budget for shipbuilding of traditional and stable design warships like the *Arleigh Burke*–class destroyers. The intent is to focus defense dollars to accelerate development of the most promising unmanned vessels and other developmental warships—for example, the next-generation destroyer DDG(X) and next-generation nuclear submarine SSN(X)—that can restore conventional deterrence of China. At the same time, current warship production planned through this decade needs to set conditions for a rapid expansion of shipyard capacity and the recruitment of sailors and workers.

The recent past is also instructive for looking at what can be achieved in the near term, until 2027. President Ronald Reagan's six-hundred-ship naval buildup of the 1980s was never achieved, but a massive rebuilding effort was accomplished by increasing defense budgets disproportionately directed to naval shipbuilding and by the return to service of ships in the inactive fleet. The combination of new shipbuilding and reactivation grew the Navy from a low of 521 ships in 1981 to 594 six years later. In 2024 there is not much in the inactive fleet to recall to service, leading to retaining ships on the Navy's list for deactivation that have more than three years of life, thereby adding thirteen warships to the fleet. Furthermore, the fleet could grow a little more should the Navy and Congress authorize the planned production of twenty-one deployable unmanned (LUSV, MUSV, XLUUV) vessels. This would deliver a fleet of 331 warships by 2027. This is not good enough, and the threat from China demands action to grow the fleet faster than conventional approaches.

SHIPYARDS

The Navy's Shipyard Infrastructure Optimization Program (SIOP), submitted to Congress in September 2018, is a $21 billion twenty-year program.[9] It does not address the Navy's four overseas shipyards (in Spain, Bahrain, and two in Japan), which complete about 70 percent of all maintenance beyond planned completion dates. In the United States, the Navy also uses twenty-six private shipyards for more than 240 conventionally powered ships, most located in proximity to the Navy's bases, but—reflecting a Cold War European theater focus—has an unbalanced drydock capacity on the East Coast despite a larger number of ships on the West Coast.[10] The result is a private, public, and overseas shipyard capacity and skilled workforce operating beyond capacity and without modern equipment, which compounds delays and increases cost.

Fully funding the Navy's SIOP is necessary but will not address the shortfall in today's fleet, let alone in a larger one the nation will need for great-power competition. Multiple GAO reports and testimony before Congress indicate there is much work needed.[11] Case in point, over the summer of 2023, almost half of the nation's nuclear submarine fleet was reportedly in port waiting for maintenance.[12] This is deeply dangerous. Today there are only four public shipyards due to aggressive closures that shuttered shipyards in the 1990s to cash in on the post–Cold War peace dividend. Between 1996 and 1997 the public shipyards in Long Beach and Mare Island, California; Charleston, South Carolina; and Philadelphia, Pennsylvania, were all closed—cutting in half the Navy's ability to maintain its nuclear submarines and aircraft carriers.[13] Failing to maintain nuclear submarines is particularly dangerous, given their ability to evade China's deadliest defenses.

Similar concerns have been raised earlier. The Heritage Foundation's Maiya Clark has called for a fifth public shipyard, calling out the Navy's antiquated four public shipyards as unable to sustain sensitive nuclear-powered submarines and aircraft carriers.[14] Even the commander of Fleet Forces Command has called for two additional nuclear maintenance shipyards.[15] While shipyard capacity is inadequate, the number of people willing and with the requisite skills to do shipyard work is too small. This situation is beginning to have a deleterious impact on naval shipbuilding, illustrated by reporting in January 2024 that the Navy's new *Constellation*-class frigate is behind schedule due to worker shortfalls.[16] Investing in human capital—sailors and shipyard workers—must be included as a third pillar of a modern naval act.

SAILORS

As of February 1, 2024, the Navy was composed of 292 warships manned by 333,708 active-duty officers and sailors stationed across the globe.

For the 355-ship fleet planned for by 2034, the Navy assesses that end-strength manpower will need to grow to more than 360,000.[17] Working against the Navy's manning plans has been a crisis in recruiting that has set in since 2021. In 2023 the Navy missed its recruiting goals by 7,464, but so far its retention numbers have stayed steady . . . for now.[18] Retired U.S. Army lieutenant general Thomas Spoehr has studied the military's recruiting crisis for years and sees it as a national security dilemma. He and many military experts agree, more needs to be done to expand high school physical fitness programs, increase the numbers of military recruiters, and provide more remedial education programs for willing recruits from underperforming school systems.[19]

To meet its recruiting needs, the Navy must visibly engage in more high schools and communities—including those not known for delivering volunteers for military service. This can introduce more people to the merits of naval service. Studies indicate that this approach would improve recruiting. A better long-term solution would be for high schools to produce more technically apt graduates—and the Junior Reserve Officer Training Corps (JROTC) has proved that it can help do that. Given this track record, some disadvantaged school districts have turned to the JROTC—a move that has improved attendance, reduced disciplinary problems, and delivered higher graduation rates.

Another avenue in which the Navy will need to do more is better preparing new recruits for a naval career between basic training and their first operational assignment. Recruits usually receive minimal remediation to ready them for demanding technical specialties such as nuclear mechanics. As the Navy struggles to attract recruits, it has increasingly lowered the standards of who it recruits by allowing in recruits with lower Armed Services Qualification Test scores and even no high school diploma.[20] The result is a shortage of recruits who possess the necessary technical aptitudes required for the most challenging and technically demanding specialties. For the Navy to expand its fleet, it is imperative to establish methods for enhancing the skills of promising new recruits for the most technically challenging specialties. This represents a cultural shift for a service that prides itself on selecting recruits with the required technical aptitude. One potential solution is to reintroduce with a renewed mandate the Broadened Opportunity for Officer Selection and Training (BOOST) program, which was discontinued in 2008. Its new mandate must be to prepare promising junior enlisted sailors for the most technically challenging specialties while also providing a path for promising sailors to pursue a commission as an officer. Failing to prepare recruits who have less technical aptitude for a life at sea is hiring in bad faith. And unless the Navy acts to prepare, it will come at personal expense to the recruit, undue loss of taxpayer resources from higher accident rates, and potentially a loss in war.

Meanwhile, as recruitment has suffered, the Navy has had to rely increasingly on retaining trained sailors. This is a short-term palliative and does nothing to solve the underlying problems. Unfortunately, with at least 22,000 junior enlisted at-sea billets unfilled in January 2024, fewer sailors have to do more than normally expected.[21] Moreover, for the past forty years the Navy has maintained approximately one hundred warships at sea, and as the overall size of the fleet has dwindled, this has meant longer deployments and greater operational demands on both ships and personnel. Under this added stress, eventually sailors and officers will vote with their feet and leave the Navy—action is needed before that becomes a flood crossing the brow out of the Navy.

Each sailor and officer represent a significant investment in capital and time for effective operation of the fleet—an investment that must not be squandered and that, if lost, cannot easily be replaced. The same is true of highly skilled shipyard workers such as welders certified to conduct welds on naval nuclear propulsion plants. For a variety of reasons, the nation's naval shipbuilders are clustered in New England, Virginia's Tidewater region, and the Gulf Coast, leaving few options for those wishing to live elsewhere to consider a career in the maritime industry. Making matters worse, since Ronald Reagan was president, the number of people working in the defense industry is today a third of what it was then, with 17,000 defense-related companies having folded.[22] At a congressional hearing in February 2023, president of the Shipbuilders Council of America, Matthew Paxton, asserted that what shipbuilders most need from the Defense Department is "a consistent, upward and adequately funded demand spiral." A modern naval act must do this for recruiting sailors as well as shipyard workers, all in support of a sustained naval shipbuilding program.

CONGRESSIONAL BUDGET PROCESSES DO NOT ENABLE BEST BUSINESS PRACTICES

In the past, Congress has mandated force levels like the 12 Carrier Act in 2019 or, in 2016, legislated a fleet of 355 warships sometime in the future—neither action had assured money attached.[23] Given the dangers before the nation, and given what little time there is to build a naval force able to deter and win a war with China, why have results been illusionary?

Politics plays a role in the prioritization of funding for the military—this is a feature of our democratic governance. That said, in order for an issue to get needed political attention for action, it must be easily understood and accessible to the public. Burying the plan for a naval shipbuilding program and efforts to grow the associated shipyard capacities within the thousands of pages of the NDAA has not helped in this regard. Moving a narrow issue with wide public support out of a larger legislative vehicle for action has happened before. Recall how Congress addressed assault rifle bans outside of wider gun control; moved border wall construction outside wider immigration reform; and, more recently, when President Trump approved the FUTURE Act, locking in funding assistance for historically black colleges and universities outside of Department of Education budgeting.[24] These accomplishments associated a singular issue with a specific legislative bill. With these acts in mind, political leadership in Congress faces a choice on a national imperative—building a fleet to deter China backed by the industry to support it. Separate and dedicated legislation can act as a lightning rod, forcing the decision-making process. Such a move may also overcome administrations unwilling to make such investments. This, in fact, has been the case since 2021, as Congress has twice overruled the president's proposed defense budgets for fiscal years 2022 and 2023, budgets that would have shrunk the Navy to 280 warships in 2027.

Part of the answer is the way budgets are built for defense. On the structural front, the NDAA is one legislative bill to govern all military resourcing annually. Treating all the military services' requests for future capabilities, near-term operational needs, and procurement on a common scale using opaque administrative processes obscures too much. For one, it places the mobility and lethality of naval forces key in a war with China on the same priority plane as heavy land-based assets appropriate for a war in Europe or the Middle East. Inside the Department of Defense since the 1986 Goldwater–Nichols Act, a joint force resourcing process has not demonstrated itself fully effective at aligning limited resources according to the threat from China—yet.[25]

Given this recent history, in a rare move, a Democrat-led Congress bucked their own party's president and overrode his proposed budget, sending more moneys to defense. At the same time, Congress demonstrated an increasingly bipartisan desire to address the nation's lackluster shipbuilding and capacity for maintaining the Navy's ships through such legislation as the Shipyard Act. Had it passed, this act would have seen $4 billion for commercial shipyard growth and $21 billion toward modernizing the Navy's four public shipyards that sustain nuclear submarines and aircraft carriers.[26] Unfortunately, these additional moneys did not come with predictable orders for warships and promises of sustained resourcing.

However, sustaining that fleet would require capital investment to grow the workforce, building and maintaining it as well as investing in additional shipyards.[27] Sustained and predictable budgets have not been the norm for the Navy, which has consistently aimed for a fleet of more than three hundred ships, a number it has not exceeded since 2003. Moreover, since 2017 the Navy has annually underdelivered, according to long-term shipbuilding plans, by an average of ten warships.[28] Bottom line, a plan is nothing without leadership and resources.

Ships are expensive to build and maintain, and the purchase of an aircraft carrier at approximately $13 billion does impact the overall defense budget. Such big-ticket items exert a constraining effect on the Navy's budget planning process, as they are subject to a predetermined maximum dollar limit with specific "must resource" guidance from the Office of Management and Budget and the Defense Department's Defense Planning Guidance, even before the Navy's planning phase commences. This in turn results in downward pressure to either buy less or spread the cost over several budgets in order to minimize the visible impact that ship procurement can have from year to year on the NDAA.[29] As a result, the Navy has come to procure its most expensive ships with incremental funding, spreading the cost of a ship over several years with Congress's consent. The effect is great uncertainty and unpredictability for the shipbuilder and the Navy force planners. *Columbia*-class ballistic missile submarines, at $15 billion a ship, pose additional challenges to a shipbuilding budget ranging from $27 to $33 billion a year through fiscal year 2027.[30] These boats must deliver on time to sustain the nation's strategic deterrence as the *Ohio*-class boats retire this decade. To enable purchasing flexibility limited to the *Columbia*-class, Congress established the National Sea-Based Deterrence Fund in the 2015 budget, which provided the Navy an account in which to hold appropriated funds for up to five years and granted several authorities within one budgetary package. Another scheme used by the Navy is contracted block buys of multiple ships with the promise to make the payments year-to-year as funds are appropriated from Congress. In both cases, these deals are subject to review and can be terminated by Congress but, historically, are more likely to be terminated by the executive branch, further undermining any predictability such financing mechanisms afforded industry to make needed capital investments. What the Navy needs is locked-in funding appropriated to cover the full cost of ship construction.

Today there is a clear need to grow the Navy given the threat from China, and there is a plan for building ships already in serial production. According to the latest long-range shipbuilding plan, ships in production today include *Arleigh Burke* destroyers, *Virginia*-class and *Columbia*-class nuclear submarines, *Ford*-class aircraft carriers, *Constellation*-class frigates, and *America*-class and *San Antonio*-class amphibious ships. The cost for ordering these planned ships is approximately $130 billion for thirty-four ships over five years.[31] That said, historically the actual costs have risen, according to the Congressional Budget Office, by 23 to 35 percent and would more realistically equate to a cost outlay closer to $167.7 billion over the same period.[32] A proposed naval act in fiscal year 2023 includes forty-five ships in Navy shipbuilding plans and of stable design. These additional purchases are in part to leverage block-buy savings in specific classes as well as a maximalist's level according to recent shipbuilding plans. The total cost of this build program is estimated at $152.3 billion before any savings are realized (see table 5). If purchased in block buys, there is potential for considerable savings—and perhaps some much-needed predictability.

TABLE 5. A MODERN NAVAL ACT OF 2023

Warship Type	Number of Warships					Cost (in billions)
	2023	2024	2025	2026	2027	
Aircraft Carrier (CVN-78)*	—	—	2	—	—	$26.0
Destroyers (DDG-51)	2	2	2	2	2	$22.0
Frigates (FFG-62)†	1	3	3	4	4	$15.3
Attack Submarines (SSN-774)	2	2	2	3	3	$46.7
Ballistic Missile Submarines (SSBN-826)‡	—	1	—	1	1	$36.3
San Antonio-class (LPD-17)	1	—	1	—	—	$3.3
America-class (LHA-6)	1	—	—	—	—	$2.6
					Total Cost	$152.3
					10% Block-Buy Savings	$137.1
					Number of Ships	45

Note: The number of ships comes from the December 2020 long-range shipbuilding plan, and procurement planned in the Future Years Defense Program (FYDP) in the April 2022 long-range shipbuilding plan.

* A block buy of the next two *Ford*-class (CVN-82 and CVN-83) was anticipated for fiscal year 2025, with an assumed cost of $13 billion per hull, not including advanced procurement already made for CVN-82.

† Does not include the $1 billion anticipated for establishing a second shipyard for frigates, which would replicate the existing shipyard.

‡ Uses the accelerated build plan in the April 2022 long-range shipbuilding plan, with an additional SSBN ordered in 2027.

A naval act using block buys following microeconomic theory enables savings and infrastructure investments. Specifically, companies invest in additional capital infrastructure as a function of their marginal revenue or anticipated profits.[33] Bottom line, if shipbuilders have the money to invest, they are inclined to expand capacity to meet future demand. While it is hard to quantify how much the Navy has saved in recent block buys, given the data on hand, it is clear that block buys have delivered savings.

A few programs for which the Navy has pursued block buys are instructive regarding the approach's benefits. The first, the procurement of the second through sixth TAO-205 oilers, saved about $45 million per ship, and $10 million of that savings was directly attributed to the block buy.[34] The second, a proposed cross-class (*America*-class and *San Antonio*-class) amphibious warship block buy in the proposed fiscal year 2022 budget, would have saved 7.1 percent of cost.[35] The third, and most notable, was a $2.9 to $4 billion savings anticipated by block buying two *Ford*-class carriers (*Doris Miller* and *Enterprise*) in the fiscal year 2020 budget.[36] However, there is a penalty when Congress refuses to appropriate contracted moneys to the Navy for planned shipbuilding. For example, in 2022 the Navy faced paying a $33 million penalty when funding was cut for a contracted destroyer.[37] Done right, according to information the Navy provided to the Congressional Budget Office, cost savings from such block buys of ships range from 5 to 15 percent.

To achieve cost savings and ensure infrastructure investments for growing shipbuilding capacity in future larger block buys, it is important to note a few points. Such block buys assume some risk, which is why proven ship designs are generally preferred for this option. That said, such an approach carries no additional legislative requirements, unlike multiyear procurement, and can cover more than five years of planned procurement, which can be important for locking in additional savings in a shipbuilding contract. Importantly, today's block buys require annual appropriations of funds in executing associated contracts. This has been true since the Navy's first block buy in fiscal year 1998 for the first four *Virginia*-class submarines.[38] Assuming the authority to make a large block buy, Congress still needs to appropriate the funds to execute the contract.

To mitigate the impact of larger appropriations on overall defense topline budgets, some costs have been stretched out through advance procurement. Using up-front full funding in the earlier years of contracted shipbuilding enables additional savings from batch orders of selected long lead-time component production. This is called economic order quantity procurement. The benefit of scaling this funding mechanism up is to provide larger up-front appropriations in full funding of a contracted ship order so there is capital on hand for the industry to make timely capital investments. These investments in turn expand shipbuilding capacity and the workforce, which enables increased follow-on shipbuilding capacity and commercial shipyard capacity for maintenance—something the GAO has pointed out is inadequate to the Navy's needs today, resulting in too frequent deferred or prolonged maintenance availabilities.[39] All this rest on a shipbuilding plan that is known, ensured, and funded.

Fully funding a block buy in the year authority is granted makes it clear to industry that the demand and resourcing are real. It critically also provides industry with the funds with which to make needed capital investments and hiring to meet a large order. This predicted demand for shipbuilding then leads to increased shipbuilding capacity to meet it. Getting the funds appropriated for such a large block buy is another matter, and its scale (i.e., over $100 billion) is likely to engender a robust public debate in Congress—something the Navy should embrace. There is some historical precedent for this—notably, the several naval acts of the 1930s and the debates surrounding them in the lead up to World War II. Amid clear indications of war with Germany and Japan, the Naval Act of 1938 directed a just-in-time 20 percent growth of the fleet, which eventually led to the victory in the Pacific.

Another important facet of a modern naval act is the potential for better congressional oversight. By simplifying the current procurement process, it is expected that compliance with legislative intent is more straightforward—a warship is bought and delivered. No annual renegotiation through legislative authorizations would be required, costs to the taxpayer are set up front, and funds for executing the purchase are appropriated. Congress would appropriate the funding of the block buy up front, directing the Department of the Navy to disperse the funds in three installments: initial, midterm, and completion. If not done in a single appropriation, another option is making naval act funding mandatory spending—something the Navy tried to get in 2001 but failed. Typically, mandatory spending or direct spending is funding that must be appropriated year to year, typically for entitlements like Social Security.

Oversight would focus on the delivery of completed warships and not on the partial annual construction costs of a warship over the three or more years of its construction. Drawn-out procurement has created a tendency for the Navy and Congress to intervene in internal industry matters of hiring, parking lots, pier expansions, and so on. It would be better to focus oversight on holding both the Navy offices managing shipbuilding and the shipbuilders accountable. Additionally, committing the Navy to purchase a warship up front makes costly design modifications and ensuing delays less likely. This dynamic and problems caused by tardy design rework is taken up in detail in *U.S. Naval Power in the 21st Century*.

CREATE A MODERN NAVAL ACT

Shipbuilders can expand capacity by building on the success of recent warship block buys and approaching full up-front funding to enable capital investment. With war clouds gathering, the historical lessons of the nation's industrial mobilization of the late 1930s show what is possible and show a way ahead.

A modern naval act would authorize and appropriate the moneys needed to execute block buys of several warships currently in production. The appropriation would be lower than that proposed in table 5 based on procurement in fiscal year 2023, but it represents the high end of what we should consider. A 2025 act would include orders for one *Ford*-class aircraft carrier, one *America*-class amphibious assault ship, ten *Arleigh Burke*–class destroyers, ten *Virginia*-class nuclear submarines, eight *Constellation*-class frigates, and four *Columbia*-class ballistic missile nuclear submarines for a total cost of $135.4 billion. Importantly, in the case of the *Columbia* class, this complements the authorities given to this specific shipbuilding program through the National Sea-Based Deterrence Fund.[40] This price does not include anticipated savings of 5 to 15 percent realized by block buys. Importantly, these ships are of approved designs and in production today, and the above numbers are already stipulated in the fiscal year 2025 Future Years Defense Program covering the next five years. This proposed act is not comprehensive of all the Navy's ship procurement; resourcing programs not listed above or in development would still reside in the NDAA.

In conjunction with shipbuilding and capital investments to expand shipyard capacities, a modern naval act must address today's recruitment crisis or there will not be enough sailors and officers to serve in those warships. Just as stable design warship construction requires a set budget, a modern naval act should set a goal to grow the Navy to 360,000 active-duty sailors and officers by 2030, with a budget to fund that growth. Congress needs to resource the Navy so it can send more recruiters into more communities, add training facilities, and establish programs such as a reimagined and expanded BOOST program.

As it did in 1938, a naval act can spur investment in growing the nation's naval shipbuilding capacity for a potential war with China this decade. At the same time, as an act separate from the NDAA, a new naval act will draw attention to a specific national security priority while not competing directly with other service budget needs. Most importantly, a modern naval act echoing the nation's historic success in preparing for war in the Pacific will galvanize and focus popular support today. Congress in recent years has indicated it is willing to make the needed investments, and a modern naval act is one way of acting on that intention.

PART THREE

REORGANIZING FOR A NEW COLD WAR TO SEIZE AND RETAIN THE INITIATIVE

Chinese Aggression = Military Balance + Secure Economy + **Effective Political Control**

FIGURE 8. Chinese aggression equation, part 3 *author illustration*

Part 3 presents initiatives that reorganize various agencies to better employ economic, diplomatic, and naval forces in a long-term competitive strategy with China. Chapter 7 focuses on securing critical shipping and regaining American maritime commercial competitiveness with the creation of a maritime department. Then, to coordinate a comprehensive naval statecraft, chapter 8 presents a new structure for the National Security Council that is tailored to executing specific strategic objectives. This structure represents a divergence from convention, shifting from managing various departments and agencies to proactively driving the whole-of-government to achieve specific strategic results. Finally, chapter 9 details an oceans-centered versus a joint force regional combatant command–aligned naval fleet structure that can better execute military operational plans and naval statecraft. The effect of these endeavors is to instill uncertainty and weaken the confidence of the CCP in its ability to exert effective political control over geopolitical events.

CHAPTER 7

A MARITIME DEPARTMENT

Days before pandemic-mandated mask policies and national lockdowns, alarms were being raised in Congress about acute national supply chain vulnerabilities. At a March 2020 hearing, the then-administrator of the Maritime Administration, retired admiral Mark Buzby, asserted that without action, American shipping would be unable to sustain military operations; 90 percent of military supplies are moved by ship.[1] It would not take long before the consequences would be felt. Within a year, China's zero-Covid policies shut down ports and tied up shipping, adding to the losses brought about by Covid-19, this time on American livelihoods. Unfortunately, there are no good alternatives since the CCP controls over 10,000 commercial vessels moving almost a fifth of global trade by weight.[2] Should the CCP decide to leverage American overreliance on foreign shipping, they could sanction and blackmail our nation. In today's new cold war, this shipping vulnerability imperils American security and prosperity. Urgent action is needed to reverse the dissolution of the American maritime sector (shipping, shipbuilding, ports) and harden the nation to Chinese economic coercion—business as usual is not an option.

A CALL TO ACTION: REORGANIZING FOR RESULTS WITH A MARITIME DEPARTMENT

On National Maritime Day, May 12, 2021, the nation was reminded of how much it relies on maritime commerce. Sadly, that reminder has not been repeated, and the nation continues its precipitous slide into what author Seth Cropsey calls "seablindness." On that Maritime Day, the

Department of Transportation published the following statistics: 70 percent of all U.S. trade by weight valued at $1.5 trillion dollars was moved by ships making 465,000 port calls (10 percent of the global total).[3] At the same time, the nation only had 180 U.S.-flagged ships it could reliably call on in a crisis; in late 2023 the number has shrunk to 177.[4] This means our nation is reliant for its livelihood on the timely servicing of its shipping needs by unfriendly countries like China. Moreover, more than trade is at stake, as the military also relies on commercial shipping. Given the lack of U.S. shipping, the military must contract from foreign entities who in a crisis may not be willing to oblige or meet the need, as they did in both Gulf Wars (1990–1991, and 2003).[5] More troubling is that in a showdown with China, the ability to secure shipping for a war effort let alone sustain a wartime economy is an open question.

The risks to the nation given its seablindness have slowly been gaining attention. First were the supply chain problems during the Covid-19 pandemic recovery, with shipping backing up at U.S. ports as store shelves were barren. Then a weeklong closure of the Suez Canal in March 2021 caused by a container ship grounding created months-long supply chain snafus. To those who were following these events, it was clear the nation's supply chains were too vulnerable. In response, Congress called for establishing commissions, sought reports, and held hearings. There were calls from within the administration, too, to grow the nation's commercial fleet, notably from the Department of the Navy. This all went to no avail without presidential leadership and with a dysfunctional mosaic of maritime agencies.

To address wider government dysfunction and reorganize for better outcomes, former policymakers, senior leaders, and industry experts gathered to produce the 2023 *Mandate for Leadership*. In it are recommendations to disestablish the Department of Homeland Security (DHS) and move the U.S. Coast Guard (USCG) into the Department of Justice; break up the National Oceanic and Atmospheric Administration (NOAA) and refocus it onto the nation's maritime industry; and have the Maritime Administration (MARAD) join the USCG.[6] Based on the research in the *Mandate for Leadership*, a more comprehensive consolidation of maritime agencies would more likely eliminate redundancies, enhance institutional focus on strengthening the nation's maritime sector, and enable more effective presidential leadership and congressional oversight and accountability.

One insight from the work of the *Mandate for Leadership* is that curing the nation's seablindness and making real progress requires more than tinkering. Any attempt to address this must focus national leadership on the problem of an inadequate maritime sector. Realizing the danger of a looming world war, President Franklin D. Roosevelt established in 1937 the Maritime Commission, whose director, Emory S. Land, had frequent, direct contact with the president. Later, President Ronald Reagan saw the danger of a too-weak navy and how its invigoration could end the Cold War; he launched a campaign to grow the Navy to six hundred ships that invigorated naval shipbuilding. Future like-minded maritime-focused presidents will need institutions able to execute the required buildup of maritime commercial strength and competitiveness. A maritime department would do this.

THE DANGER OF A TOO-WEAK NATIONAL MARITIME SECTOR

Today the charge to regulate and support the nation's commercial maritime needs resides across twenty-five different agencies represented at the U.S. Committee on the Maritime Transportation System, a staff-level body that has come to be a place where maritime initiatives too often die under the weight of existing interagency processes. Within this group, four agencies stand out as having the most day-to-day impact on the nation's maritime sector: the USCG, MARAD, NOAA, and the Federal Maritime Commission (FMC). None of these currently reside in the same department, meaning that resource decisions are filtered through a parent organization's priorities, which are often not maritime-related—case in point is the Department of Transportation, whose focus on aviation and roads dwarfs institutional focus on ports; more on this later. This situation has also diminished maritime agencies' ability to shape or push back on budgeting priorities set by the Office of Management and Budget. The result is that agencies like the FMC are unable to effectively execute their missions.

The case of the FMC is unique in that it is an independent agency not within a parent department. Its staff, authorized to reach 343, is charged with regulating maritime commerce such as cargo rates and enforcing competitive business practices.[7] Without a cabinet-level presence, it has too often been unable to gain needed resources. For example, the number of regulatory actions, contract violation litigation, and cases of unfair shipping practices has tripled since 2021, and in 2023 the FMC received a modest budget increase to hire more staff.[8] Until additional hires arrive, the FMC's staff of six investigators oversee a $6 trillion shipping sector, whereas other agencies like the U.S. Securities and Exchange Commission have more than 150 investigators per $1 trillion.[9] Only after harm was done to American consumers and businesses, was the FMC able to get long-overdue funding to begin hiring more investigators.[10] This misalignment of maritime agencies embedded within larger departments also include issues of authorities.

The Department of Transportation is overwhelmingly an aviation industry–focused department. More than 80 percent of its staff work in the Federal Aviation Agency, with MARAD only having 1.4 percent of overall employees and a budget less than 1 percent of the department's total.[11] This situation leads the secretary of transportation to focus more resources and attention on aviation. MARAD's eight hundred employees are charged with ensuring the health of the nation's merchant marine critical for commerce and defense, who are also in charge of the Merchant Marine Academy along with six training ships. These resources, sadly, are not meeting the nation's need for merchant mariners.[12]

Along with MARAD, NOAA also operates ships, a small fleet of scientific research vessels focused on monitoring fish stocks and climate change impacts. Consisting of six main offices, NOAA boasts that its 12,000 employees provide environmental information impacting over one-third of the nation's gross domestic product.[13] However, unlike MARAD, NOAA dominates its host, the Department of Commerce, accounting for over half of its 2023 budget ($6.8 billion of $12.4 billion).[14] Because of this, the agency is primarily focused on scientific work and less on the mission of commerce—economic development and trade promotion. Senator Lisa Murkowski has even called NOAA "a fish out of water" within the Department of Commerce.[15] If MARAD is underserved because it is too small in its department, NOAA is too unconstrained given its dominating place in its department, requiring more institutional discipline to be focused on commerce.

Another maritime agency that operates ships is the USCG, which is hosted within the DHS. Following the terrorist attacks of September 11, 2001, the USCG was deemed important to border security and moved into the newly created DHS.[16] The stipulation remained unchanged that, in the event of war and a declaration from Congress or the president, the USCG would become part of the Department of the Navy.[17] The USCG's mission is perhaps best summarized as protecting the nation's people and interests in waters that stretch out two hundred miles from the shoreline in internationally recognized EEZs. To accomplish this expansive mission, the USCG operates 259 cutters and 200 fixed and rotary wing aircraft to patrol and conduct rescue operations.[18] As of November 30, 2023, the USCG had conducted 14,008 search-and-rescue (SAR) missions, saving more than 5,530 lives and property valued at more than $134 million.[19] Given the rise in Chinese distant fishing fleets suspected of engaging in poaching, today's USCG is too small. Force plans to address this gap, however, are too infrequent (last updated in 2019) or obscured behind classifications (as has been conveyed to Congress in 2023) while the Navy publicly releases similar plans annually.[20] Despite the scale and scope of its mission, the USCG represents only 13 percent of the DHS budget while comprising 54 percent of all DHS personnel.[21] The strain on the USCG is showing; like the military services, it is facing a 10 percent recruitment shortfall, forcing it to remove ten cutters from service.[22] This is occurring as the USCG must confront the threat of Chinese poaching in our home waters, interdict illicit narcotics and fentanyl precursor chemicals, and execute enduring missions like SAR. Given almost twenty years of inaction by the DHS to adequately resource the USCG, it is unlikely that it would change tack now.

In truth, as long as store shelves remain stocked, nonfriendly nations sell energy to our deployed military forces, and foreign ships conduct

American trade, no one worries. Unfortunately, this apathy has enabled a post–Cold War rot that has created a massive vulnerability, exposing the nation to economic coercion and potential military defeat. For more than thirty years, approaches fixed in legacy institutional structures have not cured the nation's seablindness. Without a central authority directly answerable to the president and able to testify to Congress, leadership to address this problem will persist.

REORGANIZING FOR A NEW COLD WAR

In the face of geostrategic change, the nation has reorganized itself several times. Notable in this regard is the National Security Act of 1947 that established the Department of Defense and the Central Intelligence Agency. This act put the nation on course to wage a decades-long effective cold war with the Soviet Union. Today the nation faces even more substantial challenges from industrial giant China backed by a rapidly growing military. Time is of the essence for action. China's comprehensive challenge has metastasized into a new cold war, with a great power war increasingly likely this decade.[23] Keeping the peace and safeguarding Americans' livelihoods in this new era requires significant retooling of our government to muster limited resources to greatest effect.

However, efficiency alone is not reason enough for consolidating government agencies; it must be done to deliver better results. Even then, the added overhead and confusion in the transition too often undermines the reorganization. The rationale and metric for evaluating a reorganization into a maritime department is results through enhanced effectiveness in delivering on specific goals in a timely manner. During the first year of the Trump administration in 2017, guidance was issued that is applicable today. The administration was then considering more than thirty governmental organizational moves with the aim of bringing together offices sharing a common mission, focusing on the same customer, and able to improve effectiveness.[24] Those efforts did not pan out, but the logic used for considering and planning government reorganization remains relevant. Today the challenge is revitalizing the nation's maritime sector, given the sector's wide-ranging implications for national defense and economic resiliency. After thirty years of tinkering or drafting well-worded strategy, it is clear that the maritime sector needs a grand reorganization to focus institutions on this most pressing challenge—regaining a competitive maritime industrial sector. A reorganization into a single maritime department can bring unity of effort to accomplish what the Merchant Marine Act of 1920 has not.[25] In fact, that act's preamble, with minor updates, is a good modern departmental mission statement: "Provide for the security of the nation's maritime rights in its waters and seafloor; and ensure adequate shipping free of hostile coercion in times of crisis."

This common mission would focus actions and inform budgets of the maritime agencies. For NOAA, it would mean ensuring that its research is informing seafarers of maritime conditions, assessing the health of the nation's maritime resources on the seafloor and sea life. In turn, NOAA's work would inform USCG enforcement and policing operations. MARAD would focus on ensuring that the nation regains competitiveness in shipping and shipbuilding, with the objective of ensuring adequate numbers of ships and associated crews available to sustain a wartime economy and military. The need for regaining competitiveness would inform efforts to ensure fair treatment of American shippers supported by the FMC. As already mentioned, today's maritime agencies are buried within departments overwhelmingly focused on nonmaritime issues. In fiscal year 2023, the USCG represented 14 percent of its parent DHS budget and 31.5 percent of personnel.[26] For other agencies within their parent departments, the ratios are worse; MARAD represents 0.6 percent of the Department of Transportation's budget and comprises 1.4 percent of the department's total workforce.[27] Furthermore, subordinate maritime agencies are left without a voice at cabinet meetings and too often are unable to testify directly to Congress. Consider that $89.9 billion was passed in the November 2021 Infrastructure Investment and Jobs Act, but less than 0.7 percent of such funding found its way to ports infrastructure.[28] If money indicates priorities, then the nation is recklessly ignoring its maritime sector—to China's advantage.

A unified maritime department would also be a better steward of taxpayer dollars. With Congress-appropriated funds going to a department dedicated to the maritime sector, those moneys are assured of going to maritime issues. Likewise, this would ensure better oversight by Congress with maritime issues residing in one department that it can compel testimony before it; today maritime agencies are typically not sent to Congress without their parent department's approval or departmental leadership present. For the USCG, a maritime department would more likely support budget requests by a like-minded department resulting in fewer unfunded requests, which totaled $1.57 billion in March 2023.[29] Another challenge has been acting on congressional authority granted in 2018 using the National Defense Sealift Fund to purchase used foreign-built commercial ships to fill gaps in military sealift.[30] MARAD has decades of experience with the commercial maritime sector and management of the National Defense Reserve Fleet of government-owned commercial vessels with military utility. Nonetheless, delays ensued as the Department of Defense and MARAD were not prepared to procure shipping on the open market.[31] Several years passed before the first vessels were purchased, missing the opportunity to benefit from a buyer's market during the Covid-19 pandemic. Yet, the authority has been sustained in the fiscal year 2024 National Defense Authorization Act.[32] A maritime department–run MARAD and subject to focused secretary-level scrutiny and support would likely have procured the needed shipping on the open market more quickly.

A maritime department would also better focus on service provided to the companies and workers seeking their livelihoods in and from the maritime. Case in point, MARAD languished in drafting a 2014 congressionally mandated strategy for the sustainability of a U.S.-flagged commercial fleet, taking more than six years to produce the twenty-page document that was light on details, even after its years of drafting.[33] A January 2020 GAO report details the challenges MARAD had enlisting participation across multiple departments and agencies to draft this national maritime strategy.[34] The extra time did not result in a more complete or actionable plan for regaining the nation's maritime strength.

Had MARAD been operating within a maritime department, much of the required collaboration would have occurred seamlessly, while secretary-level action would have been used to ensure other departments' participation. Most notable in this regard is having a maritime secretary attending president-led policy meetings at the White House. This would allow the maritime department secretary to address interagency disputes and bring attention to serious issues in the maritime industrial sector that require interagency action.

The envisioned consolidation would bring the four largest maritime-focused agencies into a maritime department. Done well, NOAA would be directed to focus on environmental monitoring and scientific work that informs USCG operations. This would also ensure better operational planning and procurement of future ships by NOAA and the USCG to monitor the nation's maritime resources and police them more effectively. Additionally, moving the USCG from the DHS would alleviate structural misalignments regarding its lifesaving mission (i.e., SAR) that often requires operations far from U.S. borders. To execute SAR, the USCG operational requirements for open-ocean operations are too often seen as incongruous with the wider DHS mission and, specifically, the Customs and Border Protection focus on the border and homeland security.[35] Bringing the USCG together with MARAD in a single department would also enhance their shared mission to train and certify mariners and better manage the USCG Academy and Merchant Marine Academy and their associated training ships. Additionally, MARAD, backed by a cabinet-level secretary, would have greater voice in its budget requirements and authority to procure the needed shipping for the National Defense Reserve Fleet. That said, this reorganization would also enhance accountability for results both by Congress and by a maritime department secretary. This will be important given that MARAD has stalled at making progress in programs such as the Tanker Security Program. For two years MARAD struggled to fully implement the Tanker Security Program (it contracted nine of ten allowed tankers) and as of January 2023 had yet to meet the Department of Defense 2020 Transportation Command requirement for eighty-six tankers.[36] And returning the FMC and MARAD to the same department would align industry-sector promotion and responsible regulation with the shared goal of strengthening the nation's maritime sector.

To succeed against China in the new cold war, the nation must muster its limited resources to greatest effect. This requires reorganizing for this task, which includes ideas championed by others, like dismantling the unwieldy DHS and moving its assorted agencies to other departments.[37] Change is needed to overcome decades of nonexistent unity of effort, sluggish bureaucracies, limited advocacy for resourcing, and redundancies. Consolidating the four key agencies into a single department bound by a common mission can break this maritime bureaucratic lethargy. However, in executing such a reorganization, it is important to understand the past and how this byzantine maritime bureaucracy came to be.

HOW DID WE GET HERE?

The dysfunction in government today as it relates to the maritime sector is not due to a single decision. Much of today's maritime agency structure is a legacy to the Maritime Commission of 1936 that held both regulatory and advocacy responsibilities for American shipping and shipbuilding. The Maritime Commission and its unified approach exceeded all expectations in rapidly building a merchant marine force for World War II. Having advocacy and regulatory roles resident in one agency eventually proved problematic, leading to a review by Senator George Aiken that would see those roles divided into two independent agencies.[38] This occurred in two steps, the first in 1950 with the creation of the Maritime Administration (MARAD) within the Department of Commerce. Then regulatory responsibilities were broken out in 1961 with the creation of a five-member board of commissioners, called the Federal Maritime Commission.[39] The FMC continues to conduct its regulatory mission as an independent agency but has struggled to address the massive amount of litigation arising from the Covid-19 pandemic shipping recovery of 2021.[40] Later President Lyndon Johnson, wanting to consolidate what was perceived as transportation-related work, in 1966 moved MARAD into the Department of Transportation (DoT).[41] This reflected a national approach that viewed the American maritime sector as a predominantly transportation-centric industry.[42] While this may have been politically expedient at the time, it is evident that today's need for robust American maritime capacity and capabilities transcends transportation functions and must instead be elevated as a strategic national imperative. Yet MARAD has remained in DoT ever since, with twenty-four other maritime-related agencies and offices scattered across nine departments and two commissions.

To coordinate these various agencies and departments, the interagency U.S. Committee on the Maritime Transportation System was established in 2004, chaired by the secretary of transportation.[43] This interagency committee functions through working groups that meet monthly to coordinate integrating maritime modes of transport with other means of transport and to provide five-year reports to Congress on the adequacy of the sector to national interests. This collaborative interagency approach has facilitated information sharing but is not empowered to direct resources or focused on strengthening the nation's maritime sector beyond managing it as transportation.

Aside from the main maritime agencies like the USCG, MARAD, NOAA, and the FMC, there are several important agencies with maritime equities. Top of the list is the U.S. Maritime Service, which was created in 1938 as a provision of the 1936 Merchant Marine Act to train crews for the merchant marines. It also played a vital role in the Allied victory in World War II. While today it is defunct, its earlier success warrants renewed consideration.[44] Next is the Navy's Military Sealift Command, which manages sealift for the Department of Defense.[45] Not included in his command are thirty-seven named watercraft operated by the U.S. Army Transportation Corps that supports the Army's specific maritime logistic and riverine transport needs.[46] During coastal national disasters, the Federal Emergency Management Agency also plays a role in coordinating sealift as part of federal response. For example, during the 9/11 attacks, nonfederal maritime entities also contributed to disaster responses—notably, New York state's naval militia. These naval militia are vestiges of pre–naval reserve corps days and exist in Alaska, California, New York, Ohio, South Carolina, and Texas. These state naval militia have a primary focus on supporting disaster responses. However, similar to the National Guard, these naval militia have utility in the Department of Defense–run State Partnership Program, where they can also provide support for maritime security and disaster response training in partnership with regional nations in Southeast Asia, West Africa, and the central Pacific. Should they be needed, naval militias would be a natural complement to a reactivated U.S. Maritime Service in addressing critical needs for merchant mariners during a crisis as per the existing law (46 USC 51701). The Department of State's Office of Ocean and Polar Affairs' "Limits in the Seas" has played an important role in reviewing the legal merits of claims and assertions by other nations that impact freedom of navigation, particularly in legal competition with China (known as lawfare).[47] Several international waterways, such as the Great Lakes Saint Lawrence Seaway, are managed in concert with foreign governments, so how these relate to a future maritime department needs to be considered. Overall, these offices, agencies, and legacy organizations all merit consideration in a future reorganization, but their inclusion can wait and need not be conditional for the creation of a maritime department.

In addition to the challenges of this institutional mosaic, there is no overarching strategy or framework driving action toward a common objective. The last serious national-level direction regarding the nation's shipping was in National Security Directive 28 (NSD-28), signed by President George H. W. Bush on October 5, 1989. That directive tasked various departments to ensure adequate sealift to execute a forward defense strategy and to maintain a wartime economy.[48] Despite clearly articulated responsibilities and the strategic need to secure the nation's access to reliable sealift, no progress has been made. A revised NSD-28 can provide clear strategic direction to the various maritime-related agencies and departments. Better still, a revised NSD-28 should direct the creation of a maritime department with the authority and resources to drive a recovery of American maritime strength.

Four federal agencies from different departments could be merged into a single department with the mission of fostering and protecting U.S. maritime interests.

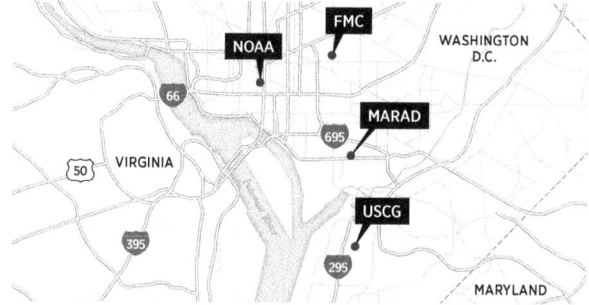

	National Oceanic and Atmospheric Administration (NOAA)	U.S. Maritime Administration (MARAD)	U.S. Coast Guard (USCG)	Federal Maritime Commission (FMC)
Department	Commerce	Transportation	Homeland Security	Independent
Primary duties	Predicts changes in climate, weather, ocean, and coasts, and conserves and manages coastal and marine ecosystems and resources.	Promotes U.S. maritime industry.	Protects U.S. maritime borders, mitigates marine disasters, and provides security against criminal and terrorist activity in the maritime domain.	Ensures a reliable international ocean transportation supply system that supports the U.S. economy and protects the public from unfair and deceptive practices.

FIGURE 9. Forming a U.S. maritime department *Heritage Foundation*

WHAT TO DO

Reorganizations are never easy, often running into parochial and political interests that distract from the original intent or result in unwieldy creations. Case in point is the massive consolidation of agencies into the DHS after the terrorist attacks of September 11, 2001. The challenges before the nation today, however, warrant urgent action to consolidate maritime-related agencies into a single cabinet-level office—a maritime department. Achieving this will require Congress and the president work together along several lines of effort.

First, Congress will need to authorize the creation of a maritime department to provide the authority to make the necessary organizational changes, including the naming of a cabinet-level secretary. This legislation will need to innumerate the new department's responsibilities for safeguarding the nation's commercial maritime interests, building new partnerships with allies to meet shipping needs, and accelerating innovation to regain American competitiveness in shipping and shipbuilding.

This should be done while stressing improved efficiencies in managing and delivering results for the nation's maritime interests. Done well—a big "if"—the creation of this department would come with little added overhead in personnel or federal budget. Success on this measure will be critical to sustaining political support, especially from fiscal conservatives in Congress. As the consolidation of existing people and resources progresses, early results will ensure broader political support. Such early successes are more likely with the prompt nomination of the new secretary, who, for example, could oversee the early creation of maritime prosperity zones, break ground on new shipyards, and announce efforts to fight against unfair shipping practices overseas.

Second, the president will need to update the NSD-28 and present a plan for consolidating all maritime-related agencies into a new department. A recommended new NSD-28 is included in the textbox at the end of this chapter. To mitigate disruptions, moves should be executed in an incremental manner, such as initially establishing a secretariat to support the new secretary and oversee the creation of the new department. A logical first move would be to align the FMC and MARAD to this new department; once completed, they could be joined by NOAA and then the USCG with the goal of consolidating the USCG, FMC, NOAA, and MARAD under a newly appointed maritime secretary within two years. Remaining true to the findings of Senator Aiken, the FMC's composition and regulatory role should remain as a separate agency within a larger unified maritime department. There is precedence for operating regulatory and advocacy within a single cabinet-level department, as was the case when MARAD and the FMC were in the Department of Commerce.

Third, the president should immediately establish a deputy assistant to the president and coordinator for national maritime issues within the National Security Council. This post would resemble the coordinator for Indo-Pacific affairs led by a deputy assistant to the president.[49] Initial tasks for a coordinator for national maritime issues would be to revise the outdated NSD-28, oversee future maritime agency reorganization, enforce coordinated action among all maritime agencies, and establish comprehensive presidential budgeting priorities for maritime agencies that the Office of Management and Budget would enact.

ORGANIZE FOR THE NEW COLD WAR

History has proven the words of Paul Hall, president of the Seafarers International Union, to be prophetic. In July 1967, testifying before Congress on MARAD's move to the DoT, Hall asserted, "History, experience, and the facts prove beyond doubt that the Maritime Administration, if included in an executive department having other duties and responsibilities, becomes submerged, is largely ignored and languishes from neglect." The same fate, one could argue, has occurred for the USCG, which is also submerged in a larger department with competing priorities. It is time the nation took seriously its maritime interests, leveraged its potential for innovation, and regained global leadership in this strategic sector. Standing up a maritime department is a critical step toward that goal to persevere in today's new cold war.

TEXTBOX 1

PROPOSED DRAFT NATIONAL SECURITY DIRECTIVE: SEALIFT AND FORMATION OF THE MARITIME DEPARTMENT

NATIONAL SECURITY DIRECTIVE ##

MEMORANDUM FOR THE VICE PRESIDENT
    THE SECRETARY OF STATE
    THE SECRETARY OF THE TREASURY
    THE SECRETARY OF DEFENSE
    THE ATTORNEY GENERAL
    THE SECRETARY OF AGRICULTURE
    THE SECRETARY OF COMMERCE
    THE SECRETARY OF HOMELAND SECURITY
    THE SECRETARY OF TRANSPORTATION
    DIRECTOR OF THE OFFICE OF MANAGEMENT AND BUDGET
    UNITED STATES TRADE REPRESENTATIVE
    THE CHIEF OF STAFF OF THE PRESIDENT FOR NATIONAL SECURITY AFFAIRS
    DIRECTOR OF CENTRAL INTELLIGENCE
    CHAIRMAN OF THE JOINT CHIEFS OF STAFF
    DIRECTOR OF FEDERAL EMERGENCY MANAGEMENT AGENCY

SUBJECT: National Security Directive on the Maritime Sector

Sealift is essential to execute this country's defense strategy, maintain a wartime economy, and avoid becoming captive to economic coercion by hostile nations—most notably, China. The United States' national sealift objective is to ensure sufficient military and civil maritime resources to meet defense needs and essential economic requirements in support of our national security strategy. The broad purpose of this directive is to ensure that the United States has the capability to meet sealift requirements and shipyard capacities to sustain naval and commercial shipping, to prevent economic coercion in peacetime, and to persevere in crisis and prolonged war. Toward this end, the following policy guidelines are established:

1. The U.S.-owned commercial maritime industry cannot alone meet today the nation's sealift and shipyard needs—correcting this requires regaining competitiveness in the strategically important maritime industrial sector. To remedy this, domestic capacities must be augmented in preparation for crisis and war using reserve fleets comprised of domestic and allied nations' ships and crews. The Maritime Department is to be established and responsible for determining and acting to secure adequate manpower and sealift; this will include assurances of adequate port connectors for most efficient shipping operations in peace and war.
2. Effective immediately the Maritime Department is established. Within thirty days of this directive, the U.S. Coast Guard, Maritime Administration, Federal Maritime Commission, and National Oceanic and Atmospheric Administration shall become part of the Maritime Department. Adjustments recommended to the formation of the Maritime Department shall be made to the deputy assistant to the president and to the coordinator for national maritime issues. Recommendations should include follow-on federal entities to join the Department of Maritime no later than six months from this directive. This reorganization will not impact existing laws allowing for the U.S. Coast Guard to become part of the Department of the Navy in times of war.
3. The Maritime Department is responsible for ensuring that the appropriate legal and procedural mechanisms necessary for exerting effective control over needed sealift are in place. The department shall lead efforts to secure commitments of sealift resources from allies to meet alliance requirements, to include the NATO Planning Board on Ocean Shipping. The Department of State and Department of Defense shall support this effort and recommend

additional formal agreements with other maritime nations to provide additional sealift.
4. The Department of Defense will determine the requirements for sealift of deploying forces, follow-on supply and sustainment, shipbuilding, and ship repair. The Department Defense and Department of Commerce shall support the Maritime Department in determining the capacity of our merchant marine industries to meet national sealift requirements in crisis and war. Within one year of this directive, the Maritime Department will begin providing annual reports on the adequacy of sealift to support deployed military operations and essential industrial activity during wartime. Additionally, the Departments of Defense, Commerce, and Transportation will support the Maritime Department to promote the incorporation of national defense features in port infrastructure, modal connectors (e.g., ports, rail lines), and new and existing commercial ships.
5. The Departments of State and Transportation, the Special Trade Representative, and other appropriate agencies shall support the Maritime Department to secure supporting international agreements and policies. This will ensure governing use of foreign flag carriers protect our national security interests and do not place U.S. industry at a competitive disadvantage in world markets. All federal agencies and departments shall promote, through efficient application of laws and regulations, the readiness of the U.S. merchant marine and supporting industries fostering competitiveness and maritime industry resiliency to crisis.
6. Development and implementation of specific sealift and supporting programs will be made with full consideration of the prompt delivery of critical sealift. Adequate sealift is a national security priority, and its requirements shall be a resource priority to ensure that adequate sealift for military operations is met no later than January 2026 and that agreements are in place to meet a wartime economy's sealift needs no later than January 2027.

CHAPTER 8

A NATIONAL SECURITY COUNCIL FOR A NEW COLD WAR

Governments, like all big institutions, have their own culture and proclivities, and the bigger they are, the more gargantuan a task to steer them onto a new course. This book is devoted to getting the national ship on course—and quickly—for the new cold war we are in with China. For such a task, presidential leadership is critical, and in supporting a president to this end, one institution will play a significant role—the National Security Council (NSC). Shifting from a business-as-usual mentality to one of naval statecraft will begin from the top with a reformulated NSC.

The NSC's origins stretch back to a similar time in our nation's history when the nation struggled to adapt to the Cold War with the Soviet Union. Presidents have always had a cabinet but have not always had a security staff dedicated to coordinating comprehensive national power. To execute a "containment" doctrine against communism required new governing structures, which were laid down in the National Security Act of 1947. That act created the Department of Defense by merging the War and Navy Departments, created the Central Intelligence Agency, and created the NSC.[1] The NSC is a place that David Rothkopf described in his 2004 book *Running the World* as "a place where great people struggle to do great things."[2] Given the nature of today's new cold war and the tasks laid out in this book, unshackling great people and institutions to achieve what is needed will again require reorganizing government.

Size matters, and an NSC staff that is too large can be a problem. President Trump's NSC numbered around 300, and President Biden grew the staff to 370 within six months.[3] These numbers are lower than President Obama's more than 400 NSC staffers. Yet inefficiencies, poorly managed crises, and missed strategic opportunities have come and gone under both small and large NSC staffs. Moreover, the world of the new cold war is placing new demands on this critical staff. Rather than just thinking about resizing the staff, a new structure of the NSC staff is required to best act in this era of great-power competition.

SYMPTOMS OF A MALADY

Since 2000 there have been indications that existing government structures were not up to the challenges of the day. The first case was the intelligence failures preceding the al-Qaeda terror attacks of September 11, 2001, which killed almost three thousand people that day. The response, acting on recommendations of the 9/11 Commission, focused primarily on effecting "unity of effort" by correcting intelligence failures and better execution of a war on terrorism. The 2004 report stated clearly: "As presently configured, the national security institutions of the U.S. government are still the institutions constructed to win the Cold War. The United States confronts a very different world today."[4]

This statement still holds true today, and hopefully adjustments can be made before another systemic failure like the one that occurred on September 11. Changes made then were for waging a war on terrorism, which is different from waging a new cold war with China. But just as our nation was unprepared for the war on terrorism on September 10, 2001, the structures of today remain similarly unready for the new cold war.

FAILING STRATEGIC CONSISTENCY

During the U.S. presidential campaign of 2000 then-candidate George W. Bush made clear his position calling for a more forceful China policy. Since the communists' Tiananmen Square massacre of June 1989, China had consistently been viewed unfavorably by a majority of Americans.[5] Bush was tapping into that public sentiment of China, as its unfavorability spiked to nearly 60 percent following a string of scandals between 1999 and 2001: human rights abuses, illegal missile technology transfers, unfair trade practices, and nuclear espionage.[6] Congress, too, acted in 1999, mandating an annual report of Chinese military developments and activities.[7] The momentum toward a competitive posture with China was sustained through the election, and a new long-term competitive strategy seemed imminent under President Bush. However, following the attacks of September 11, a massive policy reversal ensued to execute the war on terrorism. To wage this new war, the United States sought new allies, overwhelming the building consensus to confront China under prevailing political support for greater collaboration with China. This American policy reversal was in fact first characterized in 2002 as "a period of strategic opportunity" by the general secretary of the CCP—Jiang Zemin. Under the domestic and international pressures to defeat al-Qaeda, the NSC was not able to maintain appropriate focus on China. In the intervening years, this opened the door for China's entry to the WTO, fueling a rapid modernization and expansion of its military. China achieved this without ever meeting the standards of open, market-oriented principles—China's track record on WTO standards has been consistently poor.[8] There are other cases of strategic distraction too—for example, Russia's annexation of Crimea in 2014 while China, effectively unopposed, rapidly built up island garrisons in the South China Sea.

STRATEGY WITHOUT BUDGETS

Amid ongoing conflicts in Iraq and Afghanistan and the need to fund the newly passed Affordable Care Act in March 2010, and with an eye on impending reelection, President Obama attempted a pivot. This pivot, or rebalance, as it is often called, was officially known as the Defense Strategic Guidance (DSG), which sought to rebalance diminishing military spending to the Asia-Pacific.[9] In a rare move, President Obama joined his secretary of defense to announce the new strategy at the Pentagon on January 5, 2012. Almost from the beginning this pivot was doomed as the Arab Spring fanned instability across North Africa and the Middle East, sending millions of refugees into Europe.[10] Amid this regional chaos, the NSC was unready to oversee and drive a shift to the type of operations and investments required in the Asia-Pacific. Instead the effort relied on a small team at Pacific Command and the Office of the Deputy Secretary of Defense to point the way. The DSG lacked a clear prioritization of resources, causing progress to languish as they relied on reprogramming existing budgets in fiscal year 2012. This persisted for several months, until the Office of Management and Budget received budgeting guidance that directed it to prioritize resourcing the DSG. Armed with clear budgetary guidance, despite sequestration over the next two fiscal years, the Office of Management and Budget directed just over $15 billion to the region. This funded new operations, exercises, posture investments, and expansion of diplomatic presence in key nations. Unfortunately, by early 2014 White House attention was shifting, and a September 2015 joint press conference in the Rose Garden with President Obama and China's general secretary, Xi Jinping, deflated the rebalance.[11] Having already won reelection and with a supposed understanding with Xi, Obama's motivation to devote resources to the rebalance faded. Added to this, many senior advisers began departing to either retire or join the forming Hillary Clinton presidential campaign. The energy to sustain the DSG withered even as China became more aggressive; instead, efforts turned to a third offset.[12] Without a renewal of budgeting priority to the DSG, focus turned to investing in new technologies that would take years to field. Undeterred by this new effort and contrary to the 2015 Rose Garden assurances, China doubled down its militarization of the South China Sea. Within months massive airfields, missile installations, underground bunkers and port facilities at Fiery Cross, Subi, and Mischief Reefs appeared.[13] The Obama administration's shift from the region left the NSC unable to proffer a course correction as the security situation in Asia eroded. The progress that was achieved on the DSG was made possible with presidential leadership and the directed commitment of resources, such as the rebalance budget guidance.

MICRO- VERSUS MACROMANAGEMENT

Getting the balance right between overbearing management and chaos in the ranks is key for any organization. A too-large NSC is prone to becoming what many in government have called D.C.'s "thousand-mile screwdriver." In the new cold war with China, getting this balance wrong can stifle initiative and the creativity required to take advantage of opportunities emerging from fast-developing events. Likewise, without a framework like "containment" during the Cold War, there is too little guidance informing millions of daily decisions made by civilian and military staff. The U.S. Strategic Framework for the Indo-Pacific, which guided policies and actions early in the Trump administration, demonstrated the value of a strategic framework. The Trump administration declassified it in January 2021.[14] This framework provided a comprehensive approach to confronting and outcompeting China in economic, diplomatic, and military affairs. Events surrounding the Chinese intimidation of the Malaysian chartered survey ship *West Capella* proved the strength of the framework. That incident is extensively discussed in *U.S. Naval Power in the 21st Century*. Responses to this crisis serve as a model for how to run a maritime counterinsurgency in the South China Sea within a similar strategic framework—naval statecraft. However, despite the administration's unity of effort, success in this 2020 crisis was due more to luck. Had the timing of several otherwise escalatory military operations and diplomatic statements not occurred as they did, the region would have recoiled, giving China a military and diplomatic victory. The point is, strategic frameworks are important but cannot fully replace planning and coordination of significant events by the NSC.

COMPREHENSIVE COMPETITION UNREALIZED

President Biden came into office in 2021 attempting to roll back the clock with China, to a time of cooperative relations. By the end of Biden's first year as president, it was clear the effort had failed. But to make good on the attempt, a new Office of Indo-Pacific Coordinator was created at the NSC with the appointment of longtime Asia policy leader Kurt Campbell as coordinator. Despite this new office—ostensibly to actualize the administration's new, integrated deterrence detailed in the 2022 National Security Strategy—events quickly got away from Campbell.[15] Moreover, with several crises and major efforts ongoing, like the Australia–U.K.–U.S. (AUKUS) nuclear submarine initiative announced in September 2021, the full weight of the administration never seemed to coalesce. Two cases make this point: First, the U.S. government failed to bring to bear full pressure in 2022 to dissuade the Solomon Islands from going through with a security pact with China. And second, there was lackluster uptake of the May 2022 Indo-Pacific Economic Framework, which has been more discourse than delivery in new trade agreements.[16] That is not to say that the coordinator role was useless. With the underlying structure of the NSC remaining unchanged, the Office of the Coordinator needed to expend more effort over too many issues held by numerous NSC offices to meet its potential.

PROCLIVITY TO REACTION

The NSC is nominally a consensus-driven organization charged with leading various interagency decision meetings. A deputies' committee (DC) consisting of deputy cabinet secretaries and key NSC personnel debates and makes decisions of national importance. When consensus is not possible or an issue too critical, a principals' committee (PC) meets with the president. In the background to these meetings are myriad so-called interagency policy committees (IPC) and sub-IPC meetings.[17] David Rothkopf's deep analysis of the NSC came to the conclusion that this consensus-centered approach of the NSC makes it reactive to world events.[18] Events that have unfolded from the spring of 2021 through Russia's February 2022 invasion of Ukraine bear this reactive nature out. A more proactive NSC may have postulated a Ukrainian arming program that would have preempted Russia's calculations to invade or, failing that, to rapidly provide the weapons that would have prevented the descent into a war of attrition. Unchanged, the NSC will continue to give into reactive policy and initiative making instead of taking and setting the conditions of geostrategic rivalry with China.

TURF WARS

A lack of unity of effort at the NSC has often led to turf battles that require direct presidential involvement to remedy. President Jimmy Carter had campaigned in 1976 against the so-called Kissinger model of NSC-centered foreign policymaking. This and the fact that Carter was a notorious micromanager led to efforts to downgrade the NSC, only to see a reversal as crises compounded in 1979 (e.g., Iran's descent into revolution, the Soviet invasion of Afghanistan). The structure Carter and his national security advisor, Zbigniew Brezinski, would develop rested on two committees that emphasized the State Department. The results were not good. One staffer attributed the government's ineffectiveness to Carter's "terminal micro-management" and reliance on Brezinski, which fueled turf battles and rivalries.[19] In the final year of Carter's presidency this dysfunction would come to a head, leading to the resignation of Carter's secretary of state, Cyrus Vance, who was unaware of the planning for the failed April 1980 rescue attempt of American hostages in Tehran.[20] Like Carter before him, President Reagan started his presidency wanting to reverse the domineering role of the NSC. Reagan's solution to Carter's micromanagement and overreliance on a small circle of NSC advisers was to emphasize the role of cabinet secretaries. This approach also matched Reagan's hands-off approach. Unfortunately, as for Carter, in the vacuum of a strong NSC, interagency rivalry blossomed again between the Defense and State Departments. Without a strong unifying force at the NSC or a forceful president, the track record for unity of effort is poor. The lesson: effective policy execution requires an engaged president backed by an institutionally strong NSC to keep turf wars at bay and ensure unity of effort across the government.

These six maladies have bedeviled the NSC and policymaking and execution processes of all past administrations. However, we cannot pursue business as usual due to the pressures of the new cold war and the consequences of failure. The tendency toward harmful presidential micromanagement or disengagement is as much a function of the president's character as of the size of the NSC staff. A well-balanced NSC staff is not so large as to tend toward micromanagement, and not so small as to give rise to interagency turf wars or conflicts over influence on the president's decision-making. Future White House staff will need to contend with the six challenges discussed above, but the demands of the day require addressing the root cause of these maladies. Doing this and winning in the new cold war requires turning the NSC into an effective driver of proactive national action on the world stage—an attribute critical to success in this new cold war. Achieving this means that a future national security advisor, like Goldilocks, will have to find the right composition of not too large nor too small NSC staff built for nimble strategic action.

CONVENTIONAL NSC STRUCTURE

It is worth repeating that the NSC exists to serve the president. The roles of the NSC as laid out in section 101 of the National Security Act of 1947 include (1) advise the president on the integration of domestic, foreign, and military policies relating to national security; (2) assess and appraise objectives, commitments, and risks of the United States and recommend actions thereon to the president; (3) make recommendations to the president for coordinated interagency national security policies; and (4) coordinate without assuming operational authority over responses to foreign malign influence operations. These functions have remained unchanged since first enacted in 1947 and last amended in December 2023.[21] As such, various administrations have largely hewed to a single general construct for the NSC—an overwhelmingly regional focus.

The predominant regional focus of the NSC mirrors the structure of the Defense Department joint geographic military commands and the regional offices of the State Department. This alignment reinforces the NSC as the interagency manager and perpetuates institutional gaps across regions as well as in functional areas. During the final year of President George H. W. Bush's presidency in 1992, there were five regional offices (Europe and Eurasia, Asia, Africa, Latin America, Near East and South Asia), three coordinating bodies (legislative affairs, legal adviser, intelligence programs), and three functional teams (defense policy and arms control, international economic affairs, international programs). President Bill Clinton continued the regional focus (Asia, Africa, Europe, Russia/Ukraine, Inter-American, Near East and South Asia) and added the National Economic Council (NEC) to assist in executing economic policies as the communist world was being integrated into free markets.[22] The size and the scope of the NSC would reach its apex under President

Obama, with more than four hundred staffers and more than thirty teams organized into three focus areas: homeland security, national security, and strategic communications.[23] Throughout the post–Cold War era, the NSC structure functioned to mirror those of the various departments and to coordinate within regional thematic structures (e.g., arms control). The result was to reinforce a proclivity to reactive policies and focus less on advancing strategic objectives on a global scale. Moreover, past recommendations on restructuring the NSC have tended to focus on the size of the staff and which functional teams were required, but none have recommended a fundamental shift away from the regional focus.

The people who work at the NSC are dedicated patriots, often working sixteen-hour days and seven days a week for long stretches. To augment the NSC staff, subject matter experts are recruited from the various departments and agencies. In 2017, at a time when the NSC staff had grown to its largest size, 90 percent of the NSC staff were detailed from thirty federal departments and agencies.[24] However, priorities of an administration can create knowledge gaps not unlike the seams between the regional offices discussed earlier. As a presidential candidate and early in his presidency, Barack Obama strove to minimize the military aspects of American foreign policy. The president's intent was to demilitarize U.S. democracy promotion and wind down the counterinsurgency wars then raging in Iraq and Afghanistan.[25] His 2009 NSC reflected this demilitarized focus perhaps too much and created knowledge and experience gaps among an NSC largely augmented by State Department diplomats. On the eve of launching the 2012 Defense Strategic Guidance—better known as the rebalance to the Asia-Pacific, there was only one military officer in the Asia and strategic planning offices at a time when the staff was rapidly growing and implementing a new security strategy for the region. Eventually the demands of numerous security crises such as the Arab Spring and Russia's annexation of Crimea would lead to more military officers joining the NSC and filling this knowledge gap.

Whatever form it takes, the NSC is first and foremost a staff in direct support of the president. As such, it must be structured to best suit the temperament of and processes most effective for the president. In short, the NSC is a tool of the president for formulating and executing national policies. Embracing this and building an NSC around the president's top priorities, instead of regions and functional offices, would incentivize action. This would be more effective strategically and would satisfy a president chosen by an electorate demanding results on the world stage.

BUILDING A NEW NSC

A new NSC structure must be designed to do two things: serve the president and facilitate coordinated government action. This will require a staff built around the top strategic priorities articulated in the president's National Security Strategy (NSS). This strategy is mandated annually by section 603 of the Goldwater–Nichols Department of Defense Reorganization Act of 1986.[26] The administration should use this strategy as their guiding framework first and foremost, rather than treating it as a public affairs exercise, which is often the case. A proposed NSS is offered in textbox 2 at the end of this chapter. Done well, this strategy would be similar in detail and impact to Trump's Strategic Framework for the Indo-Pacific.

Past NSC staffs have created functional offices, like arms control, and regional offices to ease management (or micromanagement) of the wider executive branch. On the other hand, an action-biased NSC would enable initiative and encourage unity of effort across all departments and agencies toward specific goals. The number of these goals should be limited and of utmost national and presidential interest in order to focus the staff and not overwhelm the president's attention. The Heritage Foundation in March 2023 laid out a plan for competing with China in the new cold war, which included five lines of effort:[27]

1. Protect the homeland
2. Safeguard and advance U.S. prosperity
3. Reorient America's defense posture
4. Diminish the CCP's influence and hold it accountable
5. Exercise global leadership

These lines of effort, however, are not specific enough to be actionable or too narrowly focused on only issues relating to China. To compete over the long term requires avoiding strategic distraction. Keeping this in mind, consider these five strategic objectives to build a new NSC around:

1. Reorient military posture and operations, and develop new capabilities that undermine CCP military confidence.
2. Enhance U.S. economic resiliency to Chinese economic coercion.
3. Expel Russia from Ukraine without direct conflict, and strengthen NATO relative to Russian, Iranian, and Chinese threats (in descending order).
4. Isolate Iran from its paramilitary proxies and strategic partners (e.g., China, Russia, North Korea).
5. Establish an economic security framework among like-minded nations in Latin America and Africa to combat illicit trade (e.g., narcotics trafficking, illegal fishing) and alienate hostile influences (China, Russia, Cuba, Iran, North Korea) region wide.

Within each of these strategic objectives are numerous assumed tasks. For example, enhancing U.S. economic resiliency to Chinese economic coercion includes strengthening the nation's maritime industrial sector and access to assured shipping, discussed in chapter 5. A senior adviser to the president would lead an office for each of these five objectives. The advisers would be responsible for building a team of NSC junior staff and subject matter experts detailed from various departments and agencies. The composition, size, and expertise of each of these teams would change as a function of the actions being planned and executed. Moreover, given the comprehensive nature of the new cold war with China, each team will need experts from the military and economic statecraft. Merging the NEC with the NSC would benefit the implementation of similarly comprehensive national policies. The NEC was established in 1993 by President Clinton and has in recent years been staffed by twenty to twenty-eight economic policy experts who advise the president and coordinate economic policies.[28] Of course, presidential action will be necessary for important events outside of these five objectives or crises.

To prevent strategic distraction and remain focused on advancing the five objectives, a crisis management cell is needed. In fact, early in

President Reagan's administration, Ed Meese, acting as the president's national security advisor, established such a body—a crisis management committee chaired by the vice president.²⁹ However, supporting such a committee still requires dedicated staff and a standing body of relevant subject matter experts. This is in part backed up by the findings of the 1987 Tower Commission, which recommended strengthening NSC control over its staff.³⁰ A modern crisis management cell would act as an operational center with representatives detailed from all departments and agencies led by a small cadre of NSC staffers. This cell would oversee responses to crises of presidential interest and would oversee actions taken until it turns over responsibility to a relevant department or agency. The crisis management cell's NSC staffers would be divided into a current operations team and a crisis resolution team charged with providing updates to the president after responsibility passed out of the NSC.

The deputy national security advisor, who reports directly to the national security advisor (NSA), has responsibility for managing NSC processes and staff. Several administrative offices, such as legal counsel, public communications, legislative affairs, and administrative support, exist to support the deputy NSA. Finally, the deputy NSA would be responsible for coordinating among the NSC staff the hosting of decision-making committee meetings such as the principals' committee chaired by the president and the deputies' committee chaired by the vice president. A final coordinating and planning forum would be an interagency policy committee that would be chaired by the NSA or the deputy NSA.

To ensure unity of effort among the NSC staff and wider executive branch, the president—acting through the NSC—needs a mechanism for communicating intent and decisions. For this purpose, past presidents have issued national security decision memoranda or national security presidential directives, and national security study memoranda (NSSM), to name a few. The NSSM merits special attention as a tool for informing the NSC and cabinet offices on evolving issues and suggests ways to address them. Done right, the NSSM helps build a foundation of common knowledge and strategic framing that enables unity of effort without detailed direction from the White House. As described in *U.S.*

Naval Power in the 21st Century, the interagency response to the 2020 *West Capella* incident was not directed but guided by a common frame provided in a now-declassified ten-page memo: U.S. Strategic Framework for the Indo-Pacific.[31] Given the merging of economic and security matters in the new cold war, a modern version of this memo would be better called a strategic national interest memo released by the NSA mainly to inform the wider White House staff—the Executive Office of the President (EOP). However, conveying decisions from PC and DC meetings requires a different document laying out expectations for action and specifically directing offices to execute discrete actions. For example, a presidential strategic intent memo could articulate the use of naval statecraft in the south Pacific, with presidential strategic directive memo directing the DoD to establish an operations center in America Samoa.

The concept is that a smaller and flatter NSC staff will be nimbler in formulating and implementing presidential policies. The large NSC staff, on the other hand, is prone to micromanaging and stifling multiple levels of administrative hierarchy. At the same time, any NSC reorganization must consider congressionally mandated NSC staff positions such as the special adviser to the president on international religious freedom and the coordinator for combating malign foreign influence operations and campaigns.[32] These positions will endure without action by Congress

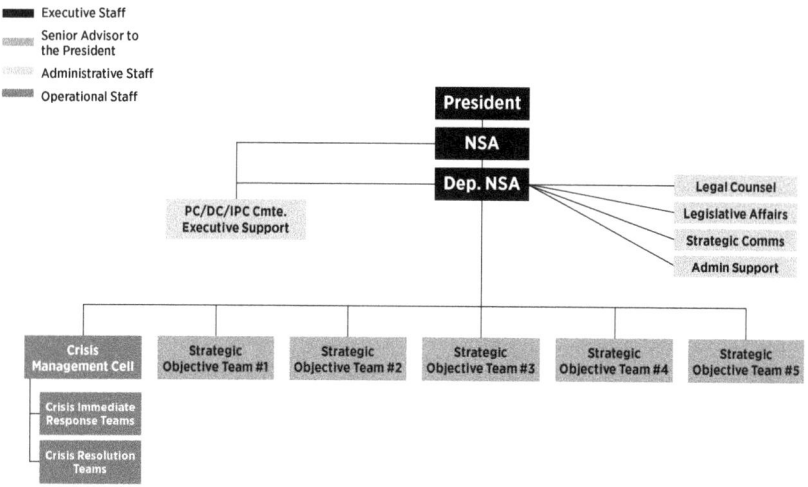

FIGURE 10. Proposed NSC structure for waging the new cold war   *Heritage Foundation*

MAP 16. REGIONAL OFFICES OF NEW COLD WAR NSC *Chris Robinson*

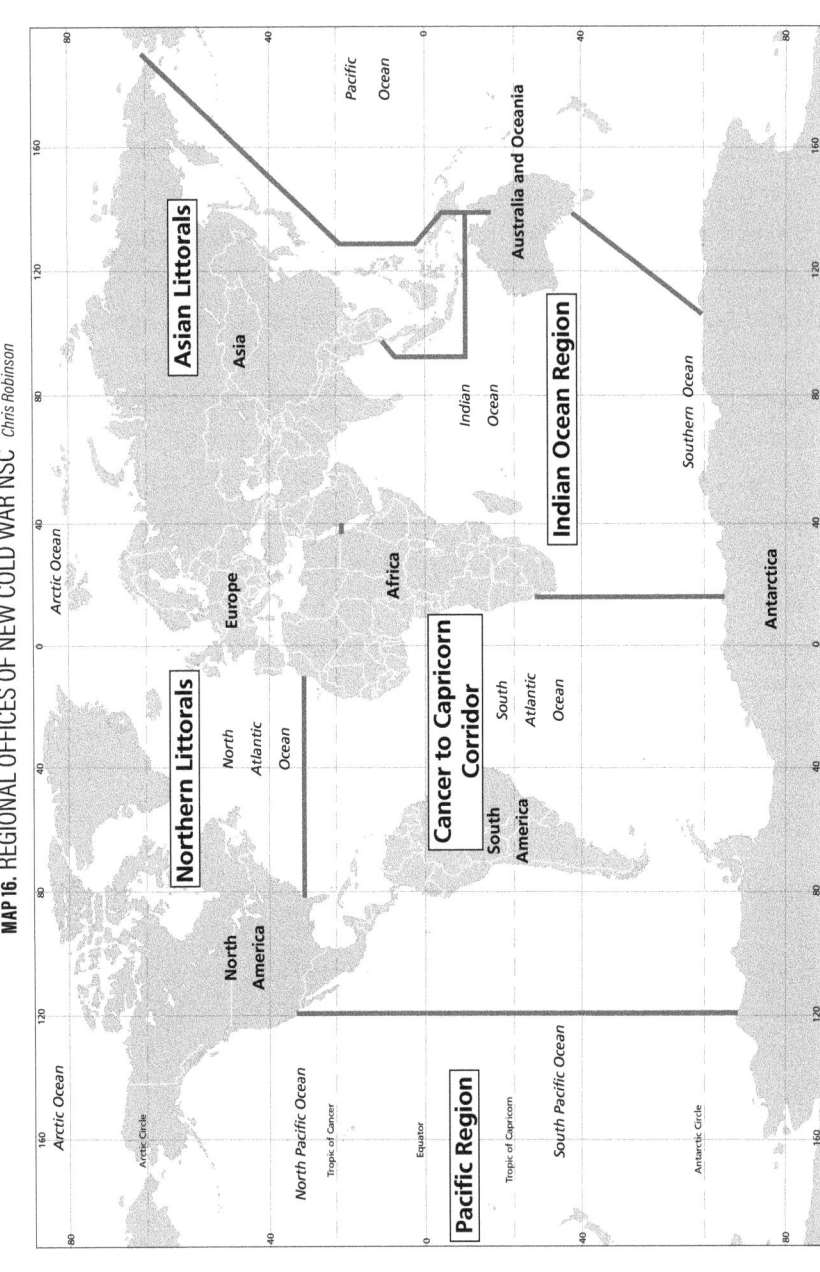

and, given their mandate, should report to one or more of the five strategic objective teams. A staff using the NSC structure recommended here would adhere to lower historic norms of about sixty NSC staffers augmented by staff of the NEC and another one hundred subject matter experts detailed from within the government.

Should any future president be reticent about doing away with regional offices, several regional adjunct offices could instead be established, led by deputy assistants to the president. These regional offices would not be aligned to State or Defense Department structures but would best support the strategic teams. Building on the first part of this book and the maritime subregions detailed in *U.S. Naval Power in the 21st Century*, five regional offices would include the Indian Ocean Region, Northern Littorals, Cancer to Capricorn Corridor, Asian Littorals, and Pacific Region.

From 2007 to 2009 the Project on National Security Reform proposed reforms to improve efficiencies in pursuit of better integrated national security policies. These reforms focused on unlikely legislative remedies and limited NSC process refinements meant to address the challenges of its day—terrorism, proliferation, failing states.[33] That said, the project contributed to the debate on the right size, composition, and role of executive orders to restructure the NSC. It was also clear that reforming the NSC for the new cold war would have to consider updating its parent body—the EOP. At the top of the list was consolidating offices with similar mandates, disestablishing offices that did not align with the president's priorities, and placing the NSC at the top of the EOP's bureaucratic hierarchy to better ensure resources devoted to presidential policy priorities.

THE NEW NSC IN ACTION—DAY 1

To implement this new NSC structure requires forethought and action well before a new administration takes office; to ensure that no time is lost, a new NSS must be published the day after inauguration along with an executive order directing a new structure for the NSC. In the recent past, strategic direction has come too late in a new administration's tenure; in the case of President Biden, his NSS was issued twenty months after his inauguration and after several crises had passed: Putin's February 2022 invasion of Ukraine and the disastrous evacuation of Afghanistan in the summer of 2021. Ideally, a new NSS and, importantly, the new NSC staff should already be named and prepared to start work on Day 1. Unfortunately, this is not the norm, but efforts like Project 2025 have worked to address this.[34] Here is how to do it.

The presidential candidates will have articulated their foreign policy and national priorities as they campaign. Statements and policy proscriptions made on the campaign trail and informed behind the scenes must be turned into an NSS that reflects the direction of a president-elect. This NSS need not be a solution to all things but rather a focus on only the top priorities, like the five listed earlier. A sample NSS is provided at the end of this chapter in textbox 2. This NSS will inform the structure of the president-elect's NSC and inform the drafting of an executive order that will be signed into force the day after inauguration. A sample executive order detailing this reorganization is provided at the end of this chapter in textbox 3.

The Day 1 executive order must direct the establishment of a task-focused structure reflecting the president's priorities and reflecting the comprehensive nature of the new cold war. Moreover, as is precedent, an associated presidential strategic decision memo should lay out NSC processes and responsibilities of the various offices within the president's NSC. This presidential strategic decision memo and associated executive order will need to be ready well before inauguration. The process of developing these documents would also serve to gather the people expected to implement them. People are policy, so the soonest the right people are identified for NSC staff and in place after the inauguration, the more likely a new administration is to make headway on the president's priorities. Ideally, the staffers for the upcoming NSC and the front offices of each cabinet secretary should participate in developing these documents. Their familiarity with the issues, the elected president's intentions, and camaraderie among staffs will be critical to quickly implementing new policies.

To get a better idea of how this new NSC would operate, let's simulate a couple of scenarios. Consider a crisis that does not fit neatly into one of the five strategic objective teams—for example, a war in Latin America instigated by Venezuela over territorial disputes with neighbor Guyana. As intelligence agencies notice an impending attack, the crisis cell would establish a monitoring team composed of subject matter experts from across the government. Since the crisis is triggered by a military intervention, additional military subject matter experts may be called to join the team. These temporary staffers would augment the monitoring team and prepare for the next iteration of action—formation of a crisis immediate response team. PC and DC meetings would propose preliminary responses for the president to consider and approve. As events unfold, the response team begins coordinating interagency actions and informs the president and NSC staff, and the NSA would propose follow-on PC and DC meetings. As events settle into predictability or are resolved, responsibility shifts to a lead department or agency directed by the president via a presidential strategic directive. Subsequent updates for the president on the receding crisis would be provided by a smaller crisis resolution team. The intent is to ensure that initial reactions align with the president's direction and then rapidly move responsibility out of the White House for managing crises.

There is more NSC oversight and action when a crisis arises that falls within one of the five strategic objective teams' purviews. In this case, once the crisis requires less immediate operational responses, the president would decide to shift responsibility to the NSC's appropriate strategic objective team to take over. The intent is to ensure policy consistency and coherency over the long term while also advancing specific strategic objectives that too often a crisis otherwise derails. Interagency policy committees would be established with representatives from relevant departments and agencies to support the strategic objective teams in executing specific initiatives. To see how this works, consider a Chinese attack on Philippine coast guard vessels with loss of life in the South China Sea, certainly a crisis warranting the president's attention as well as impacting a priority strategic objective. Initially, the crisis management cell would stand up a focused team with a representative from the appropriate strategic objective team. As the crisis subsides, the strategic objective team would coordinate sustained economic, diplomatic, and military resources to a beneficial postcrisis situation. Ideally, this approach would better ensure continuity with associated noncrisis activities such as regional naval operations and economic development projects, as detailed in chapter 2. Should narrowly focused long-term actions arising from this crisis be required, a PC or DC meeting at the NSA's request could be called seeking a presidential strategic direction. The goal is to shift specific actions and responsibilities outside the White House and free up the affected strategic objective team to remain focused on the president's overall strategic objective. If done right, a proactive NSC driving global events would have fewer unexpected crises with which to contend.

CONCLUSION

Enabling sustained and coherent national action along several of the president's strategic priorities is crucial for taking back the initiative in the new cold war. This requires a nimble and attentive NSC staff dedicated to promoting essential government restructuring such as the establishment of a maritime department, the revitalization of the nation's strategically important maritime industry, and the execution sweeping new military exercises, described in the earlier chapters. This chapter provides a potential structure for doing this and a plan for executing it. The question is, will the next president embrace this path?

TEXTBOX 2

PROPOSED DRAFT 2025 NATIONAL SECURITY STRATEGY

Our nation is midway into a decisive decade in which the risk of major war is very real, with threats to our way of life multiplying. Clear-eyed and forceful leadership is required and will be delivered by this administration to safeguard Americans, our national interests, and our way of life. To secure peace for our nation amid the rising dangers before us requires prioritizing security and our economic vitality. This National Security Strategy provides the guidance to deliver on that promise as well as a message of partnership to our allies and like-minded nations.

At this moment our national security requires the development and integration of a set of strategies, including diplomatic, informational, economic, political, and military components. The nation has been in a similar situation before, and President Ronald Reagan's historic NSDD-32 directive illustrates the scope and scale of the endeavor again before the nation.[1] As such, the United States shall be guided by the following:

a. The nation is in a new cold war with the Peoples' Republic of China, whose political and economic system are antithetical to American long-term interests. Strengthening the fundamentals of American liberty and prosperity will be critical in this comprehensive rivalry.
b. Russia, Iran, North Korea, and terrorist organizations remain committed to seeking opportunistic gains at America's cost. Confronting and dissuading future attacks will require vigilance and swift responses.
c. Allies remain a bedrock of American security, premised on mutual interests and shared commitments of resources. Bolstering these alliances will be a top priority as it relates to strengthening American defenses and burnishing trade. Likewise, attracting like-minded partner nations will be a second-order priority to the same ends.

As such, the national security policy of the United States shall be guided in the near term by the following global objectives:

1. Deter War with China. Reorient military posture and operations, and field new capabilities that diminish CCP military confidence in a confrontation with our nation.
2. Strengthen the Economy. Enhance U.S. economic resiliency to hostile nations' economic coercion (i.e., China).
3. Uphold Sovereignty over Russian Revanchism. Compel Russia to depart Ukraine and strengthen NATO to resist Russian, Iranian, and Chinese threats (in descending priority).
4. Diminish Iranian Threats to Peace. Isolate Iran from its paramilitary proxies and strategic partners (e.g., China, Russia, North Korea).
5. Limit Malign Influences. Establish an economic-security framework among like-minded nations in Latin America and Africa to combat illicit trade (i.e., narcotics trafficking, illegal fishing) and alienate hostile influences (Chinese, Russian, Cuban, Iranian, North Korean) region wide.

The theme of this National Security Strategy is America first. Previous national security strategies have made similar arguments only to be distracted by lengthy prose and short on details.[2] That said, our policies will always reflect our democratic and humanitarian values in pursuit of a future safe for Americans. These are principles enshrined in our Constitution and Bill of Rights and are our North Star going forward. Given this context, the government's plan for moving forward follows.

DETER WAR WITH CHINA
Since recognizing the People's Republic of China, our nation has consistently demonstrated an abiding interest in maintaining peace and stability across the Taiwan Strait. Any unilateral change will be resisted, but deterrence will require rebalancing the regional military presence back to a peaceful posture. This will involve assisting Taiwan

resisting potential acts of aggression against it; bolstering combined military forces with regional allies Japan, Australia, South Korea, and Philippines for common cause; and developing technologies that will offset China's military and degrade its leaders' confidence that it could prevail in a conflict now and well into the future. The decisive theater for this effort will be the Indo-Pacific, with invigorated emphasis in Southeast Asia and the south and central Pacific. The actions taken will be informed by the successful U.S. Strategic Framework for the Indo-Pacific.[3] Efforts to bolster military presence will be taken with an eye to improving trade, which will necessitate renewed emphasis on economic development that supports this goal by U.S. assistance programs (e.g., USAID, Development Finance Corporation).

STRENGTHEN THE ECONOMY
China benefits from the openness of the international economy while limiting access to its domestic market as it seeks to make the world more dependent on it while reducing its own dependence on the world. This is funding a Chinese military modernization and expansion that is well into its second decade. Recent crises—the Covid-19 pandemic and Russia's war on Ukraine—have exposed too-brittle supply chains and overreliance on our enemies for our livelihood, such as antibiotics, shipping, and rare earth minerals from China. Trade relations will be based on reciprocity and on diversification away from regimes hostile to the United States.

UPHOLD SOVEREIGNTY OVER RUSSIAN REVANCHISM
Failing to restore peace in Europe runs the increased risk of war in Asia. Putin's success in Ukraine and the bleeding of our nation's military resources benefits China as it calculates and weighs a violent adventure across the Taiwan Strait. As such, Ukraine will be assisted in its fight against Russia with equipment necessary to break the current war of attrition. This will be an all-allies effort.

DIMINISH IRANIAN THREATS TO PEACE

Hamas' barbaric assault on women, children, and the elderly on October 7, 2023, is a reminder of the terrorist organization's depravity and that of their backers in Tehran. Behind the most dangerous proxy groups to U.S. interests stands the mullahs of Iran, who are seeking nuclear weapons. As such, comprehensive efforts will be taken to isolate Iran from its proxies (i.e., Houthis, Hezbollah, Hamas, and various groups in Iraq and Syria) and roll back its overseas paramilitary presence. At the same time, invigorated efforts to expand the Abraham Accords will be undertaken in concert with efforts that expand economic relations with like-minded nations across the Middle East. To this end, initial energetic diplomatic initiatives will be undertaken to strengthen partnerships with Türkiye, Saudi Arabia, Egypt, and Kazakhstan. The goal is to turn the mullahs in Tehran inward, leading to a more representative and free society that many Iranians want for themselves.

LIMIT MALIGN INFLUENCES

At the end of the Cold War, democracy was spreading across Latin America and a more prosperous future seemed at hand. Unfortunately, socialist dictatorships persisted in Cuba and grew to include the regime in Venezuela, setting back all people in the Western Hemisphere. For a variety of reasons, Africa has likewise not broken the cycle of poverty and weak governance that is holding back its burgeoning population from reaching its full potential. Programs like Prosper Africa had modest success and show the way forward by enabling entrepreneurs at home and abroad to grow their business through mutually beneficial American trade. Together these regions offer great potential but are increasingly the target of nefarious influences—narcotics cartels, Chinese debt diplomacy and illegal fishing, Russian mercenaries, Iran terror proxies, and Cuba-inspired insurrection movements. A new Cancer to Capricorn regional economic and security framework will guide efforts to counter these nefarious influences across a region connected by the Atlantic and put the narcotics cartels out of business. Given the impacts of narcotics trafficking through Western Africa and illegal migration, several European nations are welcomed to play a role in this effort. Finally, efforts will be taken in concert with our allies to combat malign influences and illicit foreign government presence in our homeland who seek to weaken our nation and our unity.

CONCLUSION

This strategy will deliver on long-standing obligations to protect the homeland, advance American prosperity, preserve peace through strength, and advance American influence. This will be done using common sense over ideology, emphasizing delivery of results for Americans while remaining true to our founding principles. The means to this end include the five areas detailed: to deter war, strengthen our economy, push back on revisionist powers, diminish nefarious players presence on the world stage, and bring forward a more promising future shared with Latin America and Africa.

REFERENCES
1. National Security Decision Directive 32, May 20, 1982, https://irp.fas.org/offdocs/nsdd/nsdd-32.pdf.
2. National Security Strategy, October 2022, https://www.whitehouse.gov/wp-content/uploads/2022/10/Biden-Harris-Administrations-National-Security-Strategy-10.2022.pdf.
3. U.S. Strategic Framework for the Indo-Pacific, December 31, 2017, https://trumpwhitehouse.archives.gov/wp-content/uploads/2021/01/IPS-Final-Declass.pdf.

TEXTBOX 3

PROPOSED DRAFT EXECUTIVE ORDER REORGANIZING THE EXECUTIVE OFFICE OF THE PRESIDENT

EXECUTIVE ORDER #####:
Organization of the Executive Office of the President

By the authority vested in me as President of the United States by the Constitution and the laws of the United States of American, it is hereby ordered as follows:

SECTION 1. *Rationale*
The Executive Office of the President (EOP) exists to assist the president in developing and implementing national policies. This executive order is intended to focus the EOP on issues of grave importance in strengthening the nation's resiliency to nefarious influence, economic coercion, and military intimidation. Further, this new EOP is structured to enable proactive policies supportive of U.S. national interests as directed by the president.

SECTION 2. *Establishment*
The EOP was composed previously of eighteen offices;[1] it will henceforth consist of the following offices in order of seniority:

1. National Security Council
2. Office of Management and Budget
3. U.S. Trade Representative
4. Council on Environmental Quality and Health
5. Council of Economic Advisers
6. National Space, Maritime and Advancement of American Technology Council
7. Presidential Personnel Office

SECTION 3. *De-Establishment and Consolidation*
The following reorganization of the EOP is to be executed:

(a) *Council on Environmental Quality and Health.* The former Council on Environmental Quality, Gender Policy Council, Climate Policy Office, and Office of National Drug Control Policy are to be consolidated. This new office will comply with the 1969 National Environmental Policy Act (NEPA) led by a Senate-confirmed chair and supported by two assistants to the president. One assistant is charged with addressing national health issues and the second with national medical preparedness (e.g., pandemics, improved medical services, advances in medicine).

(b) *National Security Council.* Former offices created by executive order are to be consolidated within the National Security Council to better implement comprehensive national policies. The following offices are to be de-established and the appropriate responsibilities shifted to the National Security Council: National Economic Council, Office of Public Engagement, Office of the National Cyber Director, Domestic Policy Council, and Office of Intergovernmental Affairs. Composition and responsibilities of specific offices within the National Security Council will be established by Presidential Strategic Decision memorandum.

(c) *National Space, Maritime and Advancement of American Technology Council.* This office will be led by the science adviser to the president who will preside over the executive secretary of the National Space Council, and a Senate-confirmed director of the Office of Science and Technology Policy established by the National Science and Technology Policy, Organization, and Priorities Act of 1976. The Office of the Intellectual Property Enforcement Coordinator will be consolidated within this office, led by an assistant science adviser. A second assistant science adviser will be named focusing on maritime technologies.

SECTION 4. *Functions*

The president or, upon his direction, the vice president may convene meetings of any of the various offices of the EOP. Likewise, any EOP office lead or, by direction a deputy, may request ad hoc meetings of the EOP to deliberate cross-functional issues not addressed within a single office of those listed in section 2.

SECTION 5. *Administration*

Each EOP office listed in section 2 will propose a charter delineating its responsibilities and staffing needs within thirty days of this executive order being implemented. The charter and staffing requests will be approved by the White House chief of staff within forty-five days of this executive order coming into force.

REFERENCES

Executive Order 12835: Establishment of the National Economic Council, https://www.govinfo.gov/content/pkg/WCPD-1993-02-01/pdf/WCPD-1993-02-01-Pg95.pdf

1. Executive Office of the President, https://www.whitehouse.gov/administration/executive-office-of-the-president/.

TEXTBOX 4

PROPOSED DRAFT PRESIDENTIAL STRATEGIC DECISION MEMO ESTABLISHING NSC STRUCTURE AND PROCESSES

The National Security Council (NSC) will be the principal forum for deliberating and deciding issues relevant to comprehensive national security issues. As such, the national security policy of this government will comprise economic, military, diplomatic, informational, and societal elements. The functions, membership, and responsibilities of the NSC shall be as set forth in the National Security Act of 1947, and as amended in this memorandum.

The NSC will meet periodically as directed by the president or as delegated to the National Security Advisor (NSA). Membership to various NSC meetings will be agenda driven and determined by the NSA in consultation with the president, vice president, and cabinet members.

The NSA, at the direction of the president and in consultation with cabinet members, shall be responsible for determining the agenda and providing after-action updates and associated memos memorializing actions decided. To support the NSA in overseeing formal NSC meetings and associated administrative functions thereof, there shall be three assistant executive secretaries assigned as NSC Committee Executive Support Staff.

Formal NSC meetings will consist of the Principals Committee (PC), a senior interagency forum for consideration of policy issues affecting national security that the president will chair. The Deputies Committee (DC), chaired by the vice president or an alternate directed by the president, shall review interagency issues and provide guidance for NSC action or recommend presidential attention at a PC meeting for decision. Finally, development and implementation of national security policies by multiple agencies shall be accomplished by Interagency Policy Committees (IPCs) chaired by the NSA or an alternate determined by the NSA.

Informal ad hoc meetings are expected to occur on a frequent basis and shall include representatives from appropriate departments and agencies to support the NSC in executing the president's directives.

The NSC shall be structured as follows, subject to future modification upon recommendation of the NSA to best execute the president's policies:

- NSA to have overall responsibility for the conduct of the NSC staff.
- Deputy NSA to assist the NSA focusing on the conduct of functional offices in support of the wider NSC staff.
- The following functional offices will be established: NSC Committee Executive Support Staff, Legal Counsel, Legislative Affairs, Strategic Communications, and Administrative Support.
- Crisis Management Cell led by presidential executive action officers supported by a Crisis Immediate Response Team, which will oversee initial crisis response and associated interagency coordination composed of NSC staff called presidential executive action officers and representatives from each department and agency. Simply put, a Crisis Resolution Team composed of presidential executive action officers and representatives from departments and agencies, as the NSA shall deemed necessary.
- Five Strategic Objective Teams will be established, each led by a senior assistant to the president and staffed by the deputy assistant to the president and subject matter experts detailed to the NSC from government. These five teams are established to develop and implement policies as detailed in the National Security Strategy:
    1. Deter China. Reorient the posture and operations, and develop new capabilities that undermine CCP military confidence.
    2. Economic Resiliency. Enhance U.S. economic resiliency to Chinese economic coercion.

3. European Unity. Expel Russia from Ukraine without direct conflict and strengthen NATO relative to Russian, Iranian, and Chinese threats (in descending order).
4. Contain Iran. Isolate Iran from its paramilitary proxies and strategic partners (e.g., China, Russia, North Korea).
5. Compete for Africa–Latin America. Establish an economic-security framework among like-minded nations in Latin America and Africa to combat illicit trade (e.g., narcotics trafficking, illegal fishing) and alienate hostile influences (China, Russia, Cuba, Iran, North Korea) region wide.

The NSC will generate three formal documents: the Presidential Strategic Decision, the Presidential Strategic Direction, and the Strategic National Interest memoranda. These documents will convey presidential strategic intent and orders to the NSC and cabinet offices.

This structure of the NSC is intended to incentivize action and the delivery of strategic results within four years. The hierarchy is flat and intended to remain small relative to recent historic norms so the NSC can act nimbly and without getting enmeshed in internal department and agency functions.

CHAPTER 9

A FLEET STRUCTURE FOR GREAT POWER RIVALRY

Competing with China effectively in the new cold war requires operating naval forces in new ways. Part 1 lays out the importance of winning in the current competition for position, and it is this arena that will heavily rely on limited naval forces to enable strategic effects. The framework for this—naval statecraft—was first laid out in *U.S. Naval Power in the 21st Century*. It is a world the Navy must quickly adapt to. In the post–Cold War era, the Navy was largely built for waging an uncontested war from the sea, and not for competing in a peacetime competition with a great power. The post–Cold War advantages have evaporated with the recent revelations that maintaining peace will mean both retaining a war-winning military and winning the new cold war.

With the approval of the fiscal year 2023 National Defense Authorization Act, Congress and the president expanded the Navy's official role. Now, in addition to war-fighting, it is acknowledged what has been true since the American Revolution; the Navy's mandate is "for the peacetime promotion of the national security interests and prosperity of the United States."[1] Given the scale of the threat from China, a new fleet construct is required that optimizes both peacetime competition and readying for transition to major conflict. This dual approach is necessary to prevent China from winning without firing a shot as it wages an insurgency at sea to overturn the norms governing commerce and naval operations—a rules-based reordering.[2] Failing this peacetime competition would be as costly as losing a war in the long run, with far-reaching and enduring implications to the nation's security and prosperity. For the Navy to execute this peacetime mission most effectively with available forces will require reorganizing its forces in seven fleets, with an eighth fleet considered for operations detailed in chapter 2 for the south and central Pacific.

Instead of ordering the fleet along joint combatant commands, as is the case today, the Navy will need to reorganize its numbered fleets and their composition according to the threats and environments in several maritime regions. *U.S. Naval Power in the 21st Century* proposes eight maritime theaters and their strategic mission—hold, build, advance. The *hold* mission's aim is to prevent China or Russia from destabilizing a region, including the Arctic, North Atlantic, Indian Ocean region, and northeast Asia to northwest Pacific. In the Caribbean to Gulf of Guinea maritime Cancer to Capricorn Corridor, and in the south and central Pacific, the focus is to *build* access and the capacity of U.S. forces while complicating attempts by China to expand its presence, as detailed in chapter 1. In the Eastern Mediterranean and South China Sea, the focus is to *advance* U.S. interests and bolster the rules-based order. To act more urgently in deterring China, this chapter lays out a fleet reorganization of forces operating in the *build* and *advance* theaters, where the threats and opportunities are greatest. This will require redrawing existing numbered fleets' areas of operations as well as adding at least one fleet focused on operations in the South China Sea.

THE NAVY MUST REORGANIZE FOR GREAT-POWER COMPETITION WITH CHINA

Business as usual cannot continue with expectations of success in the peacetime global competition with China. According to a government-sponsored December 2022 RAND Corporation report, China is planning a network of bases that can support global military operations.[3] The scope of this is detailed in chapter 1. Already China has successfully eroded the rules-based order in the South China Sea, waging a so-called maritime insurgency using maritime militia to reset the norms there to China's liking.[4]

To recap from part 1, indications suggest that China will sharpen its comprehensive challenge over the future of Taiwan, culminating in a conflict around 2027. In line with this, recent speculation sees Chinese attempts at expanded access in the strategically important south and central Pacific as part of a "Pacific great game."[5] Such overseas bases and access agreements serve a rapidly modernizing and expanding naval force. Annual Defense Department reports on China have doubled down on these assessments, making clear that China is intent on building a global naval force supported by bases at strategic points that could imperil U.S. interests if not addressed.[6] While the threat is real, it is important to understand that China's military is limited, meaning that America can act to contest its most threatening aspirations.

Naval theorist Julian S. Corbett devoted significant time to considering how fleets should be distributed and composed, and his work is relevant still. In his 1911 book *Some Principles of Maritime Strategy*, he stressed navies' role in controlling "maritime communications"—today this would include seaborne trade, undersea cables, transoceanic airborne commerce, and naval operations.[7] For the U.S. Navy, the present challenge is securing maritime trade and security connections against China's efforts to hold them at risk. To do so, a reorganization of the Navy's numbered fleets as laid out here would tailor forces regionally to execute a global peacetime maritime strategy while better preparing for war. Since the release of the 2018 National Defense Strategy, to include the 2022 update, the Navy has yet to make significant organizational changes to adapt to the new strategic focus of competition with China.

NAVAL CAMPAIGNING AND MALLEABLE NUMBERED FLEETS

In an August 2022 article, U.S. Navy captain Joshua Taylor made the case for applying joint planning concepts to construct a South China Sea maritime campaign. To advance U.S. interests in the region, Captain Taylor recommended a persistent naval force centered around an expeditionary sea base (i.e., using existing ships like the ESB or ESD) with associated escorts and naval aircraft for intelligence, surveillance, and reconnaissance operations.[8] The type of operations and where they would be needed is detailed in chapter 3. Those forces, if employed today, executing such a maritime campaign would be commanded by the Seventh Fleet based in Yokosuka, Japan.

The principal unit for executing sustained naval operations in peacetime and war are numbered fleets like the Seventh Fleet. As of January 2025, there are six numbered fleets aligned to joint geographic combatant commands, which are based on geographic regions (e.g., European, Africa Command). The Chief of Naval Operations reiterated the centrality of numbered fleets in executing national security strategy at the naval conference WEST in January 2022, and then formally in NAVPLAN, released in July 2022.[9] The CNO's comments at WEST were pointed: "The way we fight has matured . . . transitioned to a fleet centric vice past focus on carrier strike groups . . . to best execute the national defense strategy." However, given the paucity of warships and the scale of the threat, it is inescapable that the Navy must reorganize to better focus

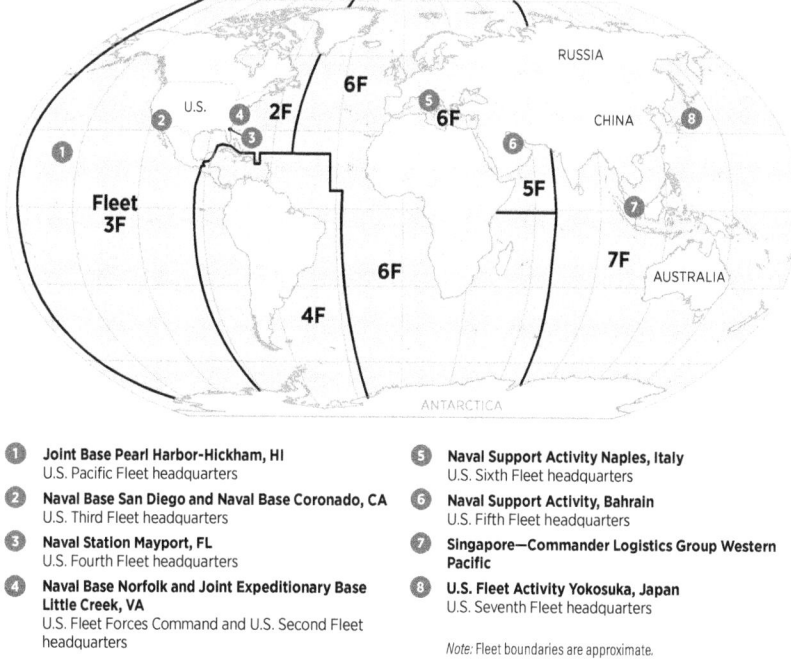

MAP 17. CURRENT U.S. NAVY FLEET BOUNDARIES *Heritage Foundation*

1. **Joint Base Pearl Harbor-Hickham, HI**
   U.S. Pacific Fleet headquarters
2. **Naval Base San Diego and Naval Base Coronado, CA**
   U.S. Third Fleet headquarters
3. **Naval Station Mayport, FL**
   U.S. Fourth Fleet headquarters
4. **Naval Base Norfolk and Joint Expeditionary Base Little Creek, VA**
   U.S. Fleet Forces Command and U.S. Second Fleet headquarters
5. **Naval Support Activity Naples, Italy**
   U.S. Sixth Fleet headquarters
6. **Naval Support Activity, Bahrain**
   U.S. Fifth Fleet headquarters
7. **Singapore—Commander Logistics Group Western Pacific**
8. **U.S. Fleet Activity Yokosuka, Japan**
   U.S. Seventh Fleet headquarters

Note: Fleet boundaries are approximate.

and tailor forces for the greatest strategic effect. This is well past due, given events in the South China Sea, where business as usual has ceded much of the rules-based order, emboldening an ever-aggressive China.[10]

Today the numbered fleets are precisely aligned with geographic joint combatant commands like Central Command, which is headquartered in Florida but responsible for military operations in the Middle East. These artificial bureaucratic lines on a map with shore-based headquarters far from the maritime theater of operations are not immutable. Recent numbered fleet changes have reflected changing world events, such as standing up the Fourth Fleet in 2008 and the reestablishment of the Second Fleet in 2018.[11] The reestablishment of the Fourth Fleet was intended to facilitate regional collective maritime structures in line with the Navy's 2007 A Cooperative Strategy for 21st Century Seapower. The establishment of the Second Fleet, however, was in response to a series of troubling Russian submarine operations off the U.S. Eastern Seaboard. Given the consequences of Chinese encroachment in the South China Sea on U.S. interests—erosion of alliances and threats to trade—calls have been made to reestablish a fleet focused on that region, most notably by the secretary of the Navy in 2020.[12] There is no impediment to realigning the Navy's numbered fleets to best execute a global maritime strategy.

MAP 18. CURRENT JOINT GEOGRAPHIC COMBATANT COMMANDS *Heritage Foundation*

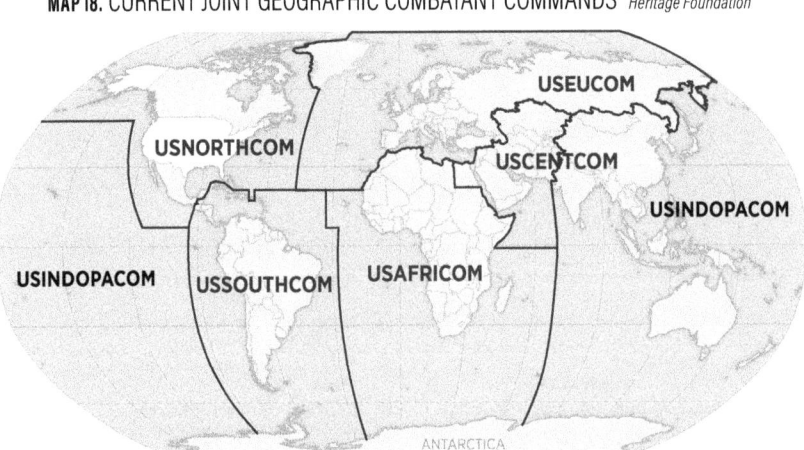

A GLOBAL MARITIME CAMPAIGN IS BEST EXECUTED USING REGIONAL NUMBERED FLEETS

The 2022 National Defense Strategy made clear that the nation is engaged in a comprehensive competition with China. The administration's approach at that time was based on a concept called "integrated deterrence." The plan aimed to use all national levers of power to influence and deter China through interagency and joint and combined campaign plans.[13] This competition and associated campaign plans will necessarily have a strong maritime component, given the global aspirations of the Chinese Communist Party and its military focus on a conflict over the island of Taiwan.[14] Organizing the Navy's numbered fleets along a maritime versus land geography, with forces tailored to specific regional strategic missions, is a better way to execute a competitive maritime strategy. *U.S. Naval Power in the 21st Century* extensively details what this would entail over a long-term strategy to 2050. The task at hand here is how to make this reorganization a reality in the near term.

The allocation of forces is based on requests from the joint geographic combatant commands to meet specific operational needs. This is done through an annual Joint Staff process—Global Force Management (GFM).[15] This necessarily prioritizes risks within and not across joint commands connected by the ocean, a prime example being three joint commands (AFRICOM, CENTCOM, and INDOPACOM) responsible for and making disparate demands on the Navy in the Indian Ocean. This situation makes it more likely that demands on the Navy are excessive and not coherent strategically.[16] In fact, during the Navy's 2016 Force Structure Assessment, duplication of mission needs across combatant commands levied a requirement for an additional 194 warships.[17] Such inefficiencies are inherent in a GFM system built to support land-based commands. Given the politics involved, pursuing a change to the joint force architecture requiring revision to the 1986 Goldwater–Nichols Act and modification to the GFM process is unlikely to succeed. Rather, reorganizing numbered fleets has a better chance of success to improve naval force strategic efficacy without requiring broad political and institutional consensus.

By using an oceans-informed force allocation, instead of by joint geographic combatant command, it is possible to assign naval forces according to maritime regions like the Indian Ocean or South China Sea. Another region ripe for rethinking numbered fleet organization is a stretch of ocean connecting the Caribbean and the Gulf of Guinea. Piracy persists and narcotic trafficking transits through this Cancer to Capricorn Corridor, as detailed in chapter 2. This single maritime region is covered by the Southern Command headquartered in Florida and by Africa Command, headquartered in Germany with associated force from the Sixth and Fourth fleets. By combining the operational needs in a geographically contiguous maritime region, a single fleet can coherently address regional strategic needs at the operational level. A refocused Fourth Fleet would be postured to combat illegal maritime activity that operates across the waterways connecting Europe, Africa, and North and South America. The Indian Ocean, covered today by Fifth, Sixth, and Seventh fleets, would likewise be consolidated into a single fleet to deter and confront Iranian aggression and enable greater cooperation with India, which can confound the growing Chinese military presence in the region.[18] These changes do not require rethinking the existing relationship between joint commands like European Command and the associated naval component commands, such as Naval Forces Europe.

Each joint geographic combatant command has an associated naval component command—for example, Indo-Pacific Command has the Pacific Fleet. This arrangement assists the joint command's control over the naval forces assigned it; likewise, it provides the Navy's component command an avenue to inform and shape the joint command's requirements for naval forces. Changing the geographic coverage of the numbered fleets will not impact the component commands' role, but numbered fleets aligned to maritime realities will better inform and improve coverage of joint command requests. The effect would be to turn the Navy into a so-called functional command that provides naval force, much like Transportation Command provides sealift and airlift for all the geographic combatant commands. This case is made in *U.S. Naval*

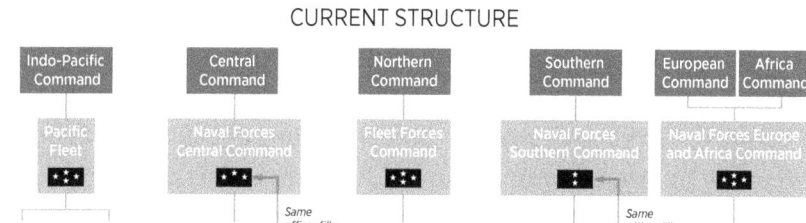

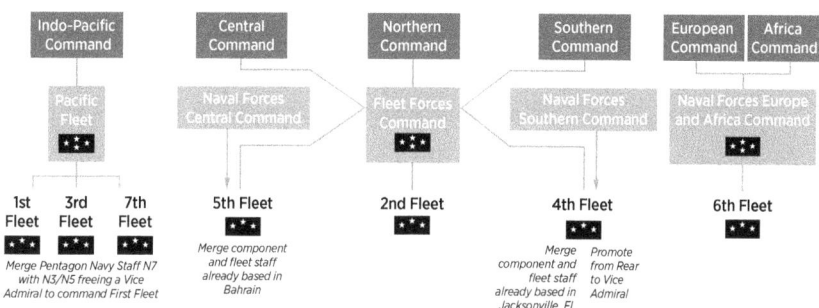

FIGURE 11. Current Navy structure versus recommended future structure

SOURCE: Authors' research Heritage Foundation

Power in the 21st Century to better enable the Navy to most economically and effectively execute global maritime campaigns.

Moreover, this arrangement will not impact joint command planning, but it will normalize numbered fleet regional operations with strengthened readiness and maintenance planning. For example, a newly constituted First Fleet in Southeast Asia would be better able to establish and sustain access to new ports for maintenance of deployed vessels. It would also be better positioned to plan increasingly effective bilateral exercises enabled by a persistent naval presence and fleet staff. Such responsibilities are today held by the Seventh Fleet, located almost three thousand miles away in Japan and with numerous competing demands, such as being ready to fight several potential wars in northeast Asia—Korean Peninsula, Taiwan, or with Russia. Such pressures on the Seventh Fleet necessarily prioritizes its presence and staff-work to northeast Asia. This dynamic is something I can personally attest to, having served on the Seventh Fleet staff and as a defense attaché in Southeast Asia.

Organizational changes envisioned in the associated tables and graphics can be achieved without congressional modification to the Goldwater–Nichols Act and would not require presidential action to adjust the Unified Command Plan (UCP).[19] However, if the Navy is reenvisioned as a functional command, a UCP change would be necessary, perhaps in the normal two-year review process that occurs on even years. The last UCP change occurred during the biennial review in 2020, when Israel was moved within CENTCOM's area of responsibility. Establishing new numbered fleets based overseas would not require a UCP change; however, it would require congressional notification at a minimum.[20]

That said, the Navy is making some adjustments to better conduct global great-power competition with China. In late 2020 the expeditionary sea base *Hershel Williams* was homeported on the Greek island of Crete and dedicated to missions in Africa. The ship is now conducting routine deployments to the Gulf of Guinea and supporting the multinational Africa Command exercise Obangame Express.[21] Southern Command, dedicated to operations in South America, has also seen increased Russian and Chinese activity in recent years. This led Congress to include in the FY 2023 defense budget a requirement for a study to validate basing up to six littoral combat ships with Fourth Fleet.[22] However, the most

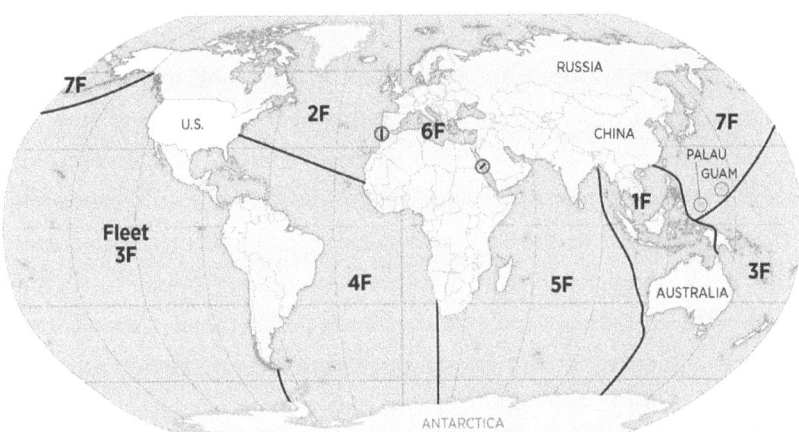

MAP 19. MODIFIED U.S. NAVAL FLEET BOUNDARIES Heritage Foundation

consequential change would be to bolster naval presence and organization in the South China Sea.

NEW FLEETS NEEDED THAT ARE FOCUSED ON CONTESTED AND STRATEGICALLY VITAL MARITIMES

Using the maritime framework laid out in *U.S. Naval Power in the 21st Century*, eight maritime regions inform revised areas of responsibility for existing and at least one new numbered fleet. Of the modifications envisioned, three merit special mention: (1) a Central Pacific Fleet focused on securing the strategic sea and air lanes that connect the mainland with forward military forces in East Asia; this would be a longer-term priority but is envisioned as a Ninth Fleet based in American Samoa carved out of the Third Fleet's area of responsibility covering the south and central Pacific; (2) an expanded operating area for Fourth Fleet to better police the nation's southern approaches principally operating in the Cancer to Capricorn Corridor; and (3), most importantly, a newly created First Fleet based in Southeast Asia to oversee a maritime counterinsurgency in the South China Sea. The modifications to the Second, Fifth, and Sixth fleets would not create new operational demands or require significant changes to existing staff. For these reasons, this chapter focuses only on the more challenging reorganizations.

As mentioned in this chapter and in part 1, the strategic importance of the South China Sea makes the creation of a dedicated fleet a top priority in the competition with China. Southeast Asia has been a focal point of great-power competition before, and it is once again an area of dispute now between the United States and China. The Navy's modest moves in recent years have set the stage for future growth. Notable is the return of littoral combat ships rotational deployments to Singapore, joining logistics ships like expeditionary fast transports that doubled as a Seventh flagship in 2018.[23] However, these deployed ships lack a regionally focused operational staff, instead relying on Seventh Fleet's Logistics Group Western Pacific. This command is led by a one-star admiral based in Singapore who supports the Seventh Fleet's logistics needs, first, with regional efforts at best a secondary consideration. Without a First Fleet, this situation would persist, and regional operations detailed in chapters 2 and 3 would remain secondary and less likely resourced, sustained, and effectively executed with regional partner maritime forces.[24]

HOW TO RESOURCE AND DEPLOY A REESTABLISHED FIRST FLEET

Reestablishing a regionally focused fleet in Southeast Asia would grow from the existing Singapore-based destroyer squadron (DESRON 7) staff. It would also leverage deployed warships and repurpose an existing ship in the region, as the Seventh Fleet did in 2018 with an expeditionary fast transport as the new fleet's command ship. A mobile command ship is ideal for a new fleet, affording it the ability to conduct fleet operations from a mobile platform free of the need to secure an overseas base before being stood up. A three-star admiral should lead this fleet to signal the significance of the region to U.S. interests, better ensure its resourcing, and gain access to regional naval and political leaders. This is important in rank-conscious Asia, where a junior flag officer would find it tough to gain access to and agreement from the more senior political and military decision makers impacting regional naval operations. This does not require increasing the number of admirals but rather reorganizing offices at the Pentagon to free up the officer needed.

When it comes to finding the vice admiral to lead this new fleet, Congress limits the numbers of flag officers. Fortunately, the Navy for years has not exceeded these levels and does have some margin and flexibility to name a new admiral; in January 2023 there were 298 flag officers within a cap of 304.[25] One option that does not require expanding the number of admirals would be to merge the recently created N7 office in the Pentagon back into N3/N5, freeing a three-star admiral for operational command of a fleet. Sending senior flag officers to operationally important commands in key contested regions is a move Congress would likely support.

With a First Fleet established, it would initially grow from existing naval forces. In future years it will gradually grow mostly from an enduring rotational presence of expeditionary sea bases, as Captain Taylor postulates, and episodic carrier strike groups operating in the

TABLE 6: A NEW U.S. NAVY FLEET STRUCTURE: MISSION TASKING

Fleet	Mission Task
First Fleet (C1F)	Execute South China Sea maritime counterinsurgency, expand access agreements for port and repair services to support wartime operations.
Second Fleet (C2F)	Protect strategic forces in Atlantic theater, monitor Russia and Chinese naval activities.
Third Fleet (C3F)	Protect strategic forces in Pacific theater, respond to Chinese and Russian out-of-area deployments, and oversee conduct of fleet problems.
Fourth Fleet (C4F)	Support counter-illicit trade (narcotics, IUU) operations, respond to Chinese and Russian out-of-area deployments, and develop regional maritime capacities.
Fifth Fleet (C5F)	Posture to deter and ready to respond to Iranian provocations, keep the Strait of Hormuz and Bab-el-Mandeb Strait open, improve maritime interoperability with Indian forces, and respond to Chinese and Russian regional deployments.
Sixth Fleet (C6F)	Posture to deter and ready to respond to Russian provocations; keep the Suez Canal open and able to rapidly reopen; respond to Chinese naval activities.
Seventh Fleet (C7F)	Posture to deter and ready to respond to China, Russian, and North Korean aggression (i.e., defense of South Korea, Japan, and Taiwan).
Ninth Fleet (C9F)	Patrol U.S. and Compact of Free Association EEZs, develop facilities to sustain fleet operations and conduct repairs.

region tied to a long-term regional maritime campaign plan executed by the First Fleet.

REIMAGINE THE FOURTH FLEET FOR PATROLLING THE CANCER TO CAPRICORN CORRIDOR

Since the publication of *U.S. Naval Power in the 21st Century*, there have been significant developments of unmanned platforms that will impact the conceptualization and composition of the future fleet. Most notable has been the performance of unmanned platforms in the Black Sea by Ukraine. However, for the U.S. Navy, the rapid maturity of the Fifth Fleet's Task Force 59 (TF 59), composed of unmanned vessels, has enabled a wider adoption of these platforms. TF 59 was established on September 9, 2021, according to Vice Adm. Brad Cooper, then commander of the Fifth Fleet, to "one, enhance our maritime domain awareness, and two, increase deterrence."[26] Several multinational unmanned exercises and successful operations near hostile Iranian naval forces has proven the merit of the approach. Since 2022, the secretary of the Navy has called for replicating TF 59's efforts at other fleets. The Fourth Fleet is setting up its own unmanned unit, and the Pacific Fleet's Adm. Samuel Paparo announced at the 2024 WEST naval conference the creation of an operational unmanned unit in addition to the May 2022 establishment of a developmental unmanned squadron—USVDIV-1.[27] Based on TF 59's performance, the Fourth Fleet is likely to benefit from expanded maritime domain awareness important to combating illicit drug trafficking and migrant flows across the nation's southern approaches.

Covering the nation's southern approaches, however, will require redrawing the lines of the Fourth Fleet's area of responsibility. Established in 1989, Joint Interagency Task Force South (JIATF-S) has had some success leveraging its twenty-one regional partners in interdicting illicit narcotics trade headed to the United States. Given the Fourth Fleet's and the JIATF-S's limited assets, to more significantly hurt the cartels' bottom line and complicate China's influence in the Global South, the Fourth Fleet will need to operate across the Cancer to Capricorn Corridor to interdict these nefarious activities. This will require an expansion of its area of operations with additional platforms that enhance its ability to police the southern approaches to the United States. This will be done in cooperation with regional partners, with regionally dedicated platforms such as the ESDs mentioned in chapter 2. A Fourth Fleet ESD could also serve as a command ship to better execute interagency and multinational maritime operations. The redrawing of areas of responsibilities and new platforms can increase interdiction performance with greater at-sea sustainment, to include unmanned aerial drones. Such drones have already demonstrated their effectiveness in extending detection ranges and persistently provide maritime domain awareness. As in the case with TF 59 in the Fifth Fleet, this combination of ESD and drones in the Fourth Fleet would greatly aid in interdicting illicit trade routes and maritime poaching.

Realizing the potential of unmanned systems in the region—South America—the secretary of the Navy announced the establishment of additional TF 59–like units. In April 2022 the CNO and secretary of the Navy announced the long-standing regional UNITAS exercise as the venue for introducing unmanned naval platforms into the region.[28] As the Fourth Fleet brings on more unmanned platforms, it will enable an effective application of naval statecraft through sustained combined counternarcotics naval operations with regional partners. Focusing the Fourth Fleet on the maritime routes that the cartels rely on will require a larger mothership than the MV *Chouest* chartered by JIATF-S, mentioned in chapter 2. Moreover, this new mothership will need the capacity to sustain partner nations' patrol craft. As detailed in chapter 2, the ideal candidates to fill this mission today are the Navy's inactive USNS *Montford Point* (ESD-1) and USNS *John Glenn* (ESD-2). Given this and the geographic proximity to the area of operations, this reorganization does not necessitate a change of home port of its fleet headquarters in Mayport, Florida.

A NUMBERED FLEET FOR THE NEW GREAT GAME OF THE PACIFIC

Today the Third Fleet, based in San Diego, California, is responsible for the waters east of the dateline to the coast of North and South America. Unfortunately, operational requirements in Asia and the Middle East, a paucity of warships, and inadequate facilities leaves large parts of the Pacific devoid of a U.S. naval presence—to include the U.S. Coast Guard. As detailed in chapter 2, the region in the south and central Pacific is a particular concern given Chinese encroachment and the potential for basing in the region. A new naval fleet based here would enhance coordination of regional operations with allies of the Pacific Quad.

While a naval fleet is one option to consider, it remains the U.S. Coast Guard's responsibility to police the nation's EEZs. However, the capacity of current Coast Guard forces is not adequate to address large-scale Chinese fishing fleets like those seen in 2020 around the Galapagos Islands. This paucity of force will persist as planned Coast Guard cutter procurement will only meet 61 percent of the need to police these waters, with over twice the planned fifty-seven offshore patrol cutters required to fill this gap.[29] Meanwhile, the Navy supports the Coast Guard in its maritime security mission by periodically (on average, twice a year) assigning ships to the Oceania Maritime Security Initiative. This effort embarks Coast Guard personnel on Navy ships to improve maritime security and maritime domain awareness in the Pacific. However, due to operational demands on the Navy, these missions have been infrequent.

Establishing one new fleet is tough, trying to stand up two is harder, but the operational necessity and logic remain sound. For decades, the central and south Pacific has been devoid of U.S. naval forces, but with increasing Chinese naval and fishing activity on the rise, a return to the region is overdue. As discussed in chapter 2, a new fleet unconventionally composed of Navy and Coast Guard platforms based in American Samoa could execute a range of naval statecraft activities. This would include infrastructure projects to support a sustained naval presence in the region and more frequent operational coordination with regional partners. Given the operational distances involved, the need for robust communications, and expeditionary sustainment capabilities, a practical first step would be basing a forward repair and command ship in American Samoa. That said, the priority is in the South China Sea, leaving the Third Fleet based in San Diego to be responsible for this vast region. However, the sooner the Navy and Coast Guard can establish a persistent naval presence in the region the better. One way forward is with an unconventional Ninth Fleet composed of deployed Navy and Coast Guard platforms within a joint command—a joint task force. Joint Interagency Task Force West (JIATF-W), based at Camp Smith in Hawaii and collocated with the Indo-Pacific Command, could provide the framework for this approach. Whatever course is taken, the gap of naval forces in this region presents a power vacuum that China is actively looking to fill, with severe and more costly consequences in the future.

CONCLUSION

Centering the global maritime competitive arm of the national defense strategy on the numbered fleets makes sense from an operational standpoint—numbered fleets are organized for sustained maritime operations. However, achieving the full benefit of this requires reorganizing the numbered fleets according to narrow strategic objectives bounded by commonsense geography of the maritime. Beginning with the work of *U.S. Naval Power in the 21st Century*, these operations can be described as holding, building, and advancing U.S. interests as the strategic environment dictates.

The shift to allocating naval forces to a numbered fleet–centric construct would take place in a phased approach. The first step to amending the GFM process is stipulating that naval forces should be allocated to numbered fleets based on operational requests of the joint geographic combatant commands. This would be done in tandem with an adjustment of numbered fleet areas of responsibility as indicated in map 19, and the allocation of platforms like repurposed ESDs. The second step is standing up new fleet staffs, such as the naming of a Commander First Fleet, with an afloat staff on a forward-deployed command ship. By realigning the numbered fleets to maritime regions with missions commensurate with the challenges and strategic objectives in each, the Navy can better employ limited forces until more warships are added to the fleet.

CONCLUSION

*A good plan violently executed now is better than
a perfect plan next week.*
—GEN. GEORGE S. PATTON JR. (1947)[1]

The time for contemplation on the rivalry with China is past. It is time for action, which at best can prevent war but certainly will better ensure America's and the free world's perseverance should there be a next great war. That said, if conflict becomes inevitable this decade, defeat will have been decided before the first shots are fired.

A goal of this book is to excite informed action to deter the CCP, who has assiduously been making every preparation for a war with the United States. The ideas here build on the strategic framework for naval statecraft laid out in the 2023 book *U.S. Naval Power in the 21st Century*. Proposals presented in this book's three parts are not comprehensive but intend to encourage even more discourse on this critical question:

HOW CAN WE PREVENT CONFLICT WHILE WINNING IN THE NEW COLD WAR WITH THE CHINESE COMMUNIST PARTY?

This is a question that can be affirmed as possible—and as irresponsible to not pursue victory. Achieving success requires operating differently, strengthening the nation's economy from coercion, and reorganizing institutions for the era's new cold war.

Given the yawning margin of military overmatch that the Chinese present across East Asia, military buildup alone will not work, and buildup beginning in 2025 would deliver needed military capacity too late. The Office of Naval Intelligence projects that China will have a fleet of four hundred warships in 2025 while, according to the annual long-range shipbuilding plan for fiscal year 2025, the U.S. Navy will shrink to 287 warships by 2027. This necessitates seizing the initiative in the positional competition playing out in the south and central Pacific and South China Sea, thereby presenting the CCP with a more daunting military challenge with the forces on hand. This will buy an added margin of peace—for a time.

Likewise, preventing additional Chinese bases in Africa or the south Pacific alone will not ensure peace. This will require a sustained military and economic national revitalization program. Top of the list—regaining the nation's maritime strength through a revolution in shipping that can defend against economic coercion and sustain a wartime economy. Together with this are actions to bolster the nation's energy sector to ensure the lights stay on, factories produce, and warships press the fight at sea. Finally, *U.S. Naval Power in the 21st Century* proposed an aggressive shipbuilding program to meet and sustain a long-term competitive strategy with a fleet of 575 warships (manned and unmanned). The math behind that fleet size and design remains valid, but without a recapitalized maritime industrial sector, meeting and sustaining that strategy will be an impossible task.

Building the fleet to the level needed will require an invigorated maritime industry driven by a clear demand signal for warships. It will be an industry strong enough to deter China, win the new cold war, or, if deterrence fails, set conditions to rapidly grow the fleet in wartime. This will require a new naval act that will begin the process of maritime industrial recapitalization while delivering to the Navy warships that have for too long been deferred. Operating naval shipbuilding and congressional processes with a business-as-usual mindset will at best get the nation a fleet of 331 warships by 2027.[2] This would require retaining every warship with service life (something the Navy has long resisted), continuing planned shipbuilding (something Congress and the president have yet to do), and building deployable armed unmanned vessels (something the Navy has delayed). This is not good enough.

Moreover, the Navy must be able to keep the ships it has now in the fight. This will require creative new methods of rearming warships at sea and conducting battle damage repairs in forward areas. The memories of the destroyer *Cole* are a stark reminder of this need. When she was attacked in the Port of Aden on October 30, 2000, the action of the sailors that day kept the ship afloat. However, she was only able to be returned to active service after she was transported for extensive repairs at a U.S. shipyard with the use of a contracted heavy-lift ship—*Blue Marlin*.[3] In June 2023 Austal began construction of a new auxiliary floating dock medium for the U.S. Navy, but it will not be able to service the Navy's aircraft carriers or amphibious assault ships (LHD/LHA).[4] Moreover, it is unclear whether the Navy will tow these new floating drydocks to forward bases where they would be of greatest utility in a future war. On the other hand, a heavy-lift ship can lift a damaged warship out of the water and transport it to a safe harbor for repairs. The Chinese navy has already taken delivery of heavy-lift repair ships as a forward-deployed repair dock—like the *Yinmahu*.[5] Repurposing ships like the Navy's two inactive ESDs for this purpose, reminiscent of floating drydocks used in World War II, will prove vital in winning the next war.

Yes, new platforms, technologies, and operational concepts will be needed, but these things alone will not ensure success in the new cold war. Like the Cold War before, this is a competition over whose system is supreme, and the winner sets the rules for trade, warfare, and diplomacy. Ideology is as relevant now as it was then, but unlike communism's grip, ideology with our contemporary foes will be more pliable. To confront the Soviet Union's systematic global challenge, the National Security Act of 1947 reorganized government for the task—creating the Central Intelligence Agency, merging separate military services into a new Department of Defense, and creating the National Security Council. Later, the 1986 Goldwater–Nichols Act further refined the military response to the Soviets by mandating joint military experience and procurement decisions. While appropriate for the times, today's blending of economic and information warfare into the mix poses new challenges that warrant new structures.

Organizational changes are never easy and always political. As such, the changes recommended in this book, while urgently required, will take several years to realize. Perhaps the most straight forward consideration in this book is reorganizing the Navy's numbered fleet structure, given that the resources and authorities overwhelmingly reside within the Department of the Navy. Top of the list is establishing a new First Fleet to oversee a maritime counterinsurgency in the South China Sea. Of course, without necessary budgets and allocation of forces, these changes will remain of limited effect. Achieving greater success requires tweaking the existing joint structure and associated budgets by recasting the Navy as a joint functional command—a provider of maritime forces. This will cross congressional, White House, and sister military service equities and authorities, making this endeavor a much more daunting task. That said, to operate effectively against new cold war foes China and Russia with the limited maritime resources we have, we will need to employ available forces in a new strategic naval statecraft framework.

Next in complexity and bucking conventional thinking is reorganizing the National Security Council to a task-centered framework. Too often its structure mirrors the executive branch, which encourages micromanagement—something witnessed during the Obama administration with its very large National Security Council staff. It is better to align this critical and extremely influential interagency body to the specific strategic objectives of the president rather than emphasize management via its own regional and functional offices. Such a change would allow for a smaller, tailored-to-task staff that would be nimbler and more focused on results. This means the White House must rely on the wider executive branch agencies and departments for the heavy lifting of daily management. The new cold war strategic framework—naval statecraft—will require new interagency leadership from the top via a remodeled National Security Council.

Most challenging will be the reorganization to better realize the revolution in shipping that can bring about an American revival in maritime industry. This will be essential for building and sustaining the navy the nation needs and securing the nation's economy from coercion or interference. That said, the merging of the four principal maritime agencies—the U.S. Coast Guard, Maritime Administration, National Oceanic and Atmospheric Administration, and Federal Maritime Commission—into a maritime department will be a worthy and necessary fight. The principal merit of this department will be better implementation of national maritime policies with nearly no growth in government. National maritime industrial weakness is a strategic vulnerability that warrants daily presidential-level attention, which can best be assured with a maritime department led by a cabinet secretary—a historic first in our nation's history.

Reorganizing a government is a slow process, but it is imperative to take action urgently to win the new cold war. Delivering tough changes will require persistent leadership to keep moving forward on the reorganizations recommended here. We must immediately begin bolstering the nation's economic resiliency to coercion and building the Navy the country needs, but achieving the fleet will be a generational task. Placing orders for the ships needed to grow our industrial capacity in the first two years will be critical for creating momentum that ensures sustained progress. Changing the manner of maritime operations into a naval statecraft framework can be realized quickly with the right leaders, who will build on such experiences as the *West Capella* incident. These captains of change will have to act urgently in waging a maritime counterinsurgency in the South China Sea, seize the initiative in the Cancer to Capricorn Corridor, and win the new great game in the south and central Pacific.

Success through naval statecraft in the near term enhances deterrence of China. As national strengthening proceeds apace, enabled by organizational changes, this will set the conditions for victory in the new cold war. Like the individual gears inside a ship's reduction gearbox, various efforts will run at different speeds and will vary in size and construction, but they will all mesh to drive the nation's ship forward.

NOTES

INTRODUCTION

1. Ronald O'Rourke, "China Naval Modernization: Implications for U.S. Naval Capabilities—Background and Issues for Congress," Congressional Research Service, updated January 30, 2024, 9–10, accessed May 21, 2024, https://crsreports.congress.gov/product/pdf/RL/RL33153/277.
2. Office of the Secretary of Defense, *Military and Security Developments involving the People's Republic of China 2020*, Annual Report to Congress, September 1, 2020, ii, vii, 38, and 143–144, https://media.defense.gov/2020/Sep/01/2002488689/-1/-1/1/2020-DOD-CHINA-MILITARY-POWER-REPORT-FINAL.PDF.
3. Samuel B. Griffith, trans., *Sun Tzu: The Art of War* (London: Oxford University Press, 1971), 49–51.
4. James Carafano, Michael Pillsbury, Jeff Smith, and Andrew Harding, eds., *Winning the New Cold War: A Plan for Countering China* (Washington, DC: Heritage Foundation, March 28, 2023), 6–15 and 116–17, https://www.heritage.org/sites/default/files/2023-07/SR270.pdf.
5. Brent D. Sadler, *U.S. Naval Power in the 21st Century: A New Strategy for Facing the Chinese and Russian Threat* (Annapolis, MD: Naval Institute Press, 2023), 73.
6. Michael Pillsbury, *The Hundred-Year Marathon: China's Secret Strategy to Replace America as the Global Superpower* (New York: Holt, 2015), 48–53.
7. Elbridge A. Colby, *The Strategy of Denial: American Defense in an Age of Great Power Conflict* (New Haven, CT: Yale University Press, 2021), 120 and 136–42.
8. Matt Pottinger, "Beijing's American Hustle: How Chinese Grand Strategy Exploits U.S. Power," *Foreign Affairs*, August 23, 2021, https://www.foreignaffairs.com/articles/asia/2021-08-23/beijings-american-hustle.
9. Zhang Liang, *The Tiananmen Papers: The Chinese Leadership's Decision to Use Force against Their Own People—In Their Own Words* (New York: PublicAffairs).
10. Rush Doshi, *The Long Game: China's Grand Strategy to Displace American Order* (New York: Oxford University Press, 2021), 47–48.
11. Aleksandr Solzhenitsyn, *The Gulag Archipelago: An Experiment in Literary Investigation*, vol. 1 (New York: Harper Perennial, 1973), 167.
12. Griffith, *Sun Tzu*, 9–10, 45–46, and 66–70.
13. Full Text of Jiang Zemin's Report at the 16th Party Congress, November 17, 2002, *China through a Lens*, http://www.china.org.cn/english/2002/Nov/49107.htm.

14. Patrick Devenny, "PLAN Procurement of Sovremenny-Class Destroyers: Developments and Repercussions," RUSI, May 23, 2005, https://rusi.org/publication/plan-procurement-sovremenny-class-destroyers-developments-and-repercussions.
15. O'Rourke, "China Naval Modernization," 24.
16. U.S. Department of Defense, "Annual Report on the Military Power of the People's Republic of China," July 28, 2003, 7, https://nuke.fas.org/guide/china/dod-2003.pdf.
17. Alfred Thayer Mahan was a nineteenth–twentieth century naval theorist famous for his 1890 book, *The Influence of Sea Power upon History*. His writing is credited with influencing all the major naval powers, to include President Theodore Roosevelt's naval modernization and buildup of the early 1900s.
18. Hu Jintao, "Hold High the Great Banner of Socialism with Chinese Characteristics and Strive for New Victories in Building a Moderately Prosperous Society in All Respects," full text of Hu Jintao's report to the Seventeenth National Congress of the Communist Party of China, October 15, 2007, http://np.china-embassy.gov.cn/eng/Features/200711/t20071104_1579245.htm; and Office of the Secretary of Defense, *Annual Report to Congress: Military and Security Developments involving the People's Republic of China, 2011*, 16–17, https://dod.defense.gov/Portals/1/Documents/pubs/2011_CMPR_Final.pdf.
19. Michael Wines and Edward Wong, "In Charged Moment, China's Political Heir Tries Introducing Himself to U.S.," *New York Times*, February 11, 2012, https://www.nytimes.com/2012/02/12/world/asia/xi-jinping-chinas-presumptive-next-leader-to-visit-us.html.
20. Benjamin Kang Lim and Megha Rajagopalan, "China's Xi Purging Corrupt Officials to Put Own Men in Place," Reuters, April 16, 2014, https://www.reuters.com/article/us-china-corruption-xi-insight/chinas-xi-purging-corrupt-officials-to-put-own-men-in-place-sources-idUSBREA3F1UT20140417/; Tom Mitchell and Gabriel Wildau, "Xi Jinping's Anti-Corruption Purge Takes Aim at China's Military," *Financial Times*, March 2, 2015, https://www.ft.com/content/09eae174-c154-11e4-88ca-00144feab7de; "Xi Jinping's 'Final Purge' ahead of Chinese Communist Party Congress," *Times of India*, October 8, 2022, https://timesofindia.indiatimes.com/world/china/xi-jinpings-final-purge-ahead-of-chinese-communist-party-congress/articleshow/94696049.cms; and Amy Hawkins, "Unsafe at the Top: China's Anti-Graft Drive Targets Billionaires and Bankers," *Guardian*, April 18, 2023, https://www.theguardian.com/world/2023/apr/19/unsafe-at-the-top-chinas-anti-graft-drive-targets-billionaires-and-bankers.
21. Keith Zhai and Chun Han Wong, "China's Xi Claims Third Term as Communist Party Leader," *Wall Street Journal*, October 23, 2022, https://www.wsj.com/articles/chinas-xi-claims-third-term-as-communist-party-leader-11666499842.
22. Markus B. Liege, *China's Use of Military Forces in Foreign Affairs* (London: Routledge, 2017), 150–51, 158, 161, 165, 169, and 176.
23. Liege, *China's Use of Military Forces*, 154.

24. Ezra F. Vogel, *Deng Xiaoping and the Transformation of China* (Cambridge, MA: Belknap Press of Harvard University Press, 2011), 274–76 and 292–93; and Liege, *China's Use of Military Forces*, 215–16.
25. Договор о добрососедстве, дружбе и сотрудничестве между Российской Федерацией и Китайской Народной Республикой [Treaty on Good-Neighbourliness, Friendship and Cooperation between the Russian Federation and the People's Republic of China], President of Russia, July 16, 2001, http://www.kremlin.ru/supplement/3418.
26. Joint Statement of the Russian Federation and the People's Republic of China on the International Relations Entering a New Era and the Global Sustainable Development, President of Russia, February 4, 2022, http://www.en.kremlin.ru/supplement/5770.
27. Chris Buckley, "China Hangs on Xi's Every Word. His Silence Also Speaks Volumes," *Japan Times*, October 22, 2022, https://www.japantimes.co.jp/news/2022/10/23/asia-pacific/politics-diplomacy-asia-pacific/xi-jinping-silence-china-listen/.
28. Frank Tang, "Explainer | What Is China's Swift Equivalent and Could It Help Beijing Reduce Reliance on the US Dollar?" *South China Morning Post*, February 28, 2022, https://www.scmp.com/economy/china-economy/article/3168684/what-chinas-swift-equivalent-and-could-it-help-beijing-reduce.
29. Jindong Zhang, Winni Zhou, and Tom Westbrook, "Yuan Overtakes Dollar to Become Most-Used Currency in China's Cross-Border Transactions," Reuters, April 26, 2023, https://www.reuters.com/markets/currencies/yuan-overtakes-dollar-become-most-used-currency-chinas-cross-border-transactions-2023-04-26/.
30. "Xi Jinping Worries That China's Troops Are Not Ready to Fight," *Economist*, November 6, 2023, https://www.economist.com/special-report/2023/11/06/xi-jinping-worries-that-chinas-troops-are-not-ready-to-fight; and Dennis J. Blasko, "PLA Weaknesses and Xi's Concerns about PLA Capabilities," U.S.–China Economic and Security Review Commission, February 7, 2019, https://www.uscc.gov/sites/default/files/Blasko_USCC Testimony_FINAL.pdf.
31. Alyssa Chen, "Purge in Chinese Nuclear Missile Force Points to Graft in Ranks," *Japan Times*, August 2, 2023, https://www.japantimes.co.jp/news/2023/08/02/asia-pacific/politics/china-pla-rocket-force-purge-xi-jinping/.
32. Phillip C. Saunders and Joel Wuthnow, "Conclusion: Assessing Chinese Military Reforms," in *Chairman Xi Remakes the PLA: Assessing Chinese Military Reforms*, ed. by Phillip C. Sauders, Arthur S. Ding, Andrew Scobell, Andrew N. D. Yang, and Joel Wuthnow (Washington, DC: National Defense University Press, 2019), 711–26, https://ndupress.ndu.edu/Portals/68/Documents/Books/Chairman-Xi/Chairman-Xi.pdf.
33. Nishan de Mel, Nilanthi Samaranayake, and Ambika Satkunanathan, "A Year after Mass Protests, Sri Lanka's Governance Crisis Continues," United States Institute of Peace, July 20, 2023, https://www.usip.org/publications/2023/07/year-after-mass-protests-sri-lankas-governance-crisis-continues.

34. Marwaan Macan-Markar, "China Keeps Sri Lanka in Debt Grip, Stalling IMF Relief," *Nikkei Asia*, October 3, 2023, https://asia.nikkei.com/Spotlight/Sri-Lanka-crisis/China-keeps-Sri-Lanka-in-debt-grip-stalling-IMF-relief.
35. Yvette Tan, "Chinese 'Spy Ship' Yuan Wang 5 Docks in Sri Lanka's Hambantota Port Despite Indian Concerns," *BBC*, August 16, 2022, https://www.bbc.com/news/world-asia-62558767.
36. Dipanjan Roy Chaudhury, "Sri Lanka Considers Permission Freeze for Chinese 'Spy' Ships," *India Times*, December 18, 2023, https://economictimes.indiatimes.com/news/international/world-news/sri-lanka-considers-permission-freeze-for-chinese-spy-ships/.
37. Thomas Hale and Tom Mitchell, "China Retreats from Sweeping Zero-Covid Policies as Economic Toll Mounts," *Financial Times*, December 7, 2022, https://www.ft.com/content/b0c2f6fa-7164-4cf5-80ad-db029a5b66de.
38. "Moody's Affirms China's A1 Rating, Changes Outlook to Negative from Stable," Moody's Investor Service, December 5, 2023, https://ratings.moodys.com/ratings-news/412128.
39. Chris Anstey, "Xi Jinping Drops Economic Growth for 'Values-Based Legitimacy,'" *Bloomberg*, October 21, 2023, https://www.bloomberg.com/news/newsletters/2023-10-21/bloomberg-new-economy-xi-jinping-drops-growth-for-values-based-legitimacy?embedded-checkout=true.
40. Kylie Atwood, "Biden Administration Looking at Arranging High-Profile Visits to China by Senior Officials," *CNN*, May 17, 2023, https://www.cnn.com/2023/05/17/politics/biden-administration-china-visits/index.html.
41. Josh Rogin, "Biden's Economic Diplomacy Push with China Is High Risk, Low Reward," *Washington Post*, April 26, 2023, https://www.washingtonpost.com/opinions/2023/04/27/china-us-economic-talks-national-security-biden/.
42. Ashley Capoot, "U.S. Commerce Secretary Says She 'Didn't Pull Any Punches' during Recent Visit to China," *CNBC*, September 3, 2023, https://www.cnbc.com/2023/09/03/us-commerce-secretary-gina-raimondo-says-she-didnt-pull-any-punches-during-recent-visit-to-china.html.
43. Joe Cash, "China Urges 'Practical' U.S. Action on Sanctions after Yellen Talks," Reuters, July 10, 2023, https://www.reuters.com/world/china-urges-practical-us-action-sanctions-after-yellen-talks-2023-07-10/; and "MOFCOM Regular Press Conference," August 31, 2023, Ministry of Commerce, People's Republic of China, http://english.mofcom.gov.cn/article/newsrelease/press/202309/20230903440119.shtml.
44. Mara Cepeda, "Philippine Coast Guard Says China Harassed, Obstructed Resupply Mission Ships in Spratlys," *Straits Times*, July 5, 2023, https://www.straitstimes.com/asia/se-asia/philippine-coast-guard-says-china-harassed-obstructed-resupply-mission-ships-in-spratlys; and Brent Sadler and Hunter Kovach, "Follow the Numbers: China Steps Up Military Activity near

Taiwan," *Daily Signal*, October 30, 2023, https://www.dailysignal.com/2023/10/30/follow-the-numbers-china-steps-up-military-activity-near-taiwan/.

45. Sarah Rumpf-Whitten, "The Biden Administration Reportedly Planned on Not Telling the Public That a Chinese Spy Balloon Had Crossed into U.S. Airspace Earlier This Year," *Fox News*, December 24, 2023, https://www.foxnews.com/politics/biden-admins-top-officials-attempted-conceal-chinese-spy-balloon-from-public-congress-exposed-report.

46. Jay Tristan Tarriela, "Why the Philippines Is Exposing China's Aggressive Actions in the South China Sea," *Diplomat*, April 19, 2023, https://thediplomat.com/2023/04/why-the-philippines-is-exposing-chinas-aggressive-actions-in-the-south-china-sea/.

47. Richard Haas, "Summing Up the Biden–Xi Summit," Australian Strategic Policy Institute, November 20, 2023, https://www.aspistrategist.org.au/summing-up-the-biden-xi-summit/.

48. Joseph Clark, "Brown Speaks with Chinese Counterpart," Department of Defense, December 21, 2023, https://www.defense.gov/News/News-Stories/Article/Article/3624242/brown-speaks-with-chinese-counterpart/.

49. Sadler and Kovach, "Follow the Numbers."

50. Ben Blanchard and Yimou Lee, "Taiwan Braces for New China Pressure Tactic in Strait," Reuters, April 6, 2023, https://www.reuters.com/world/asia-pacific/taiwan-braces-new-china-pressure-tactic-disputed-strait-2023-04-06/; and Dzirhan Mahadzir, "China Coast Guard Vessel Collides with Filipino Supply Ship in South China Sea," *USNI News*, October 22, 2023, https://news.usni.org/2023/10/22/china-coast-guard-vessel-collides-with-filipino-supply-ship-in-south-china-sea.

51. Karen Lema and Mikhail Flores, "China-Philippines Relations: Major Events in South China Sea Dispute," Reuters, December 21, 2023, https://www.reuters.com/world/asia-pacific/rift-deepens-between-philippines-china-over-south-china-sea-2023-12-21/.

52. "Fleet Tracker," *USNI News*, April 17, 2023, accessed October 28, 2024, https://news.usni.org/2023/04/17/usni-news-fleet-and-marine-tracker-april-17-2023; and U.S. Embassy Manila, "Philippine, U.S. Troops to Hold Largest Ever Balikatan Exercise from April 11 to 28," April 4, 2021, https://ph.usembassy.gov/philippine-u-s-troops-to-hold-largest-ever-balikatan-exercise-from-april-11-to-28/.

53. Nicholas R. Lardy, "How Serious Is China's Economic Slowdown," Peterson Institute for International Economics, August 17, 2023, https://www.piie.com/blogs/realtime-economics/how-serious-chinas-economic-slowdown.

54. Bonny Lin, Brian Hart, Samantha Lu, Hannah Price, and Matthew Slade, "Analyzing China's Escalation after Taiwan President Tsai's Transit through the United States," Center for Strategic & International Studies, June 29, 2023, https://www.csis.org/analysis/analyzing-chinas-escalation-after-taiwan-president-tsais-transit-through-united-states.

55. "China Announces Vessel Boarding Campaign amidst Tensions with Taiwan," *Maritime Executive*, April 6, 2023, https://maritime-executive.com/article/china-announces-vessel-boarding-campaign-amidst-tensions-with-taiwan.

CHAPTER 1. FORTIFY THE NATION, PREPARE TO STRIKE

1. Sun Tzu, *The Art of War* (Tokyo: Tuttle, 2008), 14 and 82–83.
2. James Kynge, Chris Campbell, Amy Kazmin, and Farhan Bokhari, "How China Rules the Waves," *Financial Times*, January 12, 2017, https://ig.ft.com/sites/china-ports/.
3. Michael Shoebridge, "Djibouti Shows What Sogavare's Deal with China Really Means," Australian Strategic Policy Institute, April 11, 2022.
4. Xi Jinping, Speech at the first session of the 14th National People's Congress, March 13, 2023, http://english.scio.gov.cn/m/topnews/2023-03/15/content_85168965.htm.
5. "European Business in China: Business Confidence Survey 2022," April 2022, 4–5, 15, 22, 27–30, and 39–40, accessed April 22, 2023, https://www.europeanchamber.com.cn/en/press-releases/3445.
6. Lingling Wei, "China Reins in Its Belt and Road Program, $1 Trillion Later," *Wall Street Journal*, September 26, 2022, https://www.wsj.com/articles/china-belt-road-debt-11663961638.
7. Cortez A. Cooper, "The PLA Navy's 'New Historic Mission': Expanding Capabilities for a Re-Emergent Maritime Power," Testimony presented before the U.S.-China Economic and Security Review Commission on June 11, 2009, RAND Corporation, June 2009, 4, https://www.rand.org/content/dam/rand/pubs/testimonies/2009/RAND_CT332.pdf.
8. Alison A. Kaufman, "China's Participation in Anti-Piracy Operations off the Horn of Africa: Drivers and Implications," Conference report, Center for Naval Analysis, July 2009, 1, https://www.cna.org/reports/2009/D0020834.A1.pdf.
9. Sam LaGrone, "AFRICOM: Chinese Naval Base in Africa Set to Support Aircraft Carriers," *USNI News*, April 20, 2021, https://news.usni.org/2021/04/20/africom-chinese-naval-base-in-africa-set-to-support-aircraft-carriers.
10. "An Accounting of China's Deployments to the Spratly Islands," Asia Maritime Transparency Initiative, May 9, 2018, https://amti.csis.org/accounting-chinas-deployments-spratly-islands/; and "The Ebb and Flow of Beijing's south China Sea Militia," Asia Maritime Transparency Initiative, November 9, 2022, https://amti.csis.org/the-ebb-and-flow-of-beijings-south-china-sea-militia/.
11. Olli Pekka Suorsa, "China's Artificial Islands in South China Sea: Extended Forward Presence," RSIS, no. 042 (March 19, 2020), https://hdl.handle.net/10356/137559.
12. Hunter Stires, "The Maritime Counterinsurgency Project Begins," U.S. Naval Institute *Proceedings* 148/7/1,433 (July 2022), https://www.usni.org/magazines/proceedings/2022/july/maritime-counterinsurgency-project-begins.
13. Peter Dutton, Andrew S. Erickson, and Ryan Martinson, "China's Near Seas Combat Capabilities," CMSI Red Books, Study No. 11 (2014), 8–9, https://digital-commons.usnwc.edu/cgi/viewcontent.cgi?article=1010&context=cmsi-red-books.

14. "Flooding the Zone: China Coast Guard Patrols in 2022," Asia Maritime Transparency Initiative, January 30, 2023, https://amti.csis.org/flooding-the-zone-china-coast-guard-patrols-in-2022/; and "Still on the Beat: China Coast Guard Patrols in 2020," Asia Maritime Transparency Initiative, December 4, 2020, https://amti.csis.org/still-on-the-beat-china-coast-guard-patrols-in-2020/.
15. "The Ebb and Flow of Beijing's South China Sea Militia."
16. Laura Zhou, "South China Sea: Disputed Spratly Islands Now Home to Supermarkets for PLA Soldiers," *South China Morning Post*, February 11, 2023, https://www.scmp.com/news/china/diplomacy/article/3209869/south-china-sea-disputed-spratly-islands-now-home-supermarkets-pla-soldiers.
17. Niharika Mandhana, "How Beijing Boxed America Out of the South China Sea," *Wall Street Journal*, March 11, 2023, https://www.wsj.com/articles/china-boxed-america-out-of-south-china-sea-military-d2833768.
18. "习近平总书记关心港口发展纪实" [General Secretary Xi Jinping reviews China's record of port development], *Xinhua she*, July 5, 2017, http://news.cctv.com/2017/07/05/ARTIsVj2xlPdnLiLk8p69e9j170705.shtml.
19. Isaac B. Kardon and Wendy Leutert, "Pier Competitor: China's Power Position in Global Ports," *International Security* 46, no. 4 (Spring 2022): 12–13, https://doi.org/10.1162/isec_a_00433.
20. Using the same approach as Kardon and Leutert in "Pier Competitor," an updated accounting of the three dominant China firms in overseas ports include: COSCO Shipping Ports Limited, Annual Report 2022, 22–23, https://doc.irasia.com/listco/hk/coscoship/annual/2022/ar2022.pdf; China Merchants Port Holdings, "About Us," accessed April 23, 2023, https://www.cmport.com.hk/EN/about/Profile.aspx?from=2; and Hutchison Ports, "Our Ports," accessed April 23, 2023, https://hutchisonports.com/en/About-Us/Company-Profile.html.
21. "Xi, Greek PM Visit Piraeus Port, Hail BRI Cooperation," *Xinhua*, November 12, 2019, http://www.xinhuanet.com/english/2019-11/12/c_138548572.htm; "Chinese Naval Fleet Arrives in Greece for Friendly Visit," *Xinhua*, July 23, 2017, http://www.xinhuanet.com/english/2017-07/23/c_136466322.htm; and George Georgiopoulos, "China's COSCO Acquires 51 Pct Stake in Greece's Piraeus Port," Reuters, August 10, 2016, https://www.reuters.com/article/greece-privatisation-port/chinas-cosco-acquires-51-pct-stake-in-greeces-piraeus-port-idUSL8N1AR252.
22. "COSCO Solidifies Hold on the Port of Piraeus," *Maritime Executive*, August 22, 2021, https://maritime-executive.com/article/cosco-solidifies-ownership-of-the-port-of-piraeus.
23. Plamen Tonchev, "Chinese Influence in Greece," Center for European Policy Analysis, August 24, 2022, https://cepa.org/comprehensive-reports/chinese-influence-in-greece/; and Andreas Bloom, "Greeks Wage a Court Battle against Chinese-Funded Port That May Poison the Environment," *Global Voices*, May

27, 2021, https://globalvoices.org/2021/05/27/greeks-wage-a-court-battle-against-chinese-funded-port-that-may-poison-the-environment/.
24. "Chinese Missile Destroyer 'Xi'an' Makes Technical Stop in Egypt's Alexandria," *Xinhua News Agency*, August 18, 2019, http://www.xinhuanet.com/english/2019-08/17/c_138314914.htm.
25. Haisam Hassanein, "Egypt Takes Another Step toward China," Washington Institute for Near East Policy, August 19, 2019, https://www.washingtoninstitute.org/policy-analysis/egypt-takes-another-step-toward-china.
26. Lin Noueihed and Ali Abdelaty, "China's Xi Visits Egypt, Offers Financial, Political Support," Reuters, January 20, 2016, https://www.reuters.com/article/us-egypt-china/chinas-xi-visits-egypt-offers-financial-political-support-idUSKCN0UZ05I.
27. "Xi Jinping Arrives in Cairo, Starting His State Visit to Egypt," Ministry of Foreign Affairs of the People's Republic of China, January 21, 2016, accessed April 23, 2023, https://www.fmprc.gov.cn/mfa_eng/topics_665678/2016zt/xjpdstajyljxgsfw/201601/t20160122_704473.html; and "President Xi Jinping Meets with Egyptian President Abdel Fattah El-Sisi," Ministry of Foreign Affairs of the People's Republic of China, December 9, 2022, accessed April 23, 2023, https://www.fmprc.gov.cn/mfa_eng/zxxx_662805/202212/t20221209_10987741.html.
28. Momen Saeed Atallah, "China's Xinxing to Invest $2 Billion in Suez Canal Economic Zone—Egyptian Cabinet," Reuters, March 23, 2023, https://www.reuters.com/markets/commodities/chinas-xinxing-invest-2-bln-suez-canal-economic-zone-egyptian-cabinet-2023-03-23/.
29. "Solomon Islands PM Survives No-Confidence Vote after Unrest," *Aljazeera*, December 6, 2021, https://www.aljazeera.com/news/2021/12/6/solomon-islands-pm-faces-no-confidence-vote-after-unrest.
30. Kate Lyons and Dorothy Wickham, "The Deal That Shocked the World: Inside the China-Solomons Security Pact," *Guardian*, April 20, 2022, https://www.theguardian.com/world/2022/apr/20/the-deal-that-shocked-the-world-inside-the-china-solomons-security-pact.
31. Euan Graham, "Assessing the Solomon Islands' New Security Agreement with China," IISS, May 5, 2022, https://www.iiss.org/online-analysis/online-analysis//2022/05/china-solomon-islands.
32. "Statement by NSC Spokesperson Adrienne Watson on Senior Administration Travel to Hawaii, Fiji, Papua New Guinea, and the Solomon Islands," White House, April 18, 2022, https://www.whitehouse.gov/briefing-room/statements-releases/2022/04/18/statement-by-nsc-spokesperson-adrienne-watson-on-senior-administration-travel-to-hawaii-fiji-papua-new-guinea-and-the-solomon-islands/; and Press release, U.S. Mission Papua New Guinea, Solomon Islands, and Vanuatu, March 23, 2023, https://pg.usembassy.gov/indo-pacific-coordinator-concludes-visit-to-solomon-islands/.

33. Tarcisius Kabutaulaka, "China–Solomon Islands Security Agreement and Competition for Influence in Oceania," *Georgetown Journal of International Affairs*, December 2, 2022, https://gjia.georgetown.edu/2022/12/02/china-solomon-islands-security-agreement-and-competition-for-influence-in-oceania/.
34. Cleo Paskal, "China Winning Entropic Warfare in Pacific Islands," *Sunday Guardian*, June 4, 2022, https://sundayguardianlive.com/news/china-winning-entropic-warfare-pacific-islands.
35. Shoebridge, "Djibouti Shows What Sogavare's Deal with China Really Means."
36. Andrew S. Erickson and Austin M. Strange, "Six Years at Sea . . . and Counting: Gulf of Aden Anti-Piracy and China's Maritime Commons Presence," Jamestown Foundation, June 2015, 8, 86, 151, and 161, http://www.andrewerickson.com/wp-content/uploads/2015/11/Erickson-Publication_Anti-Piracy_China_Jamestown-Book_GoA-Mission_6-Years_2015_Final.pdf; and David M. Liebenberg, "Biographies of Key Chinese Military Officers," Center for Naval Analysis, April 2013, https://www.cna.org/archive/CNA_Files/pdf/dqr-2013-u-004447-final.pdf, 2–3.
37. James Mulvenon, "And Then There Were Seven: The New, Slimmed-Down Central Military Commission," *China Leadership Monitor*, no. 56 (May 16, 2018): 4, https://www.hoover.org/sites/default/files/research/docs/clm56jm.pdf.
38. Andrew S. Erickson and Christopher Sharman, "Admiral Dong Jun Engages Friends and Foes: China's First Naval Defense Minister Brings Joint Operational Experience," *CMSI Notes*, 2, China Maritime Studies Institute, December 30, 2023, https://digital-commons.usnwc.edu/cgi/viewcontent.cgi?article=1001&context=cmsi-notes.
39. Brian Lafferty, "Civil-Military Integration and PLA Reforms," chapter 16 in *Chairman Xi Remakes the PLA: Assessing Chinese Military Reforms*, ed. by Phillip C. Saunders, Arthur S. Ding, Andrew Scobell, and Andrew N. D. Yang (Washington, DC: National Defense University Press, 2019), 648–49, https://ndupress.ndu.edu/Portals/68/Documents/Books/Chairman-Xi/Chairman-Xi_Chapter-16.pdf?ver=2019-02-08-112005-803.
40. Choi Chi-yuk, "In Unusual Move, Xi Appoints Top Party Leader to Lead Daily Affairs of Key Committee," *South China Morning Post*, June 21, 2017, https://www.scmp.com/news/china/policies-politics/article/2099248/xi-jinping-further-consolidates-power-commission.
41. "向军民融合发展重点领域聚焦用力" [Focus hard on key areas in civil-military integration development], 长江日报 [Changjiang daily], September 23, 2017.
42. Wendy Leutert and Samantha A. Vortherms, "Personnel Power: Governing State-Owned Enterprises," *Business and Politics* 23, no. 3 (2021): 419–37, https://www.cambridge.org/core/journals/business-and-politics/article/abs/personnel-power-governing-stateowned-enterprises/D0EB24902CF83B7F10A2D525CABDBCA9.
43. Kardon and Leutert, "Pier Competitor," 33–34.

44. Thomas Hale, Chuyu Liu, and Johannes Urpelainen, "Belt and Road Decision-Making in China and Recipient Countries: How and to What Extent Does Sustainability Matter?" ISEP, BSG, and ClimateWorks Foundation, April 2020, 8 and 18–19, https://sais-isep.org/wp-content/uploads/2020/04/ISEP-BSG-BRI-Report-.pdf.

45. Joel Wuthnow and Phillip C. Saunders, "Introduction: Chairman Xi Remakes the PLA," in *Chairman Xi Remakes the PLA: Assessing Chinese Military Reforms*, ed. by Phillip C. Saunders, Arthur S. Ding, Andrew Scobell, and Andrew N. D. Yang (Washington, DC: National Defense University Press, 2019), 28–29; and Fei Shiting, Zhang Junsheng, and Liu Guoshun, "揭秘新成立的中央军委国防动员部" [Demystifying the newly established CMC National Defense Mobilization Department], *China Youth Daily*, January 29, 2016, http://zqb.cyol.com/html/2016-01/29/nw.D110000zgqnb_20160129_1-06.htm.

46. H. I. Sutton, "Chinese Launch Assault Craft from Civilian Car Ferries in Mass Amphibious Invasion Drill, Satellite Photos Show," *USNI News*, September 28, 2022, https://news.usni.org/2022/09/28/chinese-launch-assault-craft-from-civilian-car-ferries-in-mass-amphibious-invasion-drill-satellite-photos-show.

47. Kardon and Leutert, "Pier Competitor," 39.

48. Agence France Presse, "China Evacuates 1,300 Citizens, Other Nationals from Sudan," *Barron's*, April 26, 2023, https://www.barrons.com/news/china-sends-navy-to-evacuate-citizens-in-sudan-defence-ministry-35f01e93.

49. Werner Globke, *Weyers Flottentaschenbuch 2020–2022: Warships of the World* (Bad Neuenahr-Ahrweiler: Bernard & Graefe, 2020), 50–51 and 66–67.

50. Wuthnow and Saunders, "Chairman Xi Remakes the PLA," 2–3.

51. Stephen Chen, "China Plots 33 Spots for Regular Research Ship Visits, in Taiwan Strait, South China Sea, Pacific and Indian Oceans," *South China Morning Post*, April 1, 2023, https://www.scmp.com/news/china/science/article/3214483/china-plots-33-spots-regular-research-ship-visits-taiwan-strait-south-china-sea-pacific-and-indian; and "A Survey of Marine Research Vessels in the Indo-Pacific," CSIS, April 16, 2020, https://amti.csis.org/a-survey-of-marine-research-vessels-in-the-indo-pacific/; 孙理想, "国内首套万米全水深声学观测潜标在马里亚纳海沟实验成功" [The first set of 10,000-meter full-water deep acoustic observation potential in China was successfully tested in the Mariana Trench], *People's Daily*, December 25, 2017, http://scitech.people.com.cn/n1/2017/1225/c1007-29727789.html.

52. Center for Strategic and International Studies, "JL-2," Missile Threat, Missile Defense Project, August 12, 2016, last modified July 31, 2021, accessed April 25, 2023, https://missilethreat.csis.org/missile/jl-2/.

53. U.S. Department of Defense, Office of the Secretary of Defense, *Military and Security Developments involving the People's Republic of China, 2021*, Annual Report to Congress, VIII, 90, and 92, https://media.defense.gov/2021/Nov/03/2002885874/-1/-1/0/2021-CMPR-FINAL.PDF.

54. Jeffrey Lewis, "China's Orbital Bombardment System Is Big, Bad News—but Not a Breakthrough," *Foreign Policy*, October 18, 2021, https://foreignpolicy.com/2021/10/18/hypersonic-china-missile-nuclear-fobs/.
55. Andrew Scobell, Michael McMahon, and Cortez A. Cooper III, "China's Aircraft Carrier Program: Drivers, Developments, Implications," *Naval War College Review* 68, no. 4 (2015) 6–7, https://digital-commons.usnwc.edu/cgi/viewcontent.cgi?article=1267&context=nwc-review.
56. Michael Dahm, "Lessons from the Changing Geometry of PLA Navy Carrier Ops," U.S. Naval Institute *Proceedings* 149/1/1,439 (January 2023), https://www.usni.org/magazines/proceedings/2023/january/lessons-changing-geometry-pla-navy-carrier-ops.
57. J. Michael Dahm and Alison Zhao, "China Maritime Report No. 28: Bitterness Ends, Sweetness Begins: Organizational Changes to the PLAN Submarine Force since 2015," *CMSI China Maritime Reports*, June 10, 2023, 13–14, https://digital-commons.usnwc.edu/cgi/viewcontent.cgi?article=1027&context=cmsi-maritime-reports.
58. Eric Wertheim, "Type 055 Renhai-Class Cruiser: China's Premier Surface Combatant," U.S. Naval Institute *Proceedings* 149/33/1,441 (March 2023), https://www.usni.org/magazines/proceedings/2023/march/type-055-renhai-class-cruiser-chinas-premier-surface-combatant.
59. Christopher Biggers, "China Launches Second Possible Type 093B Hull," *Janes*, February 1, 2023, https://www.janes.com/osint-insights/defence-news/sea/china-launches-second-possible-type-093b-hull.
60. U.S. Department of Defense, "Military and Security Development involving the People's Republic of China," Annual Report to Congress, November 29, 2022, 50–51, https://media.defense.gov/2022/Nov/29/2003122279/-1/-1/1/2022-MILITARY-AND-SECURITY-DEVELOPMENTS-INVOLVING-THE-PEOPLES-REPUBLIC-OF-CHINA.PDF.
61. "Chinese Navy's 5-Day Nigeria Visit Marks Rare West Africa Foray," *Aljazeera*, July 3, 2023, https://www.aljazeera.com/news/2023/7/3/chinese-navys-5-day-nigeria-visit-marks-rare-west-africa-foray.
62. A discussion about Bonaparte's rationale for the quote that opens this section can be found at Jake R. Jelineo, "Napoleon's Logistics; or How Napoleon Learned to Worry about Supply," Air Command and Staff College, research report, April 2012, https://apps.dtic.mil/sti/pdfs/AD1022125.pdf.
63. Stefano Ambrogi, "U.S. Navy Steps Up Fuel Deliveries to Gulf Forces," Reuters, November 23, 2007, https://www.reuters.com/article/us-tankers-gulf/u-s-navy-steps-up-fuel-deliveries-to-gulf-forces-idUKL2231306820071123.
64. David Rising, "US Aircraft Carrier Makes Da Nang Port Call as America Looks to Strengthen Ties with Vietnam," Associated Press, June 26, 2023, https://apnews.com/article/us-aircraft-carrier-da-nang-vietnam-3b5aa2d343d2e97fce27275b5c533f62.

65. Jack Lau, "Chinese Navy Hospital Ship Heads to Pacific to Show Military's 'Peaceful Development,'" *South China Morning Post*, July 3, 2023, https://www.scmp.com/news/china/military/article/3226402/chinese-navy-hospital-ship-heads-pacific-show-militarys-peaceful-development.
66. Henry Cronic, "New Zealand's Anti-Nuclear Legislation and the United States in 1985," Wilson Center, August 26, 2020, https://www.wilsoncenter.org/blog-post/new-zealands-anti-nuclear-legislation-and-united-states-1985.
67. Yvette Tan, "Chinese 'Spy Ship' Yuan Wang 5 Docks in Sri Lanka Despite Indian Concern," *BBC News*, August 16, 2022, https://www.bbc.com/news/world-asia-62558767.
68. DoD USS *Cole* Commission, *USS COLE Commission Report* (Washington, DC: U.S. Department of Defense, January 9, 2001), 3 and 8, https://irp.fas.org/threat/cole.pdf.
69. United Nations Convention on the Law of the Sea, United Nations, article 225, 113, https://www.un.org/depts/los/convention_agreements/texts/unclos/unclos_e.pdf.
70. Sam LaGrone, "Hong Kong Snub Not First Time China Turned Away U.S. Ships over Politics," *USNI News*, May 3, 2016, https://news.usni.org/2016/05/02/hong-kong-snub-not-first-time-china-turned-away-u-s-ships-over-politics.
71. "Husbanding Service Provider Program Policy," OPNAV Instruction 4400.11A, June 26, 2020, enclosure 1, 6–7, https://www.secnav.navy.mil/doni/Directives/04000%20Logistical%20Support%20and%20Services/04-400%20Supply%20and%20Material%20Services/4400.11A.pdf.
72. Blake Herzinger, "Fat Leonard Cost the U.S. Navy More Than Money," *Foreign Policy*, October 24, 2022, https://foreignpolicy.com/2022/10/24/fat-leonard-us-navy-corruption-scandal/.
73. Tuvia Gering and Heath Sloane, "Beijing's Overseas Military Base in Djibouti," *MEMRI*, July 16, 2021, https://www.memri.org/reports/beijings-overseas-military-base-djibouti; and "Djibouti: The Highly Secret Chinese Military Base Revealed," *Preligens*, 2022, https://www.preligens.com/resources/insights/insight-djibouti-highly-secret-chinese-military-base-revealed-challenges-x.
74. "Mid-Deployment Voyage Repair: Through a Maintenance Lens," 6th Fleet Public Affairs, August 3, 2022, https://www.navy.mil/Press-Office/News-Stories/Article/3115983/mid-deployment-voyage-repair-through-a-maintenance-lens/.
75. Christopher H. Sharman, "China Moves Out: Stepping Stones toward a New Maritime Strategy," Center for the Study of Chinese Military Affairs, April 2015, 12–13, https://ndupress.ndu.edu/Portals/68/Documents/stratperspective/china/ChinaPerspectives-9.pdf.
76. John T. Kuehn, *Agents of Innovation: The General Board and the Design of the Fleet That Defeated the Japanese Navy* (Annapolis, MD: Naval Institute Press, 2008), 125–26.

77. Liu Zhen, "Chinese Navy Shows New Heavy-Lift Ship Carrier, Revealing Future Role in Wartime Transport and Vessel Rescue," *South China Morning Post*, January 6, 2023, https://www.scmp.com/news/china/military/article/3205802/chinese-navy-shows-new-heavy-lift-ship-carrier-revealing-future-role-wartime-transport-and-vessel.
78. "Xin Guang Hua Semi-Submersible Vessel," *Ship Technology*, October 18, 2016, https://www.ship-technology.com/projects/guang-hua-kou-semi-submersible-vessel/.
79. Craig Whitlock, "U.S. Marine Accused in Slaying in the Philippines, Raising Old Tensions," *Washington Post*, October 15, 2014, https://www.washingtonpost.com/world/national-security/us-marine-accused-in-slaying-in-the-philippines-raising-old-tensions/2014/10/15/c3bfd588-5475-11e4-892e-602188e70e9c_story.html.
80. Didi Kirsten Tatlow, "China's Stake in World Ports Sharpens Attention on Political Influence," *Newsweek*, October 9, 2022, https://www.newsweek.com/2022/10/14/chinas-stake-world-ports-sharpens-attention-political-influence-1749215.html.
81. Kardon and Leutert, "Pier Competitor," 39–41.
82. Jeremy Page, Gordon Lubold, and Rob Taylor, "Deal for Naval Outpost in Cambodia Furthers China's Quest for Military Network," *Wall Street Journal*, July 22, 2019, https://www.wsj.com/articles/secret-deal-for-chinese-naval-outpost-in-cambodia-raises-u-s-fears-of-beijings-ambitions-11563732482.
83. Prak Chan Thul, "U.S. Presses Cambodia over Possible Chinese Military Presence," Reuters, July 1, 2019, https://www.reuters.com/article/us-cambodia-usa/u-s-presses-cambodia-over-possible-chinese-military-presence-idUSKCN1TW23W.
84. Jack Brook and Phin Rathana, "Cambodia Reveals Air Defense Plans near China-Funded Naval Base," *Nikkei*, April 1, 2023, https://asia.nikkei.com/Politics/Defense/Cambodia-reveals-air-defense-plans-near-China-funded-naval-base.
85. David Rising and Sopheng Cheang, "China, Cambodia Break Ground on Port, Dismiss US Concerns," Associated Press, June 8, 2022, https://apnews.com/article/hun-sen-thailand-beijing-china-cambodia-ac6a298e9b4d142139be99403d42f6ad.
86. David Rising, "China Stresses Ties with Southeast Asia in Cambodia Meeting," Associated Press, August 4, 2022, https://apnews.com/article/russia-ukraine-taiwan-china-beijing-asia-8867e7381c4608920901b177c383db58; Łukas Kobierski, "Wang Yi's Trip to Cambodia," Warsaw Institute, October 16, 2020, https://warsawinstitute.org/wang-yis-trip-cambodia/; and "Wang Yi Meets with King Norodom Sihamoni and Queen Mother Norodom Monineath Sihanouk of Cambodia," Ministry of Foreign Affairs of the People's Republic of China, April 4, 2019, accessed April 29, 2023, https://www.fmprc.gov.cn/mfa_eng/gjhdq_665435/2675_665437/2696_663396/2698_663400/201904/t20190409_511013.html.
87. "Crude Petroleum in China," OEC, accessed April 29, 2023, https://oec.world/en/profile/bilateral-product/crude-petroleum/reporter/chn.
88. Brent D. Sadler, "Effective Naval Statecraft Can Prevent Communist Chinese Naval Bases in Africa," *Backgrounder*, no. 3688 March 10, 2022, 4,

6–7, and 10–11, https://www.heritage.org/sites/default/files/2022-03/BG3688.pdf.

89. "Wang Yi: China-Equatorial Guinea Relations an Example of Equal, Friendly Partnership," *CGTN*, September 25, 2022, https://news.cgtn.com/news/2022-09-25/Wang-Yi-hails-China-Equatorial-Guinea-relations-as-equal-friendly--1dC9dU78p6U/index.html; and "Chinese FM Wang Yi Meets with Equatorial Guinea's FM," *Xinhua*, December 2, 2021, http://www.news.cn/english/2021-12/02/c_1310347469.htm.

90. Jennifer Staats, "Four Takeaways from China's Tour of the Pacific Islands," U.S. Institute of Peace, June 9, 2022, https://www.usip.org/publications/2022/06/four-takeaways-chinas-tour-pacific-islands.

91. "China-Pacific Island Countries Common Development Vision" (draft), accessed April 29, 2023, https://www.documentcloud.org/documents/22037011-china-pacific-island-countries-common-development-vision; and "China-Pacific Island Countries Five-Year Action Plan on Common Development (2022–2026)" (draft), accessed April 29, 2023, https://www.documentcloud.org/documents/22037012-china-pacific-island-countries-five-year-action-plan-on-common-development-2022-2026.

92. Christopher Cairns and April Herlevi, "China and the Solomon Islands: Drivers of Security Cooperation," *in depth* (blog), Center for Naval Analysis, April 13, 2022, https://www.cna.org/our-media/indepth/2022/04/china-and-the-solomon-islands.

93. "Minister Veke Hails China-SI Police Cooperation," *Solomon Star*, February 25, 2023, https://www.solomonstarnews.com/minister-veke-hails-china-si-police-cooperation/; and Kabutaulaka, "China-Solomon Islands Security Agreement."

94. AidData is a research laboratory housed at the College of William & Mary with a particular focus on using novel techniques in financial forensics, among others, to better inform policy and investment choices; see https://www.aiddata.org/about.

95. Alison A. Kaufman, "China's Participation in Anti-Piracy Operations off the Horn of Africa: Drivers and Implications," Center for Naval Analysis, conference report, July 2009, 2–3, 8, and 10, https://www.cna.org/reports/2009/D0020834.A1.pdf.

96. Joel Wuthnow and Margaret Baughman, "Selective Engagements—Chinese Naval Diplomacy and U.S.–China Competition," *Naval War College Review* 76, no. 1, art. 6 (Winter 2023): 3–6, https://digital-commons.usnwc.edu/cgi/viewcontent.cgi?article=8328&context=nwc-review.

97. Capitainerie—DPFZA, Facebook post, August 1, 2023, accessed August 2, 2023, https://m.facebook.com/story.php?story_fbid=pfbid02kz1pfF1DYnNoySyiZcqQqakG1gmMdT8A1fb8ydzSE4GAyfWXtUxyLCDeCqichgh9l&id=100069058035202&mibextid=qClgEa. Confirmed via other media posts of this drydock's arrival and capacity for handling ships weighing up to 50k gwt, 217 m long and 43.5 m wide.

98. Alexander Wooley, Sheng Zhang, Rory Fedorochko, and Sarina Patterson, *Harboring Global Ambitions: China's Ports Footprint and Implications for Future Overseas*

Naval Bases (Williamsburg, VA: AidData at William & Mary, 2023), 15–16, accessed May 19, 2024, https://www.aiddata.org/harboring-global-ambitions.
99. James McBride, Noah Berman, and Andrew Chatzky, "China's Massive Belt and Road Initiative," Council on Foreign Relations, February 2, 2023, https://www.cfr.org/backgrounder/chinas-massive-belt-and-road-initiative.
100. "Chinese Missile Destroyer 'Xi'an' Makes Technical Stop."
101. Charles A. Ray, "South Africa's Naval Exercises with China and Russia: Cause for Concern?" Foreign Policy Research Institute, April 13, 2023, https://www.fpri.org/article/2023/04/south-africas-naval-exercises-with-china-and-russia-cause-for-concern/.
102. Pete McKenzie, "Bribes, Booze and Bombs: The Brazen Plan to Create a Pacific Tax Haven," *Washington Post*, February 15, 2023, https://www.washingtonpost.com/world/2023/02/14/china-united-states-marshall-islands-rongelap/.

CHAPTER 2. NAVAL STATECRAFT OPERATIONALIZED

1. According to the United Nations Conference on Trade and Development, the Global South includes Africa, Latin America, Asia, and Oceania. However, it does not include Israel, Japan, South Korea, New Zealand, or Australia.
2. Chuin-Wei Yap, "China's Fishing Fleet, the World's Largest, Drives Beijing's Global Ambitions," *Wall Street Journal*, April 21, 2021, https://www.wsj.com/articles/chinas-fishing-fleet-the-worlds-largest-drives-beijings-global-ambitions-11619015507.
3. Manaswita Konar, Erin Gray, Lauren Thuringer, and U. Rashid Sumaila, "The Scale of Illicit Trade in Pacific Ocean Marine Resources," World Resources Institute Working Paper, October 2019, https://www.wri.org/webform/download_publication?source_entity_type=node&source_entity_id=65797.
4. Huihui Shen and Shuolin Huang, "China's Policies and Practice on Combatting IUU in Distant Water Fisheries," *Aquaculture and Fisheries* 6, no. 6 (November 2021): 27–34, https://doi.org/10.1016/j.aaf.2020.03.002.
5. Miren Gutiérrez, Alfonso Daniels, Guy Jobbins, Guillermo Gutiérrez Almazor, and César Montenegro, *China's Distant Water Fishing Fleet: Scale, Impact and Governance* (London: Overseas Development Institute, June 2020), 15–27, https://cdn.odi.org/media/documents/chinesedistantwaterfishing_web.pdf.
6. Ryan D. Martinson, *Echelon Defense: The Role of Sea Power in Chinese Maritime Dispute Strategy*, CMSI Red Books, Study No. 15, February 2018, https://digital-commons.usnwc.edu/cgi/viewcontent.cgi?article=1014&context=cmsi-red-books.
7. "United States and China Coast Guards Interdict Vessel for Illegally Fishing on the High Seas," *Coast Guard News*, June 3, 2014, https://coastguardnews.com/united-states-and-china-coast-guards-interdict-vessel-for-illegally-fishing-on-the-high-seas/.
8. Melody Schreiber, "A U.S. Coast Guard Patrol Unexpectedly Encountered Chinese Warships near Alaska's Aleutian Islands," *Arctic Today*, September 16, 2021,

https://www.arctictoday.com/a-us-coast-guard-patrol-unexpectedly-encountered-chinese-warships-near-alaskas-aleutian-islands/; and "Chinese Coast Guard Ships Depart for North Pacific on Law Enforcement Mission," *Global Times*, July 31, 2021, https://www.globaltimes.cn/page/202107/1230140.shtml.

9. Dzirhan Mahadzir, "Chinese Navy Piracy Patrol Shepherds Fishing Fleet through Gulf of Aden," *USNI News*, January 6, 2022, https://news.usni.org/2022/01/06/chinese-navy-piracy-patrol-shepherds-fishing-fleet-through-gulf-of-aden.

10. James Di Pane, "U.S. Coast Guard Readiness Will Help to Deter China and Other Threats: Congress Should Fund Select Items on Unfunded Priority List," Heritage Foundation, May 25, 2023, https://www.heritage.org/defense/report/us-coast-guard-readiness-will-help-deter-china-and-other-threats-congress-should.

11. U.S. Coast Guard, "District 14," accessed January 6, 2022, https://www.pacificarea.uscg.mil/Our-Organization/District-14/.

12. "U.S. Coast Guard Commissions Three Fast Response Cutters in Guam," *Maritime Executive*, July 29, 2021, https://www.maritime-executive.com/article/u-s-coast-guard-commissions-three-fast-response-cutters-in-guam.

13. Edward Lundquist, "USCG Report: Small Cutters Prove They Can Patrol a Big Ocean," *Marine Link*, June14, 2022, https://www.marinelink.com/news/uscg-report-small-cutters-prove-patrol-a-497335.

14. U.S. Coast Guard, "National Security Cutter," Acquisition Directorate, accessed January 14, 2022, https://www.dcms.uscg.mil/Our-Organization/Assistant-Commandant-for-Acquisitions-CG-9/Programs/Surface-Programs/National-Security-Cutter/; and U.S. Coast Guard, "Offshore Patrol Cutter," Acquisition Directorate, accessed January 14, 2022, https://www.dcms.uscg.mil/Our-Organization/Assistant-Commandant-for-Acquisitions-CG-9/Programs/Surface-Programs/Offshore-Patrol-Cutter/.

15. Ronald O'Rourke, *Coast Guard Cutter Procurement: Background and Issues for Congress*, Report for Congress, R42567 (Washington, DC: Congressional Research Service, July 15, 2024), 29, https://sgp.fas.org/crs/weapons/R42567.pdf.

16. French Ministry of Armed Forces, "France and Security in the Indo–Pacific," foreword by Florence Parly, updated May 2019, 6–7 and 12, https://franceintheus.org/IMG/pdf/France_and_Security_in_the_Indo-Pacific_-_2019.pdf.

17. Australian Department of Defense, "Pacific Maritime Security Program," accessed January 6, 2022, https://www.defence.gov.au/programs-initiatives/pacific-engagement/maritime-capability.

18. New Zealand Defense Force, Annual Report 2020, 42–44, https://www.nzdf.mil.nz/assets/Uploads/DocumentLibrary/20-099-NZDF-Annual-Report-2020-FA-WEB-1.pdf.

19. Matthew West, "Coast Guard Cutter Completes Operation Blue Pacific Patrol in Oceania," U.S. Indo–Pacific Command, December 14, 2021, https://www.pacom.mil/Media/News/News-Article-View/Article/2873281/coast-guard-cutter-completes-operation-blue-pacific-patrol-in-oceania/.

20. "Patrol Ships Bid Farewell to Portsmouth as They Begin Indo–Pacific Deployment," News release, Royal Navy [United Kingdom], September 7, 2021, https://www.royalnavy.mod.uk/news-and-latest-activity/news/2021/september/07/210907-spey-and-tamar-deploy; and Brad Lendon, "Royal Navy Warships Leave Britain for Landmark Pacific Deployment," *CNN*, September 8, 2021, https://www.cnn.com/2021/09/08/asia/british-warships-pacific-deployment-intl-hnk-ml/index.html.

21. Andrew Harding, "A Generational Opportunity to Counter China: Prioritizing the Pacific Islands through the Compacts of Free Association (COFA)," *Backgrounder*, no. 3784, August 28, 2023, 7 and 11, https://www.heritage.org/sites/default/files/2023-08/BG3784.pdf.

22. Neil Ruiz, Luis Noe-Bustamante, and Nadya Saber, "Coming of Age," International Monetary Fund, March 2020, https://www.imf.org/en/Publications/fandd/issues/2020/03/infographic-global-population-trends-picture.

23. "Our Growing Population," United Nations, https://www.un.org/en/global-issues/population.

24. Mayowa Kuyoro, Acha Leke, Olivia White, Lola Woetzel, Kartik Jayaram, and Kendyll Hicks, "Reimagining Economic Growth in Africa: Turning Divinity into Opportunity," McKinsey Global Institute, June 5, 2023, https://www.mckinsey.com/mgi/our-research/reimagining-economic-growth-in-africa-turning-diversity-into-opportunity; and "Projections by Continent," Institut National D'Etudes Démographiques, July 2024, https://www.ined.fr/en/everything_about_population/data/world-projections/projections-by-continent/.

25. Bert Wilkinson, "Guyana Asks U.S. to Help Boost Its Military as Territorial Dispute with Venezuela Deepens," *PBS News Hour*, January 10, 2024, https://www.pbs.org/newshour/world/guyana-asks-u-s-to-help-boost-its-military-as-territorial-dispute-with-venezuela-deepens.

26. International Trade Administration, U.S. Department of Commerce, "Investment Climate Statement," February 1, 2024, accessed May 17, 2024, https://www.trade.gov/country-commercial-guides/angola-investment-climate-statement.

27. Fernando Garcia and Lucila Venturi, "Argentina under a New Government: What Are the Big Economic Challenges?," *Economic Observatory*, May 8, 2024, https://www.economicsobservatory.com/what-economic-challenges-does-argentina-face-today.

28. Leonardo Palma, "Italy's New Look," *War on the Rocks*, August 17, 2023, https://warontherocks.com/2023/08/italys-new-look/.

29. Office of the Secretary of Defense, *Military and Security Developments involving the People's Republic of China, 2021*, Annual Report to Congress, November 3, 2021, 132, https://media.defense.gov/2021/Nov/03/2002885874/-1/-1/0/2021-CMPR-FINAL.PDF.

30. Christoph Nedopil Wang, "China Belt and Road Initiative (BRI) Investment Report H1 2021," IIGF Green BRI Center, 5, https://greenfdc.org/wp-content/uploads/2021/07/21_07_22_BRI-Investment-Report-H1-2021.pdf.

31. John McCauley, Margaret Pearson, and Xiaonan Wang, "Africa's Leaders Often Welcome Chinese Private Investment: How Do African Citizens Feel?" *Washington Post*, December 9, 2021, https://www.washingtonpost.com/politics/2021/12/09/africas-leaders-often-welcome-chinese-private-investment-how-do-african-citizens-feel/.
32. "Obangame Express," U.S. Africa Command, news release, March 2021, https://www.africom.mil/what-we-do/exercises/obangame-express.
33. Daniel F. Runde, Conor M. Savoy, and Janina Staguhn, "China and SMEs in Sub-Saharan Africa: A Window of Opportunity for the United States," *CSIS Briefs*, October 2021, 1–3, https://csis-website-prod.s3.amazonaws.com/s3fs-public/publication/211014_Runde_ChinaSMEs_SSAfrica_1.pdf?aezWlX6sT.dpZSJOvdKIqldRnDf8ngkX.
34. World Bank, "Small and Medium Enterprises (SMEs) Finance," accessed December 29, 2021, https://www.worldbank.org/en/topic/smefinance.
35. James M. Roberts and Brett D. Schaefer, "The U.S. Development Finance Corporation Is Failing to Counter China," *Backgrounder*, no. 3649, September 17, 2021, https://www.heritage.org/global-politics/report/the-us-development-finance-corporation-failing-counter-china.
36. Mrinalika Roy, "Exxon Mobil to Exit Equatorial Guinea," Reuters, February 8, 2024, https://www.reuters.com/business/energy/exxon-mobil-exit-equatorial-guinea-2024-02-08/.
37. "U.S. Overdose Deaths Decrease in 2023, First Time since 2018," National Center for Health Statistics, May 15, 2024, https://www.cdc.gov/nchs/pressroom/nchs_press_releases/2024/20240515.htm.
38. Channing May, *Transnational Crime and the Developing World*, Global Financial Integrity, March 2017, xi and 99, https://34n8bd.p3cdn1.secureserver.net/wp-content/uploads/2017/03/Transnational_Crime-final.pdf; and Jeremy McDermott and Steven Dudley, "GameChangers 2023: The Cocaine Flash-to-Bang in 2024," *InSightCrime*, January 5, 2024, https://insightcrime.org/news/gamechangers-2023-cocaine-flash-to-bang-2024/.
39. May, *Transnational Crime and the Developing World*, 3 and 11.
40. Based on JISTF-S presentations and interviews conducted November 2023 at the headquarters in Key West, Florida.
41. U.S. Naval Forces Southern Command, U.S. Fourth Fleet, image 211024-N-KY668-1208, October 24, 2021, https://www.fourthfleet.navy.mil/Press-Room/Image-Gallery/igphoto/2002885818/.
42. Bernadette Carreon, Aubrey Belford, and Martin Young, "Pacific Gambit: Inside the Chinese Communist Party and Triad Push into Palau," OCCRP, December 12, 2022, https://www.occrp.org/en/investigations/pacific-gambit-inside-the-chinese-communist-party-and-triad-push-into-palau.
43. Sam LaGrone, "PACFLEET CO Paparo Talks Combat Logistics, Chinese Coercion," *USNI News*, February 14, 2023, https://news.usni.org/2023/02/14/pacfleet-co-paparo-talks-combat-logistics-chinese-coercion.

44. F. E. Haeberle, *Structural Repairs in Forward Areas during World War II* (Washington, DC: Bureau of Ships, Navy Department, December 1949), 1–4, https://www.history.navy.mil/research/library/online-reading-room/title-list-alphabetically/s/structural-repairs-forward-areas-wwii.html.
45. Navy Vessel Register, USNS *Montford Point* (ESD-1), May 10, 2022, https://www.nvr.navy.mil/SHIPDETAILS/SHIPSDETAIL_ESD_2.HTML; and Navy Vessel Register, USNS *John Glenn* (ESD-2), May 10, 2022, https://www.nvr.navy.mil/SHIPDETAILS/SHIPSDETAIL_ESD_2.HTML.
46. "Expeditionary Sea Base (ESB)," Naval Sea Systems Command, January 21, 2021, accessed February 21, 2024, https://www.navy.mil/Resources/Fact-Files/Display-FactFiles/Article/2169994/expeditionary-sea-base-esb/.
47. "SECNAV Del Toro Delivers Keynote Address at WEST 2024," Press Office, February 15, 2024, https://www.navy.mil/Press-Office/Speeches/display-speeches/Article/3677940/secnav-del-toro-delivers-keynote-address-at-west-2024/.
48. On Saildrone, see Laura Heckmann, "SNA NEWS: Navy Prioritizing Hybrid Manned-Unmanned Fleet," *National Defense*, January 10, 2024, https://www.nationaldefensemagazine.org/articles/2024/1/10/navy-prioritizing-hybrid-manned-unmanned-fleet. On ScanEagle, see Insitu, "Insitu's ScanEagle Contributes to Large US Coast Guard Drug Bust," February 17, 2022, https://www.insitu.com/news/insitus-scaneagle-contributes-to-large-us-coast-guard-drug-bust. On the Navy's unmanned surface vessels, see Ronald O'Rourke, *Navy Large Unmanned Surface and Undersea Vehicles: Background and Issues for Congress* (Washington, DC: Congressional Research Service, September 5, 2023), 4–7, 12, and 16–17, https://s3.documentcloud.org/documents/23940928/navy-large-unmanned-surface-and-undersea-vehicles-background-and-issues-for-congress-sept-5-2023.pdf.
49. U.S. Department of State, Office of the Spokesperson, "Joint Statement on the Philippines-United States Bilateral Strategic Dialogue," statement, April 24, 2024, https://www.state.gov/joint-statement-on-the-philippines-united-states-bilateral-strategic-dialogue/.
50. Jim Gomez and Aaron Favila, "Sleepy Far-Flung Towns in the Philippines Will Host US Forces Returning to Counter China Threats," Associated Press, May 13, 2024, https://apnews.com/article/us-forces-philippines-south-china-sea-taiwan-f98247675dd8a808a515601a6f0c5240.
51. Jason Hung, "China's Swift Power Grows in the Philippines," *The Diplomat*, February 26, 2021, https://thediplomat.com/2021/02/chinas-soft-power-grows-in-the-philippines/.
52. Hunter Stires, "The South China Sea Needs a 'COIN' Toss," U.S. Naval Institute *Proceedings*, vol. 145/5/1,359 (May 2019), https://www.usni.org/magazines/proceedings/2019/may/south-china-sea-needs-coin-toss.
53. Henrietta Fore, Robert Gates, and Condoleezza Rice, *U.S. Government Counterinsurgency Guide*, U.S. Government Interagency Counterinsurgency Initiative,

January 13, 2009, https://2009-2017.state.gov/documents/organization/119629.pdf.

54. U.S. Energy Information Administration, "Country Analysis Executive Summary: Malaysia," January 25, 2021, https://www.eia.gov/international/content/analysis/countries_long/Malaysia/malaysia.pdf.

55. U.S. Energy Information Administration, "Vietnam," February 2017, https://www.eia.gov/international/analysis/country/VNM; and "Fisheries Country Profile: Viet Nam," Southeast Asian Fisheries Development Center, December 9, 2022, http://www.seafdec.org/fisheries-country-profile-viet-nam/.

56. Philippine Statistics Authority, "The Philippine Marine Fishery Resources," Republic of the Philippines, 2016. The last available data covered the years 1985–98, with fishing averaging 3.6 percent of GDP. Given the importance of fish in the Filipino diet and numbers employed in the fishing sector, it is highly likely that fishing remains a large segment of the domestic economy.

57. "Indonesia Election Commission Confirms Prabowo Subianto as New President," *Aljazeera*, March 20, 2024, https://www.aljazeera.com/news/2024/3/20/indonesia-election-commission-confirms-prabowo-subianto-wins-presidency.

58. Sri Yaumil Habibie, "South China Sea Conflict: Indonesia's Maritime Diplomacy," *Modern Diplomacy*, April 25, 2024, https://moderndiplomacy.eu/2024/04/25/south-china-sea-conflict-indonesias-maritime-diplomacy/; and Dewi Santoso and Fadhillah Nafisah, "Indonesia's Global Maritime Axis Doctrine: Security Concerns and Recommendations," *Jurnal Hubungan Internasional* 10, no. 2 (July–December 2017): 191–201.

CHAPTER 3. A NEW OPERATIONAL APPROACH IN DECISIVE MARITIME THEATERS

1. "Insurgency is the organized use of subversion and violence to seize, nullify, or challenge political control of a region. An insurgency is a form of intrastate conflict, and counterinsurgency (COIN) is used to counter it." Joint Chiefs of Staff, "Counterinsurgency," Joint Publication 3-24, validated April 30, 2021, xi and I-1, https://www.jcs.mil/Portals/36/Documents/Doctrine/pubs/jp3_24.pdf.

2. Hunter Stires, "The South China Sea Sees a 'COIN' Toss," U.S. Naval Institute *Proceedings*, May 2019, https://www.usni.org/magazines/proceedings/2019/may/south-china-sea-needs-coin-toss.

3. Brent Droste Sadler, *U.S. Naval Power in the 21st Century: A New Strategy for Facing the Chinese and Russian Threat* (Annapolis, MD: Naval Institute Press, 2023), 16–18 and 28–29.

4. "We all reaffirmed today that our Mutual Defense Treaty remains the bedrock of our cooperation. As Secretary Blinken and I have said clearly and repeatedly, the Mutual Defense Treaty applies to armed attacks on either of our armed forces, our aircraft, or public vessels—including our Coast Guard—anywhere in the South China Sea." Lloyd J. Austin III, quoted in "Secretary Antony J. Blinken, Secretary of

Defense Lloyd J. Austin III, Philippine Secretary of Foreign Affairs Enrique Manalo, and Philippine Senior Undersecretary and Officer in Charge of the Department of National Defense Carlito Galvez at a Joint Press Availability," U.S. Department of State, April 11, 2023, https://www.state.gov/secretary-antony-j-blinken-secretary-of-defense-lloyd-j-austin-iii-philippine-secretary-of-foreign-affairs-enrique-manalo-and-philippine-senior-undersecretary-and-officer-in-charge-of-the-departm/.

5. Niharika Mandhana, "'Only Pirates Do This': China Wields Axes and Knives in South China Sea Fight," *Wall Street Journal*, June 20, 2024, https://www.wsj.com/world/asia/only-pirates-do-this-china-wields-axes-and-knives-in-south-china-sea-fight-c2467248.

6. "Tracking China's Coast Guard off Borneo," Asia Maritime Transparency Initiative, April 5, 2017, https://amti.csis.org/tracking-chinas-coast-guard-off-borneo/.

7. "Commander, Destroyer Squadron Seven," U.S. Navy, https://www.surfpac.navy.mil/Portals/54/Documents/CDS/CDS%207/210217%20-%20About%20Us%20DESRON%207.pdf?ver=6zIP8TPL8lky_KFANlmBuA%3d%3d.

8. Vincent K. Brooks, "Pacific Pathways: Lessons and Best Practices," *Pacific Pathways Newsletter*, Center for Army Lessons Learned, September 2016, no. 16-27, 3–5, 12, 22, 42, and 94, https://api.army.mil/e2/c/downloads/2023/01/19/cf33a5a4/16-27-pacific-pathways-regional-comprehensive-engagement-and-echeloned-readiness-newsletter-sep-16-public.pdf.

9. Aaron-Matthew Lariosa, "U.S. Army Deploys New Missile Launcher to the Philippines," *Naval News*, April 15, 2024, https://www.navalnews.com/naval-news/2024/04/u-s-army-deploys-new-missile-launcher-to-the-philippines.

10. "TSP/CBP Key to Security, Deterrence in Pacific," 36th Operations Group Public Affairs, July 16, 2007, https://www.pacaf.af.mil/News/Article-Display/Article/596997/tspcbp-key-to-security-deterrence-in-pacific/.

11. Jim Gomez, "Philippines Launches Strategy of Publicizing Chinese Actions," Associated Press, March 8, 2023, https://apnews.com/article/philippines-publicize-aggression-south-china-sea-724c054eb155982a1d363a257334dd13.

12. Wendell B. Leimbach and Eric Duckworth, "Prevailing without Gunsmoke in the South China Sea," U.S. Naval Institute *Proceedings*, November 2022, https://www.usni.org/magazines/proceedings/2022/november/prevailing-without-gunsmoke-south-china-sea.

13. "Navy, Marine Corps Conclude Large Scale Exercise 2023," U.S. Fleet Forces Command Public Affairs, August 18, 2023, https://www.navy.mil/Press-Office/News-Stories/Article/3498799/navy-marine-corps-conclude-large-scale-exercise-2023/.

14. Albert A. Nofi, *To Train the Fleet for War: The U.S. Navy Fleet Problems 1923–1940* (Newport, RI: Naval War College Press, 2010), 277–80.

15. Nofi, *To Train the Fleet for War*, 285.

16. Michael Getler, "Make-Believe Mobilization Showed Major Flaws," *Washington Post*, July 23, 1980, https://www.washingtonpost.com/archive/politics

/1980/07/24/make-believe-mobilization-showed-major-flaws/e6d0c81b-22a3-4ac0-9b46-2e334d5d3f70/.

17. Francis J. H. Park, "Deconflicting Exercises and Experimentation under Global Integration," *Joint Forces Quarterly*, 3rd quarter 2021, https://ndupress.ndu.edu/Portals/68/Documents/jfq/jfq-102/jfq-102_51-57_Features-Deconflicting_Exercises.pdf.

18. Department of Defense, "Military and Security Developments involving the People's Republic of China, 2023: Annual Report to Congress," 50, 55–56, and 69, accessed April 27, 2024, https://media.defense.gov/2023/Oct/19/2003323409/-1/-1/1/2023-MILITARY-AND-SECURITY-DEVELOPMENTS-INVOLVING-THE-PEOPLES-REPUBLIC-OF-CHINA.PDF.

19. Andrew Feickert, "Defense Primer: Army Multi-Domain Operations (MDO)," *In Focus*, Congressional Research Service, January 2, 2024, accessed April 27, 2024, https://sgp.fas.org/crs/natsec/IF11409.pdf.

20. Andrew Feickert, "U.S. Marine Corps Force Design 2030 Initiative: Background and Issues for Congress," CRS Report R47614, Congressional Research Service, June 30, 2023, 1, 3, 7, and 11, accessed April 27, 2024, https://crsreports.congress.gov/product/pdf/R/R47614.

21. Anita Hofschneider, "Military Won't Proceed with Marianas Bombing Range but the New Plan Is Unclear," *Honolulu Civil Beat*, April 8, 2022, https://www.civilbeat.org/2022/04/military-wont-proceed-with-marianas-bombing-range-but-the-new-plan-is-unclear/.

22. U.S. Transportation Command, "Turbo Activation 19-Plus After Action Report," December 16, 2019, 15–16, https://www.globalsecurity.org/military/library/report/2019/ustranscom_turbo-activation19-plus_aar_20191216.pdf.

23. John F. Lehman, *Oceans Ventured: Winning the Cold War at Sea* (New York: Norton, 2018), 49–50.

24. "U.S., Allied Forces Conduct Exercise Pacific Vanguard 2023," Destroyer Squadron 15 Public Affairs, July 8, 2023, https://www.cpf.navy.mil/Newsroom/News/Article/3448397/us-allied-forces-conduct-exercise-pacific-vanguard-2023/.

CHAPTER 4. ENHANCING OPERATIONAL AND INDUSTRIAL ENERGY RESILIENCY

1. The SPR was created in 1975 when the Energy Policy and Conservation Act was enacted. It is a tool intended to alleviate market impacts such as natural disasters, political disputes, and conflicts. The SPR has a capacity of 713.5 million barrels of crude oil; in February 2023 it contained 371 million barrels of crude. Due to difficulties in storing refined petroleum products, the SPR is overwhelmingly crude oil. U.S. Department of Energy, "Strategic Petroleum Reserve: Providing Energy Security for America," February 2023, https://www.energy.gov/sites/default/files/2023-03/Infographic SPR 02_2023.pdf. In 2012 Hurricane Sandy damaged gasoline infrastructure in northeast United States, leading to the creation of the

Northeast Gasoline Supply Reserve, with the capacity for 700,000 barrels at the New York Harbor, 200,000 barrels in Boston area, and 100,000 barrels in South Portland, Maine. U.S. Department of Energy, Office of Cybersecurity, Energy Security, and Emergency Response, "Northeast Gasoline Supply Reserve," n.d., accessed October 28, 2024, https://www.energy.gov/ceser/northeast-gasoline-supply-reserve. Similarly, the Department of Energy manages a third petroleum reserve—the Northeast Home Heating Oil Reserve, which consists of ultra-low sulfur diesel for heating oil use that includes 400,000 barrels in the Boston area, 300,000 barrels at the New York Harbor, and 300,000 barrels in Groton, Connecticut. U.S. Department of Energy, Office of Cybersecurity, Energy Security, and Emergency Response, "The Northeast Home Heating Oil Reserve," n.d., accessed October 28, 2024, https://www.energy.gov/ceser/northeast-home-heating-oil-reserve.

2. "U.S. Energy Facts Explained," EIA, Chart: U.S. Energy Consumption by Source and Sector, 2022, based on EIA, *Monthly Energy Review*, April 2024, tables 1.3, 1.4c, and 2.1a–2.6, accessed January 17, 2024, https://www.eia.gov/energyexplained/us-energy-facts/.

3. Engine Technology Forum, "Trucking," n.d., accessed November 20, 2022, https://enginetechforum.org/trucking.

4. John Harper, "U.S. Military Wants Its Vehicles to Go Electric—with Detroit's Help," National Defense, February 4, 2022, accessed February 9, 2023, https://www.nationaldefensemagazine.org/articles/2022/2/4/military-wants-its--vehicles-to-go-electricwith-detroits-help; and National Defense Authorization Act for Fiscal Year 2023, 117th Congress, December 27, 2021, sec. 322 and 351, accessed February 9, 2023, https://www.congress.gov/117/plaws/publ81/PLAW-117publ81.pdf.

5. Darren W. McDew, Transportation Command testimony before Senate Armed Services Committee, April 10, 2018, 58, https://www.armed-services.senate.gov/imo/media/doc/18-32_04-10-18.pdf.

6. Cybersecurity & Infrastructure Security Agency, "Energy Sector," n.d., accessed March 18, 2023, https://www.cisa.gov/topics/critical-infrastructure-security-and-resilience/critical-infrastructure-sectors/energy-sector.

7. *Fiscal Year 2020 Fact Book*, 43rd ed. (Fort Belvoir, VA: Defense Logistics Agency, 2020), 20, https://www.dla.mil/Portals/104/Documents/Energy/Publications/DLAEnergyFactBookFY20_lowres2.pdf.

8. Office of the Under Secretary of Defense for Acquisition and Sustainment, *Fiscal Year 2020 Operational Energy Annual Report* (Washington, DC: Department of Defense, May 2021), 3, https://www.acq.osd.mil/eie/Downloads/OE/FY20 OE Annual Report.pdf.

9. Connie Braesch, "DLA Energy's International Agreements Program Supports a Network of Global Relationships," Defense Logistics Agency, January 15, 2019, https://www.dla.mil/About-DLA/News/News-Article-View/Article/1731115/dla-energys-international-agreements-program-supports-a-network-of-global-relat/.

10. "FAQs: How Much Oil Is Consumed in the United States?" EIA, last updated September 19, 2022, https://www.eia.gov/tools/faqs/faq.php?id=33&t=6.
11. *Fiscal Year 2022 Fact Book*, 44th ed. (For Belvoir, VA: Defense Logistics Agency, 2022), 27 and 31, https://www.dla.mil/Portals/104/Documents/Energy/Publications/DLAEnergyFactBook2022_2.pdf.
12. U.S. Department of Transportation and U.S. Maritime Administration, "National Defense Reserve Fleet and Services," March 31, 2024, https://www.maritime.dot.gov/sites/marad.dot.gov/files/2024-05/2024_03%20NDRF%20Inventory%20Internal.pdf.
13. U.S. Department of Transportation and U.S. Maritime Administration, "Maritime Security Program," accessed January 17, 2024, https://www.maritime.dot.gov/national-security/strategic-sealift/maritime-security-program-msp.
14. Bryan Clark, Timothy Walton, and Adam Lemon, *Strengthening the U.S. Defense Maritime Industrial Base: A Plan to Improve Maritime Industry's Contribution to National Security* (Washington, DC: Center for Strategic and Budgetary Assessments, February 12, 2020), 9–13 and 48, https://csbaonline.org/research/publications/strengthening-the-u.s-defense-maritime-industrial-base-a-plan-to-improve-maritime-industrys-contribution-to-national-security/publication/1.
15. Maritime Traffick database, accessed November 21, 2022, https://www.marinetraffic.com/en/ais/home/centerx:-12.0/centery:25.0/zoom:4.
16. U.S. Department of Defense, "Red Hill Bulk Fuel Storage Facility, Oahu, Hawaii: Defueling Plan Supplement 1.B," September 28, 2022, 12–13, https://cnrh.cnic.navy.mil/Portals/79/CNRH/Documents/red_hill/Defueling%20Plan%20page%20contents/Red%20Hill%20Defueling%20Plan%20Supplement%201.B%20plus%20Encl%201%202022-09-28.pdf.
17. Heather L. Greenley, "The Strategic Petroleum Reserve: Background, Authorities, and Considerations," Congressional Research Service, R46355, May 13, 2020, 10–11, https://crsreports.congress.gov/product/pdf/R/R46355.
18. Ty Chapman, "America's Light Sweet Problem," *Five Star Metals*, January 31, 2019, accessed March 18, 2023, https://www.fsmetals.com/about-us/blog/americas-light-sweet-problem.
19. AFPM, "U.S. Refiners Clean Up Trade as Their Own Exports Soar," *Politico*, sponsor-generated content, n.d., accessed March 18, 2023, https://www.politico.com/sponsor-content/2019/09/us-refiners-clean-up-trade.
20. "Oil Infrastructure," *ISO New England*, April 2021, 3–4, https://www.iso-ne.com/static-assets/documents/2021/04/oil_infrastructure.pdf.
21. Quoted in Brent D. Sadler, "Chinese Handcuffs: Don't Allow the U.S. Military to Be Hooked on Green Energy from China," Heritage Foundation, June 20, 2024, 6, https://www.heritage.org/sites/default/files/2024-06/BG3838.pdf.
22. The White House, "FACT SHEET: President Biden to Announce New Actions to Strengthen U.S. Energy Security, Encourage Production, and Bring Down

Costs," October 18, 2022, https://www.whitehouse.gov/briefing-room/statements-releases/2022/10/18/fact-sheet-president-biden-to-announce-new-actions-to-strengthen-u-s-energy-security-encourage-production-and-bring-down-costs/.

23. Kevin Hack, "Strong Demand for Diesel Leads to High Prices and Tight Inventories Going into Winter," Today in Energy, EIA, November 10, 2022, https://www.eia.gov/todayinenergy/detail.php?id=54619.

24. Stephanie Kelly, "US Crude Stockpiles Jump, Distillates Draw Down to 18-Mth Low—EIA," Reuters, November 22, 2023, https://www.reuters.com/markets/commodities/us-crude-stockpiles-jump-distillates-draw-down-18-mth-low-eia-2023-11-22/.

25. U.S. Department of Energy, Office of Cybersecurity, Energy Security, and Emergency Response, "DOE Issues Notice of Congressionally Mandated Sale to Purchase Crude Oil from the Strategic Petroleum Reserve," February 13, 2023, https://www.energy.gov/ceser/articles/doe-issues-notice-congressionally-mandated-sale-purchase-crude-oil-strategic.

26. Jennifer Jacobs and Ari Natter, "US to Sell 26 Million More Barrels from Strategic Oil Reserve," *Bloomberg*, February 13, 2023, https://www.bloomberg.com/news/articles/2023-02-13/us-to-sell-26-million-more-barrels-from-strategic-crude-reserve.

27. "Short-Term Energy Outlook," EIA, November 8, 2022, accessed November 20, 2022, https://www.eia.gov/outlooks/steo/.

28. "Weekly U.S. Ending Stocks of Crude Oil in SPR," EIA, January 5, 2024, accessed January 17, 2024, https://www.eia.gov/dnav/pet/hist/LeafHandler.ashx?n=PET&s=WCSSTUS1&f=W.

29. Nicolas Loris, "Why Congress Should Pull the Plug on the Strategic Petroleum Reserve," Heritage Foundation, August 20, 2015, https://www.heritage.org/environment/report/why-congress-should-pull-the-plug-the-strategic-petroleum-reserve.

30. OPEC attempted to drive U.S. shale oil producers out of business by driving crude oil prices down. The lower prices of the time, as well as increasing domestic production of domestic shale oil, diminished the public perception for needing a SPR. Clifford Krauss, "OPEC Took Aim at U.S. Oil Producers, but Hurt Itself, Too," *New York Times*, June 15, 2017, https://www.nytimes.com/2017/06/15/business/energy-environment/gas-oil-petrol-opec.html.

31. "Crude Oil Pipelines," EIA, updated January 9, 2023, accessed March 15, 2023, https://atlas.eia.gov/datasets/eia::crude-oil-pipelines/about; "Map of Petroleum Infrastructure and Resources in the U.S.," EIA, August 12, 2021, accessed March 15, 2023, https://atlas.eia.gov/apps/e1c92d7601b9490697d22dfe2da1b4ac/explore.

32. ICF International, with principal contributors Kevin DeCorla-Souza, Matt Gilstrap, and CeCe Coffey, "East Coast and Gulf Coast Transportation Fuels Markets," EIA, February 2016, 32, https://www.eia.gov/analysis/transportationfuels/padd1n3/pdf/transportation_fuels_padd1n3.pdf; and EIA, "Planned Shutdown of Philadelphia Refinery Will Change Gasoline and Diesel Supply Patterns for the U.S. East

Coast," *This Week in Petroleum*, July 3, 2019, https://www.eia.gov/petroleum/weekly/archive/2019/190703/includes/analysis_print.php.

33. Ethanol is an oxygen scavenger, meaning that it will react and degrade if it contacts water or air. Since typical American motor gasoline is blended to 10 percent ethanol, once blended, its transport via pipeline is problematic. This is why blending occurs near the point of sale or use.

34. Diana Furchtgott-Roth, "Speedier Pipeline Approvals Needed for Oil and Gas Transportation," *Forbes*, February 14, 2023, https://www.forbes.com/sites/dianafurchtgott-roth/2023/02/14/speedier-pipeline-approvals-needed-for-oil-and-gas-transportation/.

35. Alan Apthorp, "Supply Alert October 25, 2022," Mansfield Energy, October 25, 2022, https://mansfield.energy/market-news/supply-alert-october-25-2022/.

36. Chunzi Xu, "New York, New England Ration Heating Oil Even before Peak Winter," *Bloomberg*, October 21, 2022, https://www.bloomberg.com/news/articles/2022-10-21/heating-oil-being-rationed-in-us-northeast-before-winter-starts.

37. EIA, "Planned Shutdown of Philadelphia Refinery"; and "Yes, Diesel Supplies Are Tight: This Is What Refiners Are Doing about It," AFPM Communications, November 15, 2022, https://www.afpm.org/newsroom/blog/yes-diesel-supplies-are-tight-what-refiners-are-doing-about-it. The Jones Act refers to section 27 of the Merchant Marine Act of 1920 and remains in force today despite revisions to the Merchant Marine Act. The act stipulates that all shipping between U.S. ports must be conducted on ships owned, registered, and built in the United States and having a U.S. crew.

38. "Table 1: Number and Capacity of Operable Petroleum Refineries by PAD District and State as of January 1, 2022," EIA, accessed January 31, 2023, https://www.eia.gov/petroleum/refinerycapacity/table1.pdf.

39. Rebecca Elliott, "U.S. Oil Refiners Accelerate Shift to Renewables in Downturn," *Wall Street Journal*, August 12, 2020, https://www.wsj.com/articles/u-s-refiners-embrace-greener-fuels-11597251600.

40. Internation Energy Forum and S&P Global, *IEF Oil Refining Sector Insights Report: Stretched Sector Fuels Market Volatility*, September 13, 2022, https://www.ief.org/news/ief-oil-refining-sector-insights-report-stretched-sector-fuels-market-volatility.

41. Internation Energy Forum and S&P Global, *IEF Oil Refining Sector Insights Report*.

42. On the capacity of the Santa Maria refinery, see "California Oil Refinery History," California Energy Commission, March 21, 2021, accessed March 15, 2023, https://www.energy.ca.gov/data-reports/energy-almanac/californias-petroleum-market/californias-oil-refineries/california-oil. For the Phillips 66 announcement of the closure of the Santa Maria refinery, see "Santa Maria Refinery," Phillips 66, accessed March 15, 2023, https://www.phillips66.com/refining/santa-maria-refinery/.

43. EIA, "Recent West Coast Gasoline and Diesel Prices Show Significant Volatility," *This Week in Petroleum*, October 26, 2022, https://www.eia.gov/petroleum/weekly/archive/2022/221026/includes/analysis_print.php.

44. For an example of how ESG special-interest groups pressure businesses, see Brad Lander, letter to Laurence G. Fink, Re: BlackRock Inc.'s Commitment to Net Zero Emissions, September 21, 2022, https://comptroller.nyc.gov/wp-content/uploads/2022/09/Letter-to-BlackRock-CEO-Larry-Fink.pdf.
45. Sarah Ladislaw, Ethan Zindler, Nikos Tsafos, Logan Goldie-Scot, Lachlan Carey, Pol Lezcano, Jane Nakano, and Jenny Chase, *Industrial Policy, Trade, and Clean Energy Supply Chains*, Center for Strategic and International Studies, February 2021, 10–14, https://csis-website-prod.s3.amazonaws.com/s3fs-public/publication/210224_Ladislaw_Industrial_Policy.pdf.
46. Eric Ng, "Climate and Sustainability: How Impending EU Laws on ESG Disclosures Will Be a Matter of Survival for Asian Suppliers," *South China Morning Post*, February 14, 2023, https://www.scmp.com/business/article/3210126/climate-and-sustainability-how-impending-eu-laws-esg-disclosures-will-be-matter-survival-asian. A survey conducted by Deloitte of three hundred publicly owned companies with a minimum annual revenue of $500 million USD indicated 50 percent have already implemented ESG policies and controls. Deloitte, *Sustainability Action Report: Survey Findings on ESG Disclosure and Preparedness*, December 2022, 4, 15, and 18, https://www2.deloitte.com/content/dam/Deloitte/us/Documents/audit/us-survey-findings-on-esg-disclosure-and-preparedness.pdf.
47. U.S. Department of Energy, Office of Cybersecurity, Energy Security, and Emergency Response, "Energy Waiver Library," n.d., accessed March 18, 2023, https://www.energy.gov/ceser/energy-waivers-library.
48. Patrick Tyrrell, "Permanent Repeal of the Jones Act Would Be a Winning Response to COVID-19," Heritage Foundation, April 7, 2020, https://www.heritage.org/trade/commentary/permanent-repeal-the-jones-act-would-be-winning-response-covid-19.
49. "FAQs: How Much Petroleum Does the United States Import and Export?" EIA, n.d., accessed February 9, 2023, https://www.eia.gov/tools/faqs/faq.php?id=727&t=6.
50. Katie Tubb, "Biden's Radical, Anti-Fossil Fuel Energy Policy Costs Americans Dearly," *Daily Signal*, June 28, 2022, https://www.heritage.org/energy-economics/commentary/bidens-radical-anti-fossil-fuel-energy-policy-costs-americans-dearly.
51. "Sanctions Adopted Following Russia's Military Aggression against Ukraine," European Commission, n.d., accessed March 18, 2023, https://finance.ec.europa.eu/sanctions-adopted-following-russias-military-aggression-against-ukraine_en.
52. Myah Ward, "White House Is Pressed on Potential Oil Deals with Saudi Arabia, Venezuela and Iran," *Politico*, March 7, 2022, https://www.politico.com/news/2022/03/07/white-house-oil-deals-saudi-arabia-venezuela-iran-00014803.
53. Simon Read, "EU Countries Are Encouraging Voluntary Gas Cuts—Here's Why and What to Expect Next," World Economic Forum, September 14, 2022, https://www.weforum.org/agenda/2022/09/gas-energy-eu-rationing-russia/.

54. Arathy Somasekhar, "Oil Climbs 1% as Tankers Avoid Red Sea after Strikes on Houthis," Reuters, January 12, 2024, https://www.reuters.com/markets/commodities/oil-prices-rise-more-than-2-after-us-britain-strikes-yemen-2024-01-12/.
55. Derrick Morgan, "Here Are the Factors That Affect Gas Prices," *Daily Signal*, September 23, 2022, https://www.dailysignal.com/2022/09/23/what-goes-into-gas-prices-at-the-pump-lessons-from-across-the-oil-supply-chain/.
56. Office of the Under Secretary of Defense for Acquisition and Sustainment, *Fiscal Year 2019 Operational Energy Annual Report* (Washington, DC: Department of Defense, March 2020), 2 and 18, https://www.acq.osd.mil/eie/Downloads/OE/FY19%20OE%20Annual%20Report.pdf.
57. *Fiscal Year 2021 Fact Book*, 44th ed. (Washington, DC: Defense Logistics Agency Energy, 2021), 31, 39–41, and 43, https://www.dla.mil/Portals/104/Documents/Energy/Publications/DLAEnergyFactBook2021_2.pdf.
58. United Nations, *UNCTAD Handbook of Statistics* (New York: United Nations Publications, 2021), 72 and 79, https://unctad.org/system/files/official-document/tdstat46_en.pdf; and Elizabeth Connelly and Bruno Idini, "International Shipping," IEA, September 2022, accessed November 21, 2022, https://www.iea.org/reports/international-shipping.
59. Kevin Hack, "Several Refining Projects Are Scheduled in Asia and the Middle East," EIA, August 2, 2022, https://www.eia.gov/todayinenergy/detail.php?id=53279.
60. "Current Wave of Refinery Capacity Growth 'Likely to Be the last': IEA," S&P Global, October 24, 2023, https://www.spglobal.com/commodityinsights/en/market-insights/latest-news/oil/102423-current-wave-of-refinery-capacity-growth-likely-to-be-the-last-iea.
61. EIA, *Oil Market Report*, January 18, 2023, 1, 3, and 4–5, https://iea.blob.core.windows.net/assets/6b994ae3-17fe-4a44-8bb8-eb1217cc4604/-18JAN2023_OilMarketReport.pdf.
62. Willy C. Shih, "Climate Regulations Are about to Disrupt Global Shipping," *Harvard Business Review*, October 21, 2022, https://hbr.org/2022/10/climate-regulations-are-about-to-disrupt-global-shipping.
63. Costas Paris, "Shipping Industry Balks at Green Energy Transition," *Wall Street Journal*, December 22, 2022, https://www.wsj.com/articles/shipping-industry-balks-at-green-energy-transition-11671696107.
64. "Refining Capacity 101: What to Understand before Demanding 'Restarts,'" AFPM Communications, June 6, 2022, https://www.afpm.org/newsroom/blog/refining-capacity-101-what-understand-demanding-restarts.
65. "Number and Capacity of Petroleum Refineries," EIA, n.d., accessed January 17, 2024, https://www.eia.gov/dnav/pet/pet_pnp_cap1_dcu_nus_a.htm.
66. EIA, *International Energy Outlook 2021 with Projects to 2050*, October 2021, https://www.eia.gov/outlooks/ieo/pdf/IEO2021_Narrative.pdf.

67. Heavy crude oil refers to denser grades of oil that require more refining than lighter grades. Crude oil can also be "sweet" or "sour," referring to its sulfur content. See "Oil and Petroleum Products Explained: Refining Crude Oil," EIA, n.d., accessed January 31, 2023, https://www.eia.gov/energyexplained/oil-and-petroleum-products/refining-crude-oil-inputs-and-outputs.php; and EIA, "Refinery Closures Contribute to Decreased U.S. Refinery Capacity during 2020," *This Week in Petroleum*, June 30, 2021, https://www.eia.gov/petroleum/weekly/archive/2021/210630/includes/analysis_print.php.
68. "Table 3: Capacity of Operable Petroleum Refineries by State as of January 1, 2022," EIA, n.d., accessed January 31, 2023, https://www.eia.gov/petroleum/refinerycapacity/table3.pdf; and EIA, *Annual Energy Review 2011*, September 2012, 23, https://www.eia.gov/totalenergy/data/annual/pdf/aer.pdf.
69. Scott E. Wuesthoff, "The Utility of Targeting the Petroleum-Based Sector of a Nation's Economic Infrastructure," thesis, Air University Press, Maxwell AFB, Alabama, June 1994, vi, 3–4, 6–7, 12–13, 20, 27, and 29, https://media.defense.gov/2018/Jan/02/2001862444/-1/-1/0/T_WUESTHOFF_UTILITY_OF.PDF.
70. Daren Bakst and Peter St. Onge, *Inflation: Policymakers Should Stop Driving It and Start Fighting It*, Heritage Foundation, Special report, no. 252, January 20, 2022, https://www.heritage.org/sites/default/files/2022-02/SR252.pdf; and Julie Harris and Kevin Hack, "Refinery Closures Decreased U.S. Refinery Capacity during 2020," EIA, July 8, 2021, https://www.eia.gov/todayinenergy/detail.php?id=48636.
71. "East Coast and Gulf Coast Transportation Fuels Markets," EIA, February 3, 2016, https://www.eia.gov/analysis/transportationfuels/padd1n3/; and "Table 1: Number and Capacity of Operable Petroleum Refineries."
72. Robert Rapier, "Four Reasons Why the U.S. Is Grappling with a Diesel Shortage," Oil Price, November 5, 2022, https://oilprice.com/Energy/Gas-Prices/Four-Reasons-Why-The-US-Is-Grappling-With-A-Diesel-Shortage.html.
73. "U.S. Energy Facts Explained," EIA, n.d., accessed February 6, 2023, https://www.eia.gov/energyexplained/us-energy-facts/imports-and-exports.php.
74. "New Refineries Will Increase Global Refining Capacity in 2022 and 2023," EIA, *This Week in Petroleum*, July 27, 2022, https://www.eia.gov/petroleum/weekly/archive/2022/220720/includes/analysis_print.php; and "Oil Market Report—November 2022," November 2022, https://www.iea.org/reports/oil-market-report-november-2022.
75. AFPM Communications, "Refining Capacity 101."
76. Distillate inventories at the Amsterdam Rotterdam Antwerp storage hub have been well below their five-year average since the start of 2022 and were more than 1.0 million barrels below the five-year average through most of the summer (graph 4). See "IEF Oil Refining Sector Insights Report: Stretched Sector Fuels Market Volatility," International Energy Forum, September 13, 2022, https://www.ief.org/news/ief-oil-refining-sector-insights-report-stretched-sector-fuels-market-volatility;

and EIA, "Rapid Increases in Diesel Prices Reflect Low Inventories Going into Winter Demand Season," *This Week in Petroleum*, November 2, 2022, https://www.eia.gov/petroleum/weekly/archive/2022/221102/includes/analysis_print.php.
77. "LyondellBasell Announces Plans to Exit Refining Business," LyondellBasell, April 21, 2022, https://www.lyondellbasell.com/en/news-events/corporate--financial-news/lyondellbasell-announces-plans-to-exit-refining-business/.
78. Erwin Seba, "Exxon Starts New Crude Unit at Beaumont, Texas Refinery—Sources," Reuters, March 1, 2023, https://www.reuters.com/business/energy/exxon-starts-new-crude-unit-beaumont-texas-refinery-sources-2023-03-01/.
79. "FAQs: When Was the Last Refinery Built in the United States?" EIA, n.d., accessed March 18, 2023, https://www.eia.gov/tools/faqs/faq.php?id=29&t=6; and "New Refineries Will Increase Global Refining Capacity."
80. Blending motor gasoline with more than 10 percent ethanol reaches a so-called blend-wall, as most automobiles are not able to use higher-ratio ethanol fuels.
81. "The United States Produces Most of the Fuel Ethanol That It Consumes," EIA, n.d., accessed March 16, 2023, https://www.eia.gov/energyexplained/biofuels/ethanol-supply.php.
82. Estella Shi and Sean Hill, "In 2020, U.S. Exports of Fuel Ethanol Fell for the Second Consecutive Year," EIA, *Today in Energy*, May 14, 2021, https://www.eia.gov/todayinenergy/detail.php?id=47956.
83. "Product Supplied," EIA, n.d., accessed March 22, 2023, https://www.eia.gov/dnav/pet/pet_cons_psup_dc_nus_mbblpd_a.htm; and "Number and Capacity of Petroleum Refineries."
84. "Product Supplied"; and "Number and Capacity of Petroleum Refineries."
85. Matt French, "The United States Produces Lighter Crude Oil, Imports Heavier Crude Oil," EIA, October 11, 2022, https://www.eia.gov/todayinenergy/detail.php?id=54199.
86. Richard Stern, "18 Absurdities of the McConnell-Schumer Omnibus Spending Bill," *The Daily Signal*, December 20, 2022, https://www.dailysignal.com/2022/12/20/18-absurdities-of-the-mcconnell-schumer-omnibus-spending-bill/amp/.
87. "Oil and Petroleum Products Explained."
88. Walter Lohman and Justin Rhee, eds., *2021 China Transparency Report*, 27–31, Heritage Foundation, http://thf_media.s3.amazonaws.com/2021/China_Transparency_Report.pdf.

CHAPTER 5. HOW A REVOLUTION IN SHIPPING CAN REGAIN AMERICAN MARITIME STRENGTH

1. Brent Droste Sadler, *U.S. Naval Power in the 21st Century: A New Strategy for Facing the Chinese and Russian Threat* (Annapolis, MD: Naval Institute Press, 2023), 1–2 and 239–50.
2. This is based on publicly available data from China's COSCO (About CSP: Corporate Profile, n.d., https://ports.coscoshipping.com/en/AboutCSP/CorporateProfile

/Overview/) and China Merchants Group (China Merchants Port Holdings Co. Ltd., Company Profile, https://www.cmport.com.hk/EN/about/Profile.aspx?from=2); the actual figure is likely larger when other Chinese ports' operators are included.
3. Rebeca Grynspan, "Here's How We Can Resolve the Global Supply Chain Crisis," UN Trade and Development, January 18, 2022, https://unctad.org/news/blog-heres-how-we-can-resolve-global-supply-chain-crisis.
4. The Jones Act, also known as the Merchant Marine Act of 1920, is a federal statute establishing support for the development and maintenance of a merchant marine in order to support commercial activity and serve as a naval auxiliary in times of war or national emergency (46 USC § 50101). The statute requires, among other things, shipping between U.S. ports to be conducted by U.S.-flagged ships (46 USC § 50102). Cornell Law School, "Jones Act," March 2022, accessed August 2, 2023, https://www.law.cornell.edu/wex/jones_act.
5. John Frittelli, "Shipping under the Jones Act: Legislative and Regulatory Background," Congressional Research Service, updated November 21, 2019, 23, https://sgp.fas.org/crs/misc/R45725.pdf; and Testimony of General Steve Lyons, U.S. Transportation Command, before the House Committee on Armed Services, Subcommittees on Seapower and Projection Forces and Readiness, "U.S. Transportation Command and Maritime Administration: State of the Mobility Enterprise," March 7, 2019.
6. Colin Grabow, Inu Manak, and Daniel J. Ikenson, "The Jones Act: A Burden America Can No Longer Bear," Cato Institute Policy Analysis, June 28, 2018, www.cato.org/publications/policy-analysis/jones-act-burden-america-can-no-longer-bear.
7. For the purposes of this chapter, "shipping" is inclusive of naval and commercial shipbuilding, shipping, and the associated infrastructure required to conduct global trade (i.e., ports). Regaining global competitiveness in shipping—not through government subsidies or matching China's nonmarket approach but rather by redefining the terms of competition through a "blue ocean" strategy, which would increase the competitive space to include new ways of accomplishing tasks—would create an alternative to conventional, increasingly Chinese-dominated shipping. This takes advantage of American strengths, uses market bridges to kickstart innovation by addressing urgent key naval operational problems, and in the process grows industry participants and investors.
8. Brent Sadler and Peter St. Onge, "Regaining U.S. Maritime Power Requires a Revolution in Shipping," Heritage Foundation, Special report, no. 272, May 15, 2023, 11–20, https://www.heritage.org/sites/default/files/2023-05/SR272.pdf.
9. Alfred Thayer Mahan, *The Influence of Sea Power upon History* (Boston: Little, Brown, 1890), 26.
10. Andrew Gibson and Arthur Donovan, *The Abandoned Ocean: A History of United States Maritime Policy* (Columbia: University of South Carolina, 2000), 265.
11. "Number and Size of the U.S. Flag Merchant Fleet and Its Share of the World Fleet," U.S. Department of Transportation, table_01_24_062422, n.d., accessed

March 12, 2023, https://www.bts.gov/content/number-and-size-us-flag-merchant-fleet-and-its-share-world-fleet.

12. "The Economic Importance of the U.S. Private Shipbuilding and Repairing Industry," Maritime Administration, March 30, 2021, 11, https://www.maritime.dot.gov/sites/marad.dot.gov/files/2021-06/Economic Contributions of U.S. Shipbuilding and Repairing Industry.pdf.

13. *Review of Maritime Transport 2022: Navigating Stormy Waters*, United Nations Conference on Trade and Development, 2022, 46, https://unctad.org/system/files/official-document/rmt2022_en.pdf; and Ronald O'Rourke, "China Naval Modernization: Implications for U.S. Navy Capabilities—Background and Issues for Congress," Congressional Research Service, December 1, 2022, 9, accessed March 12, 2023, https://sgp.fas.org/crs/row/RL33153.pdf.

14. "U.S. Ship Force Levels 1886–Present," Naval History and Heritage Command, n.d., accessed March 12, 2023, https://www.history.navy.mil/research/histories/ship-histories/us-ship-force-levels.html.

15. Gibson and Donovan, *The Abandoned Ocean*, 208–15.

16. Joseph Trevithick, "Alarming Navy Intel Slide Warns of China's 200 Times Greater Shipbuilding Capacity," *The Drive*, July 11, 2023, https://www.thedrive.com/the-war-zone/alarming-navy-intel-slide-warns-of-chinas-200-times-greater-shipbuilding-capacity.

17. David Axe, "Thousands of Ships, Millions of Troops: China Is Assembling a Huge Fleet for War with Taiwan," *Forbes*, July 27, 2021, updated December 10, 2021, https://www.forbes.com/sites/davidaxe/2021/07/27/thousands-of-ships-millions-of-troops-china-is-assembling-a-huge-assault-flotilla-for-a-possible-attack-on-taiwan; and Lonnie D. Henley, "China Maritime Report No. 21: Civilian Shipping and Maritime Militia: The Logistics Backbone of a Taiwan Invasion," China Maritime Studies Institute, May 2022, 11, https://digital-commons.usnwc.edu/cgi/viewcontent.cgi?article=1020&context=cmsi-maritime-reports.

18. Jude Blanchette, Jonathan E. Hillman, Mingda Qiu, and Maesea McCalpin, "Hidden Harbors: China's State-Backed Shipping Industry," Center for Strategic and International Studies, July 8, 2020, https://www.csis.org/analysis/hidden-harbors-chinas-state-backed-shipping-industry.

19. Emmanuel Mourlon-Druol and Federico Romero, *International Summitry and Global Governance: The Rise of the G7 and the European Council, 1974–1991* (London: Routledge, Taylor & Francis Group, 2014), 24–25.

20. W. Chan Kim and Renee Mauborgne, *Blue Ocean Strategy: How to Create Uncontested Market Space and the Competition Irrelevant* (Boston: Harvard Business Review Press, 2015), 22.

21. "Global Labor Rate Comparisons: The Impact on Manufacturing Location Decisions and Reshoring," Reshoring Institute, September 2022, 1–2 and 4, https://reshoringinstitute.org/wp-content/uploads/2022/09/GlobalLaborRateComparisons.pdf.

22. Frittelli, "Shipping under the Jones Act," 23; and Testimony of General Steve Lyons.
23. "Global Labor Rate Comparisons"; and Mark V. Arena, Irv Blickstein, Obaid Younossi, and Clifford A. Grammich, *Why Has the Cost of Navy Ships Risen? A Macroscopic Examination of the Trends in U.S. Naval Ship Costs over the Past Several Decades* (RAND Corporation research brief, April 20, 2006), 24, https://www.rand.org/pubs/monographs/MG484.html.
24. "The Maritime Administration's First 100 Years: 1916–2016," Maritime Administration, February 25, 2023, https://www.maritime.dot.gov/history/historical-documents-and-resources/maritime-administration%E2%80%99s-first-100-years-1916-%E2%80%93-2016.
25. Merchant Marine Act of 1920, June 5, 1920, 46 USC App Ch. 24, § 861.
26. "The Development of China's Marine Programs," The State Council of The People's Republic of China, 1998, https://policy.asiapacificenergy.org/sites/default/files/White%20Paper-%20The%20Development%20of%20China's%20Marine%20Programs%20%28EN%29.pdf.
27. Panle Jim Barwick, Myrto Kalouptsidi, and Nazim Bin Zaharah, "Implementing Industrial Policy Effectively: Lessons from Shipbuilding in China," *VoxDev*, May 28, 2024, https://voxdev.org/topic/firms/implementing-industrial-policy-effectively-lessons-shipbuilding-china.
28. Axe, "Thousands of Ships."
29. Henley, "China Maritime Report No. 21," 11.
30. H. I. Sutton and Sam LaGrone, "Chinese Launch Assault Craft from Civilian Car Ferries in Mass Amphibious Invasion Drill, Satellite Photos Show," *USNI News*, September 28, 2022, https://news.usni.org/2022/09/28/chinese-launch-assault-craft-from-civilian-car-ferries-in-mass-amphibious-invasion-drill-satellite-photos-show.
31. Didi Kirsten Tatlow, "China's Stake in World Ports Sharpens Attention on Political Influence," *Newsweek*, October 9, 2022, https://www.newsweek.com/2022/10/14/chinas-stake-world-ports-sharpens-attention-political-influence-1749215.html.
32. Erik Kravets, "When China Shanghais Your Port," *Maritime Executive*, December 23, 2022, https://maritime-executive.com/magazine/when-china-shanghais-your-port.
33. Donald J. Trump, "The National Maritime Cybersecurity Plan," The White House, December 2020, 4–5, https://trumpwhitehouse.archives.gov/wp-content/uploads/2021/01/12.2.2020-National-Maritime-Cybersecurity-Plan.pdf.
34. Joseph R. Biden, "Executive Order on Amending Regulations Relating to the Safeguarding of Vessels, Harbors, Ports, and Waterfront Facilities of the United States," The White House, February 21, 2024, https://www.whitehouse.gov/briefing-room/presidential-actions/2024/02/21/executive-order-on-amending-regulations-relating-to-the-safeguarding-of-vessels-harbors-ports-and-waterfront-facilities-of-the-united-states/.
35. "Cybersecurity in the Marine Transportation System," proposed rule by the U.S. Coast Guard, February 22, 2024, https://www.federalregister.gov

/documents/2024/02/22/2024-03075/cybersecurity-in-the-marine-transportation-system.

36. National Transportation Safety Board, *Contact of Containership Dali with the Francis Scott Key Bridge and Subsequent Bridge Collapse*, Marine Investigation Preliminary Report, DCA24MM031, May 14, 2024, https://www.ntsb.gov/investigations/Documents/DCA24MM031_PreliminaryReport%203.pdf.
37. *Review of Maritime Transport 2023: Towards a Green and Just Transition*, United Nations Conference on Trade and Development (New York: United Nations Publications, 2023), 90–95, https://unctad.org/system/files/official-document/rmt2023_en.pdf.
38. Alejandra Salgado, "How the FMC Plans to Enforce the Ocean Shipping Reform Act in 2023," *Supply Chain Dive*, February 7, 2023, https://www.supplychaindive.com/news/fmc-plans-to-enforce-the-ocean-shipping-reform-act-in-2023/641643/.
39. "Cargo Preference," U.S. Department of Transportation, Maritime Administration, September 12, 2022, accessed February 20, 2023, https://www.maritime.dot.gov/ports/cargo-preference/cargo-preference.
40. "Cargo Preference: Compliance with an Enforcement of Maritime's Buy American Laws," Remote hearing before the subcommittee on Coast Guard and Maritime Transportation of the Committee on Transportation and Infrastructure, House of Representatives, 117th Congress, 2nd sess., September 14, 2022, 2, 17, and 48, https://www.govinfo.gov/content/pkg/CHRG-117hhrg50066/pdf/CHRG-117hhrg50066.pdf.
41. Blanchette et al., "Hidden Harbors."
42. Nicolas Loris, "How to Improve America's Ports," *Backgrounder*, no. 3503, June 24, 2020, 5 and 7–8, https://www.heritage.org/sites/default/files/2020-06/BG3503.pdf.
43. Diane Katz, "Curbing Abuses of a Politicized NEPA," *Backgrounder*, Heritage Foundation, no. 3524 (August 25, 2020), 1, 4–5, and 8–9, https://www.heritage.org/sites/default/files/2020-08/BG3524.pdf.
44. Maritime Security Program Fleet (MSP), August 1, 2022, https://www.maritime.dot.gov/sites/marad.dot.gov/files/2022-08/MSP%20Fleet%20%208-1-2022.pdf.
45. "National Defense Reserve Fleet Inventory for the Month Ending December 31, 2022," U.S. Department of Transportation Maritime Administration, January 1, 2023, https://www.maritime.dot.gov/sites/marad.dot.gov/files/2023-01/2022_12%20Public%20NDRF%20Inventory%20%28002%29.pdf.
46. Umair Irfan, "The Ohio Train Derailment Was an Accident Waiting to Happen," *Vox*, February 15, 2023, www.vox.com/policy-and-politics/23597778/ohio-train-east-palestine-trainwreck-accident-chemical-norfolk.
47. Justin Roczniak, "Mismanagement and 'Monster Trains' Have Wrecked American Rail," *New York Times*, October 9, 2022, https://www.nytimes.com/2022/10/09/opinion/business-economics/freight-train-mismanagement.html.

NOTES TO PAGES 139–143   291

48. Bryan Clark, Timothy Walton, and Adam Lemon, "Strengthening the U.S. Defense Maritime Industrial Base: A Plan to Improve Maritime Industry's Contribution to National Security," Center for Strategic and Budgetary Assessments, February 12, 2020, 9–13 and 48, https://csbaonline.org/research/publications/strengthening-the-u.s-defense-maritime-industrial-base-a-plan-to-improve-maritime-industrys-contribution-to-national-security/publication/1.
49. Testimony of Mark H. Buzby, Administrator, U.S. Maritime Administration, in video of "Subcommittees on Seapower and Projection Forces and Readiness Joint Hearing: 'Sealift and Mobility Requirements in Support of the National Defense Strategy,'" Committee on Armed Services, U.S. House of Representatives, March 11, 2020, https://www.transportation.gov/testimony/sealift-and-mobility-requirements-support-national-defense-strategy. See also Mark H. Buzby, Administrator, U.S. Maritime Administration, U.S. Department of Transportation, statement for "Hearing on Sealift and Mobility Requirements in Support of the National Defense Strategy," Subcommittee on Seapower and Projection Forces and Subcommittee on Readiness, Committee on Armed Services, U.S. House of Representatives, March 11, 2020, https://www.congress.gov/116/meeting/house/110720/witnesses/HHRG-116-AS28-Wstate-BuzbyM-20200311.pdf.
50. Frittelli, "Shipping under the Jones Act," 23; and Testimony of General Steve Lyons, "U.S. Transportation Command and Maritime Administration."
51. Colin Grabow, Inu Manak, and Daniel J. Ikenson, "The Jones Act: A Burden America Can No Longer Bear," in *The Case against the Jones Act*, ed. Colin Grabow and Inu Manak (Washington, DC: Cato Institute, 2020), 6; Colin Grabow, "Rust Buckets: How the Jones Act Undermines U.S. Shipbuilding and National Security," in *The Case against the Jones Act*, 27; and Daniel J. Ikenson, "Dragging the Anchor: A Look at the Myriad Costs of the Jones Act," in *The Case against the Jones Act*, 43.
52. Testimony of Mark H. Buzby, March 11, 2020.
53. Geoffrey Brown, "U.S. Strategic Sealift's Merchant Mariner Problem," *Maritime Executive*, July 2, 2021, https://maritime-executive.com/editorials/u-s-strategic-sealift-s-merchant-mariner-problem.
54. Clark, Walton, and Lemon, "Strengthening the U.S. Defense Maritime Industrial Base," 11–13.
55. Martin Stopford, *Maritime Economics*, 2nd ed. (London: Taylor & Francis, 2003), ebook, loc. 3985–4537.
56. Theo Notteboom, Athanasios Pallis, and Jean-Paul Rodrigue, *Port Economics, Management and Policy*, chapter 6.4, "Post Resilience" (New York: Routledge, 2022), https://www.taylorfrancis.com/chapters/mono/10.4324/9780429318184-41/port-resilience-theo-notteboom-athanasios-pallis-jean-paul-rodrigue?context=ubx&refId=436d85c8-6399-41c2-8080-fe7136325309.

57. Mary-Ann Russon, "The Cost of the Suez Canal Blockage," *BBC*, March 29, 2021, https://www.bbc.com/news/business-56559073.
58. Jean-Paul Rodrigue, "The Post-Panamax Syndrome: The Challenges of the Port of Cartagena," *Port Economics*, June 29, 2017, https://www.porteconomics.eu/the-post-panamax-syndrome-the-challenges-of-the-port-of-cartagena/2/.
59. John Burrow, Philip Cullom, and Michael Dana, "Additive Manufacturing Implementation Plan V2.0," Department of the Navy, May 4, 2017, 4, 8, and 12, https://apps.dtic.mil/sti/pdfs/AD1041527.pdf.
60. Joint Defense Manufacturing Council, Office of the Deputy Director for Strategic Technology Protection and Exploitation, and Office of the Under Secretary of Defense for Research and Engineering, "Department of Defense Additive Manufacturing Strategy," January 2021, 11–12, https://www.cto.mil/wp-content/uploads/2021/01/dod-additive-manufacturing-strategy.pdf.
61. "Banking Is Only the Beginning: 65 Big Industries Blockchain Could Transform," CB Insights, March 9, 2022, https://www.cbinsights.com/research/industries-disrupted-blockchain/.
62. "Banking Is Only the Beginning."
63. Greg Miller, "How Three Chinese Companies Cornered Global Container Production," *Freight Waves*, May 24, 2021, https://www.freightwaves.com/news/how-three-chinese-companies-cornered-global-container-production.
64. There is also a larger fifty-three-foot container, also called High Cube, used primarily for road or rail transport, that is reported to often have latent/unused cargo capacity. The dimensions of these larger, heavier containers make them unfit for international container shipping.
65. "What Are DOT Truck Weight Limits by State?" I.C.E. Global Transport, *Eastern Europe Shipping Blog*, January 24, 2019, https://www.icetransport.com/blog/truck-weight-limits-by-state.
66. "Smart Railroad Giants," BOSCH, n.d., accessed May 29, 2024, https://www.bosch.com/stories/smart-trains/; and Clemens Forst, "Smart Freight Solutions for a Stronger Future," *Global Railway Review*, September 5, 2019, https://www.globalrailwayreview.com/article/82990/smart-freight-solutions-for-a-stronger-future/.
67. Miller, "How Three Chinese Companies."
68. "Shipping during COVID-19: Why Container Freight Rates Have Surged," UN Trade and Development, April 23, 2021, https://unctad.org/news/shipping-during-covid-19-why-container-freight-rates-have-surged.
69. Turkey Yıldız, "Design and Analysis of a Lightweight Composite Shipping Container Made of Carbon Fiber Laminates," MDPI Logistics, July 16, 2019, http://dx.doi.org/10.3390/logistics3030018.
70. "Urban Congestion Trends and Related Reports," U.S. Department of Transportation, Operations Performance Measurement Program, n.d., accessed May 29, 2024, https://ops.fhwa.dot.gov/perf_measurement/reliability_reports.htm.

71. Jim Gorzelany, "These Are the Cities Where Motorists Lose the Most Time and Money Sitting in Traffic," *Forbes*, January 10, 2023, https://www.forbes.com/sites/jimgorzelany/2023/01/10/these-are-the-us-cities-where-motorists-lose-the-most-time-and-money-sitting-in-traffic/.
72. "Navy Successfully Demonstrated Unmanned Cargo Delivery Systems for Ship at Sea," Naval Air Systems Command, December 21, 2022, https://www.navair.navy.mil/news/Navy-successfully-demonstrated-unmanned-cargo-delivery-systems-ship-sea/Wed-12212022-1419.
73. "Rigid Airships and Blimps: Two Structural Approaches to Cargo Transport," ISOPOLAR, December 2, 2019, https://isopolar.com/rigid-airships-and-blimps-two-structural-approaches-to-cargo-transport/.
74. Julia Buckley, "This European Airline Just Ordered a Fleet of Airships," *CTV News*, June 16, 2022, https://www.ctvnews.ca/sci-tech/this-european-airline-just-ordered-a-fleet-of-airships-1.5949747.
75. Peter Lobner, "Lockheed Martin—SkyTug and LMH-1 Hybrid Airships," Lyncean Group, March 8, 2022, accessed May 29, 2024, https://lynceans.org/wp-content/uploads/2021/08/Lockheed-Martin_SkyTug-LMH-1.pdf.
76. "Aeroscraft," AEROS, n.d., accessed October 28, 2024, https://aeroscraft.com/aeroscraft.
77. Andy J. Semotiuk, "Foreign Immigration Could Relieve U.S. Trucker Shortage," *Forbes*, August 31, 2022, https://www.forbes.com/sites/andyjsemotiuk/2022/08/31/foreign-immigration-could-relieve-us-trucker-shortage/.
78. American Trucking Associations, "Economic and Industry Data," n.d., accessed May 29, 2024, https://www.trucking.org/economics-and-industry-data.
79. U.S. Bureau to Labor Statistics, *Occupational Outlook Handbook*, "Heavy and Tracker-Trailer Truck Drivers," last modified September 8, 2022, https://www.bls.gov/ooh/transportation-and-material-moving/heavy-and-tractor-trailer-truck-drivers.htm.
80. Chad Shirley, "The Status of the Highway Trust Fund: 2023 Update," Testimony before the Subcommittee on Highways and Transit Committee on Transportation and Infrastructure U.S. House of Representatives, October 18, 2023, 1, https://www.cbo.gov/system/files/2023-10/59634.pdf.
81. Weapon System Sustainment: Aircraft Mission Capable Goals Were Generally Not Met and Sustainment Costs Varied by Aircraft," Government Accountability Office, GAO-23-106217, November 10, 2022, 255 and 313, https://www.gao.gov/products/gao-23-106217.
82. "Air Freight: A Market Study with Implications for Landlocked Countries," World Bank, 2009, 1 and 3–6, https://documents1.worldbank.org/curated/en/265051468324548129/pdf/517470NWP0tp1210Box342045B01PUBLIC1.pdf.
83. "Comparing the Costs of Rail Shipping vs Truck," RSI Logistics, April 20, 2020, accessed May 29, 2024, https://www.rsilogistics.com/blog/comparing-the-costs-of-rail-shipping-vs-truck/.

84. YardView, "Average Rates for Detention & Demurrage Fees in 2022 for Yard Management," October 3, 2022, https://www.yardview.com/post/average-rates-for-detention-demurrage-fees-in-2022-for-yard-management.
85. Woodrow Bellamy III, "10 eVTOL Development Programs to Watch in 2021," *Avionics International*, February/March 2021, https://interactive.aviationtoday.com/avionicsmagazine/february-march-2021/10-evtol-development-programs-to-watch-in-2021/.
86. "Top 3 Drones You Can Actually Fly in (Weight Capacity, Range & Price)," Hobby Henry, n.d., accessed May 29, 2024, https://hobbyhenry.com/drones-you-can-actually-fly-in/.
87. "How Long Does It Take to Pick up a Container from Port?" Flexport, n.d., November 22, 2022, https://www.flexport.com/help/589-pick-up-container-from-destination/.
88. Margherita Bruno, "Ever Alot Breaks Record for World's Largest Containership," Port Technology International, June 27, 2022, https://www.porttechnology.org/news/ever-alot-breaks-record-for-worlds-largest-containership/.
89. "Global Limit on Sulfur in Ships' Fuel Oil Reduced from 01 January 2020," International Maritime Organization, December 20, 2019, https://www.imo.org/en/MediaCentre/PressBriefings/pages/34-IMO-2020-sulphur-limit-.aspx.
90. Mikal Boe, "Advanced Nuclear Power Could Transform U.S. Maritime Industry," *Maritime Executive*, March 1, 2023, https://maritime-executive.com/editorials/advanced-nuclear-power-could-transform-u-s-maritime-industry.
91. "Nuclear Power in a Clean Energy System," International Energy Agency, May 2019, 2–3, 8–9, 44–45, 84–89, https://iea.blob.core.windows.net/assets/ad5a93ce-3a7f-461d-a441-8a05b7601887/Nuclear_Power_in_a_Clean_Energy_System.pdf.
92. "NRC to Issue Rule Certifying NuScale Small Modular Reactor," press release, NRC Public Affairs, July 29, 2022, https://www.nrc.gov/reading-rm/doc-collections/news/2022/22-029.pdf.
93. "Nuclear for a Changing Energy Sector," TerraPower, 2023, accessed March 13, 2023, https://www.terrapower.com/wp-content/uploads/2023/03/TP_2023_MCFR_Technology-0216.pdf; and "Advanced Manufacturing of Embedded Heat Pipe Nuclear Hybrid Reactor," Los Alamos National Laboratory, n.d., accessed March 13, 2023, https://arpa-e.energy.gov/technologies/projects/advanced-manufacturing-embedded-heat-pipe-nuclear-hybrid-reactor.
94. Bobby Bassham, "An Evaluation of Electric Motors for Ship Propulsion" (thesis, Naval Post Graduate School, Monterey, CA, June 2003), 2, https://core.ac.uk/download/36694766.pdf.
95. Shelby S. Oakley, letter to James Inhofe and Adam Smith, "Arleigh Burke Class Destroyers: Observations on the Navy's Hybrid Electric Drive Program," November 5, 2020, 3 and 5, Government Accountability Office, https://www.gao.gov/assets/gao-21-79r.pdf.

96. Sam LaGrone, "Zumwalt Brings Mix of Challenges, Opportunities to Fleet," *USNI News*, May 23, 2016, https://news.usni.org/2016/05/23/zumwalt_mix_challgnges.
97. Carrier Hampel, "ABB Provides Azipod Drives for Five Italian Cruise Ships," *Electrive*, November 19, 2020, https://www.electrive.com/2020/11/19/abb-provides-azipod-drives-for-five-italian-cruise-ships/.
98. "What Is the Fulbright U.S. Student Program," Fulbright U.S. Student Program, n.d., accessed February 20, 2023, https://us.fulbrightonline.org/about/fulbright-us-student-program; and "About the Fellowship: Program Objective and Benefits," Mike Mansfield Fellowship Program, n.d., accessed February 20, 2023, https://mansfieldfellows.org/about-the-fellowship/.
99. Defense Innovation Unit, n.d., accessed March 19, 2023, https://www.diu.mil/.
100. Brandi Vincent, "Pentagon's Departing DIU Director Reflects on His Legacy—and What's Next," *Fed Scoop*, July 21, 2022, https://fedscoop.com/pentagons-departing-diu-director-reflects-on-his-legacy-and-whats-next/.
101. Jackson Barnett, "The Pentagon Is Failing to Scale Emerging Technology, Senior Leaders Say," *Fed Scoop*, August 7, 2020, https://fedscoop.com/dod-innovation-emerging-technology-acquisition-aspen-security-summit/.
102. Mario Kafouros, Change Wang, Eva Mavroudi, Junjie Hong, and Constantine S. Katsikeas, "Geographic Dispersion and Co-Location in Global R&D Portfolios: Consequences for Firm Performance," Research Policy 47, no. 7 (September 2018): 1243–55, https://doi.org/10.1016/j.respol.2018.04.010.
103. The White House Opportunity and Revitalization Council, n.d., accessed February 20, 2023, https://opportunityzones.hud.gov/thecouncil.
104. "Scale AI, Port of Ponce Partner to Transform FEMA-Designated Disaster Site into a Smart Port Lab," *Business Wire*, February 16, 2023, https://www.businesswire.com/news/home/20230215005967/en/Scale-AI-Port-of-Ponce-Partner-to-Transform-FEMA-Designated-Disaster-Site-into-a-Smart-Port-Lab.
105. Dr. William Roper, public event, "Can Market Bridges Speed to New Naval Fleet Capabilities?" Heritage Foundation, October 28, 2021, https://www.heritage.org/defense/event/can-market-bridges-speed-new-naval-fleet-capabilities.
106. Dakota L. Wood, ed., "2023 Index of Military Strength," Heritage Foundation, October 2022, 332, 339–40, 361–62, 374, and 436–37, https://www.heritage.org/sites/default/files/2022-10/2023_IndexOfUSMilitaryStrength.pdf.
107. Michael Gilday, "Chief of Naval Operations Navigation Plan 2022," Department of the Navy, July 26, 2022, 8, https://media.defense.gov/2022/Jul/26/2003042389/-1/-1/1/NAVIGATION%20PLAN%202022_SIGNED.PDF.
108. Mallory Shelbourne, "Marine Corps, Navy Remain Split over Design, Number of Future Light Amphibious Warship, Divide Risks Stalling Program," *USNI News*, September 14, 2022, https://news.usni.org/2022/09/14/marine-corps-navy-remain-split-over-design-number-of-future-light-amphibious-warship-divide-risks-stalling-program.

109. Alex Davies, "The Marines' Self-Flying Chopper Survives a Three-Year Tour," *Wired*, July 30, 2014, https://www.wired.com/2014/07/kmax-autonomous-helicopter/.
110. Aaron-Matthew Lariosa, "At-Sea Rearming Deemed a 'Main Priority' By SECNAV," *Naval News*, February 2, 2023, https://www.navalnews.com/naval-news/2023/02/at-sea-rearming-deemed-a-main-priority-by-secnav/.
111. Joint Defense Manufacturing Council, et al., "Department of Defense Additive Manufacturing Strategy."
112. Megan Eckstein, "Boeing Demonstrates MQ-25's Utility as Surveillance Drone," *Defense News*, September 16, 2022, https://www.defensenews.com/naval/2022/09/16/boeing-demonstrates-mq-25s-utility-as-surveillance-drone/.
113. John R. Hoehn, "Joint All-Domain Command and Control (JADC2)," Congressional Research Service, *In Focus*, updated January 21, 2022, https://sgp.fas.org/crs/natsec/IF11493.pdf.
114. Ronald O'Rourke, "Navy Large Unmanned Surface and Undersea Vehicles: Background and Issues for Congress," Congressional Research Service, December 21, 2022, 5–7, https://sgp.fas.org/crs/weapons/R45757.pdf.
115. Team Ships Public Affairs, "U.S. Navy Conducts Unmanned Logistics Prototype Trials Aboard USNS Apalachicola," Naval Sea Systems Command, July 29, 2022, https://www.navsea.navy.mil/Media/News/Article/3110266/us-navy-conducts-unmanned-logistics-prototype-trials-aboard-usns-apalachicola/; and "Expeditionary Fast Transport," U.S. Navy, last updated October 13, 2021, https://www.navy.mil/Resources/Fact-Files/Display-FactFiles/Article/2226179/expeditionary-fast-transport-epf/.
116. Blockchains are decentralized registers of transaction data that function like a traditional database but can cheaply encompass a massive network to track the movement of cargo. Blockchains can ease customs processing and security of sensitive or perishable cargo because they operate natively across borders and languages and can use customizable permissions and rules paired with verifiable, immutable data inside smart cargo containers.
117. "A Look Back at the Wright Brothers' First Flight," Space Center Houston, December 18, 2019, https://spacecenter.org/a-look-back-at-the-wright-brothers-first-flight/; and John T. Correll, "Billy Mitchell and the Battleships," *Air & Space Forces Magazine*, July 21, 2021, https://www.airandspaceforces.com/article/billy-mitchell-ostfriesland/.
118. Clayton M. Christensen, *The Innovator's Dilemma: When New Technologies Cause Great Firms to Fail* (Boston: Harvard Business Review Press, 2016), 30.
119. "Manufacturing Sector: Output for All Employed Persons," FRED, n.d., accessed February 13, 2023, https://fred.stlouisfed.org/series/OUTMS.
120. Justin Katz, "Congress Lags in Setting up Its Own 'Future Navy' Panel," *Breaking Defense*, May 10, 2023, https://breakingdefense.com/2023/05/congress-lags-in-setting-up-its-own-future-navy-panel/.

121. The Select Committee on the CCP, About page, n.d., accessed July 18, 2023, https://selectcommitteeontheccp.house.gov/about-committee.
122. Bundesrat Ignazio Cassis, *Maritime Strategy 2023–27*, Swiss Federal Department of Foreign Affairs, June 2, 2023, 8, https://www.eda.admin.ch/content/dam/eda/en/documents/publications/SchweizerischeAussenpolitik/maritime-strategie_EN.pdf.
123. Defense Innovation Unit, n.d., accessed March 5, 2023, https://www.diu.mil/.

CHAPTER 6. A TWENTY-FIRST-CENTURY NAVAL ACT FOR SHIPS, SHIPYARDS, AND SAILORS

1. Arthur Herman, *Freedom's Forge: How American Business Produced Victory in World War II* (New York: Random House, 2012), 334.
2. John Feng, "U.S. Forces Must Not Let China 'Dictate the Terms' in the Pacific: Admiral," *Newsweek*, June 9, 2022, https://www.newsweek.com/china-taiwan-american-military-admiral-philip-davidson-us-indo-pacific-command-1714118.
3. Mallory Shelbourne, "CNO Gilday: Industrial Capacity Largest Barrier to Growing the Fleet," *USNI News*, August 25, 2022, https://news.usni.org/2022/08/25/cno-gilday-industrial-capacity-largest-barrier-to-growing-the-fleet.
4. "Navigating the Navy's Future Featuring Chief of Naval Operations Admiral Michael Gilday," Heritage Foundation, August 25, 2022, video, at 34:00, https://www.heritage.org/defense/event/navigating-the-navys-future-featuring-chief-naval-operations-admiral-michael-gilday.
5. Rep. Mike Gallagher (R-WI) proposed an amendment to the National Defense Authorization Act that would codify the Navy's presence as a naval mission. The secretary of defense objected:

   The Department objects to the House provision because it would dilute the U.S. Navy's focus on combat operations at sea at a time when peer adversaries' rapid military modernization (including naval modernization) and increasingly aggressive foreign policies require a strong emphasis on the development and modernization of U.S. naval forces' tactics, forces, and capabilities for the effective prosecution of naval warfare. DoD believes the proposed language in section 912 does not align with DoD's strategic guidance. DoD's strategic guidance, as well as multiple public statements by DoD leadership, make clear that the U.S. Navy must preserve and extend, and prevent erosion of, DoD's military superiority in all domains, including the maritime and air domain, especially in the Indo-Pacific region. In order to size and shape its forces to maximize combat credibility, especially in the Indo-Pacific region, the U.S. Navy must retain a strong strategic focus on combat operations at sea and effective prosecution of war. Dilution of this focus risks hindering the U.S. Navy's clear focus and ability to develop the tactics, forces, and capabilities necessary to maintain military superiority over peer adversaries, especially the People's Republic of China. DoD urges exclusion of House section 912.

6. Dakota Wood, "2022 Index of U.S. Military Strength," Heritage Foundation, October 2022, 387–422 and 459–82, https://www.heritage.org/sites/default/files/2021-09/2022_IndexOfUSMilitaryStrength.pdf.
7. Mike Gilday, "House Armed Services Committee Holds Hearing on the Fiscal Year 2023 Navy Budget Request," Navy Press Office, May 11, 2022, https://www.navy.mil/Press-Office/Testimony/display-testimony/Article/3029896/house-armed-services-committee-holds-hearing-on-the-fiscal-year-2023-navy-budge/.
8. Mike Gilday, "Chief of Naval Operations Navigation Plan 2022," Department of the Navy, July 26, 2022, 12, https://media.defense.gov/2022/Jul/26/2003042389/-1/-1/1/NAVIGATION%20PLAN%202022_SIGNED.PDF.
9. Megan Eckstein, "Executive Summary to Naval Shipyard Recapitalization and Optimization Plan," *USNI News*, September 12, 2018, https://news.usni.org/2018/09/12/executive-summary-to-naval-shipyard-recapitalization-and-optimization-plan.
10. Bryan Clark, Timothy A. Walton, and Adam Lemon, *Strengthening the U.S. Defense Maritime Industrial Base: A Plan to Improve Maritime Industry's Contribution to National Security*, Center for Strategic and Budgetary Assessments, February 12, 2002, 19, and 22–23, https://csbaonline.org/research/publications/strengthening-the-u.s-defense-maritime-industrial-base-a-plan-to-improve-maritime-industrys-contribution-to-national-security.
11. Diana Maurer, Testimony before the Committee on Readiness and Management Support, Committee on Armed Services, U.S. Senate, "Military Readiness: Improvement in Some Areas, but Sustainment and Other Challenges Persist," Government Accountability Office, May 2, 2023, 3, 7, 9, and 17–21, https://www.gao.gov/assets/gao-23-106673.pdf; and Stenographic Transcript before the Subcommittee on Readiness and Management Support, Committee on Armed Services, U.S. Senate, "To Receive Testimony on the Current Readiness of the Joint Force," May 2, 2023, 19–20, https://www.armed-services.senate.gov/imo/media/doc/23-42_05-02-2023.pdf.
12. Anthony Capaccio, "Nearly 40% of US Attack Submarines Are Out of Commission for Repairs," *Bloomberg*, July 11, 2023, https://www.bloomberg.com/news/articles/2023-07-11/us-navy-attack-submarine-readiness-almost-40-out-of-commission-for-repairs.
13. Maiya Clark, "U.S. Navy Shipyards Desperately Need Revitalization and a Rethink," Heritage Foundation, July 29, 2020, 2–4, https://www.heritage.org/defense/report/us-navy-shipyards-desperately-need-revitalization-and-rethink.
14. Clark, "U.S. Navy Shipyards," 12–14.
15. Daryl Caudle, "U.S. Fleet Forces Commander Adm. Daryl Caudle Discussed Naval Readiness during the Surface Navy Association's National Symposium," January 11, 2023, https://www.c-span.org/video/?525300-3/admiral-daryl-caudle-remarks-naval-readiness.
16. Nick Wilson, "Fincantieri Several Hundred Workers Short, Has Yet to Begin Construction of Second Frigate," *Inside Defense*, January 11, 2024, https://insidedefense.com/share/219970.

17. Mark D. Faram, "Navy Sees Recruiting Challenges on the Horizon," *Navy Times*, November 2, 2018, https://www.navytimes.com/news/your-navy/2018/11/02/navy-sees-recruiting-challenges-on-the-horizon/.
18. Heather Mongilio, "Navy Misses All Recruiting Goals in FY 2023, Raises Goals for FY 2024," *USNI News*, October 11, 2023, https://news.usni.org/2023/10/11/navy-misses-all-recruiting-goals-in-fy-2023-raises-goals-for-fy-2024.
19. Thomas W. Spoehr, "The Administration and Congress Must Act Now to Counter the Worsening Military Recruiting Crisis," *Issue Brief*, no. 5283 July 28, 2022, 5–7, https://www.heritage.org/sites/default/files/2022-07/IB5283.pdf.
20. Lolita C. Baldor, "No Diploma? No Problem! Navy Again Lowers Requirements as It Struggles to Meet Recruitment Goals," Associated Press, January 26, 2024, https://apnews.com/article/navy-recruiting-high-school-diploma-89b9ff047556bc0d5c54fe074410b700.
21. Heather Mongilio, "At-Sea Billet Gaps Rise to 22,000 for E1-E4 Sailors, CNP Says," *USNI News*, January 10, 2024, https://news.usni.org/2024/01/10/at-sea-billet-gaps-rise-to-22000-for-e1-e4-sailors-cnp-says.
22. John Grady, "Attracting Quality Workforce Biggest Issue Facing Shipyards, Experts Tell Congress," *USNI News*, February 8, 2023, https://news.usni.org/2023/02/08/attracting-quality-workforce-biggest-issue-facing-shipyard-experts-tell-congress.
23. SHIPS Act, S.1414, 115th Congress, accessed September 20, 2022, https://www.congress.gov/bill/115th-congress/senate-bill/1414/text; and 12 Carrier Act, H.R. 700, 116th Congress, accessed September 20, 2022, https://www.congress.gov/bill/116th-congress/house-bill/700/text.
24. On assault rifle bans, see Meghan Keneally, "Understanding the 1994 Assault Weapons Ban and Why It Ended," *ABC News*, September 13, 2019, https://abcnews.go.com/US/understanding-1994-assault-weapons-ban-ended/story?id=65546858. On the border wall, see George W. Bush, "Fact Sheet: The Secure Fence Act of 2006," The White House, October 26, 2006, https://georgewbush-whitehouse.archives.gov/news/releases/2006/10/20061026-1.html. On funding for HBCUs, see FUTURE Act, H.R. 5363, 116th Congress, December 19, 2019, https://www.congress.gov/bill/116th-congress/house-bill/5363/text.
25. Mark F. Cancian, "Goldwater-Nichols 2.0," Center for Strategic & International Studies, March 4, 2016, https://www.csis.org/analysis/goldwater-nichols-20; and Charles Nemfakos, Irv Blickstein, Aine Seitz McCarthy, and Jerry M. Sollinger, *The Perfect Storm: The Goldwater-Nichols Act and Its Effect on Navy Acquisition*, Occasional paper prepared for the U.S. Navy (Santa Monica, CA: RAND Corporation, 2010), 45–49, https://www.rand.org/content/dam/rand/pubs/occasional_papers/2010/RAND_OP308.pdf.
26. Shipyard Act of 2021, S.1441, 117th Cong. (2021–2022), https://www.congress.gov/bill/117th-congress/senate-bill/1441/text.

27. Matthew O. Paxton, "Industry Perspectives on Options and Considerations for Achieving a 355-Ship Navy," testimony before Senate Armed Services Committee on Seapower, May 24, 2017, 6–7, https://www.armed-services.senate.gov/imo/media/doc/Paxton_05-24-17.pdf.
28. Matthew Hipple, "20 Years of Naval Trends Guarantee a FY23 Shipbuilding Plan Failure," CIMSEC, May 9, 2022, https://cimsec.org/20-years-of-naval-trends-guarantee-a-fy23-shipbuilding-plan-failure/.
29. Ronald O'Rourke, *Multiyear Procurement (MYP) and Block Buy Contracting in Defense Acquisition: Background and Issues for Congress*, Congressional Research Service, August 24, 2022, 10–11, https://sgp.fas.org/crs/natsec/R41909.pdf.
30. Office of Budget, "Highlights of the Department of the Navy FY 2023 Budget," 2022, https://www.secnav.navy.mil/fmc/fmb/Documents/23pres/DON_Budget_Card.pdf.
31. Office of the Chief of Naval Operations, *Report to Congress on the Annual Long-Range Plan for Construction of Naval Vessels for Fiscal Year 2024*, March 2023, 13, https://www.govexec.com/media/navy_2024_shipbuilding_plan.pdf.
32. Congressional Budget Office, *An Analysis of the Navy's Fiscal Year 2023 Shipbuilding Plan*, November 2022, 3–5, https://www.cbo.gov/system/files/2022-11/58447-shipbuilding.pdf.
33. Walter Nicholson, *Microeconomic Theory: Basic Principles and Extensions* (Fort Worth, TX: Dryden Press, 1998), 702–3.
34. Senate Armed Services Committee, "National Defense Authorization Act for Fiscal Year 2016," Report, section 118, Fleet Replenishment Oiler Program, S.1376, 114–49, November 25, 2015, https://www.congress.gov/congressional-report/114th-congress/senate-report/49/1.
35. David Berger, "Statement of General David H. Berger, Commandant of the Marine Corps, as Delivered to the Senate Armed Services Committee on the Posture of the United States Marine Corps," June 22, 2021, https://www.armed-services.senate.gov/hearings/the-posture-of-the-department-of-the-navy-in-review-of-the-defense-authorization-request-for-fiscal-year-2022-and-the-future-years-defense-program; and Frederick Stefany, James W. Kilby, and Eric M. Smith, "Statements before the Subcommittee on Seapower and Projection Forces of the House Armed Services Committee on the Department of the Navy Fiscal Year 2022 Budget Request for Seapower and Projection Forces," June 17, 2021, https://armedservices.house.gov/hearings?ID=AD6EBC91-3BCB-4BCF-A00E-3DEBAE4FF5BB.
36. Ronald O'Rourke, *Navy Ford (CVN-78) Class Aircraft Carrier Program: Background and Issues for Congress*, Congressional Research Service, August 26, 2022, 7 and 34–37, https://sgp.fas.org/crs/weapons/RS20643.pdf.
37. Ronald O'Rourke, "Multiyear Procurement (MYP) and Block Buy Contracting in Defense Acquisition: Background and Issues for Congress," Congressional Research Service, December 20, 2023, 14–15, https://sgp.fas.org/crs/natsec/R41909.pdf.

NOTES TO PAGES 183–191   301

38. O'Rourke, "Multiyear Procurement," August 24, 2022, 10.
39. Diana Maurer, "Navy Maintenance: Navy Report Did Not Fully Address Causes of Delays or Results-Oriented Elements," Government Accountability Office, October 2020, 4–8, https://www.gao.gov/assets/gao-21-66.pdf.
40. 10 USC 2218a, National Sea-Based Deterrence Fund, text includes those laws in effect on September 19, 2022, accessed September 20, 2022, https://uscode.house.gov/view.xhtml?req=(title:10%20section:2218a%20edition:prelim).

CHAPTER 7. A MARITIME DEPARTMENT

1. David Vergun, "Low Supply, Old Ships Put Sealift at Risk, DOD Officials Say," U.S. Department of Defense, March 12, 2020, https://www.defense.gov/News/News-Stories/Article/Article/2110444/low-supply-old-ships-put-sealift-at-risk-dod-officials-say/.
2. United Nations, *Review of Maritime Transport 2023: Towards a Green and Just Transition*, chap. 2, "World Shipping: Fleet, Services, and Freight Rates" (New York: United Nations Publications, 2023), 33–34, https://unctad.org/system/files/official-document/rmt2023ch2_en.pdf.
3. Bureau of Transportation Statistics, "On National Maritime Day and Every Day, U.S. Economy Relies on Waterborne Shipping," U.S. Department of Transportation, May 12, 2021, https://www.bts.gov/data-spotlight/national-maritime-day-and-every-day-us-economy-relies-waterborne-shipping.
4. Bureau of Transportation Statistics, "Number and Size of the U.S. Flag Merchant Fleet and Its Share of the World Fleet," U.S. Department of Transportation, n.d., accessed December 2, 2023, https://www.bts.gov/content/number-and-size-us-flag-merchant-fleet-and-its-share-world-fleet.
5. David S. Hilzenrath, "Supply Transfers Reflect '91 Experience," *Washington Post*, April 5, 2003, https://www.washingtonpost.com/archive/politics/2003/04/05/supply-transfers-reflect-91-experience/44da446b-3e43-4529-92fb-c9934b03a46f/.
6. Paul Dans and Steven Groves, eds., *Mandate for Leadership: The Conservative Promise*, foreword by Kevin Roberts (Washington, DC: Heritage Foundation, 2023), 110, 133, 155, 637, and 674, https://static.project2025.org/2025_MandateForLeadership_FULL.pdf.
7. *Federal Maritime Commission FY2024 Budget Justification*, March 2023, 3 and 6, https://www.fmc.gov/wp-content/uploads/2023/03/FMCFY2024CongressionalBudgetJustification.pdf.
8. "Report: Complaints to FMC Over Shipping Industry Tripled in Two Years," *Maritime Executive*, October 23, 2023, https://maritime-executive.com/article/report-complaints-to-fmc-over-shipping-industry-tripled-in-two-years; and "Score One for Carriers, HMM Wins FMC Service Complaint from US Importer," *Maritime Executive*, November 29, 2023, https://maritime-executive.com/article/score-one-for-carriers-hmm-wins-fmc-service-complaint.

9. John Gallagher, "FMC Needs More Staff to Enforce Ocean Shipping Reforms, Official Says," *Freight Waves*, July 26, 2022, https://www.freightwaves.com/news/fmc-needs-more-staff-to-enforce-ocean-shipping-reforms-official-says.
10. *Federal Maritime Commission FY2023 Budget Justification*, March 2022, 6, 14, and 17, https://www.fmc.gov/wp-content/uploads/2022/03/Federal-Maritime-Commission-CONG23-Budget-Submission.pdf; and *Federal Maritime Commission FY2024 Budget Justification*, 5–7.
11. Heather Krause, *FAA Workforce: Better Assessing Employees' Skill Gaps Could Help FAA Prepare for Changes in Technology* (Washington, DC: Government Accountability Office, May 2021), 1, https://www.gao.gov/assets/gao-21-310.pdf; and "MARAD at a Glance," Maritime Administration, last updated March 23, 2022, accessed December 3, 2023, https://www.maritime.dot.gov/about-us.
12. Statement of Ann C. Phillips, Maritime Administrator, Maritime Administration, U.S. Department of Transportation, before the Committee on Transportation and Infrastructure Subcommittee on Coast Guard and Maritime Transportation, "Assessing the Shortage of United States Mariners and Recruitment and Retention in the United States Coast Guard," May 11, 2023, https://www.transportation.gov/assessing-shortage-united-states-mariners-and-recruitment-and-retention-united-states-coast-guard.
13. "About Our Agency," NOAA, last updated March 2, 2023, accessed December 3, 2023, https://www.noaa.gov/about-our-agency.
14. Gina M. Raimondo, *The Department of Commerce Budget in Brief Fiscal Year 2024*, Department of Commerce, March 2023, 3 and 190, https://www.commerce.gov/sites/default/files/2023-03/FY2024-BIB-Introduction.pdf.
15. Lisa Murkowski, "NOAA: A Fish Out of Water in US Commerce Department," May 1, 2012, https://www.murkowski.senate.gov/press/op-ed/op-ed-noaa-a-fish-out-of-water-in-us-commerce-department.
16. United States Coast Guard, Department of Homeland Security, "Missions," n.d., accessed October 6, 2023, https://www.uscg.mil/About/Missions/.
17. "Department in Which the Coast Guard Operates," 14 USC § 103 (2018), https://www.law.cornell.edu/uscode/text/14/103.
18. "Organizational Overview," United States Coast Guard, n.d., accessed December 3, 2023, https://www.uscg.mil/About/.
19. "U.S. Coast Guard Office of Search and Rescue (CG-SAR)," United States Coast Guard, n.d., accessed December 3, 2023, https://www.dco.uscg.mil/Our-Organization/Assistant-Commandant-for-Response-Policy-CG-5R/Office-of-Incident-Management-Preparedness-CG-5RI/US-Coast-Guard-Office-of-Search-and-Rescue-CG-SAR/.
20. Ronald O'Rourke, "Coast Guard Cutter Procurement: Background and Issues for Congress," Congressional Research Service, updated July 10, 2023, 4, 17–18, and 20, accessed December 3, 2023, https://s3.documentcloud.org/documents/23870593

/coast-guard-cutter-procurement-background-and-issues-for-congress-july-10-2023.pdf.

21. According to the FY2023 DHS budget brief, there were 252,000 personnel in the department with 79,431 total personnel in the USCG: *FY 2023 Budget in Brief*, U.S. Department of Homeland Security, 1, 9, and 48, https://www.dhs.gov/sites/default/files/2022-03/22-%201835%20-%20FY%202023%20Budget%20in%20Brief%20FINAL%20with%20Cover_Remediated.pdf.

22. Craig Hooper, "Personnel Shortage at U.S. Coast Guard Sinks 10 Cutters, 29 Stations," *Forbes*, November 2, 2023, https://www.forbes.com/sites/craighooper/2023/11/02/personnel-shortage-at-us-coast-guard-sinks-10-cutters-29-stations/?sh=3778556e648c.

23. Kevin Roberts, Foreword to *Winning the New Cold War: A Plan for Countering China*, edited by James J. Carafano, Michael Pillsbury, Jeff M. Smith, and Andrew J. Harding (Washington, DC: Heritage Foundation, 2023), 1–4, https://www.heritage.org/sites/default/files/2023-07/SR270.pdf.

24. Executive Office of the President of the United States, "Delivering Government Solutions in the 21st Century," 5 and 9–10, n.d., accessed November 14, 2023, https://trumpadministration.archives.performance.gov/GovReform/Reform-and-Reorg-Plan-Final.pdf.

25. "It is necessary for the national defense and for the proper growth of its foreign and domestic commerce that the United States shall have a merchant marine of the best equipped and most suitable types of vessels sufficient to carry the greater portion of its commerce and serve as a naval or military auxiliary in time of war or national emergency." Merchant Marine Act of 1920, June 5, 1920, 46 USC chap. 24, sec. 861.

26. *FY 2023 Budget in Brief*, 1 and 48.

27. Pete Buttigieg, *Budget Highlights 2023*, U.S. Department of Transportation, March 2022, 1–3, https://www.transportation.gov/sites/dot.gov/files/2022-03/Budget_Highlights_FY2023.pdf; and "U.S. Department of Transportation Administrations," Department of Transportation, updated August 23, 2021, accessed November 15, 2023, https://www.transportation.gov/administrations.

28. "Fact Sheet: The Bipartisan Infrastructure Deal," The White House, November 6, 2021, https://www.whitehouse.gov/briefing-room/statements-releases/2021/11/06/fact-sheet-the-bipartisan-infrastructure-deal/; and "Biden-Harris Administration Invests More Than $653 Million in Ports to Strengthen American Supply Chains," Department of Transportation, Maritime Administration, November 3, 2023, https://www.maritime.dot.gov/newsroom/biden-harris-administration-invests-more-653-million-ports-strengthen-american-supply.

29. James Di Pane, "U.S. Coast Guard Readiness Will Help to Deter China and Other Threats: Congress Should Fund Select Items on Unfunded Priority List," *Issue Brief*, no. 5314, May 25, 2023, 1, https://www.heritage.org/sites/default/files/2023-05/IB5314.pdf.

30. 10 USC § 2218—National Defense Sealift Fund, https://www.law.cornell.edu/uscode/text/10/2218; and "National Defense Authorization Act Fiscal Year 2019," H.R. 5515, section 1012, "Purchase of Vessels Using Funds in the National Defense Sealift Fund," https://www.congress.gov/115/bills/hr5515/BILLS-115hr5515enr.pdf.
31. Ben Werner, "Wittman Pushing Navy to Buy Used Cargo Ships," *USNI News*, March 10, 2020, https://news.usni.org/2020/03/10/wittman-pushing-navy-to-buy-used-cargo-ships.
32. United States Senate Committee on Armed Services, "Fiscal Year 2024 National Defense Authorization Act Executive Summary," June 2023, 24, https://www.armed-services.senate.gov/imo/media/doc/fy2024_ndaa_executive_summary.pdf.
33. U.S. Department of Transportation and the Maritime Administration, *Goals and Objectives for a Stronger Maritime Nation: A Report to Congress*, February 2020, https://www.maritime.dot.gov/sites/marad.dot.gov/files/docs/outreach/policy-papers-and-fact-sheets/12561/national-maritime-strategy.pdf.
34. *National Maritime Strategy: DOT Is Taking Steps to Obtain Interagency Input and Finalize Strategy*, Government Accountability Office Report to Congressional Committees, January 2020, 2–3, 9–10, 13–14, and 16–20, https://www.gao.gov/assets/gao-20-178.pdf.
35. U.S. Customs and Border Protection, "CBP Enforcement Statistics," Department of Homeland Security, last modified November 14, 2023, accessed December 3, 2023, https://www.cbp.gov/newsroom/stats/cbp-enforcement-statistics.
36. "U.S. Department of Transportation Announces First Ships Enrolled in the Tanker Security Program," Maritime Administration, July 25, 2023, https://www.transportation.gov/briefing-room/us-department-transportation-announces-first-ships-enrolled-tanker-security-program; and Bureau of Transportation Statistics, "Number and Size of the U.S. Flag Merchant Fleet," Table 1-24.
37. Dans and Groves, *Mandate for Leadership*, 133–34 and 155–57.
38. Andrew Gibson and Arthur Donovan, *The Abandoned Ocean: A History of United States Maritime Policy* (Columbia: University of South Carolina Press, 2000), 172–73.
39. Gibson and Donovan, *The Abandoned Ocean*, 173.
40. Gallagher, "FMC Needs More Staff."
41. Gibson and Donovan, *The Abandoned Ocean*, 195.
42. Maritime Administration, "Organization Chart," U.S. Department of Transportation, last updated August 2, 2017, accessed October 6, 2023, https://www.transportation.gov/org-chart.
43. U.S. Committee on the Marine Transportation System, "Background," n.d., accessed October 5, 2023, https://www.cmts.gov/about-us/.
44. Jimmy Drennan, "Beyond Defense: America's Past and Future Interests at Sea," CIMSEC, October 25, 2021, https://cimsec.org/beyond-defense-americas-past-and-future-interests-at-sea/.

45. Military Sealift Command, "About MSC," U.S. Navy, n.d., accessed October 6, 2023, https://sealiftcommand.com/about-msc.
46. U.S. Army Transportation Corps, "Maritime Qualifications Division," n.d., accessed October 6, 2023, https://transportation.army.mil/MQD/index.html; and U.S. Army, *Army Intratheater Watercraft Systems*, Army Regulation 56–9, 1–2, October 2, 2020, https://armypubs.army.mil/epubs/DR_pubs/DR_a/ARN30488-AR_56-9-000-WEB-1.pdf.
47. U.S. Department of State, Office of Ocean and Polar Affairs, "Limits in the Seas," n.d., accessed October 6, 2023, https://www.state.gov/limits-in-the-seas/.
48. White House, *National Security Directive 28*, October 5, 1989, 1, https://irp.fas.org/offdocs/nsd/nsd28.pdf.
49. Briefing Room, "President Biden Announces Kurt Campbell as Nominee for Deputy Secretary of State, Department of State," The White House, November 1, 2023, https://www.whitehouse.gov/briefing-room/statements-releases/2023/11/01/president-biden-announces-kurt-campbell-as-nominee-for-deputy-secretary-of-state-department-of-state/.

CHAPTER 8. A NATIONAL SECURITY COUNCIL FOR A NEW COLD WAR

1. National Security Act of 1947 (chap. 343; 61 Stat. 496; approved July 26, 1947) [as amended through Pub. L. 118–31, enacted December 22, 2023], sec. 101, 104, and 201, https://www.govinfo.gov/content/pkg/COMPS-1493/pdf/COMPS-1493.pdf.
2. David Rothkopf, *Running the World: The Inside Story of the National Security Council and the Architects of American Power* (New York: Public Affairs, 2004), xvi.
3. Daniel Lippman, Nahal Toosi, and Quint Forgey, "Biden's Beefed-Up NSC," *Politico*, August 2, 2021, https://www.politico.com/newsletters/national-security-daily/2021/08/02/bidens-beefed-up-nsc-493813.
4. *The 9/11 Commission Report*, July 22, 2004, 399–428, quote at 399, https://govinfo.library.unt.edu/911/report/911Report.pdf.
5. "China," Gallup, n.d., accessed February 25, 2024, https://news.gallup.com/poll/1627/china.aspx.
6. Wolf Blitzer, "Republicans Hammer Gore over U.S. Policy toward China," *CNN*, March 10, 1999, https://www.cnn.com/ALLPOLITICS/stories/1999/03/10/president.2000/gore.china/.
7. National Defense Authorization Act for Fiscal Year 2000, Pub. L. 106-65, 106th Congress, October 5, 1999, sec. 1202, https://www.govinfo.gov/content/pkg/PLAW-106publ65/html/PLAW-106publ65.htm.
8. "2022 Report to Congress on China's WTO Compliance," U.S. Trade Representative, February 2023, 2, https://ustr.gov/sites/default/files/2023-02/2022%20USTR%20Report%20to%20Congress%20on%20China's%20WTO%20Compliance%20-%20Final.pdf.

9. Charley Keyes, "Obama Unveils Plans for Pared-Down Military," *CNN*, January 5, 2012, https://www.cnn.com/2012/01/05/politics/pentagon-strategy-shift/index.html.
10. Kali Robinson and Will Merrow, "The Arab Spring at Ten Years: What's the Legacy of the Uprisings?" Council on Foreign Relations, December 3, 2020, https://www.cfr.org/article/arab-spring-ten-years-whats-legacy-uprisings.
11. "Remarks by President Obama and President Xi of the People's Republic of China in Joint Press Conference," The White House, September 25, 2015, https://obamawhitehouse.archives.gov/the-press-office/2015/09/25/remarks-president-obama-and-president-xi-peoples-republic-china-joint.
12. Bob Work, "Remarks by Deputy Secretary Work on Third Offset Strategy," U.S. Department of Defense, April 28, 2016, https://www.defense.gov/News/Speeches/Speech/Article/753482/remarks-by-deputy-secretary-work-on-third-offset-strategy/.
13. "A Constructive Year for Chinese Base Building," Asia Maritime Transparency Initiative, December 14, 2017, https://amti.csis.org/constructive-year-chinese-building/.
14. "U.S. Strategic Framework for the Indo-Pacific," Trump White House Archives, December 31, 2017, https://trumpwhitehouse.archives.gov/wp-content/uploads/2021/01/IPS-Final-Declass.pdf.
15. Joseph Biden, "National Security Strategy," The White House, October 2022, 22, https://www.whitehouse.gov/wp-content/uploads/2022/10/Biden-Harris-Administrations-National-Security-Strategy-10.2022.pdf.
16. Cathleen D. Cimino-Issacs, Kyla H. Kitamura, and Mark E. Manyin, "Indo-Pacific Economic Framework for Prosperity (IPEF)," Congressional Research Service, *In Focus*, December 14, 2023, accessed February 25, 2024, https://crsreports.congress.gov/product/pdf/IF/IF12373; and "FACT SHEET: In Asia, President Biden and a Dozen Indo-Pacific Partners Launch the Indo-Pacific Economic Framework for Prosperity," The White House, May 23, 2022, https://www.whitehouse.gov/briefing-room/statements-releases/2022/05/23/fact-sheet-in-asia-president-biden-and-a-dozen-indo-pacific-partners-launch-the-indo-pacific-economic-framework-for-prosperity/.
17. "Memorandum on Renewing the National Security Council System," The White House, February 4, 2021, https://www.whitehouse.gov/briefing-room/statements-releases/2021/02/04/memorandum-renewing-the-national-security-council-system/.
18. Rothkopf, *Running the World*, 457–59.
19. Jon Gans, *White House Warriors: How the National Security Council Transformed the American Way of War* (New York: Liveright, 2019), 57–60.
20. Rothkopf, *Running the World*, 172 and 206–7.
21. National Security Act of 1947, sec. 101, 7–8.
22. I. M. Destler and Ivo H. Daalder, "A New NSC for a New Administration," Policy Brief #68, Brookings Institution, November 15, 2000, https://www.brookings.edu/articles/a-new-nsc-for-a-new-administration/.

23. Alexander Bobroske, "Reforming the National Security Council," American Action Forum, December 21, 2016, https://www.americanactionforum.org/research/reforming-national-security-council/.
24. Susan Rice, "Reflecting on the National Security Council's Greatest Asset: Its People," The White House, January 17, 2017, https://obamawhitehouse.archives.gov/blog/2017/01/17/reflecting-nscs-greatest-asset-its-people-0.
25. Thomas Carothers, *Democracy Policy under Obama: Revitalization or Retreat?* (Washington, DC: Carnegie Endowment for International Peace, 2012), 10 and 32–33, https://carnegieendowment.org/files/democracy_under_obama.pdf.
26. Goldwater–Nichols Department of Defense Reorganization Act of 1986, Pub. L. 99-433, October 1, 1986, sec. 603, https://history.defense.gov/Portals/70/Documents/dod_reforms/Goldwater-NicholsDoDReordAct1986.pdf.
27. James Carafano, Michael Pillsbury, Jeff Smith, and Andrew Harding, "Winning the New Cold War: A Plan for Countering China," Heritage Foundation, March 28, 2023, 30–31, 45–46, 62–64, 73–75, and 92–94, https://www.heritage.org/asia/report/winning-the-new-cold-war-plan-countering-china.
28. "National Economic Council," The White House, n.d., accessed March 7, 2024, https://www.whitehouse.gov/nec/.
29. Rothkopf, *Running the World*, 218–19.
30. Anthony Wanis-St. John, "The National Security Council: Tool of Presidential Crisis Management," *Journal of Public and International Affairs* 9, no. 1 (1998): 105–8, https://www.american.edu/sis/faculty/upload/wanis-national-security-council.pdf.
31. "U.S. Strategic Framework for the Indo-Pacific."
32. John W. Rollins, "The National Security Council: Background and Issues for Congress," Congressional Research Service, updated October 19, 2022, 7–8, accessed March 9, 2024, https://sgp.fas.org/crs/natsec/R44828.pdf.
33. Gordon Lederman, "National Security Reform for the Twenty-First Century: A New National Security Act and Reflections on Legislation's Role in Organizational Change," *Journal of National Security Law & Policy* 3, no. 363 (2009): 363–64, 367, and 370, https://jnslp.com/wp-content/uploads/2010/08/08_Lederman-Master-12-14-09.pdf.
34. "About Project 2025," n.d., accessed March 9, 2024, https://www.project2025.org/about/about-project-2025/.

CHAPTER 9. A FLEET STRUCTURE FOR GREAT POWER RIVALRY

1. National Defense Authorization Act for Fiscal Year 2023, H.R. 7776, 117th Cong. (2022), sec. 913, "Clarification of Peacetime Functions of the Navy," https://www.congress.gov/117/bills/hr7776/BILLS-117hr7776enr.pdf.
2. See note 4 for a discussion of "rules-based order."
3. Cristina L. Garafola, Stephen Watts, and Kristin J. Leuschner, *China's Global Basing Ambitions*, RAND Arroyo Center, December 8, 2022, 8–9, 11, and 23–24, https://www.rand.org/pubs/research_reports/RRA1496-1.html.

4. "Rules-based order" has been used by several U.S. administrations to roughly equate to a body of international laws and standards encapsulated in the United Nations Charter. In the context of this chapter, the rules-based order particularly deals with issues of sovereignty, military use, trade, commerce, and technical standard–setting governing these issues. See Ben Scott, "But What Does 'Rules-Based Order' Mean?" *Interpreter*, November 2, 2020, https://www.lowyinstitute.org/the-interpreter/what-does-rules-based-order-mean.
5. Didi Kirsten Tatlow, "China Outshines U.S. as Global Scramble for Bases Heats Up," *Newsweek*, December 29, 2022, https://www.newsweek.com/2023/01/13/china-outshines-us-south-pacific-global-scramble-bases-heats-1769150.html.
6. *Military and Security Developments involving the People's Republic of China 2022*, Department of Defense Annual Report to Congress, November 29, 2022, 133, 136, 138–39, and 143–45, https://media.defense.gov/2022/Nov/29/2003122279/-1/-1/1/2022-MILITARY-AND-SECURITY-DEVELOPMENTS-INVOLVING-THE-PEOPLES-REPUBLIC-OF-CHINA.PDF.
7. Julian S. Corbett, *Some Principles of Maritime Strategy* (1911; repr. Annapolis, MD: Naval Institute Press, 1988), 107–52.
8. Joshua Taylor, "A Campaign Plan for the South China Sea," U.S. Naval Institute *Proceedings* 148/8/1,434 (August 2022), https://www.usni.org/magazines/proceedings/2022/august/campaign-plan-south-china-sea.
9. WEST Conference, "Luncheon Town Hall," U.S. Naval Institute, *YouTube*, 1 hr. 36 min., February 18, 2022, https://www.youtube.com/watch?v=TKNONiSLn6w; and Michael Gilday, *Chief of Naval Operations Navigation Plan 2022*, July 26, 2022, 1 and 14, https://media.defense.gov/2022/Jul/26/2003042389/-1/-1/1/NAVIGATION%20PLAN%202022_SIGNED.PDF.
10. Hunter Stires, "The South China Sea Needs a 'COIN' Toss," U.S. Naval Institute *Proceedings*, May 2019, https://www.usni.org/magazines/proceedings/2019/may/south-china-sea-needs-coin-toss.
11. "Navy Reestablishes U.S. 4th Fleet," *CHIPS Magazine*, July–September 2008, https://www.doncio.navy.mil/Chips/ArticleDetails.aspx?ID=2767; and Sam LaGrone, "New 2nd Fleet Boundary Will Extend North to the Edge of Russian Waters," *USNI News*, August 24, 2018, https://news.usni.org/2018/08/24/cno-new-2nd-fleet-boundary-will-extend-north-edge-russian-waters.
12. Megan Eckstein, "SECNAV Braithwaite Calls for New U.S. 1st Fleet near Indian, Pacific Oceans," *USNI News*, November 17, 2020, https://news.usni.org/2020/11/17/secnav-braithwaite-calls-for-new-u-s-1st-fleet-near-indian-pacific-oceans.
13. *2022 National Defense Strategy of the United States of America: Including the 2022 Nuclear Posture Review and the 2022 Missile Defense Review*, October 27, 2022, 8–13, https://media.defense.gov/2022/Oct/27/2003103845/-1/-1/1/2022-NATIONAL-DEFENSE-STRATEGY-NPR-MDR.PDF.
14. Elbridge A. Colby, *The Strategy of Denial: American Defense in an Age of Great Power Conflict* (New Haven, CT: Yale University Press, 2021), 178–86.

15. U.S. Department of Defense, Joint Chiefs of Staff, *Deployment and Redeployment Operations*, Joint Publication 3-35, January 10, 2018, I-4 and I-5.
16. Eric Edelman and Gary Roughead, co-chairs, *Providing for the Common Defense: The Assessment and Recommendations of the National Defense Strategy Commission*, National Defense Strategy Commission, November 13, 2018, vii–viii, ix, 21–23, and 33–34, https://www.usip.org/publications/2018/11/providing-common-defense; and Mallory Shelbourne, "House Lawmakers Want Pentagon to Rethink Global Force Deployments," *USNI News*, April 5, 2021, https://news.usni.org/2021/04/05/house-lawmakers-want-pentagon-to-rethink-global-force-deployments.
17. "Executive Summary: 2016 Navy Force Structure Assessment (FSA)," December 14, 2016, https://news.usni.org/wp-content/uploads/2016/12/FSA_Executive-Summary.pdf.
18. Jeffrey Becker, "China Maritime Report No. 11: Securing China's Lifelines across the Indian Ocean," CMSI *China Maritime Reports*, no. 11 (December 2020): 5–10, https://digital-commons.usnwc.edu/cgi/viewcontent.cgi?article=1010&context=cmsi-maritime-reports.
19. Andrew Feickert, "The Unified Command Plan and Combatant Commands: Background and Issues for Congress," Congressional Research Service, updated January 3, 2013, 5, https://crsreports.congress.gov/product/pdf/R/R42077/11.
20. Feickert, "The Unified Command Plan," 4–7.
21. Paul McLeary, "Eye on Africa, Navy's New Ship Homeports in Crete," *Breaking Defense*, October 2, 2020, https://breakingdefense.com/2020/10/eye-on-africa-navys-new-ship-homeports-in-crete/; Fred Gray IV, "USS Hershel 'Woody' Williams Completes Gulf of Guinea Maritime Security Patrol," Navy Press Office, April 20, 2022, https://www.navy.mil/Press-Office/News-Stories/Article/3004507/uss-hershel-woody-williams-completes-gulf-of-guinea-maritime-security-patrol/; and "Obangame Express," U.S. Africa Command, n.d., accessed January 2, 2023, https://www.africom.mil/what-we-do/exercises/obangame-express.
22. Geoff Ziezulewicz, "Could the LCS Fleet Be Getting a New Mission?" *Navy Times*, December 27, 2023, https://www.navytimes.com/news/your-navy/2022/12/27/could-the-lcs-fleet-be-getting-a-new-mission/.
23. Chris Krucke, "USNS Millinocket and Embarked 7th Fleet Staff Pulls into Kota Kinabalu," U.S. Indo-Pacific Command, May 21, 2018, https://www.pacom.mil/Media/News/News-Article-View/Article/1527569/usns-millinocket-and-embarked-7th-fleet-staff-pulls-into-kota-kinabalu/; and Mohammad Issa, "LCS Returns to Singapore," Navy Press Office, May 3, 2022, https://www.navy.mil/Press-Office/News-Stories/Article/3018824/lcs-returns-to-singapore/.
24. Commander, Logistics Group Western Pacific, "Mission Statement," n.d., accessed January 2, 2023, https://www.clwp.navy.mil/Mission/.
25. Title 10 USC 526a: Renumbered §526, "Authorized Strength after December 31, 2022: General Officers and Flag Officers on Active Duty," accessed January 2,

2023, https://uscode.house.gov/view.xhtml?req=granuleid:USC-prelim-title10-section526a&num=0&edition=prelim; and "(Active Duty) Flag Office Biographies," U.S. Navy, n.d., accessed January 2, 2023, https://www.navy.mil/Leadership/Flag-Officer-Biographies/Customstatus/6000/.

26. Roland Franklin, "U.S. 5th Fleet Launches New Task Force to Integrate Unmanned Systems," U.S. Naval Forces Central Command, U.S. 5th Fleet, September 9, 2021, https://www.cusnc.navy.mil/Media/News/Display/Article/2768468/us-5th-fleet-launches-new-task-force-to-integrate-unmanned-systems/.

27. Mallory Shelbourne and Sam LaGrone, "Navy Will Stand Up Lethal Drone Unit Later This Year, First Replicator USVs Picked," *USNI News*, February 14, 2024, https://news.usni.org/2024/02/14/navy-will-stand-up-lethal-drone-unit-later-this-year-first-replicator-usvs-picked.

28. Justin Katz, "With UNITAS, Navy Expands Operational Unmanned Tech to 4th Fleet in SOUTHCOM," *Breaking Defense*, July 21, 2023, https://breakingdefense.com/2023/07/with-unitas-navy-expands-operational-unmanned-tech-to-4th-fleet-in-southcom/.

29. Brent D. Sadler, James DiPane, and Chad Wolf, "Securing U.S. Maritime Rights in Our Unguarded Waters," *Backgrounder*, no. 3692, March 14, 2022, 6, https://www.heritage.org/sites/default/files/2022-03/BG3692.pdf.

CONCLUSION

1. George S. Patton, *War as I Knew It* (New York: Houghton Mifflin, 1947), 354.
2. As of May 2024, there is not much in the inactive fleet to recall to service. Focusing instead on retaining ships on the Navy's list for deactivation with more than three years of life would add thirteen warships to the fleet through 2027. Furthermore, the fleet could grow a little more with the addition of twenty-one deployable unmanned (LUSV, MUSV, XLUUV) vessels. This would deliver a fleet of 331 warships by 2027 well ahead of the Navy's long-range plans. However, this would still be short of the official 355-ship fleet goal set since the 2016 Force Structure Assessment and memorialized by Congress in law (NDAA FY18 sec. 1025).
3. "The USS Cole is slowly lifted from the water by the Norwegian heavy transport ship M/V Blue Marlin off the coast of Aden, Yemen," U.S. Department of Defense, n.d., accessed February 21, 2024, https://www.defense.gov/Multimedia/Photos/igphoto/2002018917/.
4. "Austal USA Starts Construction on Navy Drydock," Austal, June 12, 2023, https://usa.austal.com/news/AFDM.
5. Liu Zhen, "Chinese Navy Shows New Heavy-Lift Ship Carrier, Revealing Future Role in Wartime Transport and Vessel Rescue," *South China Morning Post*, January 6, 2023, https://www.scmp.com/news/china/military/article/3205802/chinese-navy-shows-new-heavy-lift-ship-carrier-revealing-future-role-wartime-transport-and-vessel?campaign=3205802&module=perpetual_scroll_0&pgtype=article.

SELECTED BIBLIOGRAPHY

BOOKS

Colby, Elbridge A. *The Strategy of Denial: American Defense in an Age of Great Power Conflict.* New Haven, CT: Yale University Press, 2021.

Doshi, Rush. *The Long Game: China's Grand Strategy to Displace American Order.* New York: Oxford University Press, 2021.

Gibson, Andrew, and Arthur Donovan. *The Abandoned Ocean: A History of United States Maritime Policy.* Columbia: University of South Carolina, 2000.

Heinrich, Thomas. *Warship Builders: An Industrial History of U.S. Naval Shipbuilding 1922–1945.* Annapolis, MD: Naval Institute Press, 2020.

Herman, Arthur. *Freedom's Forge: How American Business Produced Victory in World War II.* New York: Random House, 2012.

Land, Emory S. *Winning the War with Ships.* New York: Robert M. McBride Company, 1958.

Nofi, Albert A. *To Train the Fleet for War: The U.S. Navy Fleet Problems, 1923–1940.* Newport, RI: Naval War College Press, 2010.

Notteboom, Theo, Athanasios Pallis, and Jean-Paul Rodrique. *Port Economics, Management and Policy.* New York: Routledge, 2022.

Pillsbury, Michael. *The Hundred-Year Marathon: China's Secret Strategy to Replace America as the Global Superpower.* New York: Holt, 2015.

Rothkopf, David. *Running the World: The Inside Story of the National Security Council and the Architects of American Power.* New York: Public Affairs, 2004.

Sadler, Brent Droste. *U.S. Naval Power in the 21st Century: A New Strategy for Facing the Chinese and Russian Threat.* Annapolis, MD: Naval Institute Press, 2023.

MONOGRAPHS, CASE STUDIES, AND REPORTS

Asia Maritime Transparency Initiative. Center for Strategic and International Studies. Accessed August 2, 2022. https://amti.csis.org.

DoD USS *Cole* Commission. *USS COLE Commission Report.* Washington, DC: U.S. Department of Defense, January 9, 2001. https://irp.fas.org/threat/cole.pdf.

International Institute for Strategic Studies. *The Military Balance 2021.* New York: Routledge, 2021. https://www.iiss.org/publications/the-military-balance/the-military-balance-2021/.

Maurer, Diana. "Weapon System Sustainment Aircraft Mission Capable Goals Were Generally Not Met and Sustainment Costs Varied by Aircraft." Washington, DC:

Government Accountability Office, November 10, 2022. https://www.gao.gov/products/gao-23-106217.
Office of the Secretary of Defense. *Military and Security Developments involving the People's Republic of China 2021*, Annual Report to Congress. https://media.defense.gov/2021/Nov/03/2002885874/-1/-1/0/2021-CMPR-FINAL.PDF.
Wooley, Alexander, Sheng Zhang, Rory Fedorochko, and Sarina Patterson. *Harboring Global Ambitions: China's Ports Footprint and Implications for Future Overseas Naval Bases*. Williamsburg, VA: AidData at William & Mary, 2023. Accessed May 19, 2024. https://www.aiddata.org/harboring-global-ambitions.

INTERVIEWS AND CORRESPONDENCE

Barker, Mark W., President, Interlake Maritime Service
Braithwaite, Kenneth, Secretary of the Navy (2020–21)
Buzby, Mark Howard, U.S. Maritime Administrator (2017–21)
Carrico, Todd V., Director, Lidos Gibbs & Cox
Fahle, Rich, Head of Partnerships, NewLab
Fedor, Mark, Rear Admiral U.S. Coast Guard, Director of Joint Interagency Task Force South (2022–24)
Fireman, Howard, Deputy Director, Programming Division, Naval Architect of the Navy (2009–14)
Foggo, James G., Admiral (Ret.), U.S. Navy, Commander, Naval Forces Europe and Africa (2017–20)
Grissom, Susan, Vice President and Chief Industry Analyst, American Fuel & Petrochemical Manufacturers
Keever, Jeff Jefferson, Government Affairs T. Parker Host
Klinck, Heino, Deputy Assistant Secretary of Defense for East Asia (2019–21)
LaMarre, Paul, Director, Port of Monroe, Michigan (2012–)
Lehman, John, Secretary of the Navy (1981–87)
Martin, William, Executive Secretary, U.S. National Security Council (1985–86); Special Assistant to the President for National Security Affairs (1983–85)
McCarthy, Ed, Chief Operating Officer, Georgia Ports
Middendorf, J. William, Secretary of the Navy (1974–77)
Paskal, Cleo, Non-Resident Senior Fellow, Defense of Democracies
Profumo, Alessandro, Chief Executive Officer, Leonardo (2023–)
Romualdez, Jose Manuel, Philippines Ambassador to the United States (2017–)
Roughead, Gary, Chief of Naval Operations (2007–11)
Stires, Hunter, Fellow, John B. Hattendorf Center for Maritime Historical Research (2017–)
Suidani, Daniel, Premier of Malaita Province, Solomon Islands (2019–23)
Tennant, Paul, Vice President, Huntington Ingalls Industries (2023–)
Vandroff, Mark, Deputy Assistant to the President and Senior Director for Defense Policy (2020–21)

Wills, Steven, research analyst, Center for Naval Analysis, and author
You, Si-Kun, President of the Legislative Yuan of Taiwan (2020–24)

ARCHIVES, CONGRESSIONAL HEARINGS, AND OFFICIAL FILES

Bureau of Transportation Statistics. "On National Maritime Day and Every Day, U.S. Economy Relies on Waterborne Shipping." U.S. Department of Transportation, May 12, 2021. https://www.bts.gov/data-spotlight/national-maritime-day-and-every-day-us-economy-relies-waterborne-shipping.

Department of the Navy. "Budget Materials." https://www.secnav.navy.mil/fmc/Pages/Fiscal-Year-2025.aspx.

Energy Information Administration. *Oil Market Report*. January 18, 2023. https://iea.blob.core.windows.net/assets/6b994ae3-17fe-4a44-8bb8-eb1217cc4604/-18JAN2023_OilMarketReport.pdf.

Full Text of Jiang Zemin's Report at the 16th Party Congress, November 17, 2002. *China through a Lens*. http://www.china.org.cn/english/2002/Nov/49107.htm.

Hu Jintao. "Hold High the Great Banner of Socialism with Chinese Characteristics and Strive for New Victories in Building a Moderately Prosperous Society in All Respects." Full text of Hu Jintao's report to the Seventeenth National Congress of the Communist Party of China, October 15, 2007. http://np.china-embassy.gov.cn/eng/Features/200711/t20071104_1579245.htm.

International Tribunal for the Law of the Sea. "List of Cases." Accessed January 2, 2022. https://www.itlos.org/en/main/cases/list-of-cases/.

Maritime Administration. "Maritime Security Program." Accessed January 17, 2024. https://www.maritime.dot.gov/national-security/strategic-sealift/maritime-security-program-msp.

Millennium Challenge Corporation of USA. "Our Impact." Accessed January 2, 2022. https://www.mcc.gov/our-impact.

National Oceanic and Atmospheric Administration. "Weather and Climate Resources." Accessed January 2, 2022. https://www.noaa.gov/tools-and-resources/weather-and-climate-resources.

Naval History and Heritage Command. "Archives." Accessed January 2, 2022. https://www.history.navy.mil/research/archives.html.

———. "US Ship Force Levels." Accessed January 2, 2022. https://www.history.navy.mil/research/histories/ship-histories/us-ship-force-levels.html.

NAVSEA Shipbuilding Support Office. "Naval Vessel Register." Accessed May 19, 2024. https://www.nvr.navy.mil.

Office of Management and Budget, Executive Office of the President. "Statistical Programs of the United States Government." Accessed January 2, 2022. https://www.whitehouse.gov/omb/information-regulatory-affairs/statistical-programs-standards/.

Permanent Court of Arbitration. "Cases." Accessed January 2, 2022. https://pca-cpa.org/en/cases/.

Statement of the Honorable Carlos del Toro, Secretary of the Navy, on Department of the Navy Posture before the Senate Committee on Appropriations, April 10, 2024. https://www.appropriations.senate.gov/imo/media/doc/download_testimony23.pdf.

Statement of Mark H. Buzby, Administrator, U.S. Maritime Administration. "Subcommittees on Seapower and Projection Forces and Readiness Joint Hearing: 'Sealift and Mobility Requirements in Support of the National Defense Strategy,'" Committee on Armed Services, U.S. House of Representatives, March 11, 2020. https://docs.house.gov/meetings/AS/AS28/20200311/110720/HHRG-116-AS28-Wstate-BuzbyM-20200311.pdf.

Testimony of General Steve Lyons, U.S. Transportation Command, before the House Committee on Armed Services, Subcommittees on Seapower and Projection Forces and Readiness, "U.S. Transportation Command and Maritime Administration: State of the Mobility Enterprise," March 7, 2019. https://democrats-armedservices.house.gov/_cache/files/a/6/a6517319-b2b5-49e8-9581-bcdd9af30ee3/811B38D483E8F7A660314E1E19CD1CD4.hhrg-116-as28-wstate-lyonss-20190307.pdf.

Treaty on Good-Neighbourliness, Friendship and Cooperation between the Russian Federation and the People's Republic of China, President of Russia. July 16, 2001. http://www.kremlin.ru/supplement/3418.

United Nations, UN Conference on Trade and Development. *Review of Maritime Transport 2022: Navigating Stormy Waters*. https://unctad.org/system/files/official-document/rmt2022_en.pdf.

U.S. Department of State. "Joint Statement on the Philippines–United States Bilateral Strategic Dialogue," U.S. Department of State press release, April 24, 2024. https://www.state.gov/joint-statement-on-the-philippines-united-states-bilateral-strategic-dialogue/.

U.S. Government Interagency Counterinsurgency Initiative. *U.S. Government Counterinsurgency Guide*. January 13, 2009. https://2009-2017.state.gov/documents/organization/119629.pdf.

U.S. International Development Finance Corporation. "Our Work." Accessed January 2, 2022. https://www.dfc.gov/our-impact/our-work.

U.S. Navy. "Fact Files." Accessed January 2, 2022. https://www.navy.mil/Resources/Fact-Files/.

White House. *National Security Directive 28*, October 5, 1989. https://irp.fas.org/offdocs/nsd/nsd28.pdf.

White House Opportunity and Revitalization Council. "The Council." Accessed February 20, 2023. https://opportunityzones.hud.gov/thecouncil.

World Bank. "Open Data." Accessed January 2, 2022. https://data.worldbank.org.

INDEX

additive manufacturing, 145–46, 162
Aeros, 149
Afghanistan, 162, 215, 222
Africa, 48, 66–67; South Africa, 49, 50–51; West Africa, 44–46, 66–67, 68–74, 200
Africa Partnership Station, 70
Agency for International Development, U.S., 58, 70, 70–71
AidData, 47–49, 270n94
Aiken, George, 198, 202
Air Force, U.S., 58, 88–89
air freight, 150–51
Air Nostrum, 149
aircraft: extending range of, 162–63; PLAAF operation of strategic nuclear forces, 33, 35; redesign of, xv
aircraft carriers: acquisition by China, 35–36; cost of building and maintaining, 180–83; deployment by PLAN, 36, 37; electric-drive propulsion, 156; maintenance of, 176; purchase of ex-Soviet–built by China, 8, 35; ships and submarines for protection of, 36; size and operational needs of PLAN vessels, 37, 38, 49, 50; Vietnam visit by U.S. carrier, 39
Alaska, 62, 92
American Samoa, 55, 59, 61, 64, 65–66, 250
amphibious operations, car ferries for deployment of vehicles for, 32, 134
amphibious warships: *America* class, 36, 181–83, 185–86; cost of building and maintaining, 181–83; medium landing ship, 161–62; modern naval act and building of, 185–86; peacetime missions of, 36–37; PLAN fleet, 36–37; *San Antonio* class, 181–83; size and operational needs of PLAN vessels, 37, 38, 48, 50; U.S. fleet, 4
antiaccess area denial (A2/AD) defenses, 91, 92–93, 98
Arabian Sea, 9

Army, U.S.: deployment for maritime presence and counterinsurgency operations, 88–89; first island chain littoral operations campaign plans, 93–96; Multi Domain Task Force, 58
Army Corps of Engineers, U.S., 54–55
Army Transportation Corps, U.S., 199
artificial intelligence (AI), 146, 160
Ascension Island, 44, 45, 46
Aspen Security Forum, 160
Atoms for Peace, 155
Australia: EEZ of, 59; exercises/operations with, 98; naval presence in Pacific, 55, 63–64; nuclear submarine initiative with U.S and U.K., 211–12; Pacific Quad alliance role, 55, 63; Sogavare claim of interference from, 29

Balikatan exercise, 17
Baltimore Harbor bridge collision, 135–36
Bangladesh, 50–51
bases/overseas bases: acquisition of by China, 23–24, 52–53, 55, 237–38; economic and military interests and securing more, 24–27; organizations involved in decisions and actions related to, 30–32; PLA efforts to secure, 21; PLAN warship design changes related to types of basing, 33–35; port use as building on commercial activities and relationships, 30–32; String of Pearls naval bases, 23
Belt and Road Initiative (BRI), 10, 11, 18, 25, 27, 32, 48, 60, 67, 69
Bennett, Charlie, xv
Biden administration and Joe Biden, 14, 106, 112, 123, 207–8, 211–12, 222
biofuels, 114
Black Sea, xv
Blinken, Anthony, 276–77n4
blockchain technology, 146, 163, 296n116
blue ocean strategy for shipping, 131, 287n7

315

Blue Pacific, Operation, 64
Blue Water prototype drone, 149, 151
border disputes, resolution of, 9–10
Brezinski, Zbigniew, 213
Broadened Opportunity for Officer Selection and Training (BOOST) program, 178, 186
BUILD Act, 54–55
Bush, George H. W., 200, 214
Bush, George W., 208–9
Buzby, Mark, 139, 141, 189

California climate policies and energy security, 110–11, 119, 121–22, 282n42
Cambodia, 24, 44, 49, 50–51, 52, 55, 56, 60
Cameroon, 45, 50–51
Campbell, Kurt, 29, 211–12
Cancer to Capricorn Corridor: actions for seizing the initiative in by U.S., 252–56; area included in, 56; Chinese fishing fleets in, 69–70, 71, 74–77; drug trade and narcotics trafficking in, 71–78, 248–49; fleet organization for and focus of missions in, 74–77, 237, 242, 245–46; interests and great-power competition in, 66–74; interests in and naval statecraft to increase U.S. influence in, 56, 58, 74–78, 81–82, 237; maritime resources in, 58; naval presence and maritime security in, 74–78
car ferries, 32, 134
Caribbean to the Gulf of Guinea region, 56, 237. *See also* Cancer to Capricorn Corridor
carrier battle groups, xv
carrier strike groups, 4, 8, 17, 246–47
Carter, Jimmy, 212–13
Central Commission for Integrated Military and Civilian Development, 30, 31
Central Military Commission (CMC), 30–31, 55
Central Organization Department, 30, 31–32
CH-47 Chinook helicopters, 150
China Coast Guard (CCG), 26–27
China/Chinese Communist Party (CCP): advancement of interests of, xvii–xviii; assault on and conquering Taiwan by, xviii–xix, xx; border disputes with Russia, 10; economic power/strength of, 1–2, 7–8; global reach of, 2; hiding capabilities by, 7–8; maritime statistics, 130; military modernization and expansion by, xviii–xix; national rejuvenation as objective of, 24, 27; reactive and ineffective actions toward, xvii; rivalry with Russia, 8, 10; security arrangements in the Pacific, xvii–xviii; strategic opportunism and direction of, 11–16; strategic partnership and treaty with Russia, 10; Twentieth Party Congress, 12, 15, 31; understanding strengths and weaknesses of, xiv; weakening confidence of, 99; window of time to act on Taiwan, 19–20; WTO membership and economy of, 1, 7–8, 9–10, 209
Chinese Civil War, 1–2
Chinese Coast Guard (CCG), 61–62, 87, 87–88
Chinese Maritime Militia, 17, 26–27, 87–88
Clark, Maiya, 176
Clinton, Bill, 214, 217
Clinton, Hillary, 210
Coast Guard, U.S.: authority over maritime sector, 191–94; budget for, 193, 195, 303n21; cybersecurity regulations proposal by, 135–36; enforcement of U.S. laws in EEZs by, 62–63, 249–50; force strength and mission in south and central Pacific, 62–63, 64, 249–50; mission of, 193, 197; reorganization for new cold war, 190–91, 195–98, 201–3, 255–56; tactics to challenge China's tactics, 90–96
Colby, Elbridge, 6, 24
Cold War: allies and like-minded partner nations from, 4; great-power competition similarities to, 6; naval power for winning, xv; post–Cold War agenda and era, 3, 7, 236. *See also* new cold war
Cole, 40, 254
Commerce, U.S. Department of, 166, 192
Commission on the Future of the Navy, 166
Committee on the Maritime Transportation System, U.S., 191, 199
communication of data and communications networks, 146, 163, 296n116
Compact of Free Association (CoFA), 53, 65–66, 81–82
Comprehensive Nuclear Test Ban Treaty, xviii
Congress, U.S.: budgeting and oversight processes of, 173–74, 179–85, 299n24; Commission on the Future of the Navy, 166; support for naval and maritime power in, xv

consulates and embassies, 53, 59
container shipping: common container sizes, 147–48, 292n64; container design for multimodalism, 146–48; containerization of cargo, 128, 131, 142, 167; cost of deepening harbors to accommodate container ships, 129; manufacturing and availability of containers for, 124–25, 147–48; ports and port operations for large container ships, 144–45, 151–54; stay-at-sea container ships, 152, 154–56; weakness of U.S. capacity for internodal shipping, 128. *See also* multimodalism/intermodalism
Cooper, Brad, 247–48
Cooperative Strategy for 21st Century Seapower, A (2007), 240
Corbett, Julian S., 238
COSCO, 137
COSCO Group, 28, 31–32, 42–43, 133–35, 263n20
Covid-19 pandemic: availability of containers during, 124–25, 147–48; interruptions in supply chains during, xix–xx, 23, 124–25, 127, 189, 190; low fuel demand during, 114, 115; virtual policing during, 64–65
Cropsey, Seth, 189–90
Cross-Border Interbank Payment System (CIPS), 11–12
cruisers, 36, 43
Cuba, 67
CV-22 Osprey aircraft, 150
cyber intrusion, cyberattacks, and cyber security, xix, 135–36

Dali, 135–36
Davidson, Philip, xviii
Defense, U.S. Department of: creation of, 194, 207, 254; Goldwater-Nichols Act (1986) and changes to, 180, 216, 241, 254; State Partnership Program under, 200; Transportation Command, 92, 102–3, 125, 140, 197
Defense Innovation Unit (DIU), 159–60, 168
Defense Logistics Agency, 104, 122
Defense Strategy Guidance (DSG), 209–10, 215
Deng Xiaoping, 6
Desert Shield, 92

Desert Storm, 92, 108
Destroyer Squadron 7, 88, 89, 246
destroyers: cost of building and maintaining, 181–83; DDG(X) destroyers, 175; *Luyang* class, 8, 33, 37; modern naval act and building of, 185–86; purchase of Russian-built, 8; size and operational needs of PLAN vessels, 37, 38, 48, 50; *Zumwalt* class, 156
Detroit-Toledo-Chicago multimodalism proof-of-concept, 164, 165, 167
Development Finance Corporation (DFC), 54–55, 58, 70–71, 79–80
diesel fuel supplies and production, 104–5, 112, 114–15, 119, 154
diplomacy: DIME tools, 58; improvement of China–U.S. relations, efforts for, 13–16; naval statecraft role, xvii, xx, 5, 58–59; strengthening CCP diplomatic leverage, 11–12, 13–16
dirigibles, 149, 151, 162
disaster response and evacuations, 4, 36–37, 122, 143, 199–200, 278n1
distributed maritime operations, 163
Djibouti, 23–24, 30–31, 32, 35, 42, 44, 48, 49, 50–51, 55, 57, 270n97
Dong Jun, 19, 31, 55
drones, 148, 149, 151, 167, 248–49
drug trade and narcotics trafficking, 58, 68, 71–78, 248–49
duck, shooting behind the, xvii, xxi, 20
Duterte, Rodrigo, 79, 85

East Coast and Puerto Rico multimodalism proof-of-concept, 164, 165, 167
Eastern Mediterranean theater, xv
economy/economic power: business environment in and manufacturing moving out of China, 24–25; CCP activities after McCarthy meeting with Taiwan president, 17–18; China's economic power, 1–2, 7–8; China's economic security and weakening of growth, 13–16; China–U.S. economic relations, 14; Chinese economic statecraft, 12–13, 21; collapse of 2008, 11; developmental economic programs, 58; economic statecraft, 5; industrial strengthening and prevention of enemy interference in,

xx–xxi; naval statecraft role, xvii, xx, 5, 58–59, 70–71, 79–80; overseas bases to support economic and military interests, 24–27; strengthening against coercion, xix, xx–xxi, 16, 124–26, 252–53; strengthening CCP economic influence, 11–12
Egypt, 28–29, 30, 49, 50–51
Eisenhower administration and Dwight Eisenhower, 122, 155
electric-drive propulsion, 156
electronic warfare, xiv
embassies and consulates, 53, 59
Energy Information Administration (EIA), 106–7, 111, 115, 116, 117, 118
energy/energy sector: California climate policies and energy security, 110–11, 119, 121–22, 282n42; China's domestic energy production, 101; dangers of fragmented and underresourced, 99; ESG policies and, 111, 123, 283n44, 283n46; green energy, 101, 154–56; improving national resiliency, xx, 101–2, 120–23; interruptions to or manipulation of supply of, 107–8, 121, 123; New England supplies, 105, 109, 110, 119, 121–22; overseas supplies of, 112–15; simulation/war gaming an energy crisis, 107; Strategic Petroleum Reserve (SPR), 102, 105–9, 121, 278–78n1, 281n30; transportation of and vulnerabilities of inadequate logistics, 109–11; wartime energy requirements, 18, 103–5, 120, 139
entropic warfare, 30
environmental, social, and governance (ESG) policies, 111, 123, 283n44, 283n46
Environmental Protection Agency, Renewable Fuel Standard, 114
Equatorial Guinea, 44–46, 50–51, 52, 69–71
ethanol, 109, 118, 282n33, 286n80
European Union, 112
Evergreen, 143
eVTOL (electric vertical take-off and landing aircraft), 149
exclusive economic zones (EEZs): Chinese fishing fleets and enforcement of, 58, 61–65, 249–50; Coast Guard enforcement of, 62–63, 249–50; map of, 59; naval presence and enforcement of, 85–86, 87, 89
Executive Office of the President (EOP), 219, 221, 222, 230–32

exercises: importance of, xiv, 98; large-scale exercises (LSE), 90; modern Fleet Problems to refine capabilities, 83, 90–96, 98; Nifty Nugget exercise, 92; Third versus Seventh Fleet Problem IX, 92–93
expeditionary logistics, 161–62
expeditionary sea-based ships, 74–78, 244
expeditionary transfer dock (ESD) ships, 72, 76–78, 248–49, 251, 254
experts and expertise, fostering development of, xv

Fat Leonard scandal, 87
Federal Aviation Agency, 192
Federal Emergency Management Agency, 199–200
Federal Maritime Commission (FMC), 136, 167, 191–92, 195, 197–98, 201–2, 256
fentanyl and the drug trade, 58, 68, 71–78, 248–49
Fifth Fleet Task Force 59, 77, 247–49
Finland, 130
first island chain: deterrent patrols within the, 34–35; littoral operations campaign plans, 93–96
fishing and fishing fleets: Cancer to Capricorn Corridor activity, 69–70, 71, 74–77; EEZ enforcement in the Pacific, 58, 61–65, 249–50
Fleet Forces Command, 176
fleet liaison officers, 53–54
Fleet Problems, modern to refine capabilities, 83, 90–96, 98
Fleet Structure Assessment, 174
fleet/naval forces, 251; maritime region/geography combatant commands, 19, 237, 239, 241–45; network-connected manned and unmanned platforms, 163; numbered fleets and fleet boundaries, 238–40, 243–45; ocean-centered naval fleet structure, 19, 187, 241–45; PLAN fleet, 2; reorganization for strategic objectives and mission of Navy, xiv, 236–37, 238, 245–51, 255
Flexport, 152–54
floating drydocks, 42, 48, 75–76, 254, 270n97
Force Structure Assessment, 174, 241
Foreign Dredge Act, 137
France: Caribbean interests of, 68; EEZs in south and central Pacific, 59; maritime

statistics, 130; naval presence in Pacific, 55, 63; Pacific Quad alliance role, 55, 63
frigates: *Constellation* class, 44, 176, 181–83, 185–86; cost of building and maintaining, 181–83; *Jiangkai II* class, 37; modern naval act and building of, 185–86
fuel: biofuels, 114; blending and blend-wall, 118, 286n80; conventional fuel reliance, 102–3; diesel fuel supplies and production, 104–5, 112, 114–15, 119, 154; distant operations and need for, 33–34, 103–4; distillate fuel inventories, 106–7; ethanol, 109, 118, 282n33, 286n80; foreign sources for, 103–4; jet fuel requirements and production, 104, 114–15, 119; Jones Act and transport of, 110, 111–12, 122, 282n37; logistic ships for replenishment of, 37; MARAD fleet to move, 104–5; overseas supplies of, 112–15; pipelines to transport, 109–10, 117, 121–23, 282n33; PLAN port visits and availability of, 51; port visits for replenishment of, 40–41; Red Hill fuel storage facility, 101, 105, 109, 121, 142; U.S. military's demand for, 18, 37–38, 102–4; wartime needs and domestic supply of, 103–5, 120, 139
FUTURE Act, 179

Gallagher, Mike, 297n5
Gaza, xviii, 143
Germany, 130, 134–35, 167
Gilday, Michael, 173
Glenn Marine Group, 41
Global Force Management (GFM), 241
Global South, 58, 67–68, 74, 248, 271n1
Goldwater-Nichols Act (1986), 180, 216, 241, 254
government, U.S.: integrated deterrence and foreign policy of, 57, 211–12, 241; reorganization to execute a competitive strategy against China, 19, 20, 187, 189–91, 207–14, 255–56
Government Accountability Office (GAO) reports, 172, 176, 184, 196–97
gray-zone tactics, xviii, 89
Great Lakes multimodalism proof-of-concept, 164, 165, 167
great-power competition, 237; actions for seizing the initiative in positional competition with CCP, 52–55, 237–38, 252–56; China's approach to, 6–16; China's efforts to win without firing a shot, 5–6; comprehensive power between U.S. and China, 1–2; coordinating actions that undermine military balance, economic security, and political/diplomatic control of events, 15–19; decisive theaters of, 4–5; domestic and foreign policies and setting conditions for, xix–xx; equation to deter Chinese aggression, 16–19; geostrategic position competition, 56; great power multitasking, xxi; ideology and ideological warfare, 6–7, 254; markets and infrastructure control and winning by China, xx; regaining initiative for, 2–6, 20; rivalry focus of bilateral relationship, 2; setting conditions for by China, xix; spectrum of rivalry, 16; winning positional competition through naval statecraft, xx–xxi, 5–6, 18, 57–59, 252–56
Greece, 28, 30, 130–31, 134, 167
Guam, 34, 46, 55, 61, 62, 65–66, 93
Guinea, Gulf of: base for China in, 44–46; *Hershel Williams* deployment in, 74–77, 244; map of, 45; naval statecraft application in, 70–71, 75, 77–78. *See also* Cancer to Capricorn Corridor
Gulf Wars, 7, 92, 141, 190

Hai Lu Feng (China), 69–70
Hainan Island, 26
Hall, Paul, 203
Hamas, xviii, 2–3, 4–5, 143
Hambantota, Sri Lanka, 25, 39
Harbor Maintenance Trust Fund (HMTF) duties, 136, 167
Harboring Global Ambitions (AidData), 48
Harding, Andrew, 65
Hawaii: EEZ of and Chinese fishing fleets, 59, 61, 62; naval base in, 55; Red Hill fuel storage facility in, 101, 105, 109, 121, 142; Russian operations near, 92
heavy-lift and repair ships: floating drydocks, 42, 48, 75–76, 254, 270n97; PLAN and COSCO ships, 42–43, 254
helicopters, 149, 150–51, 162
Heritage Foundation: energy crisis simulation by, 107; market bridges discussion at, 161;

plan for competition with China, 216–17; on shipyard capacity, 176
Hershel Williams, 74–77, 244
Homeland Security, U.S. Department of, 190–91, 193, 195, 197, 197–98, 201, 303n21
Hong Kong, 40
Horn of Africa operations, 25, 27, 31, 48
Hu Jintao, 9, 25, 35, 47, 56
Hu Zhongming, 19
Hundred-Year Marathon, The (Pillsbury), 5–6
Hutchison Ports, 28–29, 49

ideology and ideological warfare, 6–7, 254
immigration and illegal migrants, 68–69, 73, 179, 248
incubators and market bridges, 126, 156–63, 167–69, 287n7
India, 130
Indian Ocean: evacuation of Chinese nationals through Port Sudan, 33, 36; naval forces organization for, 242; piracy and counterpiracy operations in, 2, 33; PLAN deployment to, 2; PLAN presence in, 33; String of Pearls naval bases, 23
Indonesia, 80–81, 92, 130, 166–67
Indo-Pacific Command, U.S., xviii, 89, 242–43
Indo-Pacific region: actions for seizing the initiative in by U.S., 52–55; shift in regional military balance to U.S. in, 18; U.S. policies for, 211
industries/industrial base: inadequacies in capacity of, xix–xx, 99; rapid industrial rearmament, 19, 99; revitalization of and regaining competitive edge in maritime industries, xvii, xix; strengthening and prevention of enemy interference in, xx–xxi, 124–25
Influence of Sea Power upon History, The (Mahan), 126–27
infrastructure: development of as economic tool and to support military presence, 54–55, 58–59; PLA access to, 21
institutions, naval and maritime: agencies with authority over, 191–94, 198–200; building on strength of, xiv; creation of new, xiv; proposal for new, xiv, 19; reorganization and modernization of, xx–xxi, 16, 20, 194–98; reorganization to execute a competitive strategy against China, 19, 187, 189–91, 252–56
insurgency and counterinsurgency: counterinsurgency/maritime counterinsurgency against China, 78–81, 82, 211, 256; definition of insurgency, 84, 276n1; naval operations/presence in maritime counterinsurgency, 83, 84–90, 98; South China Sea as insurgency at-sea by China, xviii, 26, 80, 84–85, 237–38, 256
integrated deterrence, 57, 211–12, 241
International Energy Agency, 155
International Energy Forum, 110–11, 117–18
interstate highway system, 122
Iran: Hamas support from, 4; as new cold war adversary, 3; resources for military operations against, 37–38; shipping attacks by proxy of, 127, 143; undermining regional security by, 67; understanding strengths and weaknesses of, xiv
Iraq: crude oil from, 113; invasion of by U.S., 11; Obama policy on, 215
Israel, xviii, 2–3, 4–5
Italy, 68, 69, 130

Jackson, Scoop, xv
James Shoal, 86, 87
Japan: amphibious warships of, 36; exercises/operations with, 98; Jones Act and shipping between U.S. ports by, 122, 142; maritime group membership too coordinate commerce policies and regulations, 125–26, 130–31, 166–67; maritime statistics, 130; modular ship construction use by, 128; naval deployments in Pacific, 64
Jiang Zemin, 8, 11, 20, 209
John Glenn (ESD-2), 76–77, 249
Johnson, Lyndon, 198–99
Joint All-Domain Command and Control (JADC2), 163
Joint Interagency Task Force South (JIATF-S), 72–74, 77–78, 248–49, 250
Jones Act: background of, 132–33; limitations of and waiving requirements in, 122, 140–42; Merchant Marine Act section 27, 133, 282n37; reform or repeal of, 139–40; shipping protections in, 110, 111–12, 122, 125, 137, 139, 282n37, 287n4

Junior Reserve Officer Training Corps (JROTC), 177
Justice, U.S. Department of, 190–91

Keystone XL pipeline, 123
Kiribati, 39, 54, 60, 62–63, 65–66
Korean War, 150
Kwajalein, 46, 93

Land, Emory S., 191
Latin America, 48, 66
Lehman, John, 96
Lewis B. Puller, 75
Lockheed Martin's LMH-1 dirigible, 149
Logistic Request message (LOGREQ), 40–41
logistic ships, 37, 38, 41–42, 51, 161–62
logistics: additive manufacturing, 145–46, 162; Bonaparte's quote on, 37, 267n62; communication of data and communications networks, 146, 163, 296n116; expeditionary logistics, 161–62; five-year plan for civil-military integration in, 31; new framework to revolutionize shipping, xix; resilient logistics, 162
Luconia Shoals, 26, 86, 87, 89
Lyons, James A. "Ace," xvi, 96

Mahan, Alfred Thayer, 9, 126–27
maintenance and repairs: active/preventive maintenance, 42; deployable drydock capabilities, 42–43, 254; emergent port calls for, 40, 42–43; expeditionary transfer dock (ESD) ships for, 75–76; overseas ports for PLAN for, 28–29, 31, 32; PLAN port visits and ports with capabilities for, 47, 48, 49, 51, 270n97; port visits for, 41, 42–43; Tiger Teams for, 42; U.S. aircraft carriers, 176; U.S. nuclear submarines, 176; U.S.-flagged vessel maintenance in Chinese shipyards, 135
Malaysia: Chinese harassment of *West Capella* oil survey ship of, 57, 84, 85, 211, 219, 256; confrontation over South China Sea claims of, 27; counterinsurgency activities to support, 80–81, 84; fleet liaison officer posting in Kota Kinabalu, Borneo,, 54; maritime statistics, 130
Mandate for Leadership, 190–91
Mao Zedong, 9

Marcos, Bongbong, 79
Marcos, Ferdinand, 78
Marine Corps, U.S.: expeditionary advanced base operations concept, 93–96; first island chain littoral operations campaign plans, 93–96; Marine Littoral Regiment, 58
Maritime Administration (MARAD): authority over maritime sector, 138, 191–94; on cargo preferences, 136, 139; creation and focus of, 198–99; merchant marine fleet and commercial maritime strength of the U.S., 189; on merchant marine recruitment and training, 141, 159; National Defense Reserve Fleet (NDRF) under, 104–5, 139, 196, 197; reorganization for new cold war, 190–91, 195–98, 201–3, 255–56; strategy development by for sustainability of commercial fleet, 196–97; Tanker Security Program (TSP), 138, 139, 197
Maritime Commission, 191, 198
Maritime Department: creation and focus of, 19, 187; National Security Directive 28 (NSD-28) for establishment of, 200, 202, 203, 204–6; proposal for, xiv; reorganization of agencies under, 191–98, 201–3
Maritime Group, 130–31, 166–67
Maritime Security Initiative (2015), 64, 75
Maritime Security Program, 138
Maritime Service, U.S., 199–200
Maritime Silk Road, 28
maritime statecraft: concept of, xiii, xvii; investment and action for deterrence of China, xix–xx
maritime strategy: development of new national strategy, xiv–xv; national maritime strategy, 131, 137–38, 139–40, 165–70
market bridges and innovative incubators, 126, 156–63, 167–69, 287n7
Marshall Islands, 53, 54, 65
Marxism, 7
Matson, 135
Mauritania, 45, 50–51
McCarthy, Kevin, 17–18
McLean, Malcolm, 128, 142, 167
medium landing ship, 161–62
Meese, Ed, 218

Merchant Marine Act (1920), 133, 139–40, 195, 199, 282n37, 303n25
merchant mariners, 112, 130, 141, 142, 157–59, 168–69
Merz, William, 85
microelectronics, xx
Micronesia, Federated States of, 53, 54, 59, 65
Middle East: oil supplies from, 107; refineries and refining capacity in, 115; support for chaos in by China and Russia, xviii
Miguel Keith, 75
military, Chinese: aggressive transparency campaign against bad behavior by, 88–89; control of risks and use of, 10; disparity of power between U.S. and, 3; engagement between China and U.S., 14–16; misinterpretation of intent of new missions for, 9; modernization and expansion of, 1–2, 7–11; overseas bases to support economic and military interests, 24–27; shipbuilding by, 1; use of for "peacetime" strategic objectives, 10. *See also* People's Liberation Army Navy (PLAN); People's Liberation Army (PLA)
military, U.S.: capacity to wage prolonged war with China, xix, 3; disparity of power between China and, 3
military balance, xviii–xix, 12, 13–14, 15–18, 21, 171–72
military presence: ability to maintain by China, xx; CCP and PLA activities after McCarthy meeting with Taiwan president, 17–18; deterrence of Chinese assault on Taiwan through, xix; increase in to shift regional military balance from China, 16, 18; Pelosi visit to and PLA presence around Taiwan, 14, 16–17, 44; seizing the initiative in positional competition with, 52–55, 237–38
Military Sealift Command, 76, 199
missiles: antiaccess area denial (A2/AD) defenses, 91, 92–93, 98; China's arsenal and threat from, 91; China's lead in, 1; conventional ballistic and cruise missiles, 1; intercontinental ballistic missiles (ICBMs), 34; purchase of Russian-built by China, 8–9; at-sea reloading of vertical-launch systems, 162, 254; submarine-launched ballistic missiles, 34–35

Montford Point (ESD-1), 76–77, 249
Mozambique, 50–51
MQ-25 unmanned aircraft, 162–63
multimodalism/intermodalism: cargo throughput, 144–45, 151–54; communication of data and communications networks, 146, 163, 296n116; concept of, 152; container design for, 146–48; distributed production and additive manufacturing, 145–46, 162; diversified port operations for, 151–54; fundamentals of the next, 142–56; incubators and market bridges for workers for and innovation for, 126, 156–63, 167–69, 287n7; proof-of-concept and demonstration of, 163–65, 167; stay-at-sea container ships, 152, 154–56; time in port, 143; trade pathways, 143; transport methods, 148–51, 161–62; weakness of U.S. position in, 128; West Coast opportunities for, 153, 154
munitions: PLAN port visits and ports with resupply capabilities, 47, 49, 51; replenishment of in port or at sea, 41–42
munitions ships, 37
Murkowski, Lisa, 193

narcotics trafficking and the drug trade, 58, 68, 71–78, 248–49
National Defense Authorization Act (NDAA), 174–75, 179–80, 181, 186, 196, 236, 297n5
National Defense Reserve Fleet (NDRF), 104–5, 138, 139, 196, 197
National Defense Sealift Fund, 196
National Defense Strategy (2018/2022), 238, 244
National Defense University (NDU), 47–49
National Economic Council (NEC), 214, 217, 221
National Environmental Act (NEPA), 137
National Maritime Cybersecurity Plan, 135
National Maritime Day, 189–90
national maritime strategy, 131, 137–38, 139–40, 165–70
National Oceanic and Atmospheric Administration (NOAA), 190–91, 191–94, 195–98, 201–2, 255–56
National Sea-Based Deterrence Fund, 181, 186
National Security Act (1947), 194, 207, 214, 254

National Security Council (NSC): communication processes in, 218–19; consensus-driven decisions in, 212; conventional structure of, 214–16; creation/origin of, 207, 214, 254; executive order for new structure for, 221–22, 230–32; Indo-Pacific coordinator for, 29, 202, 211–12; maladies that affect function of, 208–14; national maritime issues coordinator for, 202–3; new structure based on strategic objectives, xiv, 19, 187, 207, 207–8, 216–24, 225–29, 233–35, 255–56; regional offices of, 220, 221; size and balance of staff of, 207–8, 210, 213, 214–15, 217–21, 222–24, 233–35, 255; strategic decision memo, 222, 233–35; turf wars in, 212–13

National Security Directive 28 (NSD-28), 200

National Security Directive 28 (NSD-28) update recommendation, 200, 202, 203, 204–6

National Security Strategy (2022), 211–12

National Security Strategy (2025 draft), 216, 221–22, 225–29

national security study memoranda (NSSM), 218–19

natural disasters response and evacuations, 4, 36–37, 122, 143, 199–200, 278n1

natural resources, 69

Naval Act (1938), 171–72

naval militias, 200

naval statecraft: book about, xiii; concept of, 5; diplomatic aspect of, xvii, xx, 5, 58–59; economic power aspect of, xvii, xx, 5, 58–59, 70–71, 79–80; framework for competition with China, xvii, xx; naval power and, 5; naval presence aspect of, xvii, xx, 4–5, 58–59; winning positional competition through, xx–xxi, 5–6, 18, 57–59, 252–56

Naval Strike Warfare Center, xiv

Naval War College, xiv

naval/maritime power: deterrent effects of, 5; naval statecraft and, 5; overhaul and rebirth of, xvi; seizing and retaining initiative with, 5; strike power capabilities of, 5

naval/maritime presence: Cancer to Capricorn Corridor activity, 74–78; counterinsurgency operations, 83, 84–90, 98; EEZ enforcement through, 85–86, 87, 89; Hamas attacks and eastern Mediterranean presence, 4–5; as mission of the Navy, 173, 297n5; naval statecraft role, xvii, xx, 4–5, 58–59; PLAN presence in Indian Ocean, 33

Navigation Plan (2022), 161

Navy, U.S.: mission of, 173, 236–37, 238, 297n5; modern naval act to grow, 19, 99, 171–79, 185–86; sailors, recruitment goals, and manning plans for, 171, 176–79; Seabees, 54–55, 59; tactics to challenge China's tactics, 90–96

Netherlands, 68, 130, 167

network-connected manned and unmanned platforms, 163

new cold war: adversaries in, 3; China as principal adversary in, 3; indications of CCP engagement in, 6–7; reorganization and modernization of institutions for, xx–xxi, 16, 20, 187, 189–91, 194–98, 207–14, 252–56

New England energy supplies, 105, 109, 110, 119, 121–22

New Zealand, 39, 55, 59, 63–64

Nifty Nugget exercise, 92

North Atlantic Treaty Organization (NATO), xv

North Korea, xiv, 3

Northern Mariana Islands, 62, 65, 93

Norway, 130, 167

nuclear power for merchant ships, 154–56, 157

Nuclear Regulatory Commission, U.S., 155–56

nuclear submarine fleet of PLAN, 33, 34–35, 36

nuclear weapons: Comprehensive Nuclear Test Ban Treaty, xviii; parity between China, Russia, and U.S., 34; Russian development of new, xviii; second-strike nuclear capabilities and strategic nuclear forces, 33, 34–35

NuScale Power, 155–56

Obama administration and Barack Obama, 85, 208, 209–10, 214–15, 255

Obangame Express, 70, 244

Ocean Shipping Reform Act (2022), 136

Ocean Venture 81, Operation, xiv, 96–97

Oceania Maritime Security Initiative, 250

Oceans Ventured (Lehman), xiv

oil and gas: Gulf of Guinea operations, 70, 71; heavy crude oil, 116, 119, 285n67; Middle East oil supplies, 107; pipelines to transport, 109–10, 117, 121–23, 282n33; refineries and refining capacity in U.S., 103, 105–6, 106, 109, 110–11, 114, 115–19, 120–21, 282n42; refineries and refining capacity overseas, 115, 117–18, 285–86n76; shale oil production, 107, 281n50; Strategic Petroleum Reserve (SPR), 102, 105–9, 121, 278–78n1, 281n30; *West Capella* oil survey ship incident, 57, 84, 85, 211, 219, 256

oilers, 33–34, 37, 38, 41, 50, 183

Oman, 50–51

One Belt, One Road Initiative, 11. *See also* Belt and Road Initiative (BRI)

Open Door policies, 6

operations/naval operations: analysis of and lessons learned, xv; audiences for, 83; distributed maritime operations, 163; factors in crafting new, 83; maritime counterinsurgency operations, 83, 84–90, 98; naval deployments/demonstrations, 83, 96–98

opportunity zone programs, 160

orbital bombardment system, 35

Organization of Petroleum Exporting Countries (OPEC), 107, 281n50

Pacific Pathways program, 88

Pacific Quad, 59, 63–65, 81, 249. *See also* Australia; France; New Zealand

Pacific region, south and central: actions for seizing the initiative in by U.S., 52–55, 237–38, 252–56; central Pacific patrols by PLAN, 35; Chinese fishing fleets in and enforcement of EEZs, 58, 61–65, 249–50; Coast Guard vessels and mission in, 62–63, 64, 249–50; embassies and consulates in, 53; expansion of U.S. influence in, 55; fleet organization for and focus of missions in, 237, 242, 245–46, 247, 249–50; interests in and naval statecraft to increase U.S. influence in, 56, 58, 59–66, 81–82; map of, 59; maritime security in, 62–66; naval presence in, 62–66; seabed mineral poaching in, 58, 64

Pacific Venture, Operation, xiv, 97–98

Pakistan, 50–51

Palau, Republic of, 54, 59, 65, 74

Panama and the Panama Canal, 29, 144

Paparo, Samuel, Jr., 75, 248

Papua New Guinea, 54, 66

Paskal, Cleo, 30, 65

Paxton, Matthew, 178–79

Pelosi, Nancy, 14, 16–17, 44

People's Liberation Army Air Force (PLAAF), 26, 33, 35

People's Liberation Army Navy (PLAN): capabilities and experience for operating in distant seas, 24–27, 35–37; capabilities and strength of, 2; fleet of, 2; gray-zone tactics of, xviii, 89; logistic ships to support, 37, 38, 41–42; naval warfare focus for contest over Taiwan, 19–20; new historic missions for under Hu, 9, 25–27, 35, 47, 56; Taiwan activities after McCarthy meeting with Taiwan president, 17; warship design changes related to types of basing, 33–35

People's Liberation Army (PLA): capabilities and strength of, 2; Logistics Support Department, 32; modernization and expansion of, 7–11, 20; National Mobilization Department, 32; naval warfare focus for contest over Taiwan, 19–20; political orthodoxy and purges of leaders from, 12; readiness and capabilities of, 12; structural reforms for joint warfighting, 34; Xi's appointments to, 19, 31

Philippine Sea, 34, 35, 91, 94, 95

Philippines, 87; aggressive transparency campaign against Chinese behavior by, 88–89; alliance with and security relations between U.S. and, 78–81; confrontation over South China Sea claims of, 27; counterinsurgency against China in, 80–81; economic importance of fishing in, 81, 276n56; interference and collisions with vessels from near Second Thomas Shoal, xviii, 14, 17, 86–87; Jones Act and shipping between U.S. ports by, 122; maritime group membership too coordinate commerce policies and regulations, 125–26, 130–31, 166–67; maritime statistics, 130; military exercise with U.S., 17; murder of local citizen by servicemember in, 43; Mutual Defense

Treaty to defense, 87, 276–77n4; win by in the Permanent Court of Arbitration, The Hague, 85
Pillsbury, Michael, 5–6
piracy and counterpiracy operations, 2, 9, 25, 33, 69–70
Piraeus, Greece, 28, 30, 134
Poland, 130, 139, 166–67
Pompeo, Mike, 85
ports: coercive approach to access to, 30; container shipping requirements for water depth and port operations, 144–45, 151–54; control of and improvements to by China, xx, 23–24, 43, 44–47, 52–53, 127, 134–35, 237–38; crew behavior in and Status of Forces Agreements, 43; decisions about and diplomatic and political aspects of visits to, 37–41; departure from, 43; elements of visit to, 37–43; emergent port calls, 40, 42–43; fees, bills, and paying contractors and for services, 43, 143, 150, 167; fleet liaison officers for visits to, 53–54; harbor operations and HMTF duties, 135–36, 167; logistic needs and reasons for visits to, 37–39, 40–43; military use of building on commercial activities and relationships with, 30–32; organizations involved in decisions and actions related to, 30–32; PLAN port visits, investments in commercial ports, and potential naval bases, 47–51, 270n97; pragmatism and opportunism in gaining access to/control of, 27–30, 263n20; rest and recuperation portcalls, 41; size and operational needs of PLAN vessels and planning visits to, 37, 38, 39, 49, 50–51
post–Cold War agenda and era, 3, 7, 236
Pottinger, Matt, 6
Project 2025, 222
Project on National Security Reform, 221
Prosper Africa, 70–71, 77–78, 82
Putin, Vladimir, 57

rail transport: multimodalism role of, 139, 147, 150–51; regulations related to, 139; smart rail cars, 147; train derailment, East Palestine, 109, 139
rare-earth elements, xx
Ready Reserve Fleet, 138, 139

Reagan Administration and Ronald Reagan, 96, 175, 178, 191, 213, 217–18
Ream, Cambodia, 24, 44, 49, 50–51, 52, 55, 56, 60
Red Hill fuel storage facility, 101, 105, 109, 121, 142
Red Sea, xv, 127, 143
Renhai-class Type 055 warships, 8, 33, 36, 38, 43, 50, 91
resilient logistics, 162
Roosevelt, Franklin D., 191
Roper, William, 161
Rothkopf, David, 207, 212
rules-based order, xviii, 80, 87, 90, 237, 308n4
Running the World (Rothkopf), 207
Russia: advancement of interests of, xvii–xviii; assault on/invasion of Ukraine by, xviii, 2, 3, 4, 10, 57, 112, 115, 212, 222; border disputes with China, 10; central Pacific operations on, 92; Crimea annexation by, 11, 209, 215; maritime statistics, 130; as new cold war adversary, 3; petroleum imports from, 112, 113; PLAN port visits and potential naval bases in, 49, 50–51; rivalry with China, 8, 10; sanctions on oil and petroleum from, 112, 118; strategic partnership and treaty with China, 10; undermining regional security by, 67; understanding strengths and weaknesses of, xiv

sailors, recruitment goals, and manning plans, 171, 176–79
sanctions, xix
Saudi Arabia, 29, 50–51, 113
Savannah, 155
Scarborough Shoal, 26, 84, 86
Schwarzkopf, Norman, Jr., 92
seabed mineral poaching, 58, 64
seablindness, 189–90
sealift/sealift capacity: Jones Act and constraints on, 140–42; wartime fuel needs, 104–5, 139
Second Thomas Shoal, xviii, 14, 26, 86–87, 89
Securities and Exchange Commission, U.S., 192
September 11 attacks, 8, 11, 57, 193, 201, 208–9
Shanghai Cooperation Organization (SCO), 11
Shield AI, 160

shipbuilding, 168; budget for Navy, 173–75, 179–85; China's civilian-military activities, 127, 128–31, 133–35, 137; China's lead in, 1, 124, 127, 128–31; inadequacies in industries for, xix, 124, 127–28, 140–42; incubators and market bridges for workers for and innovation in, 126, 156–63, 167–69, 287n7; modern naval act to increase shipyards and capacity for, 19, 99, 171–79, 185–86; modernization of and partnership with maritime allies, 125–26, 130–31, 166–67; modular ship construction, 128, 131; overseas shipyards of the U.S., 175–76; regaining capacity for, 18, 99, 128–31, 165–70, 256; regulations related to, 129, 132–42, 161; shipyard and shipyard capacity of U.S., 175–76; skilled shipyard workers, 156–59, 168–69, 172, 175–76, 178–79

shipping: blue ocean strategy for, 131, 287n7; capacity for and confrontation with China, xix, 124–25; cargo preferences, 136, 139; China's civilian-military activities, 127, 128–31, 133–35, 137; Chinese merchant fleet, 124, 128–31; concept and scope of discussion about, 287n7; costs related to, 132; fuel and energy transport, 104–5, 120–23; incubators and market bridges for workers for and innovation in, 126, 156–63, 167–69, 287n7; merchant marine fleet and commercial maritime strength of the U.S., 124–26, 127–28, 189–90; modernization of and regaining competitiveness in, 125–26, 128–31, 130–31, 165–70, 166–67, 287n7; number of U.S.-flagged merchant vessels, 127, 189–90; regulations related to, 129, 132–42, 161; securing vital, 18, 99; wartime fuel transport, 104–5, 139. *See also* container shipping; Jones Act

ships: block buys of, 183–84, 185–86; budget for building, 173–75, 179–85; cost of building and maintaining, 132, 180–85; design of and costs of building, 132, 185; electric-drive propulsion, 156; force strength and number of ships for mission of the Navy, xv, 172–75, 253–54, 310n2; inactive fleet, 310n2; modern naval act to increase number of, 19, 99, 171–79,

185–86; new logistics framework to revolutionize, xix; nuclear power for merchant ships, 154–56, 157; number of U.S.-flagged merchant vessels, 127, 189–90; PLAN warship design changes related to types of basing, 33–35; PLAN warships for distant operations, 35–37; procurement costs, xv; purchase of Russian-built by China, 8–9; redesign of, xv; at-sea reloading of vertical-launch systems on warships, 162, 254; six-hundred-ship Navy goal, xv, 175, 191

Shipyard Act, 180

Shipyard Infrastructure Optimization Program (SIOP), 175–76

Shugart, Thomas, 134

Singapore: Destroyer Squadron 7 at, 88, 246; maritime group membership too coordinate commerce policies and regulations, 167; maritime statistics, 130; port operations and services in, 50–51

Sogavare, Manasseh, 2, 29–30, 47, 61

Solomon Islands: embassy in, 53, 59; infrastructure available at ports, 49; port operations and services in, 50–51; security pact with China and base in, xvii–xviii, 2, 24, 29–30, 33, 46–47, 52, 55, 56, 59, 60–61, 212

Some Principles of Maritime Strategy (Corbett), 238

South Africa, 49, 50–51

South China Sea: actions for seizing the initiative in by U.S., 252–56; analysis of operations in, xv; "boiling the frog" metaphor in, 85; CCP and PLA activities after McCarthy meeting with Taiwan president, 17–18; Chinese maritime presence in, 26–27; counterinsurgency/maritime counterinsurgency against China in, 78–81, 82, 83, 84–90, 98, 211; as decisive theater, 4, 5; fleet organization for and focus of missions in, 237, 245–47; indefensibility of man-made island garrisons in, 33; insurgency/maritime insurgency in, xviii, 26, 80, 84–85, 237–38, 256; interests in and naval statecraft to increase U.S. influence in, 56, 58, 78–82; intimidation, harassment, and interference activities in, xviii, 14, 17, 57,

58, 84–87, 88–89, 211, 237–38; man-made island building in, 25–26, 57, 85, 209; militarization of reefs and man-made islands in, 8, 25–27, 60, 210; military presence of China in, xx; naval forces organization for, 242; naval presence and enforcement of EEZs in, 85–86, 87, 89; new U.S. naval fleet structure for, 82; as theater of operations for potential war over Taiwan, 82
South Korea: exercises/operations with, 98; Hanjin shipyard bankrupty, 79; Jones Act and shipping between U.S. ports by, 122, 142; maritime group membership too coordinate commerce policies and regulations, 125–26, 130–31, 166–67; maritime statistics, 130; shipbuilding in, 132
Southeast Asia: actions for seizing the initiative in by U.S., 52–55; embassies and consulates in, 53; Fat Leonard scandal in, 87; fleet organization for and focus of missions in, 245–47; interests in and naval statecraft to increase U.S. influence in, 58, 78–82; refineries and refining capacity in, 115
Southern Hook, Operation, xiv, 97
Soviet Union: fall of, 7; outspending by U.S., 1
Spoehr, Thomas, 177
spy balloon, Chinese, 14
Sri Lanka, 12–13, 25, 50–51, 52
Status of Forces Agreements, 43
Stires, Hunter, 26, 80, 84
Strategic Framework for the Indo-Pacific, U.S., 211, 216, 219
Strategic Petroleum Reserve (SPR), 102, 105–9, 121, 278–78n1, 281n30
Strategic Studies Group, xiv
String of Pearls naval bases, 23
submarines: AUKUS nuclear submarine initiative, 211–12; cost of building and maintaining, 181–83; force strength of, xv; under-ice patrols by Russian SSBNs, 35; maintenance of U.S. nuclear submarines, 176; missions of PLAN fleet, 34; modern naval act and building of, 185–86; nuclear submarine fleet of PLAN, 33, 34–35, 36; purchase of Russian-built by China, 8–9; at-sea endurance of, 36; size and operational needs of PLAN vessels, 37, 38,

48, 50; SSN(X) nuclear submarines, 175
Suez Canal and the Suez Canal Economic Zone, 28, 29, 143, 190
Sun Tzu, 23
Super CAGs, xiv
supply chains: Covid-19 pandemic interruptions, xix–xx, 23, 124–25, 127, 189, 190; interruptions to or manipulation of global, xix–xx, 18, 99, 107–8, 121, 123, 189
Switzerland, 167

tactical disposition, 23
Taiwan: bases to support operations in and around, 52–53; CCP and PLA activities after McCarthy meeting with president of, 17–18; Chinese assault on and conquering of, xviii–xix, xx; democratic national elections in, 8, 15; independence of, 8; maritime group membership too coordinate commerce policies and regulations, 130–31, 166–67; missiles fired over by China, 57; Pelosi visit to and PLA presence around, 14, 16–17, 44; PLA/PLAN naval warfare focus for contest over, 19–20; strategic positioning for conflict over, 19–20, 24, 52–53, 237–38; theater of operations for potential war over, 82; unification of mainland and as objective of CCP, 24; window of time for CCP to act on, 19–20
Taiwan crisis, third, 8–9
Taiwan Strait, xv
Tanker Security Program (TSP), 138, 139, 197
tanks, car ferries for deployment of, 32, 134
Tariff Act (1930), 141
Taylor, Joshua, 238–39, 246–47
TerraPower, 156
terrorism, September 11 attacks and war on, 8, 11, 57, 193, 201, 208–9
Thailand, 54
Thitu Island, 26
Tiananmen Square event and the Tiananmen Papers, 6–7, 208
Tiger Teams, 42
Tower, John, xv
train derailment, East Palestine, 109, 139
transportation: interstate highway system, 122; securing for wartime economy, 18; support for military units, 18

Transportation, U.S. Department of (DoT), 138, 148–49, 190, 191–92, 195, 199, 203
Transportation Command, U.S., 92, 102–3, 125, 140, 197
traumatic trifecta, 7
trucking industry, trucks, and drivers, 148–51
Trump administration and Donald Trump, 70–71, 160, 179, 194, 207, 211, 216
Tsai Ing-wen, 17–18
Tseng, Ryan, 160
Turbo Activation 10-Plus drill, 95, 139
Turkey, 130, 166–67

Uber, 163
Ukraine: artillery rounds for, xix; assault on/invasion of by Russia, xviii, 2, 3, 4, 10, 57, 112, 115, 212, 222; Crimea annexation by Russia, 11, 209, 215; maritime statistics, 130
Unified Command Plan (UCP), 244
United Kingdom, 64, 68, 130, 211–12
United Nations Convention on the Law of the Sea, 40, 85–86
U.S. Naval Power in the 21st Century (Sadler), xiii, xvii, xx, 4, 5, 19, 54, 56, 66, 82, 83, 84, 99, 174, 185, 211, 218–19, 221, 236, 237, 241, 242–43, 245, 251
United States (U.S.): allies and like-minded partner nations of, 4; China policy under Bush, 208–9; domestic and foreign policies and vigilance against China, xix–xx; EEZs in south and central Pacific, 59, 63; national power of, xx, 1
U.S.–Papua New Guinea Defense Cooperation Agreement, 66
U.S.–Philippines Bilateral Strategic Dialogue, 79
U.S.–Philippines Enhanced Defense Cooperation Agreement (EDCA), 78–79
unmanned platforms and surface vessels: budgeting for production of, 174–75; designs and concepts of operations for, 174–75; extra-large unmanned undersea vessels (XLUUVs), 174–75, 310n2; Fifth Fleet Task Force 59, 77, 247–49; large unmanned surface vessels (LUSVs), 77, 151–53, 163, 174–75, 275n48, 310n2; medium unmanned surface vessels (MUSVs), 77, 174–75, 310n2

Vanguard Bank, 26
Vanuatu, xviii, 39, 50–51, 53, 55
vertical-launch system reloading at-sea, 162, 254
vertical-lift technologies, 148, 151–52, 162–63, 167
Vietnam, 10, 39, 54, 80–81, 84, 85–86, 89, 130, 166–67

Wang Yi, 44–45, 46–47, 55
war: capacity of U.S. to wage prolonged war with China, xix, 3, 6; military posture for protracted campaigns, 23; potential sites of, 4; victory as a fait accompli, 6; war with China already underway, belief about, xx
Washington Naval Treaty, 171
weapons/weapons systems: extending range of, 162–63; inadequacies in industries for production of, xix
West Africa, 44–46, 66–67, 68–74, 200
West Capella incident, 57, 84, 85, 211, 219, 256
WEST naval conferences, 75, 239, 248
World Trade Organization (WTO), 1, 7–8, 9–10, 209
Wu Shengli, 31

Xi Jinping: business environment under, 25; CCP role of, 7; Egypt visit by, 28–29; election and uncontested leadership, 9, 15; man-made island building by, 57; military readiness concerns of, 12; Obama policy understanding with, 210; Piraeus port visit by, 28; PLA appointments by, 19, 31; port and base decision-making role of, 30–31; reformer expectations for, 9; seaborne trade and rejuvenation goals of, 27; unification of mainland and Taiwan as objective of, 24; window of time to act on Taiwan, 19–20

Yemen, 40, 50–51, 113, 127, 143
Yinmahu heavy-lift ship (China), 42–43, 254
Yuan Wang 5 (China), 13, 39

ABOUT THE AUTHOR

BRENT DROSTE SADLER is a twenty-six-year Navy veteran with numerous operational tours on nuclear-powered submarines. He has been a member of personal staffs of senior defense department leaders and was a military diplomat in Asia. He writes about the great power competition, advanced technologies, and building the Navy the nation needs. Sadler is the author of *U.S. Naval Power in the 21st Century: A New Strategy for Facing the Chinese and Russian Threat.*

THE NAVAL INSTITUTE PRESS is the book-publishing arm of the U.S. Naval Institute, a private, nonprofit, membership society for sea service professionals and others who share an interest in naval and maritime affairs. Established in 1873 at the U.S. Naval Academy in Annapolis, Maryland, where its offices remain today, the Naval Institute has members worldwide.

Members of the Naval Institute support the education programs of the society and receive the influential monthly magazine *Proceedings* or the colorful bimonthly magazine *Naval History* and discounts on fine nautical prints and on ship and aircraft photos. They also have access to the transcripts of the Institute's Oral History Program and get discounted admission to any of the Institute-sponsored seminars offered around the country.

The Naval Institute's book-publishing program, begun in 1898 with basic guides to naval practices, has broadened its scope to include books of more general interest. Now the Naval Institute Press publishes about seventy titles each year, ranging from how-to books on boating and navigation to battle histories, biographies, ship and aircraft guides, and novels. Institute members receive significant discounts on the Press' more than eight hundred books in print.

Full-time students are eligible for special half-price membership rates. Life memberships are also available.

For more information about Naval Institute Press books that are currently available, visit www.usni.org/press/books. To learn about joining the U.S. Naval Institute, please write to:

Member Services
U.S. NAVAL INSTITUTE
291 Wood Road
Annapolis, MD 21402-5034

Telephone: (800) 233-8764
Fax: (410) 571-1703
Web address: www.usni.org

www.ingramcontent.com/pod-product-compliance
Ingram Content Group UK Ltd.
Pitfield, Milton Keynes, MK11 3LW, UK
UKHW041912140426
5217IPUK00001B/6